Journal of the American Revolution

JOURNAL

OF THE

AMERICAN REVOLUTION

ANNUAL VOLUME 2021

WESTHOLME
Yardley

Westholme Publishing, LLC
904 Edgewood Road
Yardley, Pennsylvania 19067
Visit our Web site at www.westholmepublishing.com

ISBN: 978-1-59416-361-6

Printed in the United States of America.

CONTENTS

EDITOR'S INTRODUCTION

As a publication about history, *Journal of the American Revolution* seldom reflects current events. We strive to present factual information about people and events in American history from the 1760s through the early 1800s, and leave it to readers to decide how that information relates to current events. In most ways, every year since JAR began publication has been similar in terms of content—a broad and diverse selection of articles relating to a specific time period.

2020 was different.

The global pandemic that affected almost every aspect of modern life had direct impacts on JAR. A positive effect of the pandemic, not apparent to readers, is that we received more submissions than in any previous year, freely offered by historians of all backgrounds who suddenly had more time than usual to assimilate and write about their research and passions. This afforded the JAR editorial staff a wider selection of material from which to choose our daily on-line articles.

The pandemic also shaped the content of many submissions, to a greater extent than any previous event (except, of course, the events of the late eighteenth century). We received articles about disease outbreaks, especially the deadly yellow fever epidemic that ravaged Philadelphia in 1793. Very little was understood about the specific causes and mechanisms of these diseases, but the recognized ways of arresting their spread have not changed. The term "social distancing" is new, but the concept was well-known in 1793. The era's equivalent of front-line workers performed heroic deeds and often suffered for it; racial and socioeconomic divides caused disproportionate distress among some populations; there was disagreement about whether to allow public gatherings, particularly for worship; and people "who ought to be patterns for us to follow after," the reverends Absalom Jones and Richard Allen despaired, "have acted in a manner that would make humanity shudder." History repeats itself.

The United States endured unusual political events in 2020 that inspired contributions to JAR about fundamental aspects of the nation's constitution. Why is impeachment included in the provisions of the Constitution? How did the nation come to have an electoral college, rather than a more direct method of popular vote counting? In debating current events, it is essential to understand the underpinnings of the policies at issue and the principles upon which they were founded.

This year's JAR Annual, the seventh produced by Westholme Publishing, contains a wide selection of articles published online in late 2019 and throughout 2020, covering topics from the Lenape people to the Louisiana Purchase, locations from Hudson Bay to Nicaragua, and exploits from the extra-military activities of an army doctor to the opinions of Thomas Jefferson on epidemics. But more than any other year, this volume reflects the pandemic and the politics of 2020. In a way, our efforts to show how the present is influenced by history have caused history to be influenced by the present.

Alexander Hamilton's Missing Years: New Insights into the Little Lion's Caribbean Childhood

❀ RUUD STELTEN & ALEXANDRE HINTON ❀

Alexander Hamilton's life has been documented extensively and his exploits as an adult are well known. His early childhood, however, has long been a subject of debate and, until recently, was largely shrouded in obscurity. Evidence published by historian Michael Newton in 2019 has provided new insights into Alexander Hamilton's formative years. Despite this new information coming to light, a large gap still exists in our knowledge of the life of one of America's most brilliant Founding Fathers. Recent research in the Dutch National Archives in The Hague by the authors has uncovered another piece of the puzzle, thereby filling a large gap in Alexander Hamilton's "missing" years in the early 1760s.

Until recently, Alexander's own claims and a lack of evidence to the contrary led historians to believe that he was born and raised on the island of Nevis.[1] Newton's research demonstrated that the story is more complicated and that Alexander did not spend all this time, if any, on Nevis.[2] Alexander's parents, Rachel Faucett and James Hamilton, met on St. Kitts in the early 1750s. About two years later, Alexander's older brother James Jr. was born, likely on that same island.[3] Records indicate the family left for St. Eustatius in 1753 "on account of debt."[4] This has been the last documentation of the Hamiltons' place of residence until 1765, when the family moved to St. Croix. Various witness accounts

---

1. Ron Chernow, *Alexander Hamilton* (London: Penguin Books, 2005), 7.
2. Michael Newton, *Discovering Hamilton: New Discoveries in the Lives of Alexander Hamilton, His Family, Friends, and Colleagues From Various Archives Around the World* (Phoenix: Eleftheria Publishing, 2019).
3. Ibid., 13.
4. Ibid., 12,19.

and church records place the Hamilton family on St. Eustatius and St. Kitts between 1753 and 1759, but evidence of where they resided during this period has not yet been discovered.[5] Sometime in the mid-1750s, Alexander Hamilton was born. While his date of birth has been a matter of much debate, Newton provides compelling evidence for Alexander's birth date between February 23 and August 5, 1754.[6] His birthplace, however, is still in question, as lack of records has allowed multiple islands to be considered as possibilities.

Before elaborating on the newly-found evidence relating to the Hamiltons' whereabouts between 1759 and 1765, it is important to provide a short historical overview of St. Eustatius. This island, as will be demonstrated, is where young Alexander spent a significant part of his childhood. Affectionately called Statia by its current 3,200 inhabitants, St. Eustatius is an eight-square-mile volcanic island located in the northeastern Caribbean, eight miles north of St. Kitts. Statia was first permanently colonized by the Dutch in 1636 and changed hands twenty-two times between the Dutch, French, and British, until Dutch rule was permanently reinstated in 1816. The island initially developed like many other Caribbean colonies. The Dutch settlers established cotton, tobacco, and sugar plantations in an attempt to develop a plantation economy.[7] The island's relatively dry climate, however, hindered its economic development into a successful plantation colony. The Dutch eventually turned to their commercial instincts and declared the island a free port in 1756. With import duties abolished, an increase in trade activities with ports across the Atlantic World resulted in the construction of a mile-long strip of hundreds of buildings including warehouses, merchant homes, shops, trade offices, brothels and taverns along Statia's leeward shore.[8] This bustling trade center, wedged between steep cliffs on one side and the Caribbean Sea on the other, was called the Lower Town. Statia's population increased from around 2,000 people in the 1740s to 8,476 people in 1790.[9] After 1760, the number of vessels arriving on St. Eustatius ranged between 1,800 and 2,700, but on occasion this was even exceeded; in 1779 a staggering 3,551

5. Ibid., 78-80.
6. Ibid., 8.
7. Ruud Stelten, *From Golden Rock to Historic Gem: A Historical Archaeological Analysis of the Maritime Cultural Landscape of St. Eustatius Dutch Caribbean* (Leiden: Sidestone Press, 2019), 19.
8. Jan Hartog, *History of St. Eustatius* (Aruba: De Wit Stores N.V., 1976), 38.
9. Stelten, *From Golden Rock to Historic Gem*, 104. There may have been up to 20,000 people present on the island during its heyday if one considers the many visitors, temporary residents, and sailors that were attracted by Statia's economic boom.

ships were recorded.[10] Ships from Europe and North America brought manufactured goods and provisions in exchange for products such as sugar, rum and cotton from surrounding islands. Enslaved Africans were also frequently traded on the island. Moreover, St. Eustatius played an important role during the American Revolution, during which the North American rebels obtained large quantities of arms, ammunition and gunpowder from the island. The importance of St. Eustatius in the Revolutionary War is aptly illustrated by a quote from Lord Stormont, who declared in British Parliament that "This rock [St. Eustatius] of only six miles in length and three in breadth has done England more harm than all the arms of her most potent enemies and alone supported the infamous American rebellion."[11] Statia's support to the rebels eventually led to the Fourth Anglo-Dutch War (1780-1784) and the sacking of the island by the British in 1781. After another brief period of economic prosperity following the end of the war, French trade restrictions in 1795 caused the collapse of the island's economy. In the ensuing years, St. Eustatius became an almost forgotten colony.[12]

NEW DISCOVERIES

In an effort to locate additional documentation pertaining to Alexander Hamilton's early whereabouts, the archive of the Second Dutch West India Company (*Tweede West-Indische Compagnie*), held at the National Archives in The Hague, was consulted.[13] This archive holds a trove of historical information from Dutch overseas colonies. Among other things, it contains dozens of thick volumes filled with letters and reports from St. Eustatius to the *Heren X*, the board of the Second Dutch West India Company. Every year, the *Heren X* were provided with updates on the state of the island, including lists of incoming and outgoing ships, notes from the governor, the island's financial reports and census records. It is the latter category that this article is concerned with, and in which the authors found evidence of the Hamilton family living on St. Eustatius in the 1760s.

Statia's census records are organized in a table format; they are divided into free male and free single female inhabitants of the island,

10. Richard Grant Gilmore, "St. Eustatius: The Nexus for Colonial Caribbean Capitalism," in *The Archaeology of Interdependence: European Involvement in the Development of a Sovereign United States*, ed. Douglas Comer (New York: Springer, 2013), 44.

11. Franklin Jameson, "St. Eustatius in the American Revolution," *The American Historical Review* 8, no. 4 (July 1903): 695.

12. Stelten, *From Golden Rock to Historic Gem*, 21.

13. National Archives, The Hague, 1.05.01.02.

with accompanying information on additional members of the household. These include the categories of wives, sons, daughters, male slaves, female slaves, boy slaves, girl slaves and the number of taxable people in the household. This last category, named *Duytes hoofden*, refers to a head tax, known at the time in Dutch as *hoofdgelden*. This tax was levied as a fixed sum on every liable individual. It is unclear who exactly was subjected to this head tax on St. Eustatius, and under which circumstances. In some census entries, more taxable persons are listed than there were free people in the household, but less than the number of slaves. This means that slaves were partially subjected to head tax, most likely above a certain number or only a certain demographic.[14]

The St. Eustatius census records list members of the Hamilton family living on St. Eustatius from 1759 to 1767.[15] No Hamiltons are listed in the 1758 census. The 1759, 1760, 1761 and 1762 census records all contain an entry for James Hamelton by himself.[16] He was exempt from head tax in 1759 and 1761, but not in 1760 and 1762. It is unsure where Rachel, James Jr., and Alexander lived from 1759 to 1763. They may have gone to Nevis or another island not associated with the Hamilton family. If James worked as a sailor during this time, as he would later in life, his profession might have given him ample opportunity to visit his family on a nearby island. The census records from 1763, 1764 and 1765 list James Hamilton, this time spelled correctly with an 'i'. More importantly, James is now not listed alone. The records for these years show his wife and two sons listed as well. Moreover, five slaves are listed as part of their household: two adult women, one boy and two girls. During these years, the Hamilton household thus consisted of nine people. Only one person was subjected to head tax, which was most likely James.[17]

14. In the Dutch Caribbean, slaves below ten and above sixty years of age were exempt from head tax in 1854. A similar regulation may have been in place in the previous century.

15. National Archives, The Hague, 1.05.01.02-624, folio 543; 1.05.01.02-624, folio 1025; 1.05.01.02-625, folio 514; 1.05.01.02-625, folio 596; 1.05.01.02-626, folio 53; 1.05.01.02-626, folio 550; 1.05.01.02-627, folio 56; 1.05.01.02-627, folio 101; 1.05.01.02-251, folio 738.

16. In 1758, Alexander's parents were present on St. Eustatius. The island's church records show that James and Rachel Hamelton, also spelled with an 'e', stood as godparents for the baptism of a befriended couples' son.

17. In 1766 there was a shift in how the census records were organized. Until 1766, the census records were compiled early in the year, but actually referred to the previous year. This is clearly described on the first page of each census list. In 1766, the census records were compiled twice: once on May 25 (referring to 1765) and once on December 4 (referring

In 1765, the Hamiltons moved to St. Croix, 105 miles west of St. Eustatius. Here, James first worked as a sailor aboard the ship *Jægeren* from approximately February 20 to April 6, 1765. Records indicate that his family followed James in April of that year. While on St. Croix, Rachel was able to turn a profit running a store, providing her sons with a comfortable life.[18] This can be corroborated by the fact that she still owned slaves, which she likely brought with her from St. Eustatius. After his sailing contract ended, James became employed as a debt collector.[19] James and his family's paths diverged sometime in 1766. It is unknown how long James was on St. Croix, but it is believed he left between 1766 and 1768. However, in 1766 and 1767 James is still present in the St. Eustatius census records, filling in two years that were previously unknown. He may not have changed his place of residency from St. Eustatius to St. Croix because he frequently traveled or he was not sure where he would spend most of his time due to his profession. His departure from St. Eustatius in early 1765 may only have been temporary and he might have planned to return before the end of the year. In 1766 and 1767, James is listed by himself and exempt from head tax. After 1767, he disappears from Statia's census records.

For the Hamilton family, the single head tax in their entry was most likely applicable to James, as he is also listed as taxable when he was on the island by himself in 1760 and 1762. The newly-discovered records indicate that James was exempt from head tax in 1759, 1761, 1766 and 1767. The 1764 census records show that in this year, 358 out of 588 heads of households were exempted from head tax, so this was quite common. This suggests that there were probably several conditions or prerequisites that resulted in an exemption. A few possible explanations for the exemption could be that if James was still traveling between islands, doing various jobs such as sailing and debt collecting, or did not own any taxable property, head tax might not have been extracted from him on St. Eustatius.

As noted by Newton, James Hamilton was a common name in the eighteenth-century Caribbean. There were, for example, several James Hamiltons living on St. Croix at this time.[20] The fact that the James

to 1766).In 1767, they were only compiled once, on December 3. These referred again to the previous year. The following years' census records are compiled at the end of each year. They most likely refer to the previous year as was customary before, but they can also refer to the year in which they were compiled as nothing to the contrary can be discerned from the documents.

18. Newton, *Discovering Hamilton*, 107.
19. Ibid., 110.
20. Ibid., 121.

Left, the earliest entry of James Hamelton in the St. Eustatius census records in 1759, the eighth name from the bottom. (*National Archives, The Hague, 1.05.01.02-624, folio 543*) Right, the earliest entry of the entire Hamilton family in the St. Eustatius census records in 1763, the fifth entry from the bottom. (*National Archives, The Hague, 1.05.01.02-626, folio 53*)

Hamilton in the newly-discovered census records had a family of one wife and two sons is, however, highly coincidental, especially since the Hamiltons in question had spent time on St. Eustatius before and they do not appear in any known records on other islands. Moreover, James Hamilton's wife and two sons disappear from the St. Eustatius records after 1765, when the documentary record shows they moved to St. Croix. It can therefore be concluded that it is in fact Founding Father Alexander Hamilton's family that is listed in the newly-found records.

The Hamiltons did quite well for themselves on St. Eustatius. This is reflected in the fact that they accrued sufficient wealth to buy and sustain five slaves during their time there.[21] They could have worked

21. It should be noted that three out of five slaves were children; nevertheless, if these were old enough, they could have been employed in various tasks that were not physically demanding.

in and around the house or at a possible family venture. Additionally, the family may have rented out their slaves, as this was a common practice on the island. While the number of slaves one owned was by no means the only indicator of one's economic standing, acquiring slaves was a significant investment and there were several recurring costs associated with owning them, such as providing housing, food, and clothing. As such, owning slaves alludes to, at minimum, a healthy income and a decent financial position. The Hamiltons' slaves could have already been living with them on a different island prior to the entire family relocating to St. Eustatius in 1763 or the Hamiltons could have acquired them upon moving there. To place the Hamiltons' number of slaves into perspective, one has to look at the entire Statian population at this time. The island's census records from 1764 reveal 182 out of 588 heads of households to be slave owners. Some people had large numbers of slaves, such as merchant and future Governor Johannes de Graaff, who owned fifty-one, but most only owned a few. The average number of slaves owned by slave owners on the island in 1764 was 7.2. From this data, it can be concluded that the Hamiltons were among the 31 percent of families on the island who actually owned slaves, but owning slightly below the average number. This data provides some insight into the Hamiltons' standing within society and suggests they were comfortably situated within the island's middle class.

LIFE ON ST. EUSTATIUS

There were three areas on the island where the Hamiltons could have lived: the trade district of Lower Town, the residential area of Upper Town, or the countryside. Since housing in Lower Town was very expensive and there are no indications that the Hamiltons at this time were involved in extensive trading activities, it is unlikely they could afford to live in this area with a household of nine people.[22] The island's countryside was dotted with plantations and small homesteads. Since the Hamiltons owned five slaves, they may have lived on a homestead in the countryside and put their slaves to work on a small farm. They did not, however, own any adult male slaves, so this seems an unlikely scenario. Most likely, the Hamiltons lived in Upper Town, the island's main settlement on the cliffs overlooking Lower Town. This is where most middle-class citizens resided. Upper Town was very different from the hustle and bustle of its seaside counterpart, but it was still a busy place where people vended provisions and merchandise in the streets and on the market. Moreover, government buildings, places of worship,

22. Stelten, *From Golden Rock to Historic Gem*, 107.

and the island's main fort were all located in Upper Town. Eighteenth-century travelers describe most buildings in Upper Town as single-story wooden constructions topped with a shingled roof. These houses usually had three rooms: one central room that served as a public space and two bedrooms to the sides.[23] Buildings in Upper Town reflected a combination of Dutch, English and French architectural styles. Outdoor kitchens contained typically French and Dutch ovens. Houses were built close together and included small gardens. It was not uncommon to house one's slaves in Upper Town. For example, John Bailen owned six enslaved laborers who were housed in two dwellings on his urban property in Upper Town.[24] The August 17, 1792 edition of the *St. Eustatius Gazette* contains an advertisement of a house for sale in Upper Town that contained "negroe houses" as well. The Hamiltons could have housed their two adult and three child slaves on their urban property as well.

St. Eustatius in the 1760s was an interesting place to live in many respects. The following observations provide some context as to what island life must have been like for the Hamiltons. An account from Scottish Lady Janet Schaw, dating to 1775, shows St. Eustatius to have been a very cosmopolitan place: "Never did I meet with such variety; here was a merchant vending his goods in Dutch, another in French, a third in Spanish ... They all wear the habit of their country, and the diversity is really amusing."[25] With thousands of ships arriving from all over the Atlantic World in the previous decade as well, the situation must have been similar in the 1760s. St. Eustatius attracted people from all over the world who wanted to make a quick fortune. As a result, many different religions were practiced on the island. There were Anglican, Lutheran, Dutch Reformed and Roman Catholic religious groups, each with their own place of worship. The island was also home to a relatively large Jewish community, which had built an impressive synagogue in Upper Town in the 1730s.[26]

Free and enslaved people on St. Eustatius engaged in all vices imaginable. Accounts of drinking excessive amounts of alcohol abound in the documentary record, and smoking played a prominent role in island

23. National Archives, The Hague, 3.01.26-161: Narigten van St. Eustatius, 1792.
24. Richard Grant Gilmore, "The Archaeology of New World Slave Societies: A Comparative Analysis with particular reference to St. Eustatius, Netherlands Antilles" (PhD diss., University College London, 2004), 60.
25. Janet Schaw, *Journal of a lady of quality, being the narrative of a journey from Scotland to the West Indies, North Carolina, and Portugal, in the years 1774 to 1776* (New Haven: Yale University Press, 1921), 137.
26. Stelten, *From Golden Rock to Historic Gem*, 120.

life as well. The playing of games often accompanied the consumption of alcohol, and it seems that these regularly got out of hand.[27] Merchants, planters and government officials frequently organized elaborate parties where people indulged in eating, drinking and dancing. Sometimes, free and enslaved people even mingled at parties.[28] There were also several brothels on the island that were frequented by the residents and thousands of sailors calling at Statia each year. It seems daily life for many was characterized by debauchery, but there were more wholesome ways to enjoy oneself. Picnicking was a favorite pastime for visitors and residents, and a hike up the island's dormant *Quill* volcano and into its crater was enjoyed by many.[29]

St. Eustatius' demographic was very different from many other Caribbean colonies whose economies were primarily focused on agriculture. On islands such as Barbados, up to 90 percent of the population consisted of enslaved Africans. Statia's demographic was much more balanced, with enslaved people making up 54 percent of the total population of 2,489 in 1764. The reasons for this are twofold. First, the island attracted more free people engaged in commercial activities. The steady increase in trade created a demand for service workers, artisans, sailors, and dockworkers. Second, Statia's focus on trade meant that fewer people were needed in the cane fields that were not very productive to begin with. Extensive archaeological and documentary research has shown that enslaved people on St. Eustatius had more opportunities to improve their social and economic status than those on other Caribbean islands. On St. Eustatius, many enslaved laborers were employed in maritime trades. Among other jobs, they transported people and goods between ships and shore, for which they often charged fees.[30] The fact that there was a sizable group of free blacks and coloreds on the island further shows that its favorable economic climate provided opportunities even for members of the lowest classes in society.[31]

It was in this setting that the Hamilton family lived from 1763 to 1765. Young Alexander must have been exposed to a society characterized by quick money, debauchery, and loose morals where there were often more transient than permanent residents. It was, however, also a

27. Ibid., 123-126.
28. Ibid., 127.
29. Ibid., 127.
30. Jacob Schiltkamp and Jacobus Smidt, *West Indisch Plakaatboek. Publicaties en andere wetten betrekking hebbende op St. Maarten, St. Eustatius en Saba, 1648/1681-1816* (Amsterdam: S. Emmering, 1979), 408.
31. Stelten, *From Golden Rock to Historic Gem*, 104.

society that was relatively tolerant of religious minorities and where peoples' dreams could come true, even when born into slavery. It was a place where the Hamiltons' slaves may have enjoyed more freedom and opportunities than their counterparts on other islands. From 1763 to 1765, the Hamiltons lived in one of the most cosmopolitan places in the Caribbean, where they could buy almost any type of good someone in Amsterdam, London, or Paris had access to as well. While Dutch was used in most government correspondence, English was (and still is) the language most commonly spoken on the island. Given the vibrant nature of the island's society at this time, it is not hard to imagine that young Alexander's experiences on St. Eustatius made a lasting impression on him and may have contributed in some way in shaping him into the famous political figure he was to become.

CONCLUSION

The newly-discovered census records have filled a large gap in our knowledge of the Hamiltons' whereabouts. It is now clear that James Hamilton was registered on St. Eustatius from 1759 to 1767. It is, however, uncertain if he actually lived there full time during all these years. From 1763 to 1765, Rachel, James Jr., and Alexander were present with James on St. Eustatius. In addition, they owned five slaves during these years. These new discoveries, combined with Michael Newton's recent finds, demonstrate that St. Eustatius played a prominent role in the lives of Alexander Hamilton and his family. Many more questions about the Hamiltons' lives in the Caribbean still remain. What were they doing on St. Eustatius? Where exactly did they live? Which kinds of activities were their slaves involved in? More archival research is necessary to shed further light on the formative years of one of America's most influential founders.

The Lenape Origins of an Independent America: The Catalyst of Pontiac's War, 1763–1765

KEVIN A. CONN

In the wake of the Seven Years' War in North America, the costly British triumph seemed complete. Thus, when a coda to the Seven Years' War erupted in the interior of North America, it came as an unwelcome shock to the British Empire. War broke out anew, nominally led by the Ottawa chieftain Pontiac, who gathered members of many tribes in a combined war against British presence in the Great Lakes and Ohio region. One of the tribes that participated in what historians have called Pontiac's Rebellion or Pontiac's War was the Lenape, who laid an informal siege to Fort Pitt in western Pennsylvania. Lenape attacks disrupted settlement in central and western Pennsylvania and cut off trade and contact with the fort for several months, until a relief expedition under Col. Henry Bouquet won the battle of Bushy Run in August 1763 and temporarily dispersed Lenape forces, relieving the siege. Even then, the war dragged on in a stalemate that stretched into 1765.

Although many historians have focused on Pontiac himself, Pontiac's War was as much a Lenape war as Pontiac's conflict. While the Lenape had signed the Treaty of Easton in 1758, renouncing their alliance with the French and concluding peace with the British, they renewed the war in 1763, responding to direct threats to their territory, disruption of their economy due to British stinginess and pettiness, and a spiritual movement that stressed a pan-Indian creation and sought revival in rejection of English corruption. In the wake of Gen. John Forbes' 1758 expedition against Fort Duquesne, which resulted in the

French retreat from the Ohio country, Anglophone settlers poured into central and western Pennsylvania, displacing the Lenape and other nations or amalgamated groups. Rather than leaving the strategic Forks of the Ohio, the British rebuilt Fort Duquesne, calling it Fort Pitt. The Lenape thus faced a repetition of the circumstances that had pushed them into western Pennsylvania in the first place. British Commander-in-Chief Jeffrey Amherst's restrictive trade policies and unwillingness to remove British forts such as Fort Pitt in the wake of British triumph over the French also rankled. Not only did the Delawares and most other nations depend on European trade goods, but the customary "gifts" of diplomacy also represented a kind of tribute in return for permission to occupy Native land. Amherst abruptly stopped the practice of gift giving and restricted trade of such essentials as ammunition and guns, believing it would reduce the chance of Indian hostilities if Natives were unable to stockpile weaponry.[1]

Perhaps most important in the Lenape decision to instigate Pontiac's War was the spiritual dimension of resistance to Europeans preached by the Delaware prophet Neolin. Neolin's message of spiritual renewal and resistance through eschewing European temptations such as alcohol and trade goods inspired Pontiac himself and suffused his orations, melding the spiritual and political dimensions of his war into a message that united tribes of the Eastern Woodlands and the Great Lakes regions in a common war against British authority and presence.[2] While Pontiac's War ended by 1765, with Pontiac signing a formal peace in 1766, the conflict was crucial in the relations between Britain and her Atlantic Seaboard colonies. As part of the efforts to keep the Iroquois League in particular from joining Pontiac, George III promulgated the Proclamation of 1763, which set aside lands west of the Appalachians as an Indian reserve, forbidding further colonial settlement. Thus, Pontiac's War and the Proclamation of 1763 together changed the balance between Great Britain and her colonies, beginning the series of tensions leading to American independence.

THE EIGHTEENTH-CENTURY LENAPE: UNWILLING VASSALS OF THE IROQUOIS

When William Penn arrived to settle and administer his grant of Pennsylvania in 1682, the Lenape Indians whom he encountered had already had nearly two centuries of contact with Europeans, dating to an initial

---

1. Colin G. Calloway, *The Scratch of a Pen: 1763 and the Transformation of North America* (New York: Oxford University Press, 2006), 69.
2. Gregory Evans Dowd, "Thinking and Believing: Nativism and Unity in the Ages of Pontiac and Tecumseh," *American Indian Quarterly*. Summer 1992, Vol. 16, Issue 3, 309-335.

encounter with Giovanni Verrazano in 1524.[3] The name Lenni Lenape means "the Original People," as many Indian cultures have named themselves.[4] The Lenape were a collection of small matrilineal family groups speaking two related Algonquian languages, Munsee and Unami. Comprised of three major clan groups, they inhabited the area of present-day New Jersey, southeastern New York, Eastern Pennsylvania, and northern Delaware.[5] Early English settlers called the river at the center of Lenape homelands the Delaware River, after the first governor of the Jamestown colony, Lord De La Warr, and thus called the people who lived along the river the Delawares, a name the Munsees and Unamis gradually adopted for themselves.[6] Lacking the political unity of the Iroquois League and living closer to the Atlantic coastline, the Lenape suffered more rapid loss of their lands than the Iroquois to Dutch, Swedish, and English settlers.[7] By the late seventeenth century, most Lenape had moved out of New Jersey, resettling in eastern Pennsylvania, with some groups moving into central Pennsylvania and the Ohio River country. By the end of the seventeenth century, the Delawares were "props" to the Iroquois League, and generally had the appellation "nephews," reflecting subordinate kinship status, or "women." This latter epithet was not necessarily originally pejorative; it meant that the Delawares were peacemakers who left war to their allies, the Iroquois.[8] In many Eastern Woodlands cultures, while gender roles were usually separate, women had important, valued, and influential roles that European settlers did not acknowledge. Lenape society was both matrilineal and matrilocal—the husband married outside his clan and lived with his wife's family, meaning that the Lenape were generally monogamous and valued women's power and contributions.[9]

3. Gregory Evans Dowd, *The Indians of New Jersey* (Trenton, NJ: New Jersey Historical Commission, Department of State, 2001), 31.
4. Paul A. W. Wallace, *Indians in Pennsylvania* (Harrisburg, PA: The Pennsylvania Historical and Museum Commission, 1975), 16.
5. Dowd, *Indians of New Jersey*, 9.
6. Wallace, *Indians in Pennsylvania*, 16.
7. Dowd, *Indians of New Jersey*, 47, 50.
8. Wallace, *Indians in Pennsylvania*, 56-57. Richard S. Grimes, *The Western Delaware Indian Nation, 1730-1795: Warriors and Diplomats* (Lanham, MD: Lehigh University Press; copublished by The Rowman & Littlefield Publishing Group, Inc., 2017), 8-10, posits that the Lenape in southern New York became part of the "Covenant Chain" metaphorically forged by New York Governor Edmund Andros in 1677, and they allowed the Mohawks to become spokesmen for them in negotiations with English representatives.
9. Wallace, *Indians in Pennsylvania*, 30-31.

Pennsylvania and New York forged diplomatic alliances with the Iroquois League, thanks to the influence of traders and Indian agents who had lived among the Iroquois, were sympathetic to their interests, and respected their power.[10] The Iroquois set Half-Kings, or diplomatic viceroys, over many of the amalgamated Indian communities in central Pennsylvania and the Ohio country. By the middle of the eighteenth century, the Six Nations wielded a heavy hand in dealing with the Lenape. This dominance manifested most nakedly in the so-called "Walking Purchase" of 1737, in which William Penn's sons, John and Thomas, secured tens of thousands of acres along the Delaware River in eastern Pennsylvania by means that were dubious, at best.[11] When the Lenape protested what they considered fraud, the Iroquois ratified the purchase and upbraided the Lenape, who they claimed had no right to dispose of the land at all. As the Onondaga Chieftain Canasatego scornfully informed the Delawares at a public council concerning the Walking Purchase and Lenape refusal to leave the lands in 1742, "You ought to be taken by the Hair of the Head and shak'd severely . . . We conquer'd You, we made Women of you, you know you are Women, and can no more sell Land than Women."[12] The Lenape bowed to the Iroquois ultimatum and moved westward, but the cession of these lands rankled and sowed the seeds of discord a generation later.

THE PROMISE OF PEACE: EASTON, 1758

After the failure of Edward Braddock's 1755 campaign to capture Fort Duquesne at the outset of the Seven Years' War, the Lenape defied the Iroquois' initial neutrality and allied with the French. Raiding the frontiers of Pennsylvania and into New Jersey, they terrorized many British citizens and aided the French in their pursuit of dominion over the Ohio country. Yet at the height of the struggle for the North American continent, a conference between representatives of the British Crown, the Colony of Pennsylvania, the Province of New Jersey, the Eastern and Western Lenape, the member tribes of the Iroquois League, and numerous other Indian nations convened at Easton, Pennsylvania, in October 1758. Following inconclusive negotiations between the eastern

10. Fred Anderson, *The Crucible of War: The Seven Years' War and the Fate of Empire in British North America, 1754-1766* (New York: Vintage Books, 2001), 20-22. Wallace, *Indians in Pennsylvania*, 141-142. Conrad Weiser, George Croghan, and Sir William Johnson were all colonial English traders and diplomats who had extensive ties to the nations of the Iroquois League. They moved between European and Indian worlds and collectively had a great deal of influence both with Natives and on British and colonial Indian policies.
11. Anderson, *The Crucible of War*, 22. Grimes, *The Western Delaware Indian Nation*, 22-23.
12. Grimes, *The Western Delaware Indian Nation*, 1-2.

Lenape leader Teedyuscung and the Pennsylvania government in 1756 and 1757, this conference brought peace for the Lenape and many other Iroquois vassals who had been fighting for the French. After an initially rocky beginning, marked by drunken outbursts by Teedyuscung, the delegates forged a peace that not only reshaped both Pennsylvania and New Jersey land claims, but also altered the relationship between the Lenape and their nominal overlords, the Iroquois.[13] Speaking for the Six Nations and their "nephews" the Delawares, the Seneca chieftain Tagashata declared peace on the part of the Lenape:

> I now speak at the Request of *Teedyuscung*, and our Nephews the *Delawares* . . .
> *Brethren*, We now remove the Hatchet out of your Heads, that was struck into it by our Cousins the *Delawares* . . . Our Cousins the *Delawares*, have assured us they will never think of War against their Brethren the *English* any more, but employ their Thoughts about Peace, and cultivating Friendship with them, and never suffer Enmity against them to enter into their Minds again.[14]

By the terms of the Treaty of Easton, both the eastern and western Lenape renounced their alliance with the French, guaranteed peace with the British, and formally ceded all land claims in New Jersey and Eastern Pennsylvania. In return, the Lenape received 1,000 Spanish *Reales*, guarantees of land in western Pennsylvania and the Ohio country, return of some land ceded without their consent by the Iroquois, and promises of limits on colonial settlement west of the Allegheny Mountains.[15] Importantly, Pennsylvania's Gov. William Denny agreed to negotiate directly with the western Lenape, without consulting the Iroquois—effectively granting the western Lenape a renewed political independence from their former domination by the Six Nations.

The Treaty of Easton was clearly advantageous to the provincial governments of Pennsylvania and New Jersey, as well as to the British Crown. Yet while Teedyuscung was publicly humiliated and forced to reaffirm eastern Lenape subordination to the Iroquois, the Lenape also gained, at least in theory.[16] While the Delawares and their kin agreed

13. Anderson, *The Crucible of War*, 276.
14. *The Minutes of a Treaty Held at Easton, in Pennsylvania, in October, 1758. By the Lieutenant Governor of Pennsylvania, and the Governor of New-Jersey; with the Chief Sachems and Warriors of the Mohawks, Oneydos, Onondagas, Cayugas, Senecas, Tuscaroras, Tuteloes, Nanticokes and Conoys, Chugnuts, Delawares, Unamies, Mohickons, Minisinks, and Wapings*, Evans Early American Imprint Collection—Text Creation Partnership, University of Michigan, 8.
15. *The Minutes of a Treaty Held at Easton*, 26.
16. Anderson, *The Crucible of War*, 277.

to give up land claims to which they had lost "squatters rights" through increased Anglophone settlement, chiefly in New Jersey, Pennsylvania recognized the western Lenape claims to settlement and hunting grounds west of the Appalachians and agreed to prohibit white settlement in that area.[17] Direct negotiation with Pennsylvania, granting *de facto* political autonomy from the Iroquois, was also welcome to the Delawares. Although humiliated, Teedyscung could at least claim that he had secured residence for the eastern Delawares in the Wyoming Valley of Pennsylvania, together with houses built by Pennsylvania.[18]

The greatest effect of the Treaty of Easton, however, was the decisive advantage it gave to the British Army in the struggle for North America. Peace between the Lenape, other Pennsylvania Indians, and Britain ensured the success of Gen. John Forbes' expedition against Fort Duquesne. Moving methodically through the area where Gen. Edward Braddock had met with disaster at the beginning of the war, Forbes was able to count on the neutrality of the Lenape and other tribes, and the French garrison defending Fort Duquesne lost its most valuable protection. Faced with overwhelming odds, the French blew up the fort and retreated, giving the British control of the Ohio country.

THE BETRAYAL OF PEACE, 1758-1763

The Lenape peace at Easton, however, sowed the seeds of future war. With the threat of Indian raids removed, Forbes' triumph in the Ohio country gave both a physical and psychological incentive to additional Anglophone settlement. As part of his march into the Ohio country, Forbes built a military road from Philadelphia out to the ruined Fort Duquesne. With the French retreat, he secured the strategic position at the Forks of the Ohio with a larger, more strongly built fort that he named Fort Pitt in honor of Britain's prime minister. Despite British promises that the British occupation of western forts was a temporary war measure, Amherst also maintained garrisons in forts in the Great Lakes region and western Pennsylvania. These forts aroused instant opposition, as Indian leaders immediately protested British maintenance, rebuilding, and strengthening of installations such as Fort Pitt.[19]

Seeing rich land that had previously been closed to them by threats of Indian violence, settlers poured into the Wyoming Valley and the Ohio country beginning in 1759, displacing the Delawares in lands the Lenape had thought secured by the peace in 1758. Many land specu-

17. Daniel K. Richter, *Facing East from Indian Country: A Native History of Early America* (Cambridge: Harvard University Press, 2001), 192.
18. Ibid., 200.
19. Calloway, *The Scratch of a Pen*, 55.

lators from Connecticut, believing that their royal charter gave them land claims in Pennsylvania, risked conflict with both the Lenape and the Province of Pennsylvania. Forming the Susquehanna Company and moving into the Wyoming Valley, they crowded out the eastern Delawares living there. When Teedyuscung protested, travelling to Philadelphia to complain to the governor in late 1762, he paid with his life. In April 1763, he died in a suspicious house fire; many historians agree Susquehanna Company agents likely set the late-night blaze.[20] Nearly all of the Delaware settlement burned. Within weeks, settlers under the auspices of the Susquehanna Company moved into the Wyoming Valley. Similar patterns of settlement went on elsewhere in western Pennsylvania. Professor Colin Calloway describes an unprecedented wave of emigrants to the English colonies in general and to western Pennsylvania in particular.[21] In addition to the Susquehanna Company, other groups of land speculators like the Ohio Company of Virginia resumed their sales of land to which they had dubious title, encouraging even more emigrants. Forbes' military road served as a physical highway into the West of Pennsylvania. It offered settlers a direct line of travel between military installations that rapidly became local centers of trade, and despite the promises made by Governor Denny at Easton and efforts by British leaders like Col. Henry Bouquet at Fort Pitt to root out squatters, the Anglophone population west of the Alleghenies grew rapidly.[22]

Indian discontent with Anglophone settlement bubbled to the surface as the Seven Years' War concluded. Even by the fall of 1762, well before Pontiac's War broke out, officials like Governor Hamilton of Pennsylvania, Governor Denny's successor, wrote to Sir William Johnson, Indian Agent for the Northern Colonies, speaking about the potential for war if settlement proceeded.[23] Hamilton's fears were far from the only evidence that the Lenape in particular intended to resist white encroachment on their lands. Trader and British Indian Agent Alexander McKee, one of Johnson's subordinates, recorded at the beginning of November 1762 that Delaware Indians were circulating belts of wampum among the Seneca, Shawnee, Ottawa, Chippewa, and Pottawatomie, calling for a general war against the English.[24] As the

20. Ibid., 54. Richter, *Facing East*, 200. Anderson, *The Crucible of War*, 533-534, is less sure.
21. Calloway, *The Scratch of a Pen*, 56-60.
22. Anderson, *The Crucible of War*, 524-525.
23. Albert Corey and Milton Hamilton, ed., *The Papers of Sir William Johnson, Volume X* (Albany: University of the State of New York, Division of Archives and History, 1951), 552.
24. Ibid., 578-579.

Delawares were circulating war belts even before the Treaty of Paris ended the Seven Years' War and confirmed the French cession of North America, Pontiac's War was in fact from the outset a Lenape campaign as much as the brainchild of Pontiac.

AMHERST'S RESTRICTIVE POLICIES AND THE SPARK OF WAR

British Commander-in-Chief in North America Jeffrey Amherst un-intentionally did a great deal to instigate the renewed outbreak of war through his callous disregard of Indian interests and his insensitivity to Indian diplomacy. Amherst was contemptuous of Indians, even those who had been British allies throughout the Seven Years' War.[25] As that war drew to a close in North America in 1761, he issued orders limiting the practice of gift-giving in Indian diplomacy. He also attempted to restrict trade with Indian nations, particularly forbidding the sale of firearms, gunpowder and lead.[26] This policy may have been partially a reaction to the generous practices of Sir William Johnson and his deputies, such as the trader and agent George Croghan, who secured Indian alliances through the liberal distribution of gifts. Amherst and Johnson disliked one another intensely, and their rivalry may have been a factor in Amherst's disdain for Johnson's diplomacy.[27]

The effects of Amherst's restrictions undoubtedly helped drive the Lenape to renewed war. Over the course of the seventeenth and eighteenth centuries, nations such as the Iroquois and their vassals, including the Lenape, had grown adept at playing European powers against one another and extracting gifts from their agents as a sign of respect. Northeastern Indian tribes regarded the distribution of gifts as part of the reciprocal relationship of trade and alliances, a sign by Europeans that Indian presence and concerns mattered. The presents served as a sign of respect, an annual tribute for European presence on unceded lands.[28] Gift giving also helped to uphold the authority of leaders friendly to diplomacy with Europeans, as Indian agents typically gave gifts to principal chieftains, who then distributed the presents to those

---

25. J. Clarence Webster, ed., *The Journal of Jeffery Amherst: Recording the Military Career of General Amherst in America from 1758 to 1763* (Toronto: Ryerson Press, 1931), 174-175. Throughout the journal, Amherst refers to the Indians as "savages;" he makes disparaging comments about them and issues orders to them, as if they were subordinates, rather than independent allies (see Webster, 254, for an example).

26. James T. Flexner, *Lord of the Mohawks: A Biography of Sir William Johnson* (Boston: Little, Brown, and Company, 1979), 238. See as well Richter, *Facing East*, 187-188, and Anderson, *The Crucible of War*, 455, 469-471.

27. Flexner, *Lord of the Mohawks*, 200, 215-216.

28. Calloway, *The Scratch of a Pen*, 67-69.

who followed them.[29] Most importantly, Amherst's restrictions on both trade and gifts meant that the Lenape and Shawnee had difficulty obtaining the goods they needed to survive. With the collapse of the French Empire in North America, tribes were no longer able to exploit the rivalry between the English and the French. At the same time, prices of furs plummeted as a glut of hides saturated the British markets.[30] The shift in global trade angered Indians, who regarded the change in prices as the greed of Anglophone traders and complained bitterly—with much justification—of being cheated just when the option of taking their hides elsewhere had disappeared.[31] Just as the Lenape needed more hides or furs to obtain the goods on which they had come to depend, Amherst forbade trade in the firearms, powder, and lead they needed to harvest game. As Croghan warned Bouquet in December 1762, the Lenape saw Amherst's policy as evidence that the British planned to attack them:

> They say, they never Intended to make War on the English, but Say it's full time to prepare to Defend themselves & their Country from Us, who they are convinced Design to make War on them; They say, if We did not Intend that We would not Prohibit the Sale of as much Powder & Lead as would Supply them to Hunt with, not Refuse their Warriors Powder & Lead, and other Necessarys . . .. They Interpret the General's Frugality in Lessening the Expence of Presents in a Design of Revenging what is past . . . I am of Opinion it shall not be long before We have some Broyles with them.[32]

Croghan explicitly cited Amherst's ban on presents in discussing the Delaware plans for war. Bouquet endorsed Croghan's message and sent it to Amherst and Johnson, so there were multiple reports of Lenape unrest and discontent well before the final French cession of North America. Amherst's failure either to modify his policies or at least to warn British forts of the distinct possibility of war indicates a signal military failure. Historian James Flexner has stated that the conflict should, in fact, be known as "Amherst's War," as his policies were instrumental in bringing it about.[33]

29. Ibid., 109-110.
30. Richter, *Facing East*, 178-179, mentions the decline in the importance of the British fur trade throughout the mid-eighteenth century in the northern colonies, exacerbated by the growth of the Florida fur trade beginning in 1763.
31. Flexner, *Lord of the Mohawks*, 238-239.
32. Corey and Hamilton, *The Papers of Sir William Johnson*, 597 (spelling as in source).
33. Flexner, *Lord of the Mohawks*, 255.

A SPIRITUAL DIMENSION TO THE STRUGGLE: THE DELAWARE PROPHET NEOLIN

While many historians have focused on the military, economic, and political causes of Pontiac's War, recent scholarship by contemporary historians such as Daniel Richter, Fred Anderson, and Gregory Dowd has focused as well on the spiritual dimension of the conflict.[34] Even before the Seven Years' War, a century of land dispossession had had a catastrophic effect on Indian communities. Many Indians in the Ohio region were living in mixed intertribal communities, with cultures such as the western Lenape and Shawnee blending together with admixtures of other groups.[35] Their world and traditions in tatters, many Indians were receptive to religious messages that stressed Indian renewal through spiritual purification. A number of prophets emerged during the final years of the Seven Years' War, the most influential being Delaware spiritual leader Neolin, known as the Delaware Prophet. Neolin was one of many "nativists" interested in spiritual renewal; many lesser-known prophets spread a similar message in the 1750s and 1760s. Among the Lenape, there were at least three other "prophets" who claimed visions from the "Master of Life," who bid them to preach abstinence from alcohol and stressed the joining of all Indians in a spiritual and moral alliance.[36] In a time of upheaval and change brought about by war and displacement, this message resonated both in the polyglot communities of the Ohio country and among the various tribes who had cooperated against the British.[37]

Like his predecessors, Neolin blended elements of Lenape tradition and Christianity, as well as borrowed traditions from other cultures. He did not preach a simple return to an imagined ideal past, but rather a pan-Indian movement that stressed ritual purification and rejection of the corruption of European, particularly English, temptations.[38] Neolin stressed the separate creation of Indians, claiming that the Master of

---

34. Francis Parkman, *History of the Conspiracy of Pontiac and the War of the North American Tribes against the English Colonies after the Conquest of Canada* (New York: Macmillan, 1929), 114-115, and Flexner, *Lord of the Mohawks*, 254, do mention a Delaware prophet, though not by name, and their treatment of Neolin seems incidental to their discussion of Pontiac's conspiracy, as Parkman calls it. Anderson discusses Neolin's influence, 536-538; Dowd devotes much of the first section of his book *A Spirited Resistance* to a discussion of Neolin and his teachings; Richter quotes him extensively through one of Pontiac's speeches, 193-199.

35. Dowd, *A Spirited Resistance: The North American Indian Struggle for Unity, 1745-1815* (Baltimore: Johns Hopkins University Press, 1992), 23-27.

36. Anderson, *The Crucible of War*, 535-536.

37. Dowd, *A Spirited Resistance*, 24-25.

38. Alfred Cave, "The Delaware Prophet Neolin: A Reappraisal," *Ethnohistory* 46: 2 (Spring 1999), 266.

Life had created all Indians as brothers, distinct from Africans and particularly from Europeans. Placing the blame for Indian losses of land, culture, and population on the Indians themselves, Neolin preached that Indians must regain their spiritual power through rejection of European innovations and an embrace of his vision granted by the Master of Life. He stressed purification through purging, including an emetic known simply as the "black drink." To regain spiritual power and cleanse themselves of contamination, those who followed the Master of Life were obliged to renounce alcohol, give up polygamy, gradually decrease dependence on trade, and eventually relearn the use of bows and arrows for hunting, rejecting the use of firearms, along with other English innovations such as flint and steel for fire starting.[39]

Neolin's message opened an avenue to common resistance against the British and the settlers in western Pennsylvania. First appearing in 1761 or 1762, the implicit antagonism and conflict with British colonists of his teachings resonated with Lenape villages in the Ohio country along the Susquehanna, and quickly spread to other communities and tribal groups. By April 1763, the Ottawa chieftain Pontiac discussed the ideas of Neolin at a gathering of Indians near Detroit. According to historian Jon Parmenter, the war belts that Pontiac laid before the Ottawa, Ojibwa, and Pottawatomie in calling for a unified war against the English came from the Delawares, perhaps incensed at the death of Teedyuscung.[40] A passionate adherent of the French cause in the Seven Years' War, Pontiac absorbed the teachings of Neolin and allied spiritual and physical messages of renewal to resist English encroachment. Rather than cynically employing Neolin's message, Pontiac was a disciple of the Delaware Prophet. He urged war against the English both to restore Indian power and to encourage the French to return and resume the struggle against the British.[41]

---

39. Ibid., 271-273, 281. The Lenape were traditionally matrilineal and matrilocal, practices which tend to inhibit polygamy, but the practice may have arisen in the polyglot communities that arose in the seventeenth and eighteenth centuries, as Lenape, Shawnee, western Seneca/Mingo, and other refugees formed new communities in central and western Pennsylvania and as far west as present-day Ohio.

40. Jon Parmenter, "Pontiac's War: Forging New Links in the Anglo-Iroquois Covenant Chain, 1758-1766." *Ethnohistory*, Vol. 44, No. 4 (Autumn, 1997), 627.

41. Dowd, "Thinking and Believing," 309-310, states it is unclear whether Neolin himself was pro-French or more generally anti-European; therefore, whether Pontiac twisted Neolin's message into an anti-British, pro-French form or simply repeated Neolin's message is a matter of debate. Richard White, *The Middle Ground: Indians, Empires, and Republics in the Great Lakes Region, 1650-1815* (New York: Cambridge University Press, 2011), 284, discusses the difficulties of translation making it unclear whether Neolin meant all whites, or merely the English. Dowd, *A Spirited Resistance*, 35, discusses the genuine nature of Pontiac's belief in Neolin's teachings.

THE LENAPE PARTICIPATION IN PONTIAC'S WAR, 1763-1765

Traditionally, historians have emphasized Pontiac's European-style siege of Fort Detroit in speaking of the war, giving his name to the war and the beginning of the conflict to his May 9, 1763, attack on the fort. Yet Pontiac was hardly in control of the Indian forces allied against Anglophone military installations and settlements. While Detroit did form a major front, Indians across the Great Lakes and Ohio River Valley acted more or less independently, tied more by a spiritual alliance than by the coordination of any one leader. In a series of attacks, groups of Indians from a wide array of cultures destroyed or forced the British Army to abandon nine forts, butchering many of the garrisons. During 1763 and 1764, the attacks killed approximately four hundred British soldiers and two thousand Anglophone settlers.[42]

Having in many ways instigated the conflict, the Lenape were an integral part of the fighting. Delaware warriors attempted to take Fort Pitt, cutting off most communication with the fort and attacking settlers throughout the Ohio Country. The fort was largely cut off from June through August 1763, while Delaware, Shawnee, Mingo, and allied war bands ravaged settlements throughout western Pennsylvania. In late June, at the height of the siege of Fort Pitt, Capt. Simon Ecuyer, the fort's commander, met with two Lenape chieftains who offered to allow the garrison to depart in peace but, not trusting their words, Ecuyer refused. At the conclusion of negotiations, "Out of our regard to them, we gave them two Blankets and an Handkerchief out of the Small Pox Hospital. I hope it will have the desired effect."[43] In this regard, Captain Ecuyer anticipated the orders of General Amherst, who wrote to Colonel Bouquet in July, "Could it not be contrived to Send the Small Pox among those disaffected Tribes of Indians? We must, on this occasion, Use Every Strategem in our power to Reduce them."[44] While Amherst's willingness to use biological warfare against the Indians seems revolting today, it is more difficult to blame Captain Ecuyer. As Croghan wrote to Johnson, the Lenape were calling on Ecuyer to surrender, telling him that all other forts in the West had fallen, and a trader reported the garrison at Fort Pitt was receiving fugitives who spoke of the destruction of the forts at Sandusky and Presque Isle.[45] Based on reports of the massacre of British garrisons, Ecuyer and

---

42. Parmenter, "Pontiac's War," 628.

43. A. T. Volwiler, ed., *Notes and Documents: William Trent's Journal at Fort Pitt, 1763* (Philadelphia: Historical Society of Pennsylvania, N.D.), 400.

44. Calloway, *The Scratch of a Pen*, 73. Anderson, *The Crucible of War*, 542-543 discusses Amherst's desire to use biological warfare as well.

45. Corey and Hamilton, *The Papers of Sir William Johnson*, 728. Volwiler, *Notes and Documents*, 398.

those in Fort Pitt were justified in an imminent fear of death, perhaps torture, if the Lenape were successful in taking the fort. As smallpox had already broken out in the overcrowded fort, Ecuyer had some justification in attempting anything that would harm his enemies. Smallpox did spread through the Lenape and other tribes engaged in the conflict that summer, as well as through the British, but whether Ecuyer's "gifts" caused the epidemic is unknown.[46]

In response to the Lenape siege of Fort Pitt, Amherst scrambled to put together a relief force. Many regiments had been sent to the West Indies in the last years of the war, and he had relatively few troops on hand.[47] Nonetheless, he cobbled together forces of approximately four hundred sixty soldiers under Henry Bouquet and sent the expedition to relieve Fort Pitt, as well as to chastise the Indians (a force sent to relieve Fort Detroit reached the fort, but was then wiped out in an ill-advised sally against Pontiac's camp).[48] Leaving Philadelphia in mid-July, Bouquet's expedition followed Forbes' road toward Pittsburgh, leaving small detachments to garrison forts along the way in 1758. At Edge Hill, near Bushy Run Creek, about twenty-five miles from Fort Pitt, Bouquet's forces marched into an ambush by a coalition of Lenapes, Mingos, Shawnees, Wyandots, Ottawas, and Miamis. After desperate fighting, Bouquet sprung a trap of his own; two companies feigned a panicked retreat and counterattacked when the warriors pursued them. Bouquet's reports to Amherst put a good face on the action, and Amherst recorded it in tones that indicated he regarded the encounter as a decisive victory.[49] Earlier historians agreed with Amherst and Bouquet's estimation, even calling the battle a "signal victory."[50] Modern historians, however, point out that while Bouquet did drive off the attackers, he lost approximately a quarter of his men, most of his horses, and had to destroy many of the provisions he had brought for the relief of the fort.[51]

Although Bouquet's expedition made it to Fort Pitt, evacuated civilians, and lifted the siege, the victory did not mean the end of violence in the region. In October 1763, Teedyuscung's son Captain Bull destroyed the Susquehanna Company settlement in the Wyoming Valley.

---

46. Dowd, *A Spirited Resistance*, 36, argues that Ecuyer was responsible for the epidemic; Calloway, *The Scratch of a Pen*, 73, is far less certain, stating that smallpox had already broken out among Pontiac's allies in the spring.
47. Anderson, *The Crucible of War*, 541-543.
48. Ibid., 547-550.
49. Webster, *The Journal of Jeffery Amherst*, 318-319.
50. Parkman, *History of the Conspiracy of Pontiac*, 266.
51. Anderson, *The Crucible of War*, 549. Calloway, *The Scratch of a Pen*, 88, calls Bushy Run a "pyrrhic victory."

This revenge for Teedyuscung's death took a gruesome form inspired by Neolin's rejection of British goods—dead men had their eyes pierced with awls, and one woman's body was found with the remains of red-hot iron hinges placed in her hands.[52] In December 1763, a group of western Pennsylvanians calling themselves the Paxton Boys murdered six peaceful Indians, Moravian Christians living in the town of Conestoga. They then slaughtered fourteen more who had taken refuge in Lancaster, Pennsylvania. Some of the Paxton Boys had been among those who buried the mutilated bodies at Wyoming, and they revenged themselves on any who resembled the Wyoming attackers.[53] Declaring that all Indians were enemies in an ironic echo of Neolin's "separate creation," they marched on Philadelphia, both to kill Indians sheltering there and to coerce or attack the Pennsylvania Assembly, which they believed had more concern for Indians than for Anglophone settlers' interests and safety. They were convinced to disband and return home only when Benjamin Franklin met with them and promised to address their concerns in the assembly.[54] Unfortunately, the conflict in Pennsylvania and throughout the colonies became a race war.

By the beginning of 1764, the war settled into a general stalemate. At Detroit, Pontiac broke off his siege in at the end of October 1763, when an emissary from the French commander in Illinois brought definitive news of the Treaty of Paris, informing Pontiac that there would be no French attempt to reconquer the territory lost in the Seven Years' War. Disease and the difficulties of holding a coalition took their toll on the Indian alliance.[55] Without the counterweight of the French, tribes were forced to depend on trade with the British. The diplomacy of Sir William Johnson, who persuaded the Six Nations of the Iroquois to convince the Seneca to repudiate their ties to Pontiac and send messages to their vassal tribes to desist from attacks, also played a role in damping down the conflict. British expeditions in 1764 into present-day Ohio and Illinois met former enemies who were now willing to swear peace, affirming themselves as part of the Covenant Chain that linked the British and their allies.[56] By 1765, the war was generally over,

52. Richter, *Facing East*, 200.

53. Ibid., 203.

54. Ibid., 201-206. Apparently, Franklin reneged on his promise to address the Paxton Boys' concerns.

55. Calloway, *The Scratch of a Pen*, 74-75.

56. Parmenter, "Pontiac's War," 630-635. Bradstreet exceeded his instructions and negotiated generous peace terms, insisting only on the return of all captives held by the northern Indians. This generosity actually proved useful; Bouquet's expedition encountered Indians who were willing to negotiate rather than fight.

although Pontiac himself did not sign a formal peace and declare himself an ally of the British until July 1766.[57]

The Royal Proclamation and the Long-term Effects of the Conflict

Alarmed by the renewed outbreak of violence in North America, the British Crown responded in late 1763 with an attempt to separate the contending forces on the frontiers. Influenced in part by the advocacy of Sir William Johnson, George III promulgated the Royal Proclamation of 1763. This edict essentially extended the policy agreed upon in Pennsylvania at the Treaty of Easton in 1758; it declared a line running through the Appalachian Mountains beyond which colonial settlement was prohibited. The West was an Indian preserve, "To reserve under our Sovereignty, Protection, and Dominion, for the use of the said Indians . . . all the Lands and Territories lying to the Westward of the Sources of the Rivers which fall into the Sea from the West and North West as aforesaid."[58] Although the line was well-intentioned, American colonists viewed the restriction as a betrayal of the blood they had spilled in the war and an attempt to keep them from the spoils of victory. The Proclamation was unrealistic from the outset, and the declaration of the Crown to become the protector of the Indians rankled colonists who had come to believe that all Indians were enemies to be exterminated, rather than equals with their own concerns and interests.[59] The depleted state of the British treasury in the wake of Pontiac's War also induced British Ministers to attempt to lay taxes on the American colonies. American Provincials protested, evaded, and defied British laws, no longer needing British protection from the French, irked at new taxes, and incensed by being denied access to lands they considered conquered. Tensions mounted that exploded roughly a decade later in the American Revolution.

CONCLUSION

While the Seven Years' War changed the balance of power between Britain and France in favor of Britain, Pontiac's War changed the balance of power between Anglophone colonists and Indian tribes, as well as between Britain and her American provinces. At the heart of the struggle were the Lenape, led by the spiritual leader Neolin. Betrayed by British failure to keep promises guaranteed at the Treaty of Easton, pressed by unchecked colonial settlement on lands reserved for them, and suffering under restrictions on trade imposed by the collapse of the

57. Parmenter, "Pontiac's War," 638-639.
58. George III. "The Royal Proclamation—October 7, 1763." *The Avalon Project: Documents in Law, History and Diplomacy.* Yale Law School, 2008.
59. Calloway, *The Scratch of a Pen,* 90-91.

French Empire and Amherst's restrictions on the necessities of their economy, the Lenape began sending out war belts, coupled with a spiritual message of separate creation and resistance. By the time the conflict sputtered to an end, the British Empire had assumed the role of protector of the very tribes who had been murdering British subjects, prohibiting settlers from gaining title to lands they considered theirs in the wake of French defeat. Thus, the Lenape instigation of Pontiac's War was at the root of both racial war and eventual colonial rebellion. The founding of the United States was, in part, an inadvertent Lenape creation.

Countervailing Colonial Perspectives on Quartering the British Army

🙢 GENE PROCKNOW 🙠

In the years leading up to the Revolutionary War, as the British Army repositioned its forces from western frontier posts into American cities, many Americans seethed against quartering troops in urban centers. Animosity with the military occupation was rampant but was not the universal reaction in every location. In two cities, colonial anger ranged from vituperative verbal abuse to outbreaks of destructive violence. On January 19, 1770, New York residents briefly held captive several British soldiers who posted broadsides obnoxious to the radical Sons of Liberty. When additional soldiers arrived, a melee ensued with several injuries on both sides. The ruckus became known as the Battle of Golden Hill.[1] Just a few weeks later, a more serious incident occurred in Boston. On March 5, 1770, soldiers from the British garrison in Boston opened fire on a taunting group of agitators, killing three and wounding eight others (two of whom eventually died). Protesting propagandists cleverly coined the incident as the "Boston Massacre." Generally, historians depict these two violent events as representative of all colonial reactions to the quartering of British troops in American cities. Just a few weeks later, however, this was not the case in a New Jersey town located only thirty-five miles from New York City.

British military commanders posted a portion of the 26th Regiment of Foot in the commercially important trading town of Brunswick (present-day New Brunswick), New Jersey. Located on a navigable portion of the Raritan River, Brunswick consisted of one hundred and fifty houses and three churches. During the French and Indian War, the

1. For a complete account of the events leading up to the Battle of Golden Hill and its location on contemporary Manhattan Island, see allthingsliberty.com/2020/02/the-grand-affray-at-golden-hill-new-york-city-january-19-1770/.

colony of New Jersey constructed barracks on George Street near the intersection of Barracks (later renamed Patterson) Street for the use of the British Army. Purposely sited on the road out of town, the two-story stone building was designed to billet three hundred enlisted soldiers. In 1770, men from several companies of the 26th Regiment and their families had occupied the barracks for almost three years. On a voluntary basis, officers paid local residents to board in their homes. During this period, the officers and enlisted soldiers developed an excellent working relationship with the community.

A career officer, Maj. Charles Preston (not related to Capt. Thomas Preston of the 29th Regiment who was involved in the Boston Massacre), commanded the troops in Brunswick. Scottish by heritage, a contemporary described Preston's character as "worthy, decent, fine tempered."[2] The residents of Brunswick heartedly concurred. On May 14, 1770, upon learning of the redeployment of the 26th Regiment to New York City, the Brunswickers wrote a public letter to Preston which opened, "Prompted by a pleasing Reflection on the Tranquility we have enjoyed from the Harmony that has uniformly subsisted between the Inhabitants, and the Troops quartered in the Barracks here under your immediate Command, for now near three Years, we wait upon you in Order to express our unfeigned Satisfaction." The inhabitants' letter goes on to express "cordial thanks" for the "laudable Disposition" and remarkably concludes with thanks for "Peace and good Order, without the least Infringement on our Rights and Privileges." The letter ends with a wish for "your Honour and Happiness in future life."

To celebrate and give thanks, the townspeople invited Major Preston and the other officers to a gala dinner at the locally prominent Whitehall Tavern, the largest venue in town. Remarkably, residents felt free to publish without retribution from the Sons of Liberty a public notice of the letter and the dinner in a New York newspaper, albeit a Loyalist-leaning newspaper. The reporters noted that the town's citizens provided "a genteel Entertainment."[3] Occurring just a few weeks after the Battle of Golden Hill and the Boston Massacre, the Brunswick celebratory address and festive event stood in stark contrast to the extremely troubled relations between British troops and American colonists nearby New York City and in Boston.

2. James Boswell, *The Yale Editions of the Private Papers of James Boswell: Correspondence* (United Kingdom: McGraw-Hill, n.d.), 8: 168.
3. "The Address of sundry of the Magistrates, Freeholders, and Inhabitants of the city of New-Brunswick, in the Province of New Jersey," *New-York Gazette and Weekly Mercury*, Monday May 21, 1770.

What was so different about the state of affairs in New Brunswick than other locations which quartered British troops? Similar to Boston, New York City and many colonial cities, Brunswick citizens actively participated in militant organizations including the Sons of Liberty and Committees of Correspondence. Brunswick chapters of these groups were less radical but were nonetheless firm in their convictions that British taxes and ministerial retaliations against Boston should be resisted. Rather than differences in rebellious ardor, the positive Brunswick-British Army relationships emanated from other factors. First, British military planners presciently deployed the 26th Regiment in Brunswick, Perth Amboy and Elizabethtown (present-day Elizabeth) which avoided exceeding the barracks capacities and housing accommodations in any one location. Secondly, spending and participating in the local economy by the British soldiers provided a demonstrably positive financial impact for the local citizenry. Given the surrounding agricultural opportunities and commercial trading businesses, less competition existed for employment between local residents and moonlighting British soldiers. Contrary to the situations in Boston and New York City, farmers and traders welcomed access to temporary labor especially during periods of peak demand. Further, the 26th Regiment recruited quite a few Americans which added to the goodwill with the local residents.[4]

The most important reasons for the considerable harmony lay in family and personal areas. During the 26th Regiment's almost three year stay in Brunswick, "upwards of fifty Children have been born in the Barracks." This is a prodigious number of new fathers among the one hundred and sixty soldiers stationed in the town. It is likely that approximately twenty-five percent of the soldiers were married, resulting in one or two births per married soldier.[5] Further demonstrating the happiness of the regiment, "only two Men out of the one Hundred and Sixty of which they consisted have died, one a natural Death, and the other by Accident," a remarkably low death rate for British troops deployed on overseas assignments.[6] The high number of children born

4. S.M. Baule, *Protecting the Empire's Frontier: Officers of the 18th (Royal Irish) Regiment of Foot during Its North American Service, 1767–1776* (Athens, OH: Ohio University Press, 2014), 18.

5. The estimate of the number of wives posted with the 26th Regiment is derived from prisoner of war records in 1775 which listed women captured with the regiment in Canada. Kenneth Baumgardt, "The Royal Army in America During the Revolutionary War The American Prisoner Records" (Christiana, Delaware: Department of Defense, US Army Corps of Engineers, 2008), www.dtic.mil/dtic/tr/fulltext/u2/a491107.pdf.

6. "Maj. Preston's Answer," *New-York Gazette and Weekly Mercury*, Monday, May 21, 1770.

and the low death rate were indicators of less drunk and disorderly behaviors by soldiers, a problem which plagued residents of other towns housing British troops.[7]

Reactions to the laudatory Brunswick address from the two other towns quartering soldiers of the 26th Regiment ranged from supportive to neutral. When Elizabethtown residents read the Brunswick address in the Loyalist leaning *New York Gazette and Weekly Mercury*, the Elizabeth town clerk asked the editor to print their own approbatory but not previously published address to the departing troops. Not to be outdone, the Elizabethtown leaders pointed out that their address to the 26th Regiment officers preceded the Brunswickers' version.[8] No public reaction emanated from the Perth Amboy town leaders and citizens. Given that the Royal Government under the direction of Gov. William Franklin was located in Perth Amboy, one would have thought that its leadership would have also jumped on the bandwagon and sent its own letter praising the performance of the 26th Regiment.

Acknowledging the praise and appreciation from Brunswick's leaders, Major Preston responded in writing to the town's inhabitants a few days after the sendoff dinner. He thanked the residents "for the Honour you have done me, by your kind and obliging Address and receive with the greatest Pleasure this public testimony of your Approbation of my conduct, and the Behavior of the troops under my command." He went on to cite the "good Disposition of the Inhabitants" which "will always claim my Gratitude and best Wishes for their Prosperity."[9]

Five short years later, Major Preston had an opportunity to reconsider his protestations of eternal gratitude. In command of elements of the 26th Regiment and other assorted units, the major signed articles of capitulation to an invading American army in St. Johns, Canada. Stridently, his key demand during the surrender negotiations was to remove any hint of British impropriety with respect to its North American colonies.[10] Despite successfully holding off a besieging force for fifty-three-days and capitulating only because of a lack of ammunition and supplies to continue resistance, the surrender inappropriately tainted Preston's military career. Shortly after a prisoner exchange, Pre-

---

7. For a scholarly assessment of alcohol abuse in the British Army see, Paul E. Kopperman, "The Cheapest Pay: Alcohol Abuse in the Eighteenth-Century British Army," *The Journal of Military History*, Vol. 60, No. 3 (Jul., 1996): 445-470, www.jstor.org/stable/2944520.
8. "Letter to the Editor," *New-York Gazette and Weekly Mercury*, Monday May 28, 1770.
9. "Maj. Preston's Answer," Ibid.
10. Michael P. Gabriel, *Major General Richard Montgomery: The Making of an American Hero* (Madison, NJ and London: Fairleigh Dickinson University Press ; Associated University Press, 2002), 128.

ston returned to Scotland a civilian, inherited a barony, and became a loyal Tory member of Parliament.[11]

As for the Brunswickers, relations with the British Army first cooled and then inexorably shattered. The 29th Regiment, whose soldiers participated in the Boston Massacre, replaced Preston's command in Brunswick. What went through the minds of the town's residents when the 29th Regiment arrived is not recorded, but needless to say, the town held no further dinners feting the British troops. Similar to other colonies, the town's praise of the local soldiers did not translate into paying its share to financially support the British forces as required under the Quartering and Mutiny Acts.[12] Contrary to local economic interests, but supportive of their neighboring colonies, the Brunswickers joined the colonial boycott of British goods. When war erupted, any goodwill towards the soldiers now viewed as occupiers evaporated in the ensuing violence.

Strategically located between New York and Philadelphia, Brunswick and its citizens quickly became embroiled in revolutionary politics and military campaigns. While from time to time George Washington and other Rebel leaders complained about their poor turnout among New Jersey militia, leading Brunswick merchants and influential citizens joined and commanded an active militia.[13] In early 1776, the first session of the newly constituted New Jersey legislature met to plan the state's contributions to war effort in Whitehall tavern, the site of the earlier dinner honoring the 26th Regiment. A year and a half later, the 26th Regiment marched back into town past the Whitehall Tavern, not as peaceful protectors, but as attacking occupiers.[14] To defend against a surprise attack similar to the 1776 assault on the unfortified Trenton, the 26th Regiment constructed re-

11. "Preston, Sir Charles, 5th Bt. (c.1735-1800), of Valleyfield, Firth," The History of Parliament. www.historyofparliamentonline.org/volume/1754-1790/member/preston-sir-charles-1735-1800.

12. Thomas Gage to Earl of Hillsborough, November 6, 1771, K. G. Davies, *Documents of the American Revolution 1770–1783 (Colonial Office Series)* (Shannon, Ireland: Irish University Press, 1973), 3: 231.

13. One of many examples of George Washington's negative views on the New Jersey militia. In this case, he blamed their lack of mustering on his 1776 defeats in New Jersey: George Washington to Lund Washington, December 10-17, 1776," *Founders Online*, National Archives, founders.archives.gov/documents/Washington/03-07-02-0228;.original source: *The Papers of George Washington*, Revolutionary War Series, vol. 7, 21 October 1776–5 January 1777, ed. Philander D. Chase (Charlottesville: University Press of Virginia, 1997), 289–292.

14. Archibald Robertson, *Archibald Robertson: His Diaries And Sketches In America, 1762-1780* (New York: New York Public Library, 1971), Book 2, 136.

doubts and other fortifications around the city.[15] British commander Gen. William Howe sought to entice the Continental Army out of the Watchung Mountains onto the open Jersey plains for a decisive battle. Brunswick served as a key supply and communications center to support this campaign. General Washington did not take the bait, but did harass Howe's forces on their retreat to Staten Island and New York City including skirmishing in and around Brunswick. Further demonstrating that war had changed everything, British forces burned numerous homes and other buildings, devastating the area. Throughout the conflict, British army units were not safe from attack by militia in and around Brunswick.[16]

The account of local residents giving thanks to a departing military commander contrary to national political concerns is a good reminder that all politics is local and that in some cases, personal relationships can transcend broader differences. Brunswick residents were not taking sides in the larger geopolitical dispute when sending the public letter to Major Preston. Simply, they were giving sincere thanks for keeping his soldiers in order and under control. In a small town, with no other means of protection from often-unruly troops, peace and safety were paramount issues. This episode demonstrates that there was not a straight line between high-profile events such as the Battle for Golden Hill and the Boston Massacre to the War for Independence. As evidenced in Brunswick, there were countervailing episodes, just not enough to turn the colonists' attitudes back towards allegiance to the British Crown.

15. For a map of the city and the British fortifications, see Alexander Sutherland and John Hills, Sketch of Brunswick. Sketch of the ground near Mr. Low's at Rariton Landing, 1777, Map, www.loc.gov/item/gm72003593/.
16. The highest ranking Brunswicker in the Continental Army was Brig. Gen. Anthony Walton White. A leading merchant, Col. John Neilson led the Middlesex County/Brunswick militia. For an example of the local militia attempts to attack the British forces around Brunswick see allthingsliberty.com/2017/07/battle-bennetts-island-new-jersey-site-rediscovered/.

The Sons of Liberty and Mob Terror

JEFFREY D. SIMON

The day did not start out well for Andrew Oliver. The recently appointed Stamp Act Distributor for colonial Massachusetts awoke on the morning of August 14, 1765, to learn that his effigy was hanging on an elm tree in Boston by a road that everyone who traveled into town had to pass by. The initials "AO" were written on the right arm so there would be no mistake as to whom the effigy represented. On the left arm was an inscription that read, "What greater Joy did ever New England see Than a Stampman Hanging on a Tree." A sign on his chest claimed that he had betrayed his country for the sake of money. There was also a sign that warned, "He that takes this down is an enemy to his country."[1]

Oliver's job, which would not begin for a few more months when the Stamp Act took effect, was to sell the despised stamped paper to the colonists, which would be required for all types of printed material, ranging from licenses and contracts to newspapers and diplomas. Even playing cards and dice had to have the stamps embossed on them.

1. Richard Archer, *As If an Enemy's Country: The British Occupation of Boston and the Origins of Revolution* (New York: Oxford University Press, 2010), 24; Joshua Fogarty Beatty, *The Fatal Year: Slavery, Violence, and the Stamp Act of 1765* (unpublished Ph.D. dissertation), Lyon G. Tyler Department of History, The College of William and Mary, May 2014, 67-68; Alfred F. Young, "Ebenezer Mackintosh: Boston's Captain General of the Liberty Tree," in *Revolutionary Founders: Rebels, Radicals, and Reformers in the Making of a Nation*, ed. Alfred F. Young, Gary B. Nash, Rap Raphael (New York: Vintage Books, 2011), 15. There was also a boot hanging next to the effigy with a caricature of the devil peeking out from it. This was to symbolize Lord Bute (John Stuart), whom the colonists believed was responsible for the getting the British Parliament to pass the Stamp Act when he served as first lord of the treasury and prime minister. The sole of the boot was painted green to represent George Greenville, who succeeded Bute and who was actually the main architect of the Stamp Act. (Eighteenth century English grammar and spelling is used throughout this article when quoting original documents, speeches, signs, letters, etc.)

These direct, internal taxes imposed by England were naturally unpopular, and before the day was over, Oliver would feel the brunt of the colonists' anger.

The organizers of the protest managed to mix in some levity with the seriousness of the situation. As farmers coming into town stopped their wagons to view the spectacle, they had to have their goods "stamped" by the effigy.[2] But as the crowds grew larger at the elm tree, which later would become known as the "Liberty Tree," the lieutenant governor of Massachusetts, Thomas Hutchinson, who was Oliver's brother-in-law, became worried. He wanted to end this demonstration, and with the approval of Governor Francis Bernard, he directed the sheriff to order his men to take down the effigy and record the names of those who interfered so that arrest warrants could be issued. However, by the time the sheriff's officers arrived at the scene, the crowd had grown too large, with some estimates in the thousands. The sheriff told Hutchinson that his men could not take down the effigy without placing their own lives in danger.[3]

As it turned out, the leaders of the demonstration cut down the effigy themselves at dusk. Rather than ending the protest, though, it signaled the beginning of the violence. After placing the effigy on a bier, the crowd carried it in a mock funeral procession past the Town House where Bernard and other colonial officials were still meeting, trying to decide how to handle the demonstration. The crowd shouted three "huzzahs" triumphantly and chanted, "Liberty, Property, and No Stamps," as they passed by the building.[4] They then proceeded to another building that was under construction and almost completed. Oliver owned the facility and had intended to rent it out for shops, but the mob believed it was going to be the office where the hated stamped paper would be distributed. It only took five minutes to demolish the building.[5]

It was then just a short distance to Oliver's home, where the man of the hour had not fled but instead decided to stand his ground to protect his dwelling. In a scene that would make some contemporary terrorist groups proud, the leaders of the mob "beheaded" the effigy while others in the crowd threw stones at Oliver's house, breaking the windows. The mob then moved a short distance away, where they pretended to

---

2. Young, "Ebenezer Mackintosh," 16.
3. Edmund S. Morgan and Helen M. Morgan, *The Stamp Act Crisis: Prologue to Revolution.*, 3rd ed. (Chapel Hill, North Carolina: The University of North Carolina Press, 1995), 129.
4. Young, "Ebenezer Mackintosh," 16; Morgan and Morgan, *The Stamp Act Crisis*, 130. "Huzzah" was a cheer used in Colonial America to represent triumph or admiration.
5. Morgan and Morgan, *The Stamp Act Crisis*, 130.

"stamp" what was left of the effigy. Their final goodbye to the effigy was to burn it in a bonfire that they made from the wood of Oliver's torn-down facility.[6]

If Oliver thought this was the end of his evening of terror, he was mistaken. Friends persuaded him to hide with his family in a neighbor's house in case the mob returned. A few trusted friends volunteered to remain inside the house to try to ward off any potential theft and/or destruction of the Oliver family's possessions. The mob did, in fact, return and proceeded to demolish a garden fence and break down the barricaded doors and windows. After gaining entry to the house, they learned that Oliver was not there, causing some of them to shout that they would find the Stamp Distributor and kill him. This caused Oliver's friends to flee for their own safety.[7]

The mob was preparing to search the neighbors' homes when a "gentleman"[8] told them that Oliver had gone to Castle William, the British fortification at Boston Harbor, which they had no hopes of penetrating. Believing the words of this unidentified man, the mob decided to take out their anger and frustration on the inside of Oliver's home, destroying all they could find, including furniture, mirrors, and even a large part of the inner wooden covering of the walls. Some of Oliver's possessions that they were careful not to break were his bottles of liquor, which they gladly helped themselves to.[9]

By around eleven o'clock that evening, just as the mob's activities seemed to be subsiding, Lieutenant Governor Hutchinson showed up at the house with the sheriff. They tried to address the crowd and urged them to disperse, but this only incited them further. The leader of the mob shouted, "The Governor and the Sheriff!" making sure everybody knew who these two men trying to talk to them were. "To your Arms my boys," he called out, which led to a barrage of stones being hurled at Hutchinson and the sheriff, forcing them to flee. A short time later, the crowd finally went home.[10]

The next day, Oliver, still reeling from the previous night's terror and undoubtedly fearful of more to come, sent letters to several individuals he believed were associated with the mob, informing them that he had not, in fact, taken the position of Stamp Distributor. A

6. Ibid.; Standiford, *Desperate Sons*, 50.
7. Morgan and Morgan, *Stamp Act Crisis*, p. 130; Standiford, *Desperate Sons*, 50-51.
8. A "gentleman" was "a man of good behavior, well bred, amiable, high-minded, who knows how to act in any society, in the company of any man." See Gordon S. Wood, *The Radicalism of the American Revolution* (New York: Alfred A. Knopf, 1992), 194.
9. Morgan and Morgan, *Stamp Act Crisis*, 130;, Standiford, *Desperate Sons*, 50-51.
10. Morgan and Morgan, *Stamp Act Crisis*, 131; Standiford, *Desperate Sons*, 50-51.

crowd nevertheless formed again that evening at the town square and was ready to start a bonfire, signaling the beginning of potentially another night of violence. Oliver then sent another message, this time a proclamation, disowning any interest in accepting the Stamp Distributor job. This worked, as most of the crowd dispersed. Some, however, went to Lieutenant Governor Hutchinson's house, intending to have a "talk" with him. When they discovered he wasn't home, they marched around the city triumphantly, stopping at various points to read aloud Oliver's proclamation.[11]

Oliver would face the wrath of the colonists again in just a few months. When it was learned that he had received the commission from England to be Stamp Distributor, despite his not wanting the job anymore, the leaders of the mob, who were now known as the "Sons of Liberty," demanded that he "resign" again, this time in person at the Liberty Tree at noon on December 17. Trying to avoid the humiliation, Oliver offered instead to resign at the courthouse. This alternative was promptly refused, and on a dreary, rainy day in Boston, 2,000 colonists assembled at the Liberty Tree to hear Oliver, who was perched at an upper window of a house next to the tree, announce his resignation. They gave him three "huzzahs" when he finished.[12]

The Sons of Liberty's treatment of Oliver alarmed Governor Bernard. He wrote that it was "designed as an Insult upon the Kings Authority; as a Terror to the Kings Officers; and to show them that they were nothing in the Eyes or the Hands of the People. I myself must expect to be called to the Tree of Liberty, if I stay much longer in this Town."[13]

Oliver would rebound from this embarrassing day and eventually become lieutenant governor of Massachusetts in 1770. However, private letters that he, along with Hutchinson, had sent to England in the late 1760s denouncing the challenges to authority that were occurring in Massachusetts and calling for tougher measures from England to assert its rule became public in 1773. This elicited the wrath of the Sons of Liberty, among others in the colony. In one letter, Oliver

11. Standiford, *Desperate Sons*, 51.
12. Morgan and Morgan, *Stamp Act Crisis*, 143-45. Oliver said, " . . . I never will directly or indirectly, by myself or any under me, make use of the said Depuatation or take any measures for enforcing the Stamp Act in America, which is so grievous to the People." See, "420/From Andrew Oliver," *Volume 81: The Papers of Francis Bernard, Volume 2: 1759-1763*, Colonial Society of Massachusetts, www.colonialsociety.org/publications/3111/420-andrew-oliver, accessed November 8, 2019.
13. "421/To Henry Seymour Conway," *Volume 81: The Papers of Francis Bernard, Volume 2: 1759-1763*, Colonial Society of Massachusetts, www.colonialsociety.org/publications/3111/421-henry-seymour-conway, accessed November 8, 2019.

had sought ways "to take off the original incendiaries," else "they will continue to instill their poison into the minds of the people."[14] The Massachusetts House of Representatives unsuccessfully petitioned England to have Oliver removed as lieutenant governor. A broken man in spirits and in poor health, he died on March 3, 1774.[15]

Even in death, Oliver could not escape the terror of the Sons of Liberty. They warned potential mourners to stay away from the funeral, or else they would pay the consequences. It was enough to scare away Oliver's brother, Peter, who was the chief justice of the Superior Court of Massachusetts, from attending. The mourners who did attend were subjected to taunts and shouts from the Sons of Liberty, who gave three final, derisive cheers as Oliver's body was lowered into the ground.[16] Peter Oliver would later write, "Never did Cannibals thirst stronger for human Blood than the Adherents to this Faction. Humanity seemed to be abhorrent to their Nature."[17]

AWAKENING A NATION

The events of August 14, 1765, can be considered the beginning of the American Revolution. Although it would be another decade before actual military engagements commenced with the battles of Lexington and Concord, it was the terror attack on Andrew Oliver that sent shockwaves throughout the colonies and emboldened those who were challenging England's authority in America. For months preceding the attack, there were speeches and newspaper articles denouncing the Stamp Act. Patrick Henry, the fiery orator from Virginia, was just twenty-two years old when he rose up in the Virginia House of Burgesses in May of 1765 to rail against the Stamp Act, offering resolutions that declared it was the sole right of the Virginia Assembly, not England, to tax Virginians. Henry also implied that those who passed the Stamp Act were destroying American freedom. Many newspapers throughout the colonies reprinted Henry's resolutions.[18]

14. Whitfield J. Bell, Jr., *Patriot-Improvers: Biographical Sketches of Members of the American Philosophical Society, Volume One, 1743-1768* (Philadelphia: American Philosophical Society, 1997), 517-18. Benjamin Franklin, who was the Massachusetts Assembly's agent in London, had gained possession of the private letters and sent them to the House of Representatives in Boston, where they were published.

15. Ibid., 518.

16. Ibid., 519; James H. Stark, *The Loyalists of Massachusetts and The Other Side of the American Revolution* (Boston: W.B. Clarke Co., 1907), 168.

17. Douglass Adair and John A. Schutz, editors, *Peter Oliver's Origin & Progress of the American Rebellion: A Tory View,* (San Marino, California: The Henry E. Huntington Library, and Art Gallery, 1961), (Reissued 1967 by Stanford University Press), 112.

18. Morgan and Morgan, *Stamp Act Crisis,* pp. 96, 98; Standiford, *Desperate Sons,* 39, 43.

Despite the anti-Stamp Act sentiment growing in the colonies, there was still no hint of potential violence. The attack on Andrew Oliver came as a surprise to most people. It was, however, an example of "propaganda by deed," long before that term would be coined by the anarchists in Russia and other countries in the late nineteenth century. The idea was that just talking or writing about the state of affairs or about an oppressive government was not enough to bring about change or a revolution; you needed to make your point through aggressive actions. While the organizers of the attack on Oliver were not thinking at that point about revolution, they did want to do something to ensure that the Stamp Act would never come into effect. Focusing their anger on a single Stamp Distributor in Massachusetts could send signals throughout the colonies that any designated Stamp Distributor who takes office will do so in peril to his own life.

The Stamp Act originated with its passage by the British Parliament on March 22, 1765. The legislation was the brainchild of George Grenville, first lord of the treasury and prime minister. England had incurred a large debt due to the French and Indian War (1756-1763, also known as the Seven Years' War) and was also facing escalating costs in maintaining troops and administrative officials in America. A direct tax imposed on the colonies would be one way to lessen these economic and financial burdens.[19]

It was the August 14 attack, and Oliver's announcement the next day that he would not take the position of Stamp Distributor, that resonated throughout the colonies. One night of violence demonstrated what months of writings and speeches against the Stamp Act could not—namely, the power of intimidation and terror. Designated Stamp Distributors in other colonies announced that they, too, would not take office. As historian Pauline Maier points out, "Without distributors the Stamp Act could not go into effect, so the coercions of stampmen seemed rational, even efficient."[20]

Samuel Adams, who was a leading radical member of the colonial Massachusetts legislature and who would later be a signer of the Declaration of Independence, would praise those responsible for the attack on Oliver several years later in an article in the *Boston Gazette*:

> We cannot surely have forgot the accursed designs of a most de-
> testable set of men, to destroy the Liberties of America with one blow,
> by the Stamp-Act; nor the noble and successful efforts we then made

19. Standiford, *Desperate Sons*, 4, 7.
20. Pauline Maier, *From Resistance to Revolution: Colonial Radicals and the Development of American Opposition to Britain, 1765-1776* (New York: Norton, 1991), 54.

to divert the impending stroke of ruin aimed at ourselves and our posterity. The Sons of Liberty on the 14th of August 1765, a Day which ought to be for ever remembered in America, animated with a zeal for their country then upon the brink of destruction, and resolved, at once to save her, or like Samson, to perish in the ruins, exerted themselves with such distinguished vigor.[21]

Shortly after the violence in Massachusetts, groups formed in the other colonies to protest the Stamp Act. They were encouraged by the success of the Boston attacks, which were publicized by both word of mouth and by newspaper articles.[22] Newspapers played a key role in the rise and influence of the Sons of Liberty. Several of their members were the printers of colonial newspapers, which meant they could control the news they wanted the colonists to read. The dangers that the Stamp Act posed to the colonists' basic rights was continually publicized, as were the exploits of the mobs that attacked the Stamp Distributors and all who supported the Stamp Act. "By printing highly colored news of the daring deeds of other colonists, the papers encouraged similar exploits by their own subscribers."[23]

Using the model of mob terror that worked so well in Boston, it became common in other colonies to see Stamp Distributors and other officials hung in effigy, "funeral" processions for "liberty" carried out through the streets, the burning of effigies, and physical attacks on the homes of the officials. More than sixty incidents of mob terror occurred in twenty-five different locations following the Boston attacks.[24] In one instance, the Stamp Distributor for Connecticut was put into a coffin by the mob and lowered into a grave after he insisted on keeping his job. As dirt was shoveled onto the coffin, the terrified individual shouted out for his release and promptly resigned his position.[25]

While many of the groups active in mob violence after the Boston attacks referred to themselves as "Sons of Liberty," there was never a central coordinating body to plot strategy and oversee activity in all of the colonies. The Sons of Liberty were "an informal network of autonomous societies, which flourished largely in the seaport cities in the separate colonies."[26] The officers and committee members came

21. Stoll, *Samuel Adams*, 44-45.
22. Maier, *From Resistance to Revolution*, 54.
23. Morgan and Morgan, *Stamp Act Crisis*, 197.
24. David C. Rapoport, "Before the Bombs There Were the Mobs: American Experiences with Terror," *Terrorism and Political Violence*, Volume 20, Number 2, April-June 2008, 171.
25. Ibid., 172.
26. Ibid., 174.

from the middle and upper classes of society.[27] While at first most of
the Sons of Liberty branches throughout the colonies were comprised
of merchants, lawyers, and skilled craftsmen, the groups eventually also
encompassed working class people.[28] The lower classes comprised most
of the mobs that the Sons of Liberty unleashed upon the Stamp
Distributors and anybody else who supported the Stamp Act.[29]

By mid-November, twelve of the colonies' Stamp Distributors had
resigned. The distributor for Georgia did not arrive from England until
January 1766, and within two weeks, he also resigned his position.[30]
Still, threats and physical attacks continued on anyone associated with
trying to enforce the Stamp Act. Parliament finally repealed the Stamp
Act and King George III ratified the legislation on March 18, 1766.[31]

Nobody could have imagined at that time the significance that the
successful rebellion against the Stamp Act would have a decade later
when full-scale revolt against the British occurred. The Sons of Liberty
never talked or wrote about revolution during this period. They always
stressed that they were still loyal to the king and were only protesting
the actions of the British Parliament in passing the Stamp Act.[32] And
even in that regard, the protests were usually limited to the imposition
of direct, internal taxes on the colonies by a legislative body for which
they had no representation.

But the seeds for revolution had been planted. Everything the Sons
of Liberty did to unite the colonies to take action against the British,
including the calculated use of terror, would come in handy years later
as the revolution took shape. "The Sons of Liberty were keenly aware
that terror had helped nullify the Stamp Act, and, as long as there were
pressing issues surrounding British authority, they would continue to
foster the spirit of resistance whenever and wherever they could."[33]
Peter Oliver, Andrew's brother, would later write that the success of
mob terror in leading to the repeal of the Stamp Act emboldened the
colonists "to strike hard against every Man who wished well to the Authority of the british Government, & who dared to avow its Su-
premacy."[34]

27. Maier, *From Resistance to Revolution*, 86.
28. Steven L. Danver, ed., *Revolts, Protests, Demonstrations, and Rebellions in American History: An Encyclopedia, Volume 1* (Santa Barbara, CA: ABC-CLIO, 2011), 202.
29. Morgan and Morgan, *Stamp Act Crisis*, 194.
30. Standiford, *Desperate Sons*, p. 84; Morgan and Morgan, *Stamp Act Crisis*, 163.
31. Stoll, *Samuel Adams*, 53.
32. Maier, *From Resistance to Revolution*, 104.
33. Robert Kumamoto, *The Historical Origins of Terrorism in America: 1644-1880*," (New York and London: Routledge, 2014), 109-10.
34. Adair and Schutz, *Peter Oliver's Origin & Progress*, 57.

CONCLUSION

The terror of the Sons of Liberty was combined with its masterful exploitation of the media. With members of the group controlling several newspapers, the Sons had free reign to influence public opinion. They were also able to, despite their autonomous and decentralized organizational structure, keep members and sympathizers in each of the colonies aware of recent developments and propose the best strategies to use to protect their rights and liberties.

That violence was the key part of those strategies cannot be denied. From its beginnings with the attack on Andrew Oliver in 1765 to the spectacular sabotage of ships during the Boston Tea Party in 1773, the Sons of Liberty proved that the calculated use of terror can indeed change the course of history. Without the Sons of Liberty, there would likely have never been an American Revolution, and without terror, the Sons of Liberty would not have been able to accomplish their astonishing feat of awakening a nation to its potential to win a long struggle for freedom from a much stronger, and more powerful, adversary.

A "Truly Noble" Resistance: The Sons of Liberty in Connecticut

❦ DAYNE RUGH ❦

The role of Connecticut's Sons of Liberty is one that exemplifies the state's rich history of self-governance and fiercely independent spirit. Their swift reaction to the passage of the Stamp Act of 1765 shattered the political landscape of Connecticut, known ironically as "the land of steady habits. Later, a few select Sons and their respective affiliates would transition into roles on Committees of Correspondence throughout the colony. It has been often misconstrued that the Sons of Liberty were a singular angry mob that patented the art of tarring and feathering British tax collectors, but that was nowhere to be seen in Connecticut. The story of Connecticut's Sons of Liberty is a decade-long modern grassroots movement; a community-oriented example of how it was possible to permanently undermine Britain's administration of the Thirteen Colonies through careful, non-violent resistance.

To the Sons, the Stamp Act was an offensive violation to the large degree of political sovereignty granted by Connecticut's colonial charter and outrage was quick to engulf major centers of industry including New Haven, New London, and Norwich. Eastern Connecticut in particular became a revolutionary hotbed for resistance to the Stamp Act and produced many Sons of Liberty including Col. John Durkee and Brig. Gen. Jedediah Huntington both from Norwich, as well as Declaration of Independence signer William Williams of Lebanon, Maj. Gen. Israel Putnam of Pomfret, Capt. Hugh Ledlie of Windham, and the infamous Benedict Arnold, born and raised in Norwich and resident of New Haven between 1762 and 1775.[1] Other notable members

---

1. Pauline Maier, *From Resistance to Revolution: Colonial Radicals and the Development of American Opposition to Britain, 1765-1776* (New York: W.W. Norton & Company, 1991), 306-307.

of the Connecticut Sons included Jonathan Sturges of Fairfield, Rev. Stephen Johnson of Lyme, John McCurdy of Lyme, Eliphalet Dyer of Windham, and Jonathan Trumbull of Lebanon.

Born in Windham, Connecticut in 1728, John Durkee settled in the Bean Hill section of Norwich upon reaching adulthood; his heroics in battle, business, land-speculating, and leadership in the Sons of Liberty earned him status as a local legend as well as a memorable nickname: the "bold bean hiller." He had neither the privilege of wealth, nor formal education yet historian Frances Caulkins notes, "Could the life of this able and valiant soldier be written in detail, it would form a work of uncommon interest."[2] Many details of Durkee's early life remain obscure, yet being the son of renowned Deacon William Durkee, his upbringing in a devout Christian household had a big impact on his formative years. In 1756, Durkee enlisted in the militia and served in the French and Indian War earning the rank of major by the war's end in 1763. He commanded the Third Company, a Norwich unit, and served in multiple theaters of the war including Gen. Jeffrey Amherst's capture of Montreal, and the Siege of Havana in 1762.[3] After the war's conclusion, he returned to Norwich where he maintained a farm and kept an inn and tavern within his home. His experience in military leadership and personal charisma made him a perfect fit for leading the local Sons of Liberty against the Stamp Act.

Though the Stamp Act passed in March of 1765, the implementation would not occur until November, yet the Connecticut Sons wasted no time in outlining their three specific objectives: prevent the distribution of stamps in Connecticut, galvanize public opposition to the Stamp Act, and remove as many of their political opponent's from power as possible. To carry out their mission, the Sons identified their targets, namely Governor Thomas Fitch and Connecticut's chief Stamp Agent, Jared Ingersoll.

Tensions rose steadily over the summer of 1765, and little did Ingersoll know that his job would be over before it even began. On June 1, Nathaniel Wales, Jr. of Windham wrote to Ingersoll heartily offering his services as a deputy stamp agent.[4] Wales was eager and may have had every good intention, but his naiveté caused him to inadvertently

2. Frances Caulkins, *History of Norwich Connecticut from its Possession by the Indians to the Year 1866* (Gaithersburg: New London Country Historical Society, 2009), 421.
3. Amos Browning, "A Forgotten Son of Liberty" in *Records and Papers of the New London County Historical Society: Volume 3* (New London, CT: New London County Historical Society, 1906), 258.
4. Nathaniel Wales to Jared Ingersoll, June 1, 1765, *Jared Ingersoll Papers*, ed. Franklin B. Dexter (New Haven, 1918), 325.

paint a target on his back. Several weeks later in a noticeably abrupt change of heart, Wales wrote to Ingersoll again on August 19 announcing that he was no longer up to the task, stating, "I am of opinion that the Stamp Duty can by no means be Justifyed & that it is an imposition quite unconstitutional and so Infringes on Rather destroys our Libertys and previlidges that I Cant undertake to promote or encourage."[5] What Wales didn't mention at the time is how Windham's Sons of Liberty succeeded in making him reconsider this prospect through methods known only to him; years later, Wales joined Windham's Committee of Correspondence.

Just two days after Wales's resignation, Jared Ingersoll was burned in effigy on the town green in Norwich, and again in New London, Windham, Lebanon, and Lyme, an ominous foreshadowing of what his future might soon become. Additional letters to Ingersoll warned him that the targeting of Stamp Agents was proving exceedingly effective as described by Boston agent Andrew Oliver, who wrote to Ingersoll on August 26:

> Sir The News Papers will sufficiently inform you of the Abuse I have met with. I am therefore only to acquaint you in short, that after having stood the attack for 36 hours – a single man against a whole People, the Government not being able to afford me any help during that whole time, I was persuaded to yield, in order to prevent what was coming[6]

As calls for his resignation amplified in New Haven, Ingersoll dismissed the Sons and would bring his case before Governor Fitch in September. Unbeknownst to him at the time, the Sons of Liberty were already a step ahead of him. On September 18, 1765, John Durkee and Hugh Ledlie marched from Norwich to Hartford with a large band fellow Patriots, to intercept Ingersoll who was also presently riding to Hartford from New Haven by himself. The next day, Ingersoll was met in Wethersfield by the armed contingent dubbed, Durkee's "Irregulars," reported to have been anywhere from 500 to 1,000 men strong from all over eastern Connecticut.

Seated upon his valiant white steed, John Durkee and his men respectfully yet firmly confined Ingersoll in a nearby home, making it abundantly known that he would advance no further unless his resignation as Stamp Agent was formalized. The details of the entire incident were documented by Ingersoll himself in an article he published in the *Connecticut Gazette* on September 27, 1765. In spite of the fact

---

5. Nathaniel Wales to Jared Ingersoll, August 19, 1765, ibid., 325-326.
6. Andrew Oliver to Jared Ingersoll, August 26, 1765, ibid., 328.

that Ingersoll was incredibly outnumbered by the intimidating crowd, Durkee and his militia treated him with courtesy and respect worthy of a gentleman such as him. For a moment Ingersoll believed that with a little quick wit he could persuade his captors to show mercy and let him on his way, but after three hours of back-and-forth deliberation, he realized his odds were not improving. He conceded to Durkee and was subsequently escorted to Hartford in which he read his letter of resignation before the General Assembly. In a grand fashion, the Patriot crowd made a spectacle of their victory by compelling the now former stamp agent to raise his hat and shout "Liberty and Property!" three times; Ingersoll stated to the "Commandant" of the group, likely Durkee himself, "I did not think the cause worth dying for, and that I would do whatever they should desire me to do."[7] Israel Putnam called on Governor Fitch to advise him of the outcome even demanding the Governor hand over any access to stamps should they arrive from England. In their famous exchange, Fitch asked Putnam, "But if I should refuse your admission?" to which Putnam boldly replied, "In that case, your house will be leveled to the ground in five minutes!"[8] Though his duties to the Crown were finished, Ingersoll didn't fully escape the eyes of the Sons. While back home in New Haven, Ingersoll had the pleasure of reporting fairly regularly to Putnam and Ledlie while they took the liberty of combing through Ingersoll's personal correspondence, as well as the correspondence of his associates, for the better part of six months; evidently they suspected that he might still be up to no good.[9]

Not long after this major victory for the Sons, Connecticut sent Eliphalet Dyer, William Samuel Johnson and David Rowland as delegates to the Stamp Act Congress in New York on October 7, 1765. Ledlie accompanied the delegation and wrote to Samuel Gray in Windham on October 9:

> the Great councel . . . now setts Here to [determine] [the] fate of the Brittish Coloneys in North America . . . Nobody Here Knows what is to be [done] after that [fatal] Day Which is Dreded by Every [so called] thinking man . . . in Hopes the present Congress Will Do something Worthey such a Sett of Smart Men as they [appear] to me to be.[10]

---

7. Jared Ingersoll, "Communication to The Connecticut Gazette," *The Connecticut Gazette*, September 27, 1765, ibid., 346.
8. Frederick Albion Ober, *"Old Put" the Patriot* (New York: D. Appleton and Company, 1904), 122.
9. Joseph Chew to Jared Ingersoll, February 5, 1766, *Jared Ingersoll Papers*, 377-378.
10. Hugh Ledlie to Samuel Gray, October 9, 1765, CWF Rockefeller Library Special Collections.

The resolutions adopted by the Congress did little to persuade Governor Fitch who remained unyielding in his loyalty to the Mother Country; a conviction on which he would stake his political future. By the start of the new year, the Connecticut Sons of Liberty achieved two out of their three objectives. Not a single stamp was issued in the colony, colony-wide opposition to the act was widespread, and nearly all of their political opponents were out of the picture; Governor Fitch and his deputies were next.

In March 1766, the Sons of Liberty convened in Hartford, akin to a modern-day political party, to nominate a slate of candidates headed by William Pitkin and Jonathan Trumbull to run against Fitch, who previously held the governorship for over a decade. Representation by the Sons of Liberty was strong but noticeably absent was William Williams and his delegation from Lebanon; Williams expressed his disappointment claiming it was due to a miscommunication in timing. The results were a landslide victory for the Sons; Pitkin was elected governor and Trumbull as his lieutenant governor; Colonel Putnam was elected to the General Assembly that year as well. In the end, both Ingersoll and Fitch grossly underestimated the changing political climate in Connecticut yet their sufferings could be described as remarkably tame compared to their counterparts in Boston. Upon repeal of the Stamp Act, Norwich residents erected a liberty pole on the town green with great patriotic fanfare.[11]

Tactics of the Sons of Liberty changed in the latter part of the 1760s with the passage of new acts such as the Townshend Duties, prompting the Sons and their allies to engage in non-importation movements as well as well as promote the production of locally sourced goods, homespun fabrics, and more. Others took a more clandestine approach to subverting British regulations through covert smuggling operations. One of those noted smugglers was the future traitor, Benedict Arnold.

Born in Norwich in 1741, Arnold was noteworthy he was infamous even before his betrayal as his early years were both tumultuous and tragic. Forced out of private schooling in Canterbury, Arnold completed an apprenticeship by age twenty-one with his mother's cousins, Drs. Daniel and Joshua Lathrop, and in 1762 he set out for New Haven with his sister Hannah. Upon the death of his mother in 1759, his father continued to struggle with alcohol abuse and died in 1761 having

---

11. In 1769, John Durkee left Norwich and became a manager of the Susquehanna Company before returning to Connecticut to command the 20th Continental Regiment in 1776 and the 4th Connecticut Regiment in 1777. His career in the Continental Army ended shortly after the Battle of Monmouth where a musket ball shattered his right hand. He passed away in Norwich on May 29, 1782.

squandered the family's fortune. In addition to Hannah, Arnold had four other siblings who all succumbed to yellow fever at very early ages. His father's alcoholism was a mark of shame on the family and they suffered publically because of it. Once he left Norwich, Arnold was determined to remake his destiny and never returned to his home town. Though Arnold did excel as a businessman, his utter lack of bookkeeping skills plagued him consistently and he was largely burdened by debts throughout his entire life. Strapped for cash, Arnold sold his family home in Norwich in 1764 home to none other than fellow Son of Liberty Hugh Ledlie, for a sum of 700 pounds sterling.[12]

Arnold established a successful business in New Haven within walking distance of Yale College where he sold books, medicines, and an array of cosmopolitan goods "sibi totique," from the Latin meaning "for himself and for all." He personally commanded many of his merchant vessels and his smuggling efforts resulted in major hauls of contraband liquor, but his brash overconfidence failed to keep his operation a secret. As a result, one of his disgruntled sailors threatened to expose Arnold to the authorities. Arnold never took kindly to threats and had the poor sailor flogged not once, but twice, the second time being a public demonstration, and faced a fine of fifty shillings as a result.[13] Though Arnold did have many character strengths, a knack for diplomacy was not one of them.

Arnold was normally never subtle with his feelings or intentions, and on many occasions provided a clear glimpse into the profile of a man whose passion burned fervently for the American cause, standing in stark contrast to his treasonous legacy we're all familiar with. When news of the Boston Massacre reached Arnold during one of his trips to the West Indies, he wrote:

> I was very much shocked the other day on hearing the accounts of the most wanton, cruel, and in-human murders committed in Boston by the soldiers. Good God! are the Americans all asleep, and tamely yielding up their liberties, or are they all turned philosophers, that they do not take immediate vengeance on such miscreants?[14]

12. Ledlie's wife Chloe Stoughton Ledlie resided in the former Arnold house until her death in 1769 and gave birth to two children during this time, one of which likely died in infancy. Her five years spent in Norwich were fraught were turmoil and resulted in her being physically confined as described by Frances Caulkins. These circumstances, and others, have resulted in a number of whimsical ghost stories about the allegedly cursed Arnold homestead; the fact that the house was struck by lightning and destroyed in 1853 has fueled the haunted narrative.
13. Oscar Sherwin, *Benedict Arnold: Patriot and Traitor*, (New York: The Century Co., 1931), 10.
14. Ibid., 15.

When word reached New Haven that hostilities broke out on the Lexington Green in 1775, Arnold immediately marched the second company of the Governor's Foot Guards, of which he was captain, to Cambridge.

The year 1774 became the year that everything changed. Boston was now under martial law, and the punitive Coercive Acts aimed to punish the town for the destruction of the tea in 1773. Starvation quickly took root only to be compounded by a massive smallpox epidemic the following year. Desperate for aid, an appeal was circulated from Boston's Committee of Correspondence and on June 6, 1774 at a town meeting in Norwich, the Norwich Committee of Correspondence was formed consisting of Christopher Leffingwell, Jedediah Huntington, William Hubbard, Dr. Theophilus Rogers, and Capt. Joseph Trumbull; Leffingwell would head the committee.[15] A neighbor of the Arnold family, Jedediah Huntington was a noted member of the Sons of Liberty and served valiantly in the American Revolution alongside General Washington and fellow neighbors including John Durkee. Huntington became a successful merchant and served through the entire American Revolution, earning the distinctive recognition of General Washington who regarded him as one of his most trusted commanders. Washington wrote to him on October 16, 1783 stating, "Permit me, My dear Sir to take this opportunity of expressing to you my obligations for the support and assistance I have in the course of the war received from your abilities & attachment to me . . . you have always possessed my esteem & affection."[16]

In addition to Norwich, additional Committees of Correspondence were established all throughout Connecticut which embarked on a single common mission: provide relief and aid to the citizens of Boston in the form of provisions, food, money, livestock, and intelligence. The first Norwich committee meeting was held on, of all days, July 4, 1774; minutes from the meeting list the names of twenty-six individuals the committee recruited as subscribers to aid Boston.[17] Surviving records from the Norwich committee provide clear details on these proceedings and even reveals the location of where the first meeting took place, the home of prominent resident and local tavern keeper, Azariah Lathrop.[18]

15. John Stedman, ed. *The Norwich Jubilee. A Report of the Celebration at Norwich, Connecticut on the Two Hundredth Anniversary of the Settlement of the Town* (Norwich: John W. Stedman, 1859), 90.

16. George Washington to Jedediah Huntington, October 16, 1783, Papers of the New London County Historical Society.

17. Norwich Committee of Correspondence Papers, New London County Historical Society.

18. Ibid.

The first installments of aid were in place, just in time for the Sons of Liberty to flex their muscles once again on another unsuspecting victim, similar to what happened to Jared Ingersoll. On the morning of July 6, 1774, Boston loyalist and debt collector Francis Green arrived in Norwich outside Lathrop's tavern, having been previously chased out of Windham while attempting to collect certain debts on behalf of Boston's British occupiers. As Norwich sits at the halfway point on land routes between New York and Boston, the intersection of roads outside Lathrop's tavern on the Norwichtown Green was a major stage-coach stop for many years. Word spread quickly, and the Sons of Liberty were ready for Mr. Green's arrival. One could only imagine what went through Green's mind as he witnessed the massive assembly of citizens on the Town Green complete with bells ringing, drums beating, and muskets firing. Unsurprisingly, accounts of the incident from both sides differ immensely. In an affidavit submitted to Massachusetts Gov. Thomas Gage dated July 20, Green named several individuals who affronted his visit, one of them being Simeon Huntington of Norwich who reportedly threw his hands on Green.[19] Green took out the equivalent of a wanted-ad in the *Massachusetts Gazette* offering a one-hundred dollar reward for the capture of the aggressors, but none were turned in. In fact, Jedediah Huntington was so impressed with Simeon's bravado, that he wrote to Governor Trumbull on September 9, 1775 expressing his intent to appoint Simeon as a lieutenant within his regiment stating, "I want officers of a military spirit."[20]

Not long after Francis Green was chased out of Connecticut, the Norwich committee succeeded in assembling the first round of aid, a total of 291 sheep gathered at the tavern of Benjamin Burnham in nearby Newent (Lisbon), CT in a record dated August 20, 1774.[21] Earlier in July, Samuel Adams had received the Norwich committee's promissory letters and wrote a personal response fully expressing his sincerest appreciation dated July 11, 1774:

> Gentlemen: Your obliging Letter directed to the Committee of Correspondence for the Town of Boston, came just now to my hand; and as the Gentlemen who brought it is in haste to return, I take the liberty to writing you my own Sentiments in Answer, not doubting but they

19. Peter Force, *American Archives: Containing a Documentary History of the English Colonies in North America, from the King's Message to Parliament of March 7, 1774, to the Declaration of Independence by the United States.* Fourth Series (United Kingdom: M. St. Clair Clarke and Peter Force, 1837), 630-631.
20. Mary Perkins, *Old Houses of The Antient Town of Norwich 1660–1800* (Norwich: Press of The Bulletin Co., 1895), 249-250.
21. Norwich Committee of Correspondence Papers.

are but they are concurrent with those of my Brethren. I can venture to assure you that the valuable Donation of the worthy Town of Norwich will be received by this Community with the Warmest Gratitude & [disposed] of according to the true Intent of the Generous Donors . . . The Part which the Town of Norwich takes in this Struggle for American Liberty is *truly noble* [emphasis added][22]

A response to Samuel Adams's letter was written by Christopher Leffingwell to William Phillips in Boston dated August 1774 stating that future donations will be collected and forwarded to further relieve Boston.[23] For over the course of nine months, the donations continued to pour in as Leffingwell promised, not just from Norwich but from all over Connecticut. In April of 1775, Jedediah Huntington wrote on behalf of the committee to Boston stating that additional sheep were being dispatched to the city in addition to a monetary donation of twenty-two pounds and nineteen shillings delivered by Joseph Carpenter, Norwich's master silversmith.[24] The money was received by David Jeffries on April 19, 1775 and by then, the war was officially underway. The combined efforts of the Connecticut Committees of Correspondence greatly impacted the afflicted in Boston and never went unnoticed or unacknowledged.

The Connecticut committees continued to communicate with Boston and amongst themselves and after the outbreak of war conversations between the committees shifted to matters of intelligence on enemy movements. One such instance is documented on April 28, 1775 where the New London Committee of Correspondence wrote to Norwich stating, "This moment we Received a letter from [New York] letting us know that a Packitt had that moment just arrived with Dispatch's for General Gage . . . its best to keep a good look out for it."[25] As the British entrenched themselves in Boston, a series of raids were conducted on Block Island, Fisher's Island, and Long Island to resupply the regulars with badly needed food and provisions. Christopher Leffingwell wrote to General Washington on August 7, 1775 informing

22. Samuel Adams to the Norwich Committee of Correspondence, July 11, 1774, in *A Historical Discourse Delivered in Norwich, Connecticut, September 7, 1859, at the Bi-Centennial Celebration of the Settlement of the Town*, ed. Daniel Coit Gilman (Boston: Geo. C. Rand and Avery, City Printers, 1859), 104.
23. Christopher Leffingwell to William Phillips, August 1774, Massachusetts Historical Society, Series 4 Vol. 4, 45-46.
24. Jedediah Huntington to the Boston Committee of Correspondence, April 1775, Norwich Committee of Correspondence Papers.
25. New London Committee of Correspondence to the Norwich Committee of Correspondence, April 28, 1775, Norwich Committee of Correspondence Papers.

him that the British had seized upwards of 2,000 sheep and cattle from the islands and were transported by ship back to Boston.[26] For Washington and his new army, there was nothing that could have been done to prevent the raids. Though these channels of communication and coordinated efforts were largely disorganized and wholly incomparable to the British, they nevertheless represented a budding foundation for future intelligence operations in the region.

In a way, Connecticut's Sons of Liberty were ahead of their time, focused on the clear objective of transforming the colony's future under British rule. They looked after themselves, their families, their neighbors, and brethren in neighboring colonies in a manner which proved that civil disobedience could effect change, even under the threat of death. In one of his many firebrand sermons against the Stamp Act, Rev. Stephen Johnson stated boldly, "O my Country. My dear distressed country! For you I have wrote; for you I daily mourn, and to save your invaluable Rights and Freedom, I would willingly die."[27] In a letter written in April of 1766, the Norwich Sons stated almost prophetically that they were willing "to Risk even our Lives and fortunes in Defending . . . our Just writes and Liberties against a Wicked and trechirus Ministry."[28] These words represent a nearly divine vision that would be realized a decade later in the Declaration of Independence, the resolved affirmation that the future of Americans, and of greater mankind, would not live as subjects of a King, but rather as free people governed by the principles of freedom.

---

26. The Committee of Correspondence Norwich to George Washington, August 7, 1775, *Founders Online*, National Archives, founders.archives.gov/documents/Washington/03-01-02-0169; original source: *The Papers of George Washington*, Revolutionary War Series, vol. 1, *16 June 1775–15 September 1775*, ed. Philander D. Chase (Charlottesville: University Press of Virginia, 1985), 262–264.
27. Jim Lampos and Michaelle Pearson, *Revolution in the Lymes: From the New Lights to the Sons of Liberty* (Charleston: The History Press, 2016), 43.
28. Maier, *From Resistance to Revolution*, 102.

A Moonlighting British Army Surgeon

GENE PROCKNOW

During the American War of Independence, the British Army officer corps routinely relegated its surgeons and physicians to a secondary status among its ranks. A few regimental surgeons made contributions to medical science, but the vast majority were relatively unknown both in their time and today.[1] American military doctors fared a bit better, but are mostly remembered for their interpersonal squabbles. Dr. Hammond Beaumont, surgeon to the British Army 26th Regiment of Foot, broke the mold and became remarkably well known and respected during the American Revolution. His prominence, however, emanated from extracurricular activities outside of normal military duties.

A career officer, Dr. Hammond joined the 26th Regiment as its surgeon in 1761 and during the summer of 1767 embarked from Ireland for garrison duty in colonial North America. Gen. Thomas Gage first deployed the regiment to three towns in the New Jersey. Dr. Hammond found New Jersey to be agreeable and on December 7, 1768 he married Elizabeth Trotter at the St. John's Church in Essex (now Union) County.[2] Two years later, British commanders repositioned the 26th Regiment to New York City. Soon after, Dr. Beaumont first ventured beyond his regimental duties into a profit-making private medical practice. Venereal disease ran rampant among both soldiers and the general

---

1. From a professional medical perspective, Tabitha Marshall argues that British Surgeons Thomas Dickson Reide, Robert Jackson and Robert Hamilton stand out for making significant contributions to medical science during the Revolutionary Era.

2. New Jersey Historical Society, *Documents Relating to the Colonial, Revolutionary and Post-Revolutionary History of the State of New Jersey* (Press printing and publishing Company, 1900), 408, books.google.com/books?id=qEBKAQAAMAAJ. The couple's marriage license is dated November 17, 1768.

population. Suffering from the afflictions associated with syphilis, Thomas Flackfield, a private in the 26th Regiment, sought medical care from the regimental surgeon as treatments from local physicians failed to alleviate his distress.

Dr. Beaumont prescribed a multi-stage regimen featuring Keyser's Pills. Developed and marketed by Jean Keyser, a French military surgeon, the widely distributed pills consisted of a mixture of mercuric oxide and acetic acid. The private suffered from one hundred and twenty-nine ulcers covering all parts of his body. After a taking eleven hundred and seven Keyser's Pills over a four-month period, the private's symptoms disappeared. With this "miraculous recovery," Dr. Beaumont sensed a profit-making opportunity and entered into a cooperative relationship with a famous newspaper editor and drug distributor. Publisher of the *New York Gazetteer or the Connecticut, New Jersey, Hudson's River, and Quebec Weekly Advertiser,* James Rivington imported Keyser's Pills from Dr. James Cowper in London and advertised the pills and the services of Dr. Beaumont to afflicted readers and other members of the community. In newspaper advertisements throughout the colonies, Rivington assured the authenticity of his pills and attested to Dr. Beaumont's curative services.[3] In addition to syphilis, the Dr. Keyser's Pills were advertised to combat a host of afflictions including rheumatism, asthma, and sciatica, all common afflictions of eighteenth century soldiers. The pills were even thought to cure "giddiness of the head."[4] Demonstrating their popularity, American general Henry Knox also sold Dr. Keyser's Pills provided by Rivington in his Boston book store.[5]

Anticipating additional profitable ways to augment his regimental income, Dr. Beaumont engaged in a business venture with Dr. James Latham (c. 1734-1799) surgeon to the 8th Regiment of Foot. Latham held a lucrative franchise for the northern colonies to administer a smallpox inoculation using the propriety Suttonian method. In the 1760s, Dr. James Sutton and his son David developed the Suttonian system of inoculation. The process started with abstaining from meat and alcohol for two weeks prior to the inoculation. In week three, a charged lancet was held slantwise to create a one sixteenth of an inch-deep incision in the skin to insert some of the disease. Afterwards, reg-

3. James Rivington to Messieurs Bradford, *Pennsylvania Journal or Weekly Advertiser*, November 10, 1773.
4. *New York Gazette and Weekly Mercury*, June, 22, 1772, Supplement, 2.
5. John L. Smith, "Henry Knox, Drug Dealer?," *Journal of the American Revolution*, February 25, 2014, allthingsliberty.com/2014/02/henry-knox-drug-dealer/.

ular purges, exercise in the open air, a bland diet and cold-water baths were ordered. With a bit of mystery, the attending physician administered a secret remedy to cap off the treatment regimen. No one is sure of its exact ingredients, but later physicians believe Sutton's confidential remedy consisted of mercury and antimony, two common medical components of the period. The undisclosed remedy added a perceived competitive advantage and a barrier to entry to a procedure viewed both as dangerous and controversial by the general public. By stressing the secret remedy and the extensive regimen, Dr. Sutton sought to disadvantage physicians who had not purchased a franchise.

During an earlier posting in Canada, Dr. Latham first practiced the Suttonian method. Given its notable and immediate success, Latham "sub-franchised" the system to other physicians throughout New York, Connecticut and Massachusetts. When Dr. Beaumont learned that the 26th Regiment was to be transferred to Montreal, he purchased the right to administer the inoculation in Canada from Dr. Latham. It was a profitable business. In addition to the pills, the standard treatment charge for a British soldier was one guinea and likely more for a civilian. Doctors practicing the Suttonian method developed a reputation for highly successful inoculations with few deaths and mild cases, attracting many patients. For Dr. Latham, the practice became so lucrative that he quit the British Army to attend to his growing network of franchised physicians and his burgeoning private practice.

As the Revolutionary War intervened, Dr. Beaumont would not experience the same level of financial success as Dr. Latham. Beaumont's outmanned 26th Regiment attempted to stem the determined 1775 American invasion of Canada. The Americans overwhelmed the widely dispersed components of the 26th Regiment at Fort Ticonderoga, Fort St. Johns, Montreal and the St. Lawrence Valley. The American Rebels captured Beaumont at the latter location on November 18 and sent him to a prisoner of war camp in Reading, Pennsylvania.[6] During his captivity, he continued to inoculate prisoners. After a year of captivity, Beaumont and the 26th Regiment returned to New York City under terms of a negotiated prisoner exchange.

In occupied New York City, Dr. Beaumont's life and career took a "dramatic" turn. British commanders reassigned him to the garrison's hospital as one of the eight attending physicians and surgeons.[7] Beaumont, however, turned most of his attention to the dramatic stage, be-

6. *Philadelphia Gazette*, December 27, 1775.
7. "Promotions, War Office July 22, 1777," *Pennsylvania Ledger, or the Virginia, Maryland, Pennsylvania, and New Jersey Weekly Advertiser*, October 22, 1777.

coming a thespian. Theater enthusiastic British officers organized an acting troupe to entertain the officer corps and to generate funds to be donated to stranded widows and children of British soldiers. The officer troupe appropriated the red-painted John Street Theater and renamed it the Royal Theater. More senior British officers played the male parts with the junior or younger officers playing female roles. Mistresses and professional actresses sometimes became cast members. Joining the 1777 season, Dr. Beaumont performed as the principle "low comedian" engendering raucous laughter from satire, bawdy language, double entendras and crude jokes. He became a hit during the well-attended, five-month theater season of weekly plays. In a bow to the actors' professional responsibilities, several of the performances were cancelled as result of military operations.

When Gen. Sir William Howe launched his campaign to capture Philadelphia in the fall of 1777, Dr. Beaumont accompanied the invasion force and re-focused on his duties as a regimental surgeon. In January, 1778, he participated in a curious mission into Rebel territory. To provide clothing, supplies, and medical aid to captured British soldiers, he received a pass from Gen. George Washington to pass Rebel lines and attend prisoners in Reading, Pennsylvania. The planned humanitarian mission got caught up in the politics between Washington and the Board of War led by Maj. Gen. Horatio Gates. Although the British supply force received a pass for safe transit from Washington, the Board of War ordered their detention. During the detention dispute, Rebel officers discovered counterfeit Continental currency in the British supply wagons. This breach of protocol and gentlemanly honor infuriated the Rebels and tainted the entire British mission. Even though Washington eventually straightened out the conflicting orders and allowed the British mission to proceed, Dr. Beaumont and the supply force abandoned their efforts to reach Reading and returned to Philadelphia.

Rebuffed in his efforts to care for sick and wounded prisoners, Dr. Hammond quickly returned his attention to the stage. Transformed from a place to care for the sick and wounded, the red brick and wood Southwark Theatre on Philadelphia's South Street reopened as a playhouse for the amateur thespian British officers. Oil lamps lit the stage and Capt. John André and Capt. Oliver Delancey painted the background scenery.[8] In a season stretching from January 19 to May 19, the

---

8. Darlene Emmert Fisher, "Social Life in Philadelphia During the American Revolution," *Pennsylvania History: A Journal of Mid-Atlantic Studies* 37, no. 3 (July 1970): 249.

cast performed thirteen different plays. The British officer troupe charged admission prices of one dollar for the box or the pit and fifty cents for the gallery. In general, the performances were well attended and well received. Demand for seats was so high that newspaper notices had to be placed to warn patrons without tickets not to bribe the door keepers.[9]

Critics regarded Dr. Beaumont as the star of the troupe. Audiences especially hailed Beaumont's performance in the comedy farce *The Mock Doctor, or the dumb lady cured*, a Henry Fielding adaption of Moliere's *Le Médecin malgré lui*.[10] Beaumont played the lead role, Gregory, the husband impersonating a doctor at the request of his wife. British Capt. John Peebles remarked in his diary that "Dr. Beaumont shin'd in the mock Doctor."[11] Given the critical acclaim, the troupe restaged the play several times over the subsequent months. A fan of the theater, General Howe regularly sat in the "Royal Box" with his mistress. In a peculiar turn of events, Rebel Maj. Gen. Charles Lee, who at the time was a British prisoner, accompanied General Howe to a March performance.[12]

At the end of the theater season, British officers staged an opulent outdoor pageant known as "The Meschianza" in honor of the departing General Howe. Beaumont played a prominent role in this over-the-top extravaganza. He acted the part of a herald in the center of a square of knights and their lady escorts. After a flourish of trumpets, Dr. Beaumont, in his best theatrical voice, exclaimed, "Knights of the Blended Rose by me the Herald, proclaim and assert that the Ladies of the Blended Rose excel in wit, beauty, and every accomplishment, those of the whole world; and should any Knight or Knights be so hardy as to dispute or deny it, they are ready to enter the lists with them and maintain their assertions by deeds of arms, according to the laws of ancient chivalry."[13]

Dr. Beaumont evacuated Philadelphia with the British Army, now under the command of Gen. Henry Clinton, and returned to New York City. Once back in New York, Beaumont resumed medical duties at

9. *Philadelphia Ledger*, January 26, 1778.

10. *Philadelphia During the Revolution*, 371.

11. John Peebles, *John Peebles' American War: The Diary of a Scottish Grenadier, 1776-1782*, ed. Ira D. Gruber(Mechanicsburg, PA: Stackpole Books, 1998), 172.

12. Jared A. Brown, "'Howe's Strolling Company': British Military Theatre in New York and Philadelphia, 1777 and 1778," *Theatre Survey* 18, no. 1 (1977): 39, doi.org/10.1017/S0040557400005184.

13. David Hamilton Murdoch, ed., *Rebellion in America: A Contemporary British Viewpoint, 1765-1783* (Santa Barbara, CA: Clio Books, 1979), 623.

"A Side Box," published in London, December 6, 1781.

the garrison's hospital. Over the next two years, his interest and devotion to the theater intensified. In addition to acting, he became the playhouse treasurer and then in 1779 he assumed the role of co-manager of the theater. Soon after, a personal tragedy struck Beaumont. In the spring of 1780, Elizabeth (Trotter) Beaumont passed away in her thirty-seventh year after twelve years of marriage.[14]

Despite his personal loss, Dr. Beaumont remained highly engaged in public entertainment events. The next year he organized evening walks at Fort George for gentlemen and their ladies. Offered by subscription of one guinea, a band serenaded the strolling couples.[15] Also during this period Beaumont devoted his time to dealing with the increasing complexity of the growing and prosperous theater business generating almost four thousand pounds per season. The highly active theatre remained in production through 1782. Nearing the end of its annual run, Beaumont solicited nominations from regimental commanding officers of deserving widows and children to receive surplus

14. *New-York Gazette and Weekly Mercury*, May 29, 1780.
15. *Royal Gazette*, Wednesday, July 25, 1781.

funds generated by theater performances. Under his management, a record of over eight hundred pounds was raised in the 1781-2 season to support the families of deceased British soldiers, the highest amount in any of the seven years of theater operation. After this successful season, tragedy again struck. Dr. Hammond Beaumont died on October 1, 1782. An obituary in the *Royal Gazette* remembered Beaumont as, "a Gentleman of infinite pleasantry and humour, very respectable in his profession, and greatly esteemed by a numerous acquaintance."[16] After his death, the theater floundered.[17]

Initially, like many other physicians and officers, Dr. Beaumont sought to leverage his situation in North America for personal financial gain. He energetically pursued a lucrative private medical practice while holding an active army surgeon's commission. But he found his true passion in the theater. Acting and theater management engendered respect and acclaim from his fellow officers that Beaumont's normal regimental duties did not provide. While there is no evidence that the theater interfered with the doctor's military duties, the demands of weekly theater productions consumed a predominance of his time. As a result, Dr. Beaumont was not known for being an outstanding army surgeon but he was well liked and esteemed for his captivating thespian roles. While many people find satisfaction from their advocations and careers, to follow your true passion is a good life lesson for all!

16. *New-York Gazette and Weekly Mercury*, October 7, 1782.
17. After the war, the Royal Theater would regain its original name and become a major force in the rebirth of the American stage.

An Economist's Solution to the War: Adam Smith and the Rebelling Colonies

BOB RUPPERT

Adam Smith, considered by many to be the Father of Modern Economics, was born in Kirkcaldy, Scotland on June 16, 1723. His father, also Adam Smith, was a senior solicitor and judge advocate; his mother, Margaret Douglas, was the daughter of a well-landed gentleman. Smith entered the University of Glasgow when he was fourteen years old and studied under Francis Hutcheson. In 1740, as a graduate scholar, he pursued his postgraduate studies at Oxford. He gradually became dissatisfied with the style of education at Oxford and left in 1746. Two years later, he was giving rhetoric lectures at the University of Edinburgh. He was assisted in securing the position by Lord Kames and the Philosophical Society of Edinburgh. In 1750, Smith met David Hume. Until his death, Hume and Smith would regularly converse on such topics as history, politics, philosophy, economics and religion. In 1752, Smith became a professor at the University of Glasgow where he taught logic and became a member of the Philosophical Society of Edinburgh. Before the year was out, he was asked to become the head of Moral Philosophy. In 1759, Smith published *The Theory of Moral Sentiments* and three years later, the University of Glasgow conferred upon him the degree of Doctor of Laws (LL.D.).

In 1763, his life began to move in another direction. David Hume, four years earlier, had sent presentation copies of *Theory of Moral Sentiments* to notable politicians including his friend Charles Townshend. Townshend was so impressed with Smith's work that he travelled to Glasgow to meet him. He asked Smith to consider being

tutor and chaperone to his stepson, Henry Scott, the young Duke of
Buccleugh, on the young man's Grand Tour of the continent his
graduation from Eton. In October of 1763, with Henry Scott in his
final term at Eton, Townshend contacted Smith and asked him for his
decision.[1] Smith accepted the offer[2] and with permission from the
university, took up his new position in January of 1764.

At the time, a wealthy young man from the gentry class finished his
education by going on a tour of the continent; it was an educational
rite of passage. The tour had two purposes: first, to expose him to the
cultural legacy of both Classical Antiquity and the Renaissance, and
second, to experience the aristocratic societies on the continent. For
the first year and a half Scott and Smith toured the south of France,
then spent two months in Geneva and finally ten months in Paris. The
tutelage was cut short in 1766 when Henry Scott's brother died. Shortly
after returning to London, Smith's services were required by Lord
Shelburne, the Secretary-of-State for the Southern Department and
the American Colonies,[3] and Charles Townshend, now the Chancellor
of the Exchequer; the former sought advice on the Roman Colonial
Model of Government,[4] the latter needed annotation of a document
that he had prepared on the concept of a "Sinking Fund."[5] In time, the
document would evolve into the Revenue (or Townshend) Acts of
1767. Smith headed back to Scotland, but instead of returning to the
University of Glasgow, he returned to his home in Kirkcaldy and began
work on what would become his magnum opus, *An Inquiry into the
Nature and Causes of the Wealth of Nations*. Smith spent most of the next
six years working on the text.

In 1773 he returned to London where he hoped to finish the text
and express his gratitude to the Royal Society for his recent election.
During his time in London, he visited Shelburne frequently. The first
edition of *Wealth of Nations* was published on March 9, 1776. Smith
sent a copy to Shelburne. It was clear by the time of its publication that
Smith was preoccupied with the American colonies. He had devoted

1. "Correspondence No. 76, Charles Townshend to Smith, 25 October 1763," in Ernest
Campbell Mossner and Ian Simpson Ross, eds., *The Glasgow Edition of the Works and
Correspondence of Adam Smith* (Oxford: Clarendon Press, 1987), 95.
2. "Correspondence No. 78, Adam Smith to Hume, 12 December 1763," ibid., 98.
3. Ian Simpson Ross, *The Life of Adam Smith* (Oxford: Oxford University Press, 1995),
116, 134-36; Smith had also tutored Shelburne's second son, Thomas Petty Fitzmaurice,
at the University of Glasgow from 1759 thru 1761.
4. "Correspondence No. 101, Adam Smith to Shelburne, 12 February 1767," in *The
Glasgow Edition of the Works and Correspondence of Adam Smith*, 122.
5. "Correspondence No. 302, Charles Townshend to Smith, Oct.—Dec. 1766," ibid., 328.

Chapter VII of Book IV, entitled "Of Colones" and Chapter III of Book V, "Of Public Debts," or nearly thirty percent of Volume II, to the present conflict between Britain and America. Among the many arguments that Smith presented in his work, there were three that directly impacted the colonists.

First, he believed the colonies should be taxed.

> It is not contrary to justice that . . . America should contribute to-wards the discharge of the publick debt of Great Britain. That debt was contracted in support of government . . . to which several of the colonies of America owe their present charters, and consequently their present constitution, and to which all the colonies of America owe the liberty, security, and property, which they ever since enjoyed. That publick debt has been contracted in the defence, not of Great Britain alone, but of all the different provinces of the empire.[6]

Second, he believed the colonies should be granted representation in Parliament. Taxes imposed on the colonies

> could scarce, perhaps, be done, consistently with the principles of the British constitution, without admitting into the British Parliament, or if you will into the states-general of the British Empire, a fair and equal representation of all those different provinces, that of each province bearing the same proportion of the produce of its taxes, as the representation of Great Britain might bear to the produce of the taxes levied upon Great Britain"[7]

Third, he believed that there should be free trade within the empire.

> The extension of the custom-house laws of Great Britain [to America] . . . would be in the highest degree advantageous to both. All the invidious restraints, [that is,] the distinctions between the enumerated and non-enumerated commodities of America would be entirely at and end . . . The trade between all the different parts of British empire, would in consequence, be as free as the coasting trade of Great Britain at present. The British empire would thus afford within itself an immense internal market for every part of the produce of all its different provinces.[8]

In April Smith headed back to Kirkcaldy. Over the next four months, he and Hume exchanged numerous letters. Hume had recently

---

6. Adam Smith, *An Inquiry into the Nature and Causes of the Wealth of Nations*, R.H. Campbell and S.S. Skinner, eds. (Carmel, IN: The Liberty Fund, 1981), 2: 944.
7. Ibid., 933.
8. Ibid., 935.

finished a short autobiography entitled *My Own Life*. On August 22, Smith asked him if he could "add a few lines to your account of your own life;"[9] on the 23, Hume, with the assistance of his caretaker, wrote back, "You have entire liberty to make what Additions you please to the account of my Life."[10] Sadly, on August 25, David Hume died. On November 19, Smith sent a letter to Hume's publisher, William Strahan; it was a stirring eulogy in honor of his friend.[11] Two months later, the autobiography and letter were published together for the first time.[12]

By January 1777, Smith was back in London. He wanted to be in town for the printing of the second edition of *Wealth of Nations* and had been asked by Lord North, the Prime Minister and Chancellor of the Exchequer (he had succeeded Charles Townshend), to serve as an advisor to Sir Grey Cooper, the Secretary to the Treasury, who put together the nation's budget. Smith's connection with Lord North probably came about through Alexander Wedderburn, a former student and now friend as well as the Solicitor-General in North's administration. Smith had been in communication with Wedderburn during the previous summer.[13] Due to the war, the government of England was falling deeper in debt and needed additional sources of revenue. Smith's ideas considerably influenced Cooper's thinking on the matter. He recommended the imposition of two new taxes in the 1777 budget, one on manservants and another on property sold at auction. The former was projected to bring in 105,000 pounds and the latter, 37,000 pounds. These became part of North's budget speech that was delivered in the House of Commons in August. The following year Cooper recommended two more taxes, one on inhabited house duty and another on malt. The former was projected to bring in 264,000 pounds and the latter, 310,000 pounds.[14]

9. "Correspondence No. 166, Adams Smith to David Hume, 22 August 1776," in *The Glasgow Edition of the Works and Correspondence of Adam Smith*, 206.
10. "Correspondence No. 168, David Hume to Adams Smith, 23 August 1776," ibid., 208.
11. "Correspondence No. 179, Adams Smith to William Strahan, 9 and 13 November 1776," ibid., 217, 221.
12. *Scots Magazine*, Volume 39 (January, 1777), 1-7.
13. "Correspondence No. 159, Alexander Wedderburn to Adam Smith, 6 June 1776," in *The Glasgow Edition of the Works and Correspondence of Adam Smith*, 197; "Correspondence No. 163, Adam Smith to Alexander Wedderburn, 14 August 1776," ibid., 203; "Correspondence No. 185, Alexander Wedderburn to Adam Smith, 30 October 1776," ibid., 226.
14. John Rae, *The Life of Adam Smith* (London: Macmillan and Company, 1895), 320-21; *The London Magazine, Or, Gentleman's Monthly Intelligencer* (London: R. Baldwin, 1778), 46: 393-94.

On October 23, Archibald Menzies, the Commissioner of Customs in Scotland, died. In November, at the recommendation of William Strahan, Alexander Wedderburn, the Duke of Buccleugh, Sir Grey Cooper and Henry Dundas, the Lord Advocate of Scotland, Lord North agreed to appoint Smith to be the new Commissioner of Customs.[15]

On December 2, news reached London of Burgoyne's defeat at Saratoga. The loss of 6,000 men immediately changed the military calculus of the war. England needed to consider a different approach with regard to her American colonies. North wrote in a letter to King George, "The consequences of this most fatal event may be very important and serious and will certainly require some material change of system. No time shall be lost, and no person who can give good information left unconsulted in the present moment."[16]

The reality of the moment was not lost on Smith. In February of 1778, he wrote a memorandum to Wedderburn that condensed his thoughts on England's future options.[17] It was entitled "Smith's Thoughts on the State of the Contest with America." The memorandum read:

> There seems to be four, and but four, possible ways in which the present unhappy War with our Colonies may be conceived to end.
>
> First, it may be conceived to end in the complete submission of America; all the different colonies, not only acknowledging, as formerly, the supremacy of . . . the mother country; but contributing their proper proportion towards defraying the expence of the general Government and defence of the Empire.
>
> Secondly, it may be conceived to end in the complete emancipation of America; not a single acre of land, from the entrance into Hudson's Straits to the mouth of the Mississippi, acknowledging the supremacy of Great Britain.
>
> Thirdly, it may be conceived to end in the restoration, or something near to the restoration, of the old system; the colonies acknowledging the supremacy of the mother country, allowing the Crown to appoint the Governors, the Lieutenant-Governors . . . and submitting to certain regulations of trade; but contributing little or nothing towards defraying the expence of the general Government and defence of the empire.

15. His Letters Patent appointing him commissioner were not officially signed on January 24, 1778; they were first published in the *London Gazette*, January 29, 1778.

16. John Fortescue, *The Correspondence of King George III From 1760 to December 1783* (London: Macmillan and Company, 1927-28), 3: No. 2095.

17. G.H. Guthridge, "Smith's Thoughts on the State of the Contest with America," *American Historical Review*, 38 No. 4 (July, 1933), 714-20; The memorandum was not discovered and attributed to Smith until 1933.

Fourthly, and lastly, it may be conceived to end in the submission of a part, but of a part only, of America; Great Britain, after a long, expensive and ruinous war, being obliged to acknowledge the independency of the rest.

The probability of some of these events is very small; and it may not, perhaps, be worthwhile to say anything about them. For the sake of order and distinctness, however, I shall say a few words concerning the advantages and disadvantages which might be expected from each.

If the complete submission of America was brought about altogether by Conquest, a military government would naturally be established there; and the continuance of that submission would be supposed to depend altogether upon the continuance of the force which had originally established it. But a military government is what, of all others, the Americans hate and dread the most. While they are able to keep the field they never will submit to it; and if, in spite of their utmost resistance, it should be established, they will, for more than a century to come, be at all times ready to take arms in order to overturn it . . .

Whatever could be extorted from them . . . would be spent in maintaining that military force which would be requisite to command their obedience. By our dominion over a country, which submitted so unwillingly to our authority, we could gain scarce anything but the disgrace of being supposed to oppress a people whom we have long talked of . . . as our brethren and even as our children . . .

A plan of this kind would be agreeable to the present humour of Great Britain where, if you except a few angry speeches in Parliament, it would meet with scarce any opposition.

If the complete submission of America was brought about altogether by treaty, the most perfect equality would probably be established between the mother country and her colonies; both parts of the empire enjoying the same freedom of trade and sharing in their proper proportion both in the burden of taxation and in the benefit of representation

The principal security of every government arises always from the support of those whose dignity, authority and interest, depend upon its being supported . . . The leading men of America, being either members of the general legislature of the empire, or electors of those members, would have the same interest to support the general government of the empire which the Members of the British legislature and their electors have at present to support the particular government of Great Britain . . .

That the complete submission of America, however, should be brought about by treaty only, seems not very probable at present. In their present elevation of spirits, the ulcerated minds of the Americans are not likely to consent to any union, even upon terms the most advantageous to themselves. One or two campaigns, however, more successful than those we have hitherto made against them, might bring them perhaps to think more soberly upon the subject of their dispute with the mother country . . . however, the plan of a constitutional union with our colonies and of an American representation seems not to be agreeable to any considerable party of men in Great Britain. The plan which, if it could be executed, would certainly tend most to the prosperity, to the splendour, and to the duration of the empire, if you except here and there a solitary philosopher like myself, seems scarce to have a single advocate. After the unavoidable difficulty, however, of reconciling the discordant views both of societies and of individuals

The complete emancipation of America from all dependency upon Great Britain would at once deliver this country from the great ordinary expence of the military establishment necessary for maintaining her authority in the colonies, and of the naval establishment necessary for defending her monopoly of their trade. It would at once deliver her likewise from the still greater extraordinary expence of defending them in time of war . . . If, with the complete emancipation of America, we should restore Canada to France and the two Floridas to Spain; we should render our colonies the natural enemies of those two monarchies and consequently the natural allies of Great Britain. Those splendid, but unprofitable acquisitions of the late war, left our colonies no other enemies to quarrel with but their mother country. By restoring those acquisitions to their antient masters, we should certainly revive old enemies and old enemies . . . yet the similarity of language and manners would in most cases dispose the Americans to prefer our alliance to that of any other nation. Their antient affection for the people of this country might revive, if they were once assured that we meant to claim no dominion over them; and if in the peace which we made with them, we insisted upon nothing, but the personal safety, and the restoration to their estates and possessions, of those few unfortunate individuals who have made some feeble, but ineffectual efforts to support our authority among them. By a federal union with America we should certainly incur much less expence, and might, at the same time, gain as real advantages, as any we have hitherto derived from all the nominal dominion we have ever exercised over them.

But tho' this termination of the war might be really advantageous, it would not, in the eyes of Europe appear honourable to Great Britain; and when her empire was so much curtailed, her power and dignity would be supposed to be proportionably diminished. What is of still greater importance, it could scarce fail to discredit the Government in the eyes of our own people, who would probably impute to mal-administration what might, perhaps, be no more than the unavoidable effect of the natural and necessary course of things.

The restoration, or something near to the restoration, of the old system would sufficiently preserve, both in the eyes of foreign nations and of our own people, the credit and honour of the government. Our own people seem to desire this event so ardently, that what might be the effect of mere weakness and inability, would by them be imputed to wisdom, tho' too late wisdom, and moderation. But this event would not preserve the honour of the British Government in the eyes of the Americans. After so complete a victory, as even this event would amount to; after having, not only left their own strength, but made us to feel it, they would be ten times more ungovernable than ever; factious, mutinous and discontented subjects in time of peace; at all times, upon the slightest disobligation, disposed to rebel . . . This event, however, does not at present seem very probable. The Americans, I imagine, would be less unwilling to consent to such a union with Great Britain than to the restoration, or anything like the restoration, of the old system . . .

The Americans . . . when they compare the mildness of their old government with the violence of that which they have established in its stead, cannot fail both to remember the one with regret and to view the other with detestation. That these will be their sentiments when the war is over and when their new government, if ever that should happen, is firmly established among them, I have no doubt. But while the war they will impute, and with appearance of reason too, the greater part of the oppressions which they suffer to the necessity of the times. Those oppressions will serve to animate them, not so much against their own leaders, as against the government of the Mother country to which they will impute the causes of the necessity.

An apparent restoration of the old system, so contrived as to lead necessarily, but insensibly to the total dismemberment of America, might, perhaps, satisfy the people of Great Britain . . . It might, at the same time, gradually bring about an event which, in the present distressful situation of our affairs, is, perhaps, of all those which are likely to happen, the most advantageous to the state. But the policy, the secrecy, the prudence necessary for conducting a scheme of this kind, are such as, I apprehend, a British Government, from the nature and essence of our constitution, is altogether incapable of.

The submission or conquest of a part, but of a part only, of America, seems of all the four possible terminations of this unhappy war, by far the most probable; and unfortunately it is the termination which is likely to prove most destructive to Great Britain. The defence of that part, from the attacks of the other colonies, would require a much greater military force than all the taxes which could be raised upon it could maintain. The neighborhood of that part would keep alive the jealousy and animosity of all the other provinces, and would necessarily throw them into an alliance of the enemies of Great Britain.

Smith knew the plan that was most advantageous to the empire was the one that promoted a constitutional union with American representation, but he also knew it was unlikely to be adopted. There were two primary reasons for this: First, most members of Parliament were Landed Gentry and were not of the mindset to do so. "We, on this side of the water, are afraid lest the multitude of American representatives should overturn the balance of the constitution, and increase too much either the influence of the crown on one hand, or the force of democracy on the other."[18] Second, two men who he believed supported him brushed aside his notion of a constitutional union. They were North and Shelburne. North wanted to restore relations to the status quo of 1763. On February 17, 1779, he introduced two conciliatory bills in the House of Commons. The purpose of the first, entitled "Taxation of Colonies Act 1778," was

> To remove the said uneasiness, and to quiet the minds of his Majesty's Subjects, who may be disposed to return to their allegiance, and to restore the peace and welfare of all his Majesty's dominions, it is expedient to declare that the King and Parliament will not impose any duty, tax, or assessment, for the purpose of raising a revenue within any of the said Colonies, Provinces, or Plantations . . . Except only such duties as it may be expedient to impose for the regulation of commerce; the net produce of such duties to be always paid and applied to and for the use of the Colony, Province, or Plantation, in which the same shall be respectively levied.

The purpose of the second, entitled "Royal Instructions to the Peace Commission 1778" was

> That persons to be appointed by his Majesty . . . shall have full power, commission, and authority, to treat, consult and agree, with such body or bodies political and corporate, or with such assembly or assemblies of men, or with such person or persons . . . concerning any grievance . . . . existing or supposed to exist, in the government of any of the said Colonies, Provinces, or Plantations. That in order to facilitate the good purposes of this Act, it shall and may be lawful for the said Commissioners,[19] from time to time . . . To order or proclaim a cessation of hostilities on the part of his Majesty's troops in any of the said Colonies . . .

18. Smith, *An Inquiry into the Nature and Causes of the Wealth of Nations*, 2: 625.
19. The three commissioners were Frederick Howard, the 5th Earl of Carlisle, George Johnstone, the former governor of West Florida, and William Eden, an undersecretary of state.

To suspend the operation and effect of a certain Act of Parliament . . .
To grant a pardon or pardons to any number or description of persons
within the said Colonies . . . [and] are hereby authorized and empowered to suspend in such places, and for such times as they shall think
fit . . . The operation and effect of all or any of the Acts or Act of Parliament, which have been passed since the 10th day of February, 1763.[20]

Nowhere in the Act or the Instructions were the commissioners
granted power to negotiate a constitutional union or independence.
There was, however, in the final version of the Instructions an
additional concession concerning representation. Unfortunately, it
described a "mutual representation:"

By a reciprocal deputation of an agent or agents from the different
states, who shall have the privilege of a seat and voice in the Parliament
of Great Britain; or, if sent from Britain, to have in that case a seat and
voice in the assemblies of the different states to which they may be deputed respectively, in order to attend to the several interests of those
whom they are deputed.[21]

Smith believed that the Continental Congress, who had declared
the colonies free and independent almost a year and half earlier, would
find most of the commissioners' powers meaningless. Shelburne, on the
other hand, wanted the mercantile system to remain in place.

Never adopt any scheme which would go to dissever our colonies
from us; for as soon as that event should take place . . . The Sun of Great
Britain is set and we shall no longer be a powerful or respectable people
. . . Treaties of Commerce [are] the most ridiculous things in the whole
world; showing, by a variety of historical precedents, that those which
had at the time of making them been deemed the wisest, have always
failed, and turned out to no effect . . . Trade laws were quite a different
nature, they were solemn compacts, in which the interests of the con-
tracting parties were reciprocal, and founded, on the same basis . . . Such
were the connections between all states and their colonies; and such
were the obligations of interest and good faith . . . He advised the ministers eternally to . . . Never give up the Navigation Act[s].[22]

Adam Smith knew what North and Shelburne failed to grasp—if a
constitutional union and representation in Parliament were not strongly
considered, it was too late for anything but independence.

20. 18 Geo. 3 c. 12; *The Papers of George Washington, Revolutionary War Series, 1 March
1778—30 April 1778*, David R. Hoth, ed. (Charlottesville, VA: University of Virginia Press,
2004), 546-48.
21. teachingamericanhistory.org/library/document/response-to-british-peace-proposals/.
22. *The Parliamentary History of England, From the Earliest Period to the Year 1803* (London:
T.C. Hansard, 1814), 850-56.

Ethan Allen's Mysterious Defeat at Montreal Reconsidered

❀❦ MARK R. ANDERSON ❦❀

On September 25, 1775, three weeks into the American invasion of Canada, the legendary Ethan Allen fought a fierce battle outside Montreal with about one hundred Canadians and Continental soldiers at his side. The result was bitter defeat at the hands of a larger British-Canadian force that had sortied from the city to confront them at Longue Pointe. The self-penned *Narrative of Colonel Ethan Allen's Captivity* claimed that another party was committed to join him in taking Montreal that day, but somehow, he and his men had been inexplicably left to fend for themselves. Over the centuries, historians have had remarkably few primary sources to help unravel this mystery.

Only Ethan Allen's *Narrative*, written in 1779, provides substantial details from the American perspective. As a result, historiographical explanations of his misadventure have generally split into two distinct camps. One faction follows dominant contemporary views that Allen's "imprudence and ambition" had unnecessarily exposed his party to defeat in a rash, uncoordinated attempt on the city, and emphasizes inconsistencies in the self-serving *Narrative* account.[1] Other historians and biographers hew close to the *Narrative*, focusing on Allen's claim

---

1. James Livingston to Richard Montgomery, September 27, 1775, i153 v1 r172 p196, RG360, M247, National Archives and Records Administration (NARA), also in Peter Force, ed. *American Archives, Fourth Series* (AA4) (Washington, DC: M. St. Clair Clarke and Peter Force, 1837-1846), 3: 953; Henry Beekman Livingston to Robert R. Livingston, October 6, 1775, *Magazine of American History* 21 (1889): 258; Timothy Bedel to Richard Montgomery, September 18 [sic], 1775, i153 v1 r172 p202, RG360, M247, NARA [AA4 3: 954 transcription with a presumably correct date of September 28]; Benjamin Trumbull, "A Concise Journal or Minutes of the Principal Movements Towards St. John's ... in 1775," *Collections of the Connecticut Historical Society* 7 (1899): 147; Richard Montgomery to Philip Schuyler, September 27, 1775, Philip Schuyler Papers, New York Public Library [also AA4 3: 952]; "Extract of a letter from Tionderoga [sic], October 5," *Rivington's Gazette*, October 26, 1775.

that Maj. John Brown had committed to a coordinated, supporting attack on Montreal with many more men but did not arrive, leaving Allen
to his fate.[2] Long-overlooked Canadian primary sources, however, shed
significant light on Allen's mysterious predicament and suggest an alternative explanation for his "single-handed" battlefield defeat at
Longue Pointe on September 25.

An important point in Ethan Allen's road to Montreal came on July
27, 1775, when he was left without a commission or command after
township leaders surprisingly selected Seth Warner to command their
new Continental Green Mountain Rangers Regiment. Still eager to
contribute to the Patriot cause, Allen joined the September invasion of
Canada as a volunteer officer. Maj. Gen. Philip Schuyler and Brig. Gen.
Richard Montgomery focused the Northern Army's main efforts on a
siege of British Fort Saint Johns, just inside the Canadian border, but
dispatched the energetic and charismatic Allen on a productive six-day
mission behind enemy lines. He served as a liaison with Richelieu Valley Canadian patriots and Indians. Allen returned to headquarters on
September 14, and four days later, General Montgomery sent him out
once again to promote Canadian partisan recruiting efforts and procure
supplies.[3]

Allen ventured down the Richelieu River, north towards the St.
Lawrence, and made a last report to Montgomery from St. Ours on
September 20. Only the hero's own *Narrative* offers an account of his
activities thereafter, when he was sidetracked to participate in an attack
on Montreal:

> On the morning of the 24th day of September, I set out with my
> guard of about eighty men, from Longueil, to go to La Prairie . . . but
> had not advanced two miles before I met with Major Brown . . . who
> desired me to halt, saying that he had something of importance to com-
> municate to me and my confidants; upon which I halted the party, and

2. Most Ethan Allen and Green Mountain Boy-focused works—especially early ones—
follow the thesis that Brown abandoned Allen. In 1798, Ethan's brother Ira added Seth
Warner to this story, essentially accusing both Brown and Warner of deliberate betrayal
out of jealousy. Ira Allen, *History of the State of Vermont* [reprint of *The Natural and Political
History of the State of Vermont . . .* (1798)] (Tokyo: Charles E. Tuttle, 1969), 46. In contrast,
the Allen-blaming camp has usually emphasized Brown's distinguished patriotic military
record and proven commitment to the cause to counter the *Narrative*'s implied claim
against him.
3. Ethan Allen to Philip Schuyler, September 6, 1775, AA4 3: 742-43; Ethan Allen, *Narrative of Col. Ethan Allen's Captivity* (Albany: Pratt and Clark, 1804), 13-15; Schuyler to
George Washington, September 20, 1775, AA4 3: 752; Richard Montgomery to Schuyler,
September 19, 1775, AA4 3: 797; Schuyler to Washington, September 20, 1775, AA4 3:
752; Trumbull, "Concise Journal," 145-46.

went into an house, and took a private room with him and several of my associates, where . . . Brown proposed that, "Provided I would return to Longueil, and procure some canoes, so as to cross the river St. Lawrence a little north of Montreal, he would cross it a little to the south of the town, with near two hundred men, as he had boats sufficient; and that we would make ourselves masters of Montreal."—This plan was readily adopted by me and those in council; and in consequence of which I returned to Longueil[,] collected a few canoes, and added about thirty English Americans to my party, and crossed the river in the night of the 24th, agreeable to the before proposed plan.[4]

To this point, John Brown had been an Allen ally who had joined in the capture of Fort Ticonderoga four months earlier. In the Canadian invasion, Brown was given a similar role to Allen's, but in a more official role as a Continental major; he too led remote army missions north of Fort Saint Johns, often in conjunction with the local irregulars.[5] There is no documentary record from Brown or the other participants of this council to verify or contest Allen's *Narrative* account of this meeting or the ensuing plans.

In the fateful morning of September 25, Allen anxiously waited to hear the "three huzzas" that Brown's force would allegedly use to signal a successful crossing from La Prairie and readiness to attack Montreal from the south. After two hours, he concluded that Brown's force was not arriving. Allen was in a predicament, isolated on the island with just his one hundred men, lacking sufficient watercraft to evacuate the entire force at once. When British and Loyalist forces unexpectedly marched out of Montreal to meet him later that day, he opted for a pitched battle against the odds, until ultimately convinced to surrender.[6]

SANGUINET'S "EYEWITNESS ACCOUNT"

As historians have diligently searched for sources that might expand on Allen's streamlined *Narrative,* many have overlooked intriguing details in an otherwise well-known Canadian source—the *Témoin oculaire,*

4. Allen to Montgomery, September 20, 1775, AA4 3: 754; Allen, *Narrative,* 15-16.

5. John Brown was the major of Easton's Massachusetts Regiment. He had been very active in Canada in 1775, conducting a fact-finding mission to Montreal in the spring before Ticonderoga, and then conducting several scouting missions across the border to gather intelligence, gage Canadian support, and communicate with Richelieu Valley Patriot cells before the invasion.

6. Allen, *Narrative,* 15-17. Historian David Bennett offered a detailed critique of the alleged plan described in the *Narrative,* concluding that Allen's account is "dubious" and that such a plan would have been "preposterous," in large part based on the Montreal-area geography. David Bennett, *A Few Lawless Vagabonds: Ethan Allen, the Republic of Vermont, and the American Revolution* (Havertown, PA: Casemate, 2014), 79-80.

or "eyewitness account" of the 1775-1776 invasion, written by Montreal notary-lawyer Simon Sanguinet and published in French in the nineteenth century. As an active Loyalist and inquisitive government official, Sanguinet was particularly well-informed of events in and around the city. His most enlightening contributions to the Allen story involve prebattle activities in the dark hours of September 24-25.[7]

While Allen's *Narrative* offered just a one-sentence account of that night's St. Lawrence passage after the party "collected a few canoes," Sanguinet identified that it was Montreal citizen Jacques Roussain—owner of a canoe service at Allen's mainland departure point in Longueuil—who "loaned them canoes to facilitate their crossing." Roussain continued to be intimately involved with the mission that night. He "went, with seven or eight others" to meet the rebel force in Longue Pointe after Allen's ten o'clock crossing.[8]

Then, Sanguinet's 'eyewitness account' added a particularly intriguing element to the story. "In the course of the night," Ethan Allen "visited several houses in the Quebec suburb, particularly Jacques Roussain's." The Montreal suburbs were known havens for Patriot Canadian activity, and the Quebec (or Sainte-Marie) suburb sat outside the city's northern walls, closest to Longue Pointe. While Sanguinet did not describe specific topics in Allen's conversations that night, British sources hint at them. A couple weeks after the battle, Indian Superintendent Guy Johnson recounted that, "*relying on some persons said to be disaffected in the City* [author's emphasis], Col: Allen, their most daring partizan, advanced with a body of about 140 Rebels very near Montreal." Gov. Guy Carleton also related claims from the Canadians captured with Allen, who had said "they expected all the suburbs, some in the town, and many from the neighbouring parishes, would have joined them and that they were to march in without opposition."[9]

7. Yves-Jean Tremblay, "Sanguinet, Simon," *Dictionary of Canadian Biography*,www.biographi.ca/en/bio/sanguinet_simon_4E.html; Justin H. Smith, *Our Struggle for the Fourteenth Colony: Canada and the American Revolution* (New York: G. P. Putnam's Sons, 1907), 1: 387.
8. Simon Sanguinet, "Témoin Oculaire de l'Invasion du Canada par les Bastonnois: Journal de M. Sanguinet," in Hospice-Anthelme Verreau, ed., *Invasion du Canada: Collection des Mémoires Recueillis et Annotes* (Montréal: Eusèbe Senécal, 1873), 49 (author's translation); Claude Perrault, ed., *Montréal en 1781: Déclaration du fief et seigneurie de L'île de Montréal* (Montréal: Payette Radio, 1969), 100-1; Alex Jodoin and J. L. Vincent, *Histoire de Longueuil et da la Famille Longueuil* (Montreal: Gebhardt-Berthiaume, 1889), 547.
9. Sanguinet, "Témoin Oculaire," 52, 61 (translation from E.B. O'Callaghan Papers, New-York Historical Society, p31); Guy Johnson to Earl of Dartmouth, October 12, 1775, Edmund B. O'Callaghan, ed., *Documents Relative to the Colonial History of the State of New-York* (Albany: Weed, Parsons and Company, 1857), 8: 637; Guy Carleton to Earl of

Until events on September 25 proved them wrong, nobody—Loyalist or Patriot—appears to have expected Montreal's citizens to defend the city if threatened by American forces that week. Continental intelligence reports described British government preparations to evacuate the city, and even erroneously suggested that the governor had already departed. Carleton, too, confided that he believed the city was "defenceless" before Allen's defeat.[10] The details of overnight discussions from Sanguinet's journal, combined with widespread assumptions about Montreal's vulnerability, create a scene in which suburban Patriot friends might have easily convinced Allen that Montreal was ripe for the taking—even with just his own small party. These factors could be construed to support the theory that Allen acted rashly in an attempt to claim victory on his own. On the other hand, these additional elements of the story do nothing to disprove the competing *Narrative*-aligned theory that Brown negligently or deliberately abandoned Allen to face defeat alone. Sanguinet adds important details, but offers little to solve the core mystery behind Allen's alleged abandonment.

THE L'ASSOMPTION MOBILIZATION

Other long-ignored sources—from French Canadian depositions and a priest's memoirs—describe a substantial effort to cooperate with Allen at Montreal. They make it clear that on the very day of the Battle of Longue Pointe, a Continental captain was deliberately coordinating efforts with Canadian patriot leaders in L'Assomption Parish, twenty-six miles north of Montreal. When integrated into the established story, these accounts complicate the traditional explanations for Allen's "single-handed" fight.

Early on September 25, Repentigny postmaster Joseph Deschamps brought a carriage to receive two ferry passengers approaching from the north end of the Island of Montreal. He soon met "two strangers, an Acadian, who acted as a French interpreter to the other, who he said was a Bostonian officer wore a blanket overcoat and had a feather in his hat" (French Canadians used the term "Bostonian" to describe Americans from any of the old English colonies). After perhaps an hour's ride, passing over ten miles of farmland along the L'Assomption

Dartmouth, October 25, 1775, Kenneth Davies, ed., *Documents of the American Revolution, 1770-1783 (Colonial Office Series)*, volume 11 (Dublin: Irish University Press, 1976), 165.
10. "Extract of a letter from a gentleman in Quebeck" September 30, 1775, AA4 3: 845; Montgomery to Schuyler, September 19, 1775, AA4 3: 797; Montgomery to Schuyler, September 20, 1775, i153 v1 r172 p184, RG360, M247, NARA; Marie-Thérèse Benoist to François Baby, October 3, 1775, Verreau, *Invasion*, 317; Allen, *Narrative*, 18.

River, Deschamps delivered these men at the home of notorious Canadian Patriot Thomas Walker. [11]

Walker had been an outspoken and obnoxious agitator for traditional English rights in Montreal since his arrival from Boston in the early 1760s. As the Revolution brewed, he unsurprisingly took an active role in the city's Patriot committee of correspondence. In May 1775, partisan tensions flared in Montreal after the controversial Quebec Act went into effect and even more so after rebel Americans raided Fort Saint Johns, so Walker left for his country estate in L'Assomption. There, far from government eyes and Loyalist enemies, Walker kept a covert correspondence with rebel American leaders at Ticonderoga. He provided intelligence and encouraged an invasion of Canada. Even though British authorities intercepted several letters and arrested messengers, they incredibly permitted Walker to remain at liberty, even after the rebel American army entered Canada. [12]

On September 25, Thomas Walker welcomed the visiting Continental captain and interpreter who had been brought to L'Assomption. Walker met with the officer in a separate room for about an hour and a half. The two emerged midway through their discussions to find that six or seven locals had since arrived. Walker purposefully asked them, "is it not true that I have three or four hundred inhabitants at my disposal? to which the said persons replied unanimously, yes sir"—apparently validating claims of support that he had made in private conversation with the captain. L'Assomption's parish priest, Pierre Huet de la Valinière, later recounted that Walker "had won the confidence of most of the parish & even of many from the surrounding areas." When the military visitors prepared to leave Walker's house, the American captain shook hands with all the local guests while the Acadian interpreter told them in French, "come to see us, we will be above Long Point." [13]

Walker took his rebel guests to visit a Patriot neighbor named Correy, perhaps Edward Correy. Militia captain Jean-Baptiste Bruyère de Belair was at the house and later recounted: "the Bostonian officer, who spoke a little French, said to him: Good-day, Captain, will you do me the favor of inviting your people to come *to-morrow* with me to look

12. Lewis H. Thomas, "Walker, Thomas (d. 1788)," in *Dictionary of Canadian Biography*, www.biographi.ca/en/bio/walker_thomas_1788_4E.html; "Extract of another Letter from Quebec, dated Oct. 25," J. Almon, ed., *The Remembrancer; or Impartial Repository of Public Events. . . Part 1* (London: 1776), 138.
13. Deschamps deposition, 93-94; Memoires sur l'état actuel de Canada [la Valinière], MG7 VI, Library and Archives Canada (translation by Teresa Meadows).

on *while I will take the town of Montreal* [author's emphasis]." Belair obliged and left to prepare men for action the next morning.[14]

Traveling on from Correy's house, the party encountered the parish priests of L'Assomption and neighboring St. Sulpice along the road. The American officer stepped down from the carriage, saluted the clergymen and spoke briefly in English with La Valinière, the "fiery factious and turbulent" L'Assomption priest who was already developing a reputation for being too friendly with Walker's Patriot faction and the invading rebels. The Continental captain apparently informed La Valinière that Walker had "convinced the Militia captain [Belair] to join his company with the Insurgents & to show up *the next day* on the very island of Montreal [author's emphasis]." The carriage driver Deschamps also heard the Acadian tell the priests "*we have a hundred men above Long Point* [author's emphasis]." After this, Deschamps took the visitors back to the ferry landing and coordinated their return passage to the Island of Montreal and beyond. Throughout the day, everyone in L'Assomption remained ignorant of the battle already taking place outside Montreal, even though Allen's *Narrative* said that he sent a messenger to Walker early that day, beseeching "speedy assistance."[15]

The following morning, September 26, Thomas Walker and militia captain Belair met near L'Assomption church, prepared to lead their followers to join Allen outside Montreal—still oblivious to his defeat. They found "eighty or one hundred men" assembled for the undertaking. Belair had told them not to bring weapons, so all but three were unarmed—they clearly believed that they would not have to fight to take the city. The L'Assomption men never left their parish that day, though. Allen later reported that Walker disbanded the "considerable number of men" he had raised "upon hearing of my misfortune."[16]

The Canadian narratives from L'Assomption clearly show that Walker and Belair had assembled nearly one hundred men to join Allen in taking Montreal on September 26, one day after the actual battle

14. Deschamps deposition, 94; "Edouard Curry [Correy]," individual #571003, Programme de recherche en démographie historique, Université de Montréal; Deposition of Jean-Baptiste Bruyères [de Belair] (Translation), October 4, 1775, Historical Section, *History*, 2: 86-87.

15. Deschamps deposition, 94; Memoires [la Valinière] (translation by Teresa Meadows); Lucien Lemieux, "Huet de la Valinière, Pierre," in *Dictionary of Canadian Biography*, www.biographi.ca/en/bio/huet_de_la_valiniere_pierre_5E.html; Allen, *Narrative*, 17. Four years later, Gov. Frederick Haldimand would also describe the troublesome La Valinière as "a perfect rebel in his Heart"; Haldimand to George Germain, October 24, 1779, Add. Mss 21714, fo. 226, Haldimand Papers (Microfilm H-1436), LAC.

16. Belair deposition, 87; Allen, *Narrative*, 18; Memoires [la Valinière].

outside that city. Postmaster Deschamps also took note of the rebel Acadian interpreter's repeated references to Ethan Allen's Longue Pointe landing site, indicating the Continental captain's familiarity with Allen's general role in the otherwise nebulous plan to advance into Montreal.

Unfortunately, none of the primary sources identify the name of the Continental captain who made the circuit around L'Assomption that day. His identity might offer new connections to further unravel the mystery behind Allen's defeat. The most useful distinguishing detail mentioned in the L'Assomption accounts was the visitor's rank—eliminating the possibility that it was Major Brown or Lieut. Col. Seth Warner. Walker's visitor was presumably one of a dozen or so American captains ranging north of the Saint Johns siege with diverse, scattered detachments that week, including company commanders from the New Hampshire rangers, 2nd New York Regiment, and Green Mountain Rangers. It is also noteworthy that Sanguinet mentioned the captain and his interpreter having crossed to the Island of Montreal from Varennes, not from Longue Pointe or Allen's crossing point at Longueuil, and that they returned on the same path.[17]

A RECONSIDERATION

These long-neglected Canadian sources expand the Battle of Longue Pointe story far beyond the Green Mountain Boys hero's streamlined *Narrative*. Although the L'Assomption accounts appear to be disconnected from the *Narrative*, in combination they suggest a simpler, more practical explanation for Ethan Allen and his hundred men being left to fight on their own outside Montreal. Beyond the traditional "blame Allen" and "blame Brown" camps, it appears that the fog and friction of war were likely at the root of Allen's alleged abandonment and defeat.

In the week preceding the Battle of Longue Pointe, a handful of dynamic, intrepid but militarily inexperienced American officers were quite busy ranging a 400-square-mile area of operations—a wedge of

17. Belair deposition, 87; Deschamps deposition, 94; Memoires [la Valinière]; "Extract of another Letter from Quebec, dated Oct. 25," Almon, *Remembrancer* (1776, part 1), 139-40; Sanguinet, "Témoin Oculaire," 55. The captain who visited L'Assomption was clearly not Ethan's brother Heman Allen though; he was still waiting to join the campaign after suffering from "the camp disorder" (dysentery); Heman Allen letters, September 16 and October 20, 1775, W18285, pp 37-38, 45-46, RG15, M804, NARA. Circumstantially, the Acadian interpreter was almost certainly Pierre Granger. Deposition of Pierre Charlan, August 6, 1775, Historical Section, *History*, 2: 67; "Pierre Granger," individual #216625 and family records, Programme de recherche en démographie historique, Université de Montréal.

land defined by Fort Saint Johns, the Richelieu River, the St. Lawrence, and La Prairie. As seen in the chance meeting between Allen and Brown outside Longueuil, these detachment leaders had inconsistent, happenstance communication with each other. Senior commanders had only nominal command and control over these roving operations, with reports arriving at headquarters two or three days after the fact. Even though General Montgomery was aware that his subordinates had been discussing plans for Montreal, time and distance kept him from directly influencing their activities.[18]

It clearly appears that Major Brown, Ethan Allen, and the captains involved in the Montreal scheme failed to properly coordinate key de-tails—the most obvious error being the day for the attack. In contrast to the well-documented L'Assomption mobilization, there are no pri-mary sources that describe Brown making any preparations to cross from La Prairie at that time—suggesting that Allen might also have misunderstood Brown's promise for support, assuming that it was com-ing directly from the major's detachment at La Prairie, when Brown could theoretically have been preparing Walker's Canadians at L'As-somption instead. The inherent confusion, and perhaps embarrassment, behind such fatally flawed coordination might also explain the remark-able void in the documentary record from any of the other alleged plan-ners. More than one hundred years ago, historian Justin H. Smith thoroughly evaluated many of these same primary sources and rhetor-ically asked, "Was there a misunderstanding then?" He followed with a similar conclusion: "Apparently there was."[19]

An anecdote from Ethan Allen's own *Narrative* could even be in-terpreted to support the possibility of a critical coordination error. De-scribing his subsequent captivity in England, he wrote: "great numbers of people . . . came to the [Pendennis] castle to see the prisoners . . . one of them asked me what my occupation in life had been? I answered him, that in my younger days I had studied divinity, but was a conjurer by profession. He replied that I conjured wrong at the time that I was taken; and *I was obliged to own, that I mistook a figure at that time* [au-thor's emphasis], but that I had conjured them out of Ticonderoga." In the *Narrative*, Allen represented this as a clever riposte, but it raises the question of what his "mistaken figure" might have been—was it misleading information from his friends in the Montreal suburbs, John

18. Montgomery to Schuyler, September 28, 1775 [a.m.], Philip Schuyler Papers, New York Public Library [also AA4 3: 954].
19. Smith, *Our Struggle for the Fourteenth Colony*, 1: 388.

Brown's character and reliability, confusion over the date or other details of the attack, or perhaps really just a witty retort.[20] The failed Montreal operation remains open to interpretation, but Sanguinet's journal, the L'Assomption depositions, and La Valinière's memoirs provide important historical elements behind Allen's unfortunate defeat that should not be ignored in future treatments of the topic.

20. Allen, *Narrative*, 44.

Who Said, "Don't Fire Till You See the Whites of Their Eyes"?

J. L. BELL

"Don't fire till you see the whites of their eyes!" is one of the most famous quotations to come out of the Revolutionary War. According to hallowed American tradition, the provincial commander at the Battle of Bunker Hill bellowed those words to his soldiers, warning them to preserve their gunpowder until their muskets could do the most damage to the British regulars.[1]

Phrased in that way, the order to hold fire gained poetic qualities that make it memorable: assonance (those long I sounds) and hyperbole (no provincials literally waited until they could see the enemy's eyeballs). Since ultimately the British chased the provincials off the field, remembering how American fighters had bravely watched the redcoats march closer and closer erased some of the sting of losing.

For over a century, American popular culture attributed the "whites of their eyes" line to Col. Israel Putnam of Connecticut. In more recent decades, however, a new pattern emerged. Many authorities now say that the quotation could be no more than a myth, and that if any officer at Bunker Hill gave that order, it came from Col. William Prescott of Massachusetts. This article examines how that quotation became popular, how scholars developed doubts about it, and finally what the printed record tells us about its actual origin in the eighteenth century.

The book that promulgated the "whites of their eyes" story most widely in early America was Mason Weems's *Life of George Washington*.

---

1. In this article I call the Battle of Bunker Hill by that traditional name while referring to different parts of the battlefield under their period names of Breed's Hill and Bunker's Hill. I thank Yoni Appelbaum, Alexander Rose, Liz Covart, Todd Andrlik, George Wildrick, and others for helping me over the years think through the questions raised by this quotation.

The 1808 edition of that bestseller stated:

> *"Don't throw away a single shot, my brave fellows,"* said Old Putnam,
> ["]*don't throw away a single shot, but take good aim; nor touch a trigger, till*
> *you can see the whites of their eyes."*[2]

As with his legends of young Washington and the cherry tree and middle-aged Washington praying in the snow, Weems included no source for this anecdote. But his biography was immensely popular in the early republic and helped to form the public understanding of Bunker Hill.

The next major source for the quotation was Samuel Swett's "Historical and Topographical Sketch of Bunker Hill Battle," an appendix to an 1818 edition of David Humphreys's *An Essay on the Life of the Honourable Major General Israel Putnam.* Swett wrote:

> General Putnam rode through the line, and ordered that no one should fire till they [the British soldiers] arrived within eight rods, nor any one till commanded. "Powder was scarce and must not be wasted. They should not fire at the enemy till they saw the white of their eyes, and then fire low, take aim at their waistbands. They were all marksmen, and could kill a squirrel at a hundred yards; reserve their fire, and the enemy were all destroyed. Aim at the handsome coats, pick off the commanders." The same orders were reiterated by Prescott at the redoubt, by Pomeroy, Stark, and all the veteran commanders.[3]

Swett provided no source for this statement, but he probably relied on a deposition that Revolutionary War veteran Philip Johnson provided in Newburyport, Massachusetts, on August 6, 1818. Swett had that document printed in the *Boston Daily Advertiser* at the end of 1825. The relevant portion of Johnson's recollection was:

> While he was at the rail fence, and just before the battle commenced, he saw Gen. Putnam on horseback very near him, and distinctly heard him say, "Men, you know you are all marksmen; you can take a squirrel from the tallest tree; don't fire till you see the whites of their eyes."[4]

---

2. Mason Weems, *Life of George Washington* (R. Cochran, Philadelphia: 1808), 74-5. Weems did not include that anecdote in the "third edition improved" printed for him by John Bioren in Philadelphia sometime after 1800.

3. David Humphreys, *Life of Putnam* (Boston: Samuel Avery, 1818), 229-30.

4. The *Boston Daily Advertiser* published a letter from Swett enclosing testimony from Joseph Whitmore on December 20, 1825. I could not locate the following days' issues online, but the *New York Daily Advertiser* of December 26 reprinted the Philip Johnson letter, saying it came from the Boston newspaper. It is thus apparent that Swett sent both letters to the *Boston Daily Advertiser* at the same time, and the newspaper published the Johnson document sometime between December 21 and 25.

When Swett issued his *Notes to the Sketch of Bunker Hill Battle* in 1825, he included a portion of Johnson's newspaper statement and quotations from two more men who recalled the "whites of their eyes" order:

> Elijah Jourdan of "Bucksfield" (now Buckfield, Maine): "While we were waiting for the British to come up the Hill, orders were given to us not to fire till we could see the whites of their eyes; and this order, I was then told, came from Gen. Putnam; but I did not hear it from him."
>
> John Stevens of Andover, Massachusetts: "Was in the fort. Saw Putnam in the fort before small arms fired; told them, not to fire till they saw the white of their eyes. Threatened to kill some who fired too soon."[5]

We thus have two men who said they were at the battle and heard Putnam give the "whites of their eyes" order, plus a third who recalled hearing the order credited to him on that day. Those men were not in the same regiments. They described fighting on different parts of the battlefield. After the war they settled in separate towns, hundreds of miles apart. It seems highly unlikely that they coordinated their stories for Putnam's sake.

Still, those recollections were not enough to convince all historians that Putnam said, "Don't fire till you see the whites of their eyes." One problem was suspicion about veterans' colorful tales. In 1842 the Rev. George E. Ellis of Charlestown examined notebooks of testimony taken down from elderly men who came to the fiftieth anniversary of the Bunker Hill battle. He later described those volumes this way:

> Their contents were most extraordinary, many of the testimonies extravagant, boastful, inconsistent, and utterly untrue,—mixtures of old men's broken memories and fond imaginings with the love of the marvellous. Some of those who gave in affidavits about the battle could not have been in it, nor even in its neighborhood. They had got so used to telling the story for the wonderment of village listeners, as grandfathers' tales, and as petted representatives of "the spirit of '76," that they did not distinguish between what they had seen and done and what they had read, heard, or dreamed.[6]

Seen through that lens, the appearance of the "whites of their eyes" phrase in Weems's biography becomes a red flag for fraud. What if the veterans Swett quoted had tailored their story to fit with that widely

5. Samuel Swett, *Notes to His Sketch of Bunker-Hill Battle* (Boston: Munroe & Francis, 1825), 14-5, 17.
6. *Massachusetts Historical Society Proceedings*, 2 (1880), 231-2.

published account? With so many Americans already thinking they knew what Putnam had said at Bunker Hill, the old men might have inserted that quotation into their stories to appear more authentic.

A second factor in making historians doubt the story of a "whites of their eyes" order was that it depicted Putnam as issuing a crucial order to all the provincial forces. Exactly which commander was in charge of the New England troops on the battlefield was a topic of long and bitter argument in the nineteenth century. Was it Putnam, Connecticut's general and hero? Colonel Prescott, in the redoubt? Gen. Seth Pomeroy, in the ranks as a volunteer? Dr. Joseph Warren, who had also been commissioned a general? Indeed, one big limitation of Samuel Swett's historical work is that instead of printing veterans' full accounts of the battle, he published material "for the defence of Gen. Putnam, did he need any," cutting down the quotations to focus on what the old soldiers said about who was in command.[7]

Historians who felt Prescott was the most important battlefield leader therefore had an impetus to doubt the story of Putnam's instruction and to play it down. In his monumental *History of the Siege of Boston*, first published in 1849, Richard Frothingham, Jr., listed a variety of orders rather than emphasize only one:

> "Powder was scarce, and must not be wasted," they said; "Fire low;" "Aim at the waistbands;" "Wait until you see the white of their eyes;" "Aim at the handsome coats;" "Pick off the commanders."

In a footnote Frothingham added, "These phrases occur frequently in the depositions, the same one being often ascribed to different officers." He then quoted some of the words that Philip Johnson had ascribed Putnam, though not exactly: "Men, you are all marksman— don't one of you fire until your see the white of their eyes."[8]

As the centenary of the battle approached, a new voice entered the discussion over the "whites of their eyes" quotation. The influential British historian Thomas Carlyle published his massive biography of Frederick the Great from 1858 to 1865. American readers noticed that Carlyle quoted orders to Prussian soldiers not to shoot "till you see the whites of their eyes" from decades before Bunker Hill. He mentioned forms of that order on three occasions: at the Battle of Mollwitz in 1741, not credited to a particular commander (or cited to a particular source); at the Battle of Jägerndorf in 1745, by Margraf Karl; and at

---

7. Phrase taken from *Boston Daily Advertiser*, December 20, 1825, 2.
8. Richard Frothingham, *History of the Siege of Boston, and of the Battles of Lexington, Concord, and Bunker Hill* (Boston: Little, Brown, 1849), 140. See also Frothingham, *History of Charlestown, Massachusetts* (Boston: Little, Brown, 1845), 341.

the Battle of Prague in 1757, by Frederick himself.[9]

That publication changed how American authors described the famous quotation. In his section of the *Memorial History of Boston* (1881), Edward Everett Hale wrote: "All along the American lines the order had been given which the officers remembered in the memoirs of Frederick's wars: 'Wait till you can see the whites of their eyes.'" Hale added an explanatory footnote for contemporary readers that began: "Prince Charles, when he cut through the Austrian army, in retiring from Jägendorf, gave this order to his infantry: 'Silent, till you see the whites of their eyes.'"[10]

There are weak spots in Hale's analysis. First, he introduced two errors into what Carlyle had written. Hale turned Margraf Karl not into Margrave Carl but "Prince Charles," and Jägerndorf into "Jägendorf" with only one R. Subsequent authors who relied on Hale instead of checking back further reproduced those errors, showing us the exact spread of his idea that the "whites of their eyes" line was just borrowed from the German.

Secondly, Hale's telling rested on the idea that the provincial New England officers of 1775 were familiar with the "memoirs of Frederick's wars." There is no evidence for that. British colonists with military interests had undoubtedly heard of Frederick the Great's victories in the Seven Years' War, but American newspapers almost never quoted Prussian military sources, and American booksellers did not advertise translations of them. No material printed in colonial America quoted Frederick the Great or his subordinates issuing orders with any variations of the "whites of their eyes." Nonetheless, Hale's analysis took hold.

As the credulous Colonial Revival gave way to the early-twentieth-century debunking of America's unsupported historical legends, the traditional story of "the whites of their eyes" appeared very shaky. Allen French exemplified how historians became suspicious of traditions and demanded stronger evidence:

> All the late tales give stories of the setting of marks and the measuring of distances, and the warning to hold the fire until the men could see the whites of the eyes, or the buttons, or the gaiters appearing over a rise in the ground . . . But none of these things are told in contemporary stories.[11]

9. Thomas Caryle, *History of Friedrich II. of Prussia, Called Frederick the Great* (Leipzig: Bernhard Tauchnitz, 1862-65), 6:328, 8:138, 10:41.

10. *The Memorial History of Boston*, Justin Winsor, editor (Boston: Ticknor, 1881), 3:85.

11. Allen French, *The First Year of the American Revolution* (Boston: Houghton Mifflin, 1934), 230.

The scholarly consensus now held that the famous quotation may never had been uttered at Bunker Hill after all. If any battlefield commander really did give that command, it had to be Colonel Prescott, regardless of what earlier sources had said about Colonel Putnam. And the quotation wasn't an American original—those officers were just copying an older German expression.

We see that muddled understanding in recent reference books. For example, *The Oxford Dictionary of American Quotations* attributed the words to Prescott and adds, "Also attributed to Israel Putnam, but he was probably relaying the order from Prescott."[12] *The Dictionary of Military and Naval Quotations* credited "Don't fire 'til you see the whites of their eyes" to Prescott and "Men, you are all marksmen—don't one of you fire until you see the whites of their eyes" to Putnam "relaying Prescott's order."[13] *The Yale Book of Quotations* pushed back toward Putnam, citing an 1825 reference while acknowledging the other attributions.[14] In *Founding Myths*, Ray Raphael noted that the *American National Biography* reference series quotes the words in its entries on both Putnam and Prescott, the former definitely and the latter as "Tradition has" it.[15]

Some authorities emphasize the legendary aspect of the quotation, saying that neither Putnam nor Prescott nor any other commander spoke that famous line. Paul F. Boller's *They Never Said It: A Book of Fake Quotes, Misquotes, and Misleading Attributions* lists the traditional quote under Prescott's name, with no mention of Putnam, but then reports earlier uses by Prussian royalty.[16] *The Quote Verifier* lists Prescott first "By tradition," mentions how "Others attribute" the words to Putnam, and concludes that they were "Probably a common military

12. *The Oxford Dictionary of American Quotations,* Hugh Rawson and Margaret Miner, editors (New York: Oxford University Press, 2006), 48. Formerly published as *The American Heritage Dictionary of American Quotations.*
13. *The Dictionary of Military and Naval Quotations,* Robert Debs Heinl, editor (Annapolis: Naval Institute Press, 1966), 116.
14. *The Yale Book of Quotations,* Fred R. Shapiro, editor (New Haven: Yale University Press, 2006), 623.
15. Ray Raphael, *Founding Myths: Stories that Hide Our Patriotic Past* (New York: New Press, 2004), 200. In his long-reprinted *Dictionary of Catch Phrases,* the London-based Eric Partridge attributed the line to "the US General Israel Pitman [sic] or, according to other authorities, General Joseph Warren or Colonel William Prescott"; Paul Beale, editor (London: Routledge, 2013), 108.
16. Paul F. Boller, *They Never Said It: A Book of Fake Quotes, Misquotes, and Misleading Attributions* (New York: Oxford University Press, 1989), entry for "William Prescott."

command."[17] In *Men of War*, Henry I. Kurtz wrote, "Did anyone say 'Don't fire 'till you see the whites of their eyes?' Probably not."[18]

The past century of histories of the Bunker Hill battle have also treated the tradition uncertainly. In *Now We Are Enemies*, Thomas Fleming wrote that the quotation was "All I really knew about" the battle when he began his research, and ultimately he found that "The 'whites of their eyes' was not original with Putnam."[19] Richard M. Ketchum in *Decisive Day* included the phrase among other orders not quoted directly or ascribed to particular officers.[20] John R. Elting called the line an "old legend" and noted that taking it literally "would be too close for comfort."[21]

In *With Fire and Sword*, James T. Nelson quoted Johnson on hearing Putnam say those words but added: "Others would claim to have heard that same order, and it is certainly possible that Putnam said it. It would not have been original to him."[22] Paul Lockhart titled his study of Bunker Hill after the quotation, but inside he wrote:

> Prescott quietly ordered his men to cease fire and to maintain silence. Don't fire, he cautioned, until the Redcoats draw within thirty yards of the walls. He may—*may*—have uttered the immortal words, "Don't fire until you see the whites of their eyes." The phrase has been attributed to Stark and Putnam, too, but it makes little difference who said it or even if it was said at all. It was common sense, and all the veteran commanders in the American lines would have said the very same thing in different ways.[23]

Finally, in his *Bunker Hill*, Nathaniel Philbrick kept the "whites of their eyes" order in an endnote alongside other orders.[24]

---

17. Ralph Keyes, *The Quote Verifier* (New York: St. Martin's, 2006), 64-5.

18. Henry I. Kurtz, *Men of War: Essays on American Wars and Warriors* (Bloomington: Xlibris, 2006), 31.

19. Thomas Fleming, *Now We Are Enemies: The Story of Bunker Hill*, 50th anniversary edition (Franklin, Tenn.: American History Press, 2010), xiii, 200.

20. Richard M. Ketchum, *Decisive Day: The Battle for Bunker Hill*, expanded edition (Garden City, N.Y.: Doubleday, 1974), 155-8.

21. John R. Elting, *The Battle of Bunker's Hill* (Monmouth Beach, N.J.: Philip Freneau Press, 1975), 31.

22. James T. Nelson, *With Fire and Sword: The Battle of Bunker Hill and the Beginning of the American Revolution* (New York: St. Martin's, 2011), 275.

23. Paul Lockhart, *The Whites of Their Eyes: Bunker Hill, the First American Army, and the Emergence of George Washington* (New York: HarperCollins, 2011), 280.

24. Nathaniel Philbrick, *Bunker Hill: A City, A Siege, a Revolution* (New York: Viking, 2013), 341-2.

We have thus reached a cultural consensus that one of the Revolutionary War's most famous sayings may not have been said at all, and was credited to the wrong person based on questionable evidence and "tradition."

In fact, the digitization of printed sources that were once difficult to find sheds new light on the famous "whites of their eyes" quotation. It shows:

1) The evidence for that order being given at Bunker Hill predates Mason Weems, and in fact comes closer to the period of the war than the evidence for many other spoken words we attribute to figures of the Revolution.

2) That evidence leads directly to Israel Putnam.

3) The "whites of their eyes" phrase indeed has deeper roots, but they lie not in Prussia but in a tradition of the British military.

The story of the first printing of the "whites of their eyes" story begins back with David Humphreys's publication of *An Essay on the Life of the Honourable Major-General Israel Putnam* in 1788. In describing the Battle of Bunker Hill (which happened before he became Putnam's aide), Humphreys did not include the "whites of their eyes" line. In fact, he suggested that the man in charge of the New England forces that day was Dr. Joseph Warren in his new capacity as a Massachusetts major general.[25]

That prompted the Rev. Josiah Whitney to ask Putnam, his most famous parishioner in Brooklyn, Connecticut, about the battle. The retired general said that Doctor Warren had come onto the battlefield as a volunteer and did not presume to take command. Putnam died in 1790, and Whitney described their conversation in a footnote to *A Sermon Occasioned by the Death of the Honorable Major-General Israel Putnam, of Brooklyn.*[26] This publication did not discuss the "whites of their eyes" quotation either, but it shows that Whitney and Putnam talked about Bunker Hill.

Ten years later, the Rev. Elijah Parish of Byfield, Massachusetts, published *An Oration, Delivered at Byfield, February 22d, 1800, the Day of National Mourning for the Death of General George Washington.* On page 15 he added a footnote describing the Battle of Bunker Hill. Parish, who originally came from Lebanon, Connecticut, said he had discussed that battle with his older colleague Whitney and from him learned:

25. Humphreys, *Life of Putnam*, 107, 109.
26. Josiah Whitney, *Sermon on the Death of Putnam* (Windham, Conn.: John Byrne, 1790).

Putnam was the commanding officer of the party, who went upon the hill the evening before the action: he commanded in the action: he harangued his men as the British first advanced, charged them to reserve their fire, till they were near, "*till they could see the white of their eyes,*" were his words.—At the second assault he commended their former calmness, assured them "they would now do much better," and directed them "to aim at the officers." They obeyed. The fire was tremendous. "*My God,*" said Putnam, in telling the story, "*I never saw such a carnage of the human race.*" These things he related to the Reverend Mr. Whitney, his Minister, by whose permission they are now published.[27]

That story was picked up in *The Columbian Phenix and Boston Review* magazine in June 1800.[28] Parish repeated the tale with more drama in a history textbook he cowrote in 1804 with the Rev. Dr. Jedidiah Morse, *A Compendious History of New England.*[29]

Thus, we have a clear line of transmission for the quotation: from Putnam to Whitney between 1788 and 1790, and from Whitney to Parish in the next ten years. Weems probably borrowed from Parish's textbook to create the even more dramatic form of the story in the 1808 expansion of his life of Washington. Ten years later, Philip Johnson's deposition provided the now-famous phrasing, "Don't fire till you see the whites of their eyes." We cannot be sure exactly what Putnam said on the battlefield—indeed, he may have used somewhat different words at different times—but we have solid evidence he used a "whites of their eyes" phrase that many men heard.

That order implies little about who was in command at Bunker Hill. The consensus among historians now is that there was no unified command on the provincial side. Prescott certainly led the contingent in the Breed's Hill redoubt, the main focus of combat. Col. John Stark of New Hampshire basically had an independent command at the rail fence on another part of the peninsula. And Putnam was riding all round the battlefield—shouting encouragement in one place, helping to load a cannon in another, trying to rally reinforcements off Bunker's Hill to the rear. In that context, it is certainly plausible for Putnam to have bellowed "Don't fire till you see the whites of their eyes" and then ridden off to another corner of the field to repeat the instruction. Officers relayed the same orders in their own ways, as Revolutionary War veterans remembered.

27. Elijah Parish, *Oration at Byfield* ([Newburyport]: Angier March, 1800), 15.
28. "Historical Sketch," *Columbian Phenix and Boston Review,* 1 (1800), 331-2.
29. Jedidiah Morse and Parish, *A Compendious History of New England* (Charlestown, Mass.: Samuel Etheridge, 1804), 342.

But that does not mean Putnam originated the "whites of their eyes" phrase. In fact, there are precedents going back decades within the British military—but not in the army. Rather, holding fire for that long was said to be a tradition of the Royal Navy.

The London magazine *The Monitor: or, British Freeholder,* for July 10, 1756, included a long letter with this anecdote:

> you must needs have heard, Sir Andrew, how the French captains are reported to have addressed their crews in the last war when they spied any of our great ships; "Chear, my good boys; you are in no danger, the ships look formidable indeed, but they have p–l–y captains; very worthy peaceable men, who will do you little harm; possibly they may make a flourish and give you a broadside or two at a distance; but they have dropt their old way of not firing till they see the whites of your eyes."[30]

The following year, *The Monitor* for December 10, 1757, referred to the same tradition:

> there is no doubt . . . that our admirals would become as terrible, as their predecessors, who never fired till they could see the white of their enemy's eye, and were not daunted at a superior force.[31]

Those quotations state that even earlier generations of Royal Navy officers established a "whites of their eyes" tradition. Delving deeper into sources of the early eighteenth or even seventeenth centuries might therefore uncover more examples.[32]

The Royal Navy tradition also continued after the American War. On June 14, 1794, the *Gentleman's Magazine* published a detailed account of the recent naval battle that became known (in Britain, anyway) as the Glorious First of June. The author, credited as "a Naval Correspondent of high Rank," described the action like this:

> Never was so much havock, and so complete a victory, gained in so short a time. Earl Howe plainly convinced the Sans culottes that he

---

30. *The Monitor, No. 49,* July 10, 1756, 469. Thanks to Yoni Appelbaum for pointing me to these pre-Revolutionary references.

31. *The Monitor, No. 57,* December 10, 1757, 760.

32. There are also later accounts based on tradition of the "whites of their eyes" being used by British military officers during the eighteenth century. Examples include Gen. Sir Andrew Agnew at the Battle of Dettingen in 1743 (Thomas Maccrie, *The Memoirs of Sir Andrew Agnew of Lochnaw* [London: Johnstone & Hunter, 1850], 9); Capt. Robert Faulknor, R.N., commanding the *Bellona* in 1761 (Letter from "W.P.," *Gentleman's Magazine,* 76 [1806], 36); and Adm. Lord Hawke at an unspecified date (Horace Walpole and Thomas Park, *A Catalogue of the Royal and Noble Authors of England, Scotland, and Ireland* [London: John Scott, 1806], 4:397).

could yet shew them the Old English way of fighting, "not to fire before he could see the whites of their eyes." The crews of the ships that sunk all perished; a fine gang for Old Davy indeed![33]

A collection titled *The Spirit of the Public Journals for 1797* included an open letter to Lord Chatham, First Lord of the Admiralty, signed "A Yellow Admiral" and said to be taken from the *Gazetteer*. This letter was supposedly the cause of Chatham's resignation from the Admiralty, which occurred in December 1794. At one point the letter says:

> Was not I with Commodore Elliot, when we took all Thurot's squadron, after a brisk action of seven glasses? D-mme! we laid them close along-side, and did not fire a gun till we could see the white of their eyes.[34]

The "whites of their eyes" command therefore appears to have developed as a command for the Royal Navy's cannon crews, not infantrymen. Captains told their men to wait until their warships closed in before unleashing a broadside against the enemy. Israel Putnam may have heard the saying from ships' officers when he participated in the British attack on Havana in 1762.[35] As for the German phrase, that was probably a simultaneous, independent development within the Prussian army.

Just as Americans celebrate Bunker Hill despite it not being an American victory, we claim "Don't fire till you see the whites of their eyes" despite it not being an original American saying. But just as the losses sustained at Bunker Hill eventually convinced British commanders to leave Boston, so Americans have waited out older "whites of their eyes" traditions and claimed the quotation for our own.

33. *The Gentlemen's Magazine*, 54 (1784), 494. Earl Howe was Adm. Richard Howe, in 1776 the commander-in-chief of the North American Station for the Royal Navy.
34. *The Spirit of the Public Journals for 1797*, 3rd edition (London: James Ridgeway, 1802), 79. A "yellow admiral" was a navy captain given the rank of rear admiral on retirement.
35. William Cutter, *The Life of Israel Putnam, Major-General in the Army of the American Revolution* (New York: Derby & Jackson, 1861), 112-4.

Smoking the Smallpox Sufferers

✵ KATIE TURNER GETTY ✵

At about midnight on September 29, 1792, Ashley Bowen and his young assistant, Tucker Huy, heard a carriage clatter up the Boston Road and arrive at the Marblehead gate. Upon learning the "coach-full of men" had come from Boston, Bowen brooked no complaints when he approached the carriage and informed the passengers, "You must be smoke[d]."[1]

Practiced in Boston and its environs during the American Revolution and in the decades following, the art of smoking was rooted in "the ancient records of physic"[2] as a purification method. According to Dr. James Lind's 1774 *Dissertation on Fevers and Infections*, "a judicious and proper application of fire and smoke is the true means appropriated for the destruction and utter extinction of the most malignant sources of disease."[3] In particular, smoking was thought to neutralize the great mortal terror of human history—smallpox.

As ineffectual as it might strike twenty-first century minds, smoking was believed to bestow salutary effects by cleansing individuals so that they could travel freely and interact with others without communicating disease. During the siege of Boston by Patriot forces in 1775-76, smoking was employed as a prophylactic measure to prevent people displaced by the war from spreading smallpox through the Massachusetts countryside and infecting the Continental Army.

1. Ashley Bowen, "The Journals of Ashley Bowen (1728-1813) of Marblehead," ed. Philip Chadwick Foster Smith, *Publications of the Colonial Society of Massachusetts* Vol. 45, Chapter XIX, (1973): 583-584, www.colonialsociety.org/node/744#ch08.
2. Encyclopaedia Britannica, 3rd ed., s.v. "medicine," books.google.com/books?id=Ath-TAAAAYAAJ&pg=PP9#v=onepage&q&f=false.
3. James Lind, *An Essay On The Most Effectual Means of Preserving the Health of Seamen in the Royal Navy* (London: D. Wilson and G. Nicol, in the Strand, 1774), 232, books.google.com/books?id=w1l125boAIcC&printsec=frontcover&source=gbs_ge_summary_r&cad=0#v=onepage&q&f=false.

One instance of smoking that occurred during the civilian exodus from Boston in the beginning of the siege was vividly recalled by Josiah Quincy, son of attorney Josiah Quincy, Jr. and his wife, Abigail (Phillips). Only three years old when his family fled besieged Boston, Quincy with his widowed mother and her sisters piled into a carriage and trundled down Boston Neck, the only land route out of Boston.[4]

The siege of Boston had begun in April 1775, when inflamed Massachusetts militiamen drove the British back into Boston from Lexington and Concord. Militia companies from the surrounding countryside poured into the Boston area, locking thousands of British troops on the Boston peninsula, then laid siege to the city. As spring turned to summer, disease ravaged the population trapped in Boston. People succumbed to illness, sickening due to food shortages, subsistence on salt provisions and the scarcity of supplies.

During the siege, Gen. Thomas Gage, senior British officer in Boston, permitted some of Boston's inhabitants to leave the town. The process, however, was erratic and unpredictable. If and when allowed out, civilians crossed Boston Neck and entered the countryside in a state of uncertainty and carried few possessions. A common sight was "parents that are lucky enough to procure papers, with bundles in one hand & a string of children in the other, wandering out of the town (with only a Sufferance of one days provision) not knowing whither they'll go."[5]

The carriage carrying Josiah and his mother and aunts in their flight from Boston did not simply pass uninterrupted through the lines and wheel into the countryside. Decades later, Josiah recounted what happened when he and his family reached the Roxbury lines. "At the line which separates Boston and Roxbury there were troops stationed, and a sentry-box on the east side of the street erected. At this point the carriage was stopped, all its inmates made to descend and enter the sentry-box successively. On each side of the box was a small platform, round which each of the inmates was compelled to walk, and remain until our clothes were thoroughly fumigated with the fumes of brimstone cast upon a body of coals in the centre of the box. This operation was required to prevent infection."[6]

---

4. J. L. Bell, "Smoking Little Josiah," Boston 1775 (blog), boston1775.blogspot.com/2016/01/smoking-little-josiah.html, accessed September 29, 2019. Also see Edmund Quincy, *Life of Josiah Quincy of Massachusetts* (Boston: Ticknor and Fields, 1868), 20-21.

5. John Andrews, *Letters of John Andrews, Esq., of Boston, 1772-1776*, ed. Winthrop Sargent (Cambridge: Press of J. Wilson and Sons, 1866), 93, archive.org/details/lettersofjohnand00andr.

6. Quincy, *Life of Josiah Quincy*, 21.

As Quincy recalled, smoking entailed the use of a structure called a smokehouse about the size of a sentry box or perhaps a modern garden shed—intended not for meats or tools, but for people. A fire of wood or charcoal would be lit inside the smokehouse and then topped with materials thought to possess disinfecting properties—particularly brimstone (sulphur). People entered the smokehouse and the door would be closed behind them. The smokehouse would then fill with sulphurous fumes from the fire which would fumigate the occupants and—at least in theory—destroy any traces of smallpox. Individuals would then emerge from the smokehouse and be declared safe to circulate through the countryside without communicating any lingering smallpox contagion from Boston.

PASSING THROUGH THE LINES

That summer and fall, boatloads of fleeing civilians from Boston started landing unexpectedly at Winnisimmet Ferry in Chelsea, just across Boston Harbor. Their arrival startled the American soldiers stationed there serving under Lt. Col. Loammi Baldwin.[7] These soldiers, along with a committee dispatched by the Massachusetts Provincial Congress, managed the refugees landing at Winnisimmet in an effort to prevent any potential smallpox-carriers from passing through the lines.

Even more refugees came out of Boston in November and December 1775 when Gen. William Howe (now senior British officer in Boston after replacing General Gage) loaded hundreds of Bostonians onto transport ships and forced them to disembark on Point Shirley, a remote, beachy peninsula to the east beyond Chelsea. Some of these civilians were infected with smallpox.

By this time, winter had settled over Massachusetts and smallpox was flaring in Boston. Gen. George Washington and the provincial congress scrambled to provide shelter and provisions to the displaced Bostonians at Point Shirley. Yet despite these efforts, illness raged among the refugees and some died right on the beach. As the tide of desperately-ill refugees threatened to spill into the countryside from Boston, General Washington grew even more concerned about smallpox permeating the Continental lines. "I have order'd Provision to them till they can be remov'd, but am under dreadful apprehension's of their communicating the small Pox as it is Rief in Boston."[8] General Wash-

7. Loammi Baldwin to George Washington, July 29, 1775, *Founders Online*, National Archives, founders.archives.gov/documents/Washington/03-01-02-0120, accessed September 29, 2019.
8. Washington to Joseph Reed, November 27, 1775, *Founders Online*, National Archives, founders.archives.gov/documents/Washington/03-02-02-0401, accessed September 29, 2019.

ington knew that if smallpox broke out among his troops, the army could be decimated.

Earlier in the season, in an effort to keep the army and surrounding countryside as contagion-free as possible, the provincial congress had resolved, "And whereas . . . the Small-Pox is now in Boston . . . [The committee] are strictly enjoined to make use of every precaution, by smoking, cleansing, airing, and detaining persons or effects, as they may judge necessary to prevent a communication of that distemper to the Army and Inhabitants of this Colony."[9] The refugees who came out at Winnisimmet Ferry and nearby Point Shirley were accordingly smoked.

To modern minds, the level of trust placed in the efficacy of smoking is unfathomable. Even the army—whose existence might have hinged upon being spared the ravages of smallpox—trusted smoking to eradicate any smallpox contagion that might cling to recent escapees from Boston. In December, Capt. Richard Dodge, stationed at Chelsea under Lieutenant Colonel Baldwin, wrote to General Washington that eight men had escaped Boston by boat the previous night and landed at Winnisimmet Ferry where they were received by the main guard. Captain Dodge noted that one of the escaped men expressed eagerness to see Maj. Thomas Mifflin whom he had previously served under. Major Mifflin, however, as quartermaster general of the Continental Army, was headquartered in the heart of the army at Cambridge. And yet, the committee dutifully cleansed the men "by Smooking them and Lett them pass," trusting in the purifying power of the smoke despite smallpox prevailing in Boston.[10]

Since taking command at Cambridge in July 1775, General Washington had guarded against the ever-present threat that smallpox posed to the army, its potential for destruction never far from his mind. "If we escape the Small Pox in this Camp, & the Country round about, it will be miraculous."[11]

A HUBBUB

It is no surprise that getting shut in a smokehouse and nearly suffocated with brimstone fumes would elicit strong reactions from individuals.

9. Peter Force, ed., *American Archives*, Ser. 4, 3:1516, Digital Collections, Northern Illinois University.
10. Richard Dodge to Washington, December 16, 1775," *Founders Online*, National Archives, founders.archives.gov/documents/Washington/03-02-02-0512-0001, accessed September 29, 2019.
11. Washington to Reed, December 15, 1775," *Founders Online*, National Archives, founders. archives.gov/documents/Washington/03-02-02-0508, accessed September 29, 2019.

Josiah Quincy carried the vivid memory of his being smoked as a toddler at the Roxbury lines well into adulthood.

But not everyone reacted to their experience in a smokehouse with the equanimity evinced by three-year-old Josiah. The "coach-full of men" who arrived at the Marblehead gate on the night of September 29, 1792, certainly did not. Instead, these men from Boston interrupted Ashley Bowen's streak of routine smoking and caused "a hubbub."[12]

Sixty-four-year-old Bowen and his sixteen-year-old assistant, Tucker Huy, served as operators of the smokehouse at the gated entrance to the town of Marblehead, a fishing village about sixteen miles northeast of Boston. Due to an ongoing smallpox epidemic in Boston, the town selectmen had tasked Bowen with smoking any travelers who approached Marblehead on the Boston Road before permitting them through the town gate. Though the hubbub at the gate occurred several years after the end of the siege, it provides a glimpse of the smoking process—albeit, a smoking process gone awry.

In addition to working as a sailor, rigger and smokehouse operator, Bowen was a prolific diarist and kept a journal for decades. In his diary, he diligently recorded the names of the dozens of individuals he smoked during his tenure at the smokehouse. Bowen, an active, hardworking man, attacked smoking with no less than his usual vigor.

"Came from Boston Philip LeGrow and Dismore and were smoked. Ditto John Lewis, smoked. Ditto Mr. George Clark and Knapp both smoked . . . This day came from Boston Stephen Blaney, smoked. Came from Boston a stranger, smoked. Ditto come from Boston two strangers, smoked."[13] As during the siege, the smoking was intended to purify the travelers' bodies and clothes and render them contagion-free—especially important in light of the mass inoculations which were occurring in Boston in September 1792.[14]

Having already been bluntly informed by Bowen upon their arrival that they "must be smoked," a couple of the coach's passengers acquiesced to entering the smokehouse but would not let Bowen shut the

---

12. Bowen, *Journals*, 583.
13. Ibid., 582.
14. John B. Blake, *Public Health in the Town of Boston 1630-1822* (Cambridge: Harvard University Press, 1959), 135-140. According to Blake, mass smallpox inoculations were occurring in Boston in September 1792. Blake calculates that by the end of that month, 8,114 Bostonians and 1,038 "outsiders" had been inoculated out of a population of 19,000 (138-139). The town of Marblehead was likely aware of the high number of smallpox sufferers in Boston as Bowen was asked by the Selectmen to take over the smokehouse on September 10. It is unclear whether the smokehouse was in operation all of the time or whether it operated only during epidemics.

door. Then, upon double-checking the carriage, Bowen discovered two more passengers still sitting in it. He managed to get these two recalcitrant men to enter the smokehouse but they quickly re-emerged, exclaiming—no doubt due to the generous application of brimstone to the fire—"The old fellow hath an Hell! Let's see how he likes it!" One of the men pulled Bowen by the arm and challenged him to "Come and smoke us!"[15]

At that moment, one of the other men dragged Tucker from the gate and broke open the lock. The coach-full of insufficiently-smoked men then rolled through the forced gate and on to Marblehead. Bowen grabbed his hat and started to race into town on foot but the carriage quickly overtook him and he returned to the smokehouse, only momentary defeated.[16] Bowen stormed into town at dawn the following morning, still fuming from the night before. He reported the transgressors to the Marblehead Selectmen. If Bowen knew what action, if any, the selectmen took against them, he did not record it in his journal.

A few days later, Bowen happened to meet up with a man named Swisher whom Bowen knew operated the smokehouse at Malden Bridge, located just outside Boston. Malden Bridge spanned the Mystic River and would have been the logical route for travelers from the Boston area to take to the North Shore.[17] Bowen's indignation at the forcing of the Marblehead gate and nearly being dragged into the smokehouse must have still rankled in his mind. He asked Swisher about "the coach which came out of Boston last Saturday evening—if he had smoke[d] all of them." Swisher recalled the carriage and told Bowen that he had smoked a few of the men, but some of them "were so obstinate that they would not come out of the coach."[18]

In the end, the smoking was all for naught. From a modern perspective, it is unlikely if Bowen's generous applications of brimstone or hot-footed pursuit of transgressors played any role in keeping the residents of Marblehead safe from smallpox. Likewise, the smoking of displaced persons at Winnisimmet Ferry, Point Shirley and the Roxbury lines during the siege must have had no bearing on whether smallpox was communicated through the countryside.

General Washington did receive his miracle—smallpox failed to make significant inroads against the Continental Army in the winter of 1775-76. But the efficacy of smoking is too doubtful to modern

15. Bowen, *Journals*, 584.
16. Ibid., 584.
17. Ibid., 585.
18. Ibid.

minds to be credited with saving the army or the inhabitants from the scourge of smallpox. The fumigation of people during the siege and in the years afterward likely had no salutary effects at all. To a modern-day observer, the health benefits bestowed by smoking are as hazy and nebulous as tendrils of smoke curling into the air from a brimstone fire, lingering for only a moment before dissipating in the winds of time.

The Revolutionary War Origins of the Whistleblower Law

❦ LOUIS ARTHUR NORTON ❦

The so called "whistleblower law" had a salty source. It did not emanate from the shrill sound of a boatswain's pipe, but rather a Revolutionary War naval episode. Its origin can be traced to the Continental Congress's 1775 appointment of Ezek Hopkins, formerly a merchantman and privateer, as commander-in-chief of the Continental Navy. As a naval commodore, he formed and led a fleet of eight small merchant ships that had been reconfigured into warships: the *Alfred*, *Andrea Doria*, *Cabot*, *Columbus*, *Providence*, *Hornet*, and *Wasp*.[1] Hopkins sailed his task force south on February 17, 1776 to New Providence (Nassau) in the Bahamas whose fort was deemed vulnerable and poorly guarded. The commodore planned to capture the fort to furnish badly needed arms, gunpowder and other supplies for the Continental Army and, at the same time, as a show the force of the nascent Continental Navy.

The Hopkins raid on New Providence took place on March 3. It was the first amphibious landing of American marines and sailors that successfully captured munitions. "The town & fort surrendered to us with the ships & vessels in the harbor, without making any resistance we secured all the cannon, Morter shells etc., that was there and left the island. On return we had bad weather."[2] The diminutive fleet returned to New London, Connecticut on April 8 and, during their return trip, made prizes of two British merchantmen and a six-gun schooner. Unfortunately, on April 6, they failed to capture HMS *Glas-*

---

1. Among his officers were several who gained Revolutionary War notoriety: John Paul Jones, Dudley Saltonstall, Nicholas Biddle, John Hopkins, John Hazard, Abraham Whipple and the then Masters Mate, Joshua Barney.
2. William B. Clark et al., eds. *Naval Documents of the American Revolution*, 13 volumes (Washington, DC: Government Printing Office, 1964-2019), 4: 598 (NDAR).

gow, although they severely damaged her. Attacking the British on their territory became an American naval tactic employed by Captains John Paul Jones, Gustavus Conyngham and Lambert Wickes.

The Continental Congress shortly thereafter decided to supplement their new navy with a fleet of privateers, letter of marque vessels under private commanders. They were relatively successful in capturing British shipping, especially in or near North American waters. This proved to be a lucrative enterprise for the colonial seamen. The downside was that it also made it very difficult to recruit sailors for Hopkins' navy where the combat was usually more onerous and delivered less appealing monetary rewards. The commander-in-chief spent the next year or so fighting a vastly superior naval force with few triumphs and many failures. As a result, he threatened to resign his commission. When asked to continue, he gradually transformed into a sadistic martinet. Discontent emerged among his men that subsequently would have legal repercussions echoing throughout American history.

On February 11, 1777 ten officers and men of the Continental frigate *Warren* sent a letter to Robert Treat Paine, Massachusetts delegate to the second Continental Congress, proclaiming their fidelity to the American cause. In their letter they also asked for his advice in light of "our present perplexed unhappy situation." This letter continued in a more formal manner:

> Accusations against commodore Hop[kin]s
>
> First, he is a man that ridecules religion, and Seemes very apparently to despise every virtue: he does not hesitate to blaspheme and take the name of God in vain: in this respect he Sets his officers and men a most irreligious and impious example, and when on board, is oftener guilty of profane Swearing than any Jack Tar that belongs to the Ship.
>
> Secondly, he allowes himself to Speak publickly in the most profane and disrespectful manner concerning the continental congress, the guardians of our rights and priviledges, calling them a pack of damn'd fools, ignorant fellows, lawyers darks &c, a company of men wholly unacquainted with mankind, and perfectly unacquainted with their business, and that if their measures were complied with the country would be undone this he asserted not only among our own folks, but also in the presence of two captains, who were prisoners, on their passage to newport in order to be exchanged.
>
> Thirdly, he is a man, if possessed of any principles at all, possessed of the most dangerous principles conceivable, especially when we consider his Station, for he positively declares that all mankind are exactly alike: that no Man yet ever existed who could not be bought with money; who could not be hired with money to do any action whatso-

ever: this he also asserted in the presence of the above mentioned prisoners, for what reason we can't determine, unless he meant to inform Sr peter Par[ke]r that he wanted an opportunity in order to Sell himself.

Fourthly, he has treated prisoners in the most inhuman and barbarous manner.

Fifthly when a british frigate, a few days ago, was on ground, either for the want of wisdom, or designedly he conducted in a very blamable manner indeed—

Sixthly, he i[s an] effectual obsticle to the fleets being properly maned, and perhaps, on that very account, in his present Station, does his country more damage than he possibly could do in any other capacity.

Many more very criminal things might be alledged and easily proved but the present opportunity will not Suffer us to be very particular.[3]

The letter continued with similar accusations against the commodore's son John B. Hopkins, then captain of the Continental warship *Warren*. The letter was signed by Lieutenants Richard Marvin and James Sellers, three marine officers, the sailing master, the ship's chaplain, and three others. Although unaware of the petition filed by his officers, Hopkins was cognizant of the loss of confidence in him by the Marine Committee. He wrote a letter on February 14 giving the status of the various ships under his command, saying that "I desire no Command further than you Approve off—and whenever you think my Command is of no service to the Publick, I will not only agree, but in Justice to the Publick think you Should give the Command to some man that can do more for the Public Benefit."[4]

Paine apparently advised the conspirators to send their complaints to the Marine Committee and to limit their remarks only to the commodore's conduct.[5] Without authorization, Captain of Marines John Grannis left the *Warren* on February 19 and traveled to Philadelphia with a petition signed by the same officers.

Hopkins' days as the Continental Navy's commander-in-chief became numbered. The Marine Committee heard Grannis reiterate the complaints that he and others had brought to them in their papers.[6] Subsequently on March 26 the committee laid the charges before the Continental Congress. The next day, a resolution was passed "That

3. Clark et al., eds. *Naval Documents of the American Revolution*, 7: 1167.
4. Ibid., 1200.
5. This was not a mutiny, a revolt or insurrection, but the filing of a legal grievance to and through the chain of command.
6. NDAR, 8: 191.

Ezek Hopkins be immediately, and he hereby is, suspended from his command in the American Navy."[7] On March 29 John Hancock, President of the Continental Congress, wrote, "I have it in Charge from Congress to transmit the above Resolve, which is so explicit that I shall not enlarge any further than to direct, that you do not after receipt hereof in any way whatever exercise an Act of Authority or Command over any of the Vessels belonging to or in the Service of the United States of America."[8]

Hopkins was indignant over his treatment. He was unaware of the charges that were made against him in the petition and had no hearing or trial. Communications were slow and compounded by the fact that Hopkins spent a great deal of time at sea. Finally, he received a copy of the papers that had been taken to Philadelphia in the fall. Hopkins discovered that the third lieutenant of the *Warren*, Richard Marvin, was among the signers of the petition and probably the chief conspirator onboard that ship. Hopkins ordered Marvin and Samuel Shaw be tried by a court-martial. Abraham Whipple presided over the trial, a fellow Rhode Islander as were several other jury members. The plaintiffs stated that they had been arrested for doing what they believed was their right to draft a remonstrance.[9] The court-martial board, however, convicted Marvin of signing unjust and false complaints and he was ordered to give up his commission.[10] This court-martial was held on April 3 before the news of Hopkins' suspension on March 26 had reach the commander-in-chief.

The sentence of suspension remained in force until January 2, 1778, when the following entry was made in the journals of the Continental Congress: "Congress having no further occasion for the service of Esek Hopkins, Esq. who, on the 22 December 1775, was appointed commander-in-chief of the fleet fitted out by the Naval Committee. Resolved, That Esek Hopkins, Esq., be dismissed from the service of United States."[11] This decision had significant consequence; the title of Commander-in-Chief of the Fleet was never again conferred upon any other naval officer.[12]

---

7. NDAR, 8: 206.
8. Ibid., 8: 223.
9. Sheldon S. Cohen, *Commodore Abraham Whipple of the Continental Navy* (Gainesville, FL: University of Florida Press, 2010), 74.
10. NDAR, 8: 265-66.
11. Ibid., 11: 20.
12. The five-star Fleet Admirals of World War II and now the Chief of Naval Operations are approximately the more modern equivalent titles.

Immediately after his dismissal, Hopkins attempted to prove his innocence of the charges and brought a libel suit against the allegations in the document asking for damages of £10,000.

Samuel Shaw and Richard Marvin were the only original plaintiffs that they were able to find. During the trial that lasted five days, Congress furnished the defendants with copies of all relevant acts that referred to the career of Captain Hopkins. Hopkins brought many influential men before the court who had known him for a long time and testified in regard to his character. It was impossible, however, to prove that the signers of the petition "did wickedly and maliciously" conspired together "to injure Hopkins' reputation."[13] In response to their petition for help in defending suit, Congress resolved on July 30, 1778 that it was "the duty of all persons in The service of the United States, as well as all other the inhabitants thereof, to give the earliest information to Congress or other proper Authority of any misconduct, frauds, or misdemeanors committed by any officers or persons in the service of the states, which may come to their knowledge." "Resolved, That the reasonable expenses of defending the said suit be defrayed by the United States."[14] The jurors doubtlessly realized that the defendants had the support of Congress and, as noted in the resolution, the decision was for the defendants and their costs. Congress, on May 22, 1779, provided $1,418 to cover costs associated with the whistleblowers' defense. Samuel Adams, delegate to the Continental Congress from Massachusetts, was directed to ensure that their Rhode Island lawyer, William Channing, was paid.

Executions related to disobedience and grievances permeated the British Navy for many years. Justifiable complaints led to mutinies and dire consequences on HMS *Culloden* (eight hanged), HMS *Defiance* (eleven hanged) and those that took part in the so called "Revolution at Spithead" (twenty-nine hanged). They became pretexts for multiple reforms, but those were very slow in coming.[15] In contrast, because of a unique Revolutionary War legal incident, the American government provided for citizen dissent without recriminations, a concept that has resonated for over two hundred and forty years. This is an assurance even though some people may be reluctant to do so because of the untoward consequences that could befall them.

13. NDAR, 13: 112-17.
14. Ibid., 13: 593.
15. Stephen Taylor, *Sons of the Waves* (New Haven, CT: Yale University Press, 2010), 222-294.

On September 25, 1789, the Continental Congress transmitted a Bill of Rights to the nascent states for their approval and these ten amendments were adopted on December 15, 1791. The First Amendment guaranteed freedom of speech. The Civil Service Reform Act of 1978, however, was the first federal law that formally codified whistleblower rights and protections. This was followed in 1989 by the Whistleblower Protection Act to "strengthen and improve protection for the rights of federal employees, to prevent reprisals, and to help eliminate wrongdoing within the Government," and clarified the procedure by which employees could report fraud, misconduct and wrongdoing sheltered from workplace retaliation. It also separated the agencies representing whistleblowers matters. But these important Acts had their genesis from humble seamen who served in the Continental Navy during the Revolutionary War.

How Did John Adams Respond to Abigail's "Remember the Ladies"?

JANE HAMPTON COOK

Women in all states won the universal right to vote one hundred years ago through the ratification of the United States Constitution's 19th Amendment in 1920. Though women in Seneca Falls, New York, launched the women's rights movement in 1848 when they claimed that the Declaration of Independence applied to women in the Declaration of Sentiments, the first mention of women's rights took place during the American Revolution.

Abigail Adams's call to "remember the ladies" is well known. Less familiar is how her husband, John Adams, responded. The debate he held on voting rights reveals a desire for independence to mean unbiased, and the role that class played in society during the nation's founding. Adams's remedy also expressed a form of self-sufficiency still embraced today.

Often taking initiative, Abigail wrote to a London bookseller at her husband's request to build support in England for America's cause. "I need not tell you, Sir, that the distressed state of this province calls for every excursion of every member of society," Abigail had written to Edward Dilly shortly after the battles of Lexington and Concord in April 1775. Her choice of words showed her egalitarianism. "The spirit that prevails among men of all degrees, all ages and sexes is the spirit of liberty. For this they are determined to risk all their property and their lives nor shrink unnerved before a tyrant's face."[1]

At this time, John and Abigail Adams were physically but not emotionally separated. She was living like a single parent, with the full care

---

1. Abigail Adams to Edward Dilly, May 22, 1775, National Archives, founders.archives. gov/documents/Adams/04-01-02-0135.

of their four children in war-torn Massachusetts. Hundreds of miles away in Philadelphia, John was consumed with his new passions—patriotism, public policy, and politics.

John saw Abigail as his intellectual equal. Though women did not attend school in this era, Abigail had learned to read and write at home as a child growing up in Weymouth, Massachusetts, about twelve miles from Boston. A minister of a church, her father had a large library, which he encouraged Abigail to use. She indulged in books.

Adams viewed his wife with great respect and admiration. "I think you shine as a stateswoman, of late as well as a farmeress. Pray where do you get your maxims of state, they are very apropos."[2]

Their relationship and chemistry were built on their mutual intellect. "This has been the cheering consolation of my heart, in my most solitary, gloomy and disconsolate hours. In this remote situation, I am deprived in a great measure of this comfort. Yet I read, and read again your charming letters, and they serve me, in some faint degree as a substitute for the company and conversation of the writer."[3]

His longing for her during their war-enforced separation led him to write that he wanted to see her think. Yes, watch her think. "Is there no way for two friendly souls, to converse together, although the bodies are 400 miles off?—Yes by letter.—But I want a better communication. I want to hear you think, or to see your thoughts."[4]

Think she did. Abigail gave him her frank thoughts on a variety of issues, from the lack of silver to the unfairness of a liquor tax. Knowing that he was contemplating the great issue of declaring independence from England, she weighed in on a matter that meant a great deal to her. "And by the way in the new code of laws which I suppose it will be necessary for you to make, I desire you would remember the ladies, and be more generous and favorable to them than your ancestors,"[5] she wrote John on March 31, 1776. If the war was affecting every member of society, and each was fighting for liberty, then shouldn't all adults have a say in who represented them? That was her natural conclusion.

Abigail didn't hold back. "Do not put such unlimited power into the hands of the husbands. Remember all men would be tyrants if they could," she continued, underscoring her point with teasing and hyper-

2. John Adams to Abigail Adams, May 27, 1776, National Archives, founders.archives. gov/documents/Adams/04-01-02-0270.
3. John Adams to Abigail Adams, May 22, 1776, National Archives, founders.archives. gov/documents/Adams/04-01-02-0267.
4. John Adams to Abigail Adams, April 28, 1776, National Archives, founders.archives. gov/documents/Adams/04-01-02-0258.
5. Abigail Adams to John Adams, March 31, 1776, National Archives, founders.archives. gov/documents/Adams/04-01-02-0241.

bole. "If particular care and attention is not paid to the ladies, we are determined to foment a rebellion, and will not hold ourselves bound by any laws in which we have no voice, or representation."[6]

She wanted her husband to protect women from those who didn't respect women the way that he did. "Why then, not put it out of the power of the vicious and the lawless to use us with cruelty and indignity with impunity. Men of sense in all ages abhor those customs which treat us only as the vassals of your sex," she continued, using the feudal term *vassal* to underscore her point that all men were not uniformly lords over all women. "Regard us then as beings placed by Providence under your protection and in imitation of the Supreme Being make use of that power only for our happiness," she concluded.[7]

Abigail could trace her interpretation to scripture and John Locke, who had pointed out in his famous 1690 work, *Two Treatises of Government*, that "whatever God gave by the words of this grant, Genesis 1:28, it was not to Adam in particular, exclusive of all other men: whatever dominion he had thereby, it was not a private dominion, but a dominion in common with the rest of mankind."[8]

Locke saw mankind as humanity, both male and female. God didn't give dominion to Adam alone: "For it was spoken in the plural number, God blessed them, and said unto them, have dominion. God says unto Adam and Eve, have dominion." He asked this question about Eve: "Must not she thereby be lady, as well as he lord of the world? . . . for shall we say that God ever made a joint grant to two, and one only was to have the benefit of it?"[9]

Abigail obviously agreed. But did her Adam concur? On the surface, John responded to Abigail's *remember the ladies* with playful banter. "As to your extraordinary code of laws, I cannot but laugh. We have been told that our struggle has loosened the bands of government everywhere," he wrote to her on April 14, 1776. "But your letter was the first intimation that another tribe more numerous and powerful than all the rest were grown discontented.—This is rather too coarse a compliment but you are so saucy, I won't blot it out." He tried to soften the blow. "Depend upon it, we know better than to repeal our masculine systems. Although they are in full force, you know they are little more than theory."[10]

6. Ibid.
7. Ibid.
8. John Locke, *Two Treatises of Government* 1689 (London: George Routledge and Sons, 1887), 96.
9. Ibid.
10. John Adams to Abigail Adams, April 14, 1776, National Archives, founders.archives. gov/documents/Adams/04-01-02-0248.

Though Adams didn't appear to take his wife seriously, he in fact did think about it. In May 1776 he engaged in a debate over the question of who had the right to vote with James Sullivan, a Massachusetts lawyer. Sullivan was excited because leaders in Massachusetts were creating a new legislature, which the king had previously abolished.

"A new assembly is at hand in which there will be the most full and equal representation that this colony ever saw. This assembly will undoubtedly suppose it to be their duty to provide for a future less unwieldly and more equal representation than themselves," Sullivan stated.[11]

"Every member of society has a right to give his consent to the laws of the community or he owes no obedience to them," he wrote, noting that this was a true republican principle. But Sullivan saw a huge flaw in the old system. "And yet a very great number of the people of this colony have at all times been bound by laws to which they never were in a capacity to consent not having estate worth 40/ per annum &c."[12]

What was he talking about? In order to vote in Massachusetts, one had to own land worth forty shillings a year. The result was that only sixteen percent of the population was eligible to vote. Of those eligible, only three and a half percent of the population had voted in the decade before 1774, when the king implemented martial law under a British general.[13] Sullivan saw the contradiction. If only landowners could vote, then more than eighty percent of the people had no voice in choosing their representatives. The resulting system exclusively favored the upper class and left out white working class men, women, free blacks and slaves.

"But yet by fiction of law every man is supposed to consent. Why a man is supposed to consent to the acts of a society of which in this respect he is absolutely an excommunicate, none but a lawyer well dabbled in the feudal system can tell,"[14] Sullivan criticized. The current system was blind to this injustice.

Where did this voting structure come from? Originating in the medieval era of knights and lords, this voting practice was based on the feudal system. A landlord owned property. His wife, children, servants, and renters, called vassals, all depended on the landlord. The relation-

11. John Adams to James Sullivan, May 26, 1776; see note for Sullivan's May 17, 1776 letter, National Archives, founders.archives.gov/documents/Adams/06-04-02-0091.
12. Ibid.
13. Donald Ratcliffe, "The Right to Vote and the Rise of Democracy, 1787-1828," *Journal of the Early Republic* 33, No. 2 (Summer 2013), 219-254.
14. John Adams to James Sullivan, May 26, 1776; see note for Sullivan's May 17, 1776 letter, National Archives, founders.archives.gov/documents/Adams/06-04-02-0091.

ship between landlord and vassals was more than just a financial obligation to pay rent once a month. The renter also owed his landlord his military service and political allegiance.

Imagine in our modern culture if you rented a house or an apartment. You would pay your property owner a monthly amount in rent. That's it. You wouldn't depend on your owner for food or a job. If the feudal system were in place, your landlord would also be your boss, giving you instructions on farming and overseeing your work and food supply. Your landlord would be your captain in the military, who could order you to the battlefield. Your landlord could tell you how to vote. Imagine being required to vote the same way your apartment owner voted today.

Though the medieval era had died out in the 1400s, it still influenced the 1700s. Men and women who did not own land depended on someone who did. Children depended on women. Women depended on husbands, fathers and brothers. Artisans, such as silver smiths, depended on patrons, who were landowners. Renters depended on landowners for their food and homes. Working-class men often rented land. All depended on the landlord. They could not theoretically vote of their own free will because they had a bias, a debt to a landowner. The result was that only people who were not dependent could vote. This discrimination included thousands of European males as well as women, free blacks and slaves.

Hence, in John Adams's day, landlords or freeholders were the only class in society who were free and clear of dependency. Owing no one anything, landowners theoretically went into the voting booth without bias and could therefore vote their conscience.

In John Locke's original treatise, he used the word property more than 180 times. He frequently referred to "life, liberty and estate."[15] In the Declaration of Independence, Thomas Jefferson expanded Locke's philosophy by changing the emphasis on property to the pursuit of happiness. In this way he broadened the theory of natural rights to those who didn't own property. He generalized, equalized and democratized the concept. Sullivan wanted to do the same when it came to voting.

"The scars and blotches of the feudal system, the footsteps of vassalage, and the paths to lawless domination compose so great a part of it, that no friend to his country can wish to see it ever put in exercise again," Sullivan wrote, wanting to unshackle his fellow patriots.[16]

15. Locke, *Two Treatises of Government*, 234.
16. John Adams to James Sullivan, May 26, 1776; see note for Sullivan's May 17, 1776 letter, National Archives, founders.archives.gov/documents/Adams/06-04-02-0091.

Sullivan saw a problem with only landowners voting. He understood the contradiction inherent in declaring that rights come from God and creating a government based on the people when not all people had a say in their consent. If everyone had to obey the law, shouldn't they have a say in who makes the law? "For where there is a personal or corporal punishment provided, all subjects are equally concerned—the persons of the beggar, and the prince being equally dear to themselves respectively," he wrote. "Thus, Sir, the poor and rich are alike interested in that important part of government called legislation."[17]

How did John Adams respond to Sullivan? He showed he'd been thinking about his wife's call to remember the ladies. "It is certain in theory, that the only moral foundation of government is the consent of the people. But to what an extent shall we carry this principle? Shall we say, that every individual of the community, old and young, male and female, as well as rich and poor, must consent, expressly to every act of legislation? No, you will say. This is impossible," Adams wrote to Sullivan on May 26, 1776.[18]

Adams thought about the eighty-four percent of society that couldn't vote. "But let us first suppose that the whole community of every age, rank, sex, and condition, has a right to vote. This community is assembled—a motion is made and carried by a majority of one voice. The minority will not agree to this. Whence arises the right of the majority to govern, and the obligation of the minority to obey? From necessity, you will say, because there can be no other rule."[19]

Though he didn't refer to slaves or free blacks explicitly here, John and Abigail Adams didn't own slaves and both opposed slavery. He supported a passage that Thomas Jefferson wrote for the Declaration of Independence opposing slavery: "The Christian king of Great Britain [is] determined to keep open a market where men should be bought and sold, . . . suppressing every legislative attempt [by the American colonists] to prohibit or to restrain this execrable commerce."[20] Twenty-five percent of Jefferson's original draft was cut, including this passage.

Adams gave Sullivan his views on women voting. "But why exclude women? You will say, because their delicacy renders them unfit for practice and experience, in the great business of life, and the hardy enter-

17. Ibid.
18. John Adams to James Sullivan, May 26, 1776, National Archives, founders.archives. gov/documents/Adams/06-04-02-0091.
19. Ibid.
20. "Jefferson's 'original Rough draught' of the Declaration of Independence," Library of Congress, www.loc.gov/exhibits/declara/ruffdrft.html.

prises of war, as well as the arduous cares of state."[21] While his views on women do not reflect today's standards, he held a similar view of men who didn't own land.

"Is it not equally true, that men in general in every society, who are wholly destitute of property, are also too little acquainted with public affairs to form a right judgment, and too dependent upon other men to have a will of their own?" he asked. "If this is a fact, if you give to every man, who has no property, a vote, will you not make a fine encouraging provision for corruption by your fundamental law?" He saw non-landowners as a biased special interest loyal to those they depended on. "Such is the frailty of the human heart, that very few men, who have no property, have any judgment of their own. They talk and vote as they are directed by some man of property, who has attached their minds to his interest."[22]

Adams understood the problem that non-landowners had to follow the laws. "Your idea, that those laws, which affect the lives and personal liberty of all, or which inflict corporal punishment, affect those, who are not qualified to vote, as well as those who are, is just. But, so they do women, as well as men, children as well as adults." "The same reasoning, which will induce you to admit all men, who have no property, to vote, with those who have, for those laws, which affect the person will prove that you ought to admit women and children," he pointed out, acknowledging the logic of opening up the vote to non-landowners.[23]

He viewed men without property in the same way that he viewed women and children. "For generally speaking women and children, have as good judgment, and as independent minds as those men who are wholly destitute of property: these last being to all intents and purposes as much dependent upon others, who will please to feed, clothe, and employ them, as women are upon their husbands, or children on their parents."[24]

Adams feared that if Massachusetts gave all men, regardless of class or lack of land ownership, the right to vote, "there will be no end of it. New claims will arise. Women will demand a vote. Lads from 12 to 21 will think their rights not enough attended to, and every man, who has not a farthing, will demand an equal voice with any other in all acts of

21. John Adams to James Sullivan, May 26, 1776, National Archives, founders.archives. gov/documents/Adams/06-04-02-68540091.
22. Ibid.
23. Ibid.
24. Ibid.

state. It tends to confound and destroy all distinctions, and prostrate all ranks, to one common level,"[25] he wrote, believing that it would be wise not to change voting qualifications. "If the multitude is possessed of the balance of real estate, the multitude will have the balance of power, and in that case the multitude will take care of the liberty, virtue, and interest of the multitude in all acts of government."[26]

Adams had a solution to the contradiction of declaring all equal but not allowing all to vote. He wanted to turn the multitudes into landowners, making them more independent. "The only possible way then of preserving the balance of power on the side of equal liberty and public virtue, is to make the acquisition of land easy to every member of society: to make a division of the land into small quantities, so that the multitude may be possessed of landed estates."[27]

Years later the members of the Constitutional Convention also debated the question of allowing only landowners to vote. Unable to reconcile the issue, they left the power of voting rights to the states. Most states initially required land ownership in their voting laws. One state remembered the ladies.

New Jersey allowed women landowners to vote for thirty years starting in 1776. Party politics took the vote away from these women because they largely voted for the Federalist Party. Democratic-Republican party leaders added the word *male* to their voting laws in 1807 to steal votes from the Federalists.

Voting was originally a right given to the culturally independent, theoretically unbiased landowners. It serves as the starting point of a long history with non-landowning white males, former male slaves, and ultimately women of all races and ethnicity gaining the right to vote over the years.

In hindsight, it is tempting to disregard the landowning voting requirement of the founding era because it is a form of discrimination, especially by today's standards. It's also easy to criticize Adams for his lack of foresight. But Adams's remedy of making it easier for people to own land gave Americans a vision for self-sufficiency and class mobility. The concept of owning a house, land, or property is still very much a part of the American dream today, a pursuit of happiness that millions of diverse Americans continue to seek.

Likewise, today's society defines diversity in many ways, such as sex, race, ethnicity, and class. Some tend to view the founding era as lacking

25. John Adams to James Sullivan, May 26, 1776, National Archives, founders.archives. gov/documents/Adams/06-04-02-68540091..
26. Ibid.
27. Ibid.

diversity. But that's not how John Adams saw it. Adams believed there was much diversity in the founding era. In fact, to him the United States was so diverse that it was a miracle it came together in the first place. Diversity to Adams was found in religion, primarily the different sects or denominations of Christianity as well as Judaism. Defining diversity by religion is a hard concept to grasp in the world today, where all denominations of Protestant and all Catholics are lumped into the category of Christian. But understanding Adams's view of diversity and the challenges it posed puts independence and the lack of universal voting practices into better context.

"But what do we mean by the American Revolution? Do we mean the American war? The revolution was affected before the war commenced," Adams asked a newspaper editor in 1818. "The revolution was in the minds and hearts of the people. A change in their religious sentiments of their duties and obligations," he continued, before concluding, "This radical change in the principles, opinions, sentiments and affection of the people, was the real American Revolution."[28]

Adams saw a difference between Maryland, which was founded by Catholics, and Pennsylvania, which welcomed all religions, from Jews to Quakers. Religion had influenced the different charters of the colonies. "The colonies had grown up under constitutions of government, so different, there was so great a variety of religions, they were composed of so many different nations, their customs, manners and habits had so little resemblance, and . . . their knowledge of each other so imperfect, that to unite them in the same principles in theory and the same system of action was certainly a very difficult enterprise."[29]

To Adams, European Americans were very diverse. A French Catholic was different from an Irish Catholic, and an Irish Catholic was different from an Irish Protestant. "By what means, this great and important alteration in the religious, moral, political and social character of the people of thirteen colonies, all distinct, unconnected and independent of each other, was begun, pursued and accomplished, it is surely interesting to humanity to investigate, and perpetuate to posterity."[30]

Adams wrote these words in February 1818. By this time, more men had gained or were gaining the right to vote without owning land. A few months later, in October, Abigail died at the age of seventy-three. She had continued to remember the ladies throughout her life, showing

28. John Adams to Hezekiah Niles, February 13, 1818, National Archives, founders. archives.gov/documents/Adams/99-02-02-6854.
29. Ibid.
30. Ibid.

her resilience and her steadfast faith in women's capabilities. On one occasion, in 1793, her sister Elizabeth said to her, "I wish you would be so kind as to lend me the *Rights of Women*—the first opportunity."[31] The *Rights of Women* was a book by British author Mary Wollstonecraft, who advocated for women's education. John had teased Abigail that she was a disciple of Wollstonecraft.

Indeed, education for women paved the path for ladies, motivating them to fight for the right to vote, which culminated in the 19th Amendment to U.S. Constitution that celebrated its centennial in August 2020.

31. Elizabeth Shaw to Abigail Adams, December 29, 1793, National Archives, founders.archives.gov/documents/Adams/04-09-02-0285.

Opposing the Franco-American Alliance: The Case of Anne-Robert Jacques Turgot

RICHARD J. WERTHER

The participation of the French on the side of the newly declared independent American colonies is widely acknowledged as the factor that tipped the balance in the American Revolution and ultimately led to the defeat of the British. This alliance, actually two alliances—one of commerce and one of military cooperation—was concluded in early 1778, but it was the result of many years of monitoring and assessment of the situation in British North America that commenced almost immediately after France's stinging defeat in the Seven Years' War. The alliance idea had to be sold to young King Louis XVI, and most of his inner circle supported it. I would like to tell you about the one who didn't, and why he opposed it. Though he did not prevail, his reasons for opposing it add to the understanding of how the alliances came to be.

When all the intelligence reports, diplomatic maneuvering, etc. were complete, the decision boiled down to a final assessment made by the King Louis XVI (just twenty-three years old when the alliance was concluded) and his closest advisors. The most prominent supporter was the Charles Gravier, comte de Vergennes. His thinking concerning the role of France in the war were first recorded for the King in late 1775, in a document called *Reflections* (actually written by Vergennes' secretary Gerard de Rayneval). His stance is further crystalized in a second document, *Considerations*, penned in March 1776. However, one advisor remained unconvinced: His name was Anne-Robert Jacques Turgot, the Finance Minister. Turgot lost the battle, and the French and Americans eventually won the war. Given this outcome, was Turgot wrong in opposing the alliance?

I will summarize each scenario Vergennes imagined for the war in the colonies in *Considerations*, why he thought they necessitated French involvement, and how Turgot attempted to refute his arguments. Vergennes' *Reflections*, meant for the King's eyes only, enumerated three reasons for intervening—Diminishing Britain's power while increasing France's, diminishing Britain's commercial advantages while increasing France's, and regaining some of France's North American possessions (though no mention of Canada). He further raised questions and proposed answers as to the type of assistance to be provided (money, supplies, and naval), the timing of that assistance, and the projected benefits. In *Considerations*, he outlined four possible scenarios for the outcome of the conflict and why France should intervene to achieve the goals outlined in *Reflections*. It is these scenarios that Turgot directly addressed.

As you can imagine, with Turgot's role as Finance Minister, his objections contained a heavy dose of financial considerations, but his arguments were a little more nuanced than simply saying it would cost too much. It is difficult to speculate what would have happened had Turgot won the argument, but anti-British fervor in France was such that there was a low probability of this happening.

There should be no mistake, however, that Turgot's argument against involvement would ultimately rise or fall on financial considerations and their overall economic impact on France. He reportedly warned the King that "The first gunshot will drive the state to bankruptcy."[1] However, the non-monetary concerns of "International power politics and considerations of national prestige took precedence over domestic reform."[2] France's inferiority complex coming out of the Seven Years' War surfaced in *Reflections* and in *Considerations*, both of which dripped contempt for the British, calling her France's "natural enemy . . . an enemy at once grasping, ambitious, unjust, and perfidious".[3] "Experience has shown," claimed Vergennes, the British "regard as honorable at just everything which they consider beneficial to themselves and damaging to their rivals."[4]

Turgot was given the text of *Considerations* and wrote his point-by-point refutation entitled *Reflections written on the occasion of a memoir*

1. H.A Scott Trask, "What Brought on the French Revolution?," Von Mises Institute, mises.org/library/what-brought-french-revolution.
2. Ibid.
3. Charlemagne Tower, *The Marquis de Lafayette in the American Revolution* (Philadelphia, J.D Lippincott Company, 1895), 1: 93. This volume (in English) has the full texts of both Vergennes' *Reflections* and *Considerations*.
4. Ibid., 109.

given by de Vergennes to the King on how France and Spain should consider the aftermath of the quarrel between Great Britain and its colonies. Translated to English, his detailed argument, dated April 6, 1776, runs some 14,000 words.[5]

Unfortunately for Turgot, he was not arguing from a position of strength. Besides fighting against the growing tide favoring support of the Americans, some his prior efforts to put the country's financial house in order did not go over well with many influential people. He issued a number of unpopular edicts, the most (in)famous of which were his six edicts in 1776, to which the King assented, over strong opposition by the clergy and the nobility. The most controversial of the edicts were those suppressing forced unpaid labor and suppression of certain rules by which the craft guilds maintained their privileges. Turgot attempted to subject all three estates (Clergy, Nobility, all others) to taxation. Taxes on the clergy were soon lifted, but the to-be-expected hatred of his actions by the nobles and the parliaments was heaped upon him. Even the queen disliked him for opposing the grant of favors to her proteges.[6] The edicts, combined with his losing stance on the Franco-American alliance, brought his career as Finance Minister to a swift close.

As mentioned, in *Considerations* Vergennes presented four points that in his opinion argued for French intervention. All four scenarios in his view "point with almost equal certainty to a war, more or less remote, with France and Spain."[7] In other words, the arguments were all crafted with the same end result, French involvement, in mind. Let us take them point-by-point:

1. Britain and the Colonies Reconcile.

Perhaps Vergennes' greatest fear, and the fear that had driven French policy up to that time, was that the British ministry "finding itself unable to continue, may hold out its hand toward a reconciliation"[8] Indeed, there were rumors flying that Benjamin Franklin and the American delegation in France might be amenable to an accomodation, rumors Franklin did nothing to dispel and may have even fanned to keep the French engaged in alliance discussions. Reconciliation would

5. From a French version of this document from the book Oeuvres de Turgot (see note 10). It was translated to English via the Microsoft Word translation program.
6. Turgot, Radical Reform Approach, courses.lumenlearning.com/suny-hccc-worldhistory2/chapter/efforts-at-financial-reform/.
7. Tower, *The Marquis de Lafayette in the American Revolution*, 108.
8. Ibid.

create an even stronger British empire, maintaining the world balance of power that diminished France's role. More than reconciliation itself, Vergennes feared that such an easy way out of the conflict would lead the British to set their sights on the French and Spanish possessions in the New World, "employ[ing] the forces it has [already] collected together [in America] in the too easy conquest offered by the West India Islands."[9] Spain was led by fellow Bourbon King Carlos III, and the two countries were linked by a defensive alliance called the Family Compact. Spain was an integral part of all Vergennes' plans.

Timing was also an issue—a quick reconciliation would catch the French, still recovering fiscally and militarily from the Seven Years' War, unprepared. By supporting the American revolt, first clandestinely and later openly, France could forestall the possibility of a reconciliation, especially a quick one.

Turgot's Response

Though long on record as predicting American independence, Turgot acknowledged the possibility of reconciliation. He agreed it was the worst possible outcome for France, and assumed it would mean restoration of the colonies to their pre-Stamp Act position and rather than granting the colonies independence, a fear shared by some colonists. His main argument, though, had to do with the economic value, or really the lack thereof, of the sugar colonies. This theory was crucial to how he addressed the other points made by Vergennes; he wrote that "this discussion must therefore be the principal object of the third part of these reflections; it must conclude this Memoir."[10] I will do the same, and defer this discussion to later in this article. Turgot failed to address concerns about the balance of power, a non-financial consideration, probably because he thought reconciliation unlikely.

2. British Defeat of the American Colonies

Vergennes' second scenario was that "the King of England, by conquering British America, may turn it into an instrument with which to subjugate European England."[11] England's victory in the war would create a North American juggernaut which would not only threaten the mother country (it's not clear to me why Vergennes thought this would be problematic for France), but also threaten France, Spain, and their

---

9. Tower, *The Marquis de Lafayette in the American Revolution*, 108.
10. Gustave Schelle, *Oeuvres de Turgot et documents le concernant, avec biographie et notes*, Volume 5 (Paris: Felix Alcan, 1923), 386, babel.hathitrust.org/cgi/pt?id=uc1.$b810956& view=1up&seq=433. This book is in French. Translations used in this article were done via DeepL Translator. Where clarification was needed, Microsoft translation was also consulted.
11. Tower, *The Marquis de Lafayette in the American Revolution*, 108.

possessions, among these being portions of Florida, Cuba, western Canada, the West Indies Sugar islands, and Louisiana. France's, and hopefully Spain's, presence on site would prevent Britain from exerting this leverage.

One aside: Vergennes posited a danger to the French and Spanish possessions whether the British reconciled, won, or lost. If they reconciled, the threat would come from a newly-powerful alliance in the vicinity (the first scenario). If they won (this scenario), their national arrogance and accusations of France and Spain providing assistance to the colonies would cause them to go after those countries' sugar colonies. If they lost (the next scenario), they would need to lash out against the nearest targets, those islands, to placate the rage of their people and salvage some national pride.

These rhetorical gymnastics had two purposes. The "heads I win, tails you lose" nature of his arguments served to make war seem inevitable. As one historian observed "In the *Considerations* Vergennes was confronted with the task of demonstrating the superior urgency of his diplomatic program to that of Turgot's program of financial retrenchment, and this task could only be performed by representing war with England as virtually inevitable."[12] It also would scare Spain into taking a much more active role by emphasizing the threat to Spain's New World possessions, but at this point in the game, the Spanish would not take the bait. Eventually they would be involved because of their own possessions.

Turgot's Response

This could never happen because conquering the colonies would be too difficult for Great Britain and could not be done without "the total ruin of the country,"[13] rendering the British military unable to pursue such adventurism. Nor would the Americans, who "form the least corrupt part of the nation, and, at the same time, the least susceptible to the illusions which dazzle the vanity or greed of the people" be inclined to "drag England into enterprises beyond her strength."[14]

Further, the Americans, "enthusiastic for liberty, could be overwhelmed by force; but their will would not be tamed."[15] Thus, they could not truly be defeated. They could "sink and disperse themselves in the immense deserts that lie behind their settlements,"[16] essentially

12. Edward S. Corwin, The French Objective in the American Revolution, The American Historical Review, Vol. 21, No. 1 (October 1915), 36.
13. Schelle, *Oeuvres de Turgot*, 387.
14. Ibid.
15. Ibid.
16. Ibid.

resorting to a guerrilla war, beyond the capability of a European army to win. This anticipated the types of actions that thwarted Britain's strategy in the southern colonies later in the war. Should Britain somehow win, he allowed, the mother country would be significantly weakened and vulnerable as a "national bankruptcy would break the present mainsprings of the British Government and deprive it of the greater part of its means of acting externally and of dominating internally."[17]

To keep the colonies under its thumb, Britain would need an excessive level of economic and military investment, which would create unrest at home as well as being financially unsustainable. Rather than increase the threat to France and Spain, it would result in "the absolute impotence of England to form any enterprise. If my view in this respect is correct, if the complete success of the views of the English Ministry is precisely what France and Spain could wish for most happily,"[18] as it would actually *decrease* the threat to both of them.

3. The British are Defeated and Take Revenge

The British, should they be defeated in North America, would seek revenge and save "not only the heads of the ministers themselves, but even the person of the King, against the rage of the English people"[19] by turning their sights on conquering French and Spanish possessions, particularly the sugar islands. Once these were conquered, they would seek conciliation with the Americans "to whom they would open the markets and secure the trade of the Islands." [20]Presumably, a French and Spanish involvement in securing Britain's defeat in the American Revolution, and their subsequent military presence in (formerly) British North America, would discourage Britain from pursuing such a course.

Turgot's Response

First, although emotion might indeed stir a taste for revenge, he found such a scenario unlikely. "I confess that it seems difficult to me that the English Government, succumbing in its hostile plans against the settlers, succumbing, presumably, after painful and costly efforts which will have considerably weakened its means, should suddenly determine to multiply its enemies, and to form new enterprises." Further, if the colonists had just defeated the British "It is highly doubtful that they would quietly let their enemies make conquests in their vicinity." If the British government were to pursue such an action, it would only be

17. Schelle, *Oeuvres de Turgot*, 387.
18. Ibid., 390.
19. Tower, *The Marquis de Lafayette in the American Revolution*, 109.
20. Ibid., 108.

after it had "made peace with its colonies and joined forces with its own, which is absolutely within the first supposition."[21]

In other words, it got back to his refutation of Vergennes' first point, on the danger of a reconciliation between Britain and the colonies, i.e. that there was no other way they could pursue further conquests. This in turn was based on his argument about the lack of value of the colonies to their owners, a supposition he thought the American Revolution would make clear to the world. In one way or another, Vergennes' case was based on fear—the fear of losing the French colonies and his attempts to lure Spain into the conflict over fear of losing its own possessions. This all came together in the fourth point.

4. America Wins Independence on its own; seeks to conquer French and Spanish holdings

"That the Colonies, once having become independent, and retaining no attachment to England, might become conquerors by necessity; because, being overstocked with their own products, they might seek by force an outlet in the sugar islands and in Spanish America, which would destroy the relations of our colonies to the central Government."[22] In other words, if the colonies secured their independence unaided, they might turn their sights on the French and Spanish sugar islands as conquests to serve as an outlet for their surplus of goods (food, timber, etc.). Winning with the French and Spanish as allies would avert this possibility.

Turgot's Response

Turgot made two arguments. First, he questioned the American appetite for such conquest. Second, he entered into a long-winded and technical economic argument asserting that colonies in general provided little to no value to the home country. If this was true, it undermined any argument that Vergennes made that was based on threats to French and Spanish colonies coming either from the Americans or the British themselves, as pointed out in his refutation of the first scenario. Turgot saw these arguments as being based upon fear rather than rational considerations, and it is true that Vergennes attempted to exploit this fear to coax the Spanish into the alliance. Running through both of these was an early free trade argument as well as an explosion of the premise of the colonial model. To some extent, it was an argument ahead of its time. As would befit a Minister of Finance, Turgot's argument against colonial ownership relied heavily on pecuniary con-

21. Schelle, *Oeuvres de Turgot*, 391.
22. Tower, *The Marquis de Lafayette in the American Revolution*, 108.

siderations and was light on non-monetary factors such as strategic presence and national prestige.

As to the first point, he doubted the Americans would fall into the trap of becoming conquerors. "Much will depend on the consistency of the new constitution of government . . . it is possible, especially if the war is long, that the generals will take too much ascendancy for the glory which they will have acquired. It is possible that . . . they may try to perpetuate their power and prepare themselves from afar for a high fortune, by insinuating into their nascent republic a taste for conquest."[23] However, knowing the thinking of Franklin and the reputation of Washington, Turgot believed the Americans would avoid the trap that had entangled so many other revolutionaries: "It may, however, be anticipated from the prudence which seems to have hitherto presided over the conduct of the Americans, from the courage and enlightenment spread among them, and from their confidence in the wise advice of the famous Franklin, that they will have foreseen the trap, . . . that they will think above all of giving a solid form to their government, and that consequently they will love peace and will seek to preserve it."[24]

Vergennes undercut his own argument in his earlier *Reflections*, acknowledging that "Republics rarely have the love of conquest" and America would be more interested in commerce than conquest, and thus it was in France's interest for America to win.[25] Furthermore, according to Turgot, trade between America and the sugar colonies (of all nations) already occurred in the form of smuggling, and America would not have to conquer these colonies in order to dispose of excess production. The Americans would merely have to "open their ports to all nations, who would hasten to bring them everything they needed in exchange for their superfluous goods."[26]

The second argument was based on three factors which have traditionally been considered part of the value of owning colonies: 1. The price advantage gained by the owning country selling goods to the colony at a higher price and securing raw materials from the colony at a lower one; 2. The economic value that exclusive access to trade with the colony that accrues to the owning country's trader class; 3. The power that colonial ownership projects (the one non-economic factor he cited). I will avoid going into all the pedantic and technical detail but suffice to say Turgot refuted all three. "Wise and happy," he con-

---

23. Schelle, *Oeuvres de Turgot*, 391.
24. Ibid., 391.
25. Tower, *The Marquis de Lafayette in the American Revolution*, 94.
26. Schelle, *Oeuvres de Turgot*, 392.

cluded, "will be the nation which first will know how to bend its policy to the new circumstances, which will agree to see in its colonies only allied provinces, and no longer subject to the metropolis [owning country]!"[27] However, the revolution he foresaw in the perception of the colonial model would take place much later, and unfortunately only after much additional suffering and bloodshed around the world. The American Revolution would provide inspiration for some of these colonial revolts but would not bring an expeditious end to the colonial model.

The American Revolution, which Turgot thought the colonists would eventually win, even without French and/or Spanish help, would "force everyone to recognize this truth, and has corrected the European nations from the jealousy of trade, there will be one less great cause of war among men, and it is very difficult not to desire an event which must do this good to the human race."[28] While he thought this would be yet another world-changing impact of the Revolution, he saw the British as being one of the last to recognize his view on colonial ownership, writing, "It is not probable that the English will be the first to leave the prejudices which they have long regarded as the source of their greatness. In that case there can be no doubt that their obstinacy will lead to the union of their sugar colonies with those of the northern continent."[29] Spain would also have difficulty letting go, finding it "less easy than any other power to leave a road it has been following for two centuries, in order to form a brand-new system adapted to a new order of things."[30]

Vergennes cited these four possible outcomes and envisioned each as justifying an alliance with the Americans. Further, he dangled the proposal of going on the offensive, invading the British mainland while the British were otherwise occupied in North America. Turgot also turned to this in his own *Reflections* and argued against it. His three main reasons were the sad state of French finances, the equally sad state of the French Navy (which even combined with Spain did not yet not have the firepower to overcome even a distracted Britain), and the worry that such an action would serve to unite the British and Americans, resulting in a reconciliation, to the disadvantage of France. For these reasons and others (primarily logistical), the invasion of England was aborted.

27. Ibid., 398.
28. Ibid., 398.
29. Ibid., 398.
30. Ibid., 399.

Having (in his view) proved folly the unwise aspects of Vergennes' case, did Turgot have anything to offer in terms of positive recommendations? He did offer ideas, consisting primarily of the following:[31]

"The accurate and vigilant observation of events and of the designs and preparations of Great Britain."

"The letter of the Marquis de Grimaldi announces the measures that Spain is taking to watch over everything that may enter the Gulf of Mexico."

A "safe and faithful correspondence in the English colonies, so as to be always informed of events and of the present disposition of minds. This article is delicate because it would, I believe, be dangerous to have an agent who would appear to be authorized."

Providing military supplies to the Americans, rationalizing the turning of a blind eye to neutrality by saying "Our traders are free to sell to anyone who buys from them. We do not distinguish between the settlers and the English themselves."

Quietly rebuilding French forces (especially the navy) for readiness (the Spanish were doing the same). "We must therefore be prepared at that moment: either to defend, if possible, our possessions in the event that they are attacked, or to attack our enemy ourselves, taking away part of his resources, and at least forcing him to recall part of his forces for his own defense." Given France's already precarious financial situation, however, this would require some creative financing, financing that Turgot would not be around to arrange.

When all was said and done, Turgot lost both the debate and his job (to a much more accommodating finance minister, Jacques Necker[32]). Vergennes won the battle for the King's support, and the Franco-American alliance won the war. The fortunes of France itself would not turn out quite so well. The war was, as Turgot predicted, financially ruinous, by one estimate costing France over one billion livres.[33] As historian Jonathan Dull writes, "In a very real sense Britain came out of the American Revolution a winner, France a loser,"[34] with its own much more ruinous revolution not far down the road. Addi-

---

31. Schelle, *Oeuvres de Turgot*, 411-412.
32. Larrie D. Ferreiro, *Brothers at Arms* (New York, Alfred A. Knopf, 2016), 90
33. Jonathan Dull, *The French Navy and American Independence* (Princeton, NJ: Princeton University Press, 1975), 350.
34. Jonathan Dull, *France and the American Revolution Seen as Tragedy, published as part of the book Diplomacy and Revolution: The Franco-American Alliance of 1778* (Charlottesville, VA: University Press of Virginia, 1981), 90.

tionally, America's relationship with France was soon on the wane, while its relationship with Britain strengthened, especially as far as trade.[35] Perhaps the peace route would have tuned out differently, but for Vergennes, as historian Jonathan Dull puts it:

> Peace . . . was not a live option. Herein lies the essential difference in the perceptions of Vergennes and Turgot. If Turgot could have persuaded Louis XVI and Vergennes that peace, not war was a necessity if the monarchy was to survive, the history of Louis XVI's reign would have been very different. But Vergennes never saw peace with England in this light. The area of his professional concern became, therefore, strategic: when and under what conditions could France best fight the war?[36]

On the other hand, America, whose independence Turgot had long foreseen, had a bright future: In a letter written late in his life, he noted, "It is impossible not to wish ardently that this people may attain to all the prosperity of which they are capable. They are the hope of the world . . . The Asylum they open to the oppressed of all nations should console the earth."[37]

35. Ferreiro, *Brothers at Arms*, 307-308.
36. Dull, *France and the American Revolution Seen as Tragedy*, 120.
37. Turgot to Richard Price, March 22, 1778, Online Library of Liberty, oll.libertyfund.org/title/1788.

Longhouse Lost: The Battle of Oriskany and the Iroquois Civil War

❧ BRADY J. CRYTZER ❧

The coming of the American Revolution traumatized the North American frontier, and many old orders were left shattered in its wake. While historians often focus on the establishment of a new nation, few recognize the destruction of one of the continent's oldest superpowers. The battle of Oriskany in New York's Mohawk River Valley stands out for many reasons—it was one of the bloodiest days of the entire war, and one of the few battles that was made up almost entirely of North American participants. But perhaps its greatest legacy is the one discussed the least. On that day, the member nations of the Iroquois Confederacy waged war on one another for the first time, and the gruesome battle marked the beginning of a terrible civil war from which the People of the Longhouse would never recover.

THE PEOPLE OF THE LONGHOUSE

From the beginning of the American Revolution the vast and mighty Iroquois Confederacy attempted to walk the fine line of neutrality. Made up of six member nations known respectively as the Haudenosaunee (*People of the Longhouse*), the Mohawk, Cayuga, Onondaga, Oneida, Tuscarawas, and Seneca each believed that the rebellion had the potential to disrupt their long-standing alliance with the British Empire. Although each had their own perspectives on the conflict, the Six Nations relied on their ancient system of governance to establish an official policy toward the two warring sides. Employing a pseudo-federal system, sachems representing each tribe met in council to negotiate terms and gather consensus, ultimately developing a confederacy-wide policy of absolute neutrality. From the earliest months of the war, even before the volleys at Lexington Green, the Iroquois Confederacy found themselves balancing on a tightrope of revolutionary proportions.

Tradition was paramount to the Haudenosaunee, but even the weight of history was not immune to the shifting political ground of revolutionary North America. Since the 1740s the Iroquois had been staunch allies with the Crown, and that agreement was instrumental to the British conquest of New France at the end of the Seven Years' War. In the decade leading to the Revolution, though, some member nations had grown in prominence in the new British North America and a strong sense of localized autonomy had weakened the influence of the Great Council Fire. While the tribal elders stressed neutrality, the warriors of the western-most Seneca and Cayuga had flourished alongside the Redcoats, and Fort Niagara on Lake Ontario had become a royal headquarters on the frontier. Thus, with a prominent fort now on Seneca land and a wealth of trading opportunities, the renegade warriors had little interest in remaining impartial despite their tribal leadership's wishes.[1]

The British were not the only ones to benefit from the waning influence of the Great Council Fire, and the Patriots found themselves with their own allies in the unlikeliest of circumstances. Just before the outbreak of the Revolution, Presbyterian minister Samuel Kirkland made the decision to abandon his life in New Hampshire and set up shop in the Mohawk Valley. As a test of faith and patriotic virtue, Kirkland dedicated his life to proselytizing and preaching in the heart of Iroquoia. As a general truth throughout the history of Colonial America, Haudenosaunee villages in the east tended to be more open to European interaction than their more autonomous brethren in the west; true to form, Kirkland found a welcome audience amongst the villages of the Oneida. While it appears simplistic, Kirkland fostered an intensely loyal bond with the Oneida as well as with the cause of liberty, and his connections became an asset for the struggling Continental Congress.

Despite the efforts of British and Patriot agents, unbeknownst to them the fabled "Longhouse" was suffering a catastrophe of its own. In January of 1777, an Onondaga sachem relayed to the commandant of Fort Stanwix, the primary post in the Mohawk Valley, that ninety of their most powerful chiefs had suddenly died. Clearly the result of an infectious disease, most likely smallpox, the Onondaga claimed that until new leaders could be chosen, "the Central Council fire is extin-

---

1. Timothy J. Shannon, *Iroquois Diplomacy on the Early American Frontier* (New York: Penguin, 2008), 185.

guished ... and can no longer burn." With this development, a startling revelation jolted the Iroquois world: with no council fire, there would be no centralized governing body to bind its member nations. Thus, the Haudenosaunee were free to act on their own in the larger saga of the American Revolution.[2]

By 1777, British operatives at Fort Niagara were successfully breaking the Iroquois' tenuous neutrality and attracting most warriors to their side. At the same time the Oneida were quietly aligning themselves with the Patriot cause, and providing Kirkland with valuable intelligence as spies. The minister would relay those developments to Gen. George Washington, and soon became one of the Patriots' most trusted agents on the frontier. Although the Longhouse remained intact, it was being pushed to a breaking point yet unseen in its centuries-old history.[3]

INTO THE WILDERNESS

By the spring of 1777 the state of the American rebellion was grim. After Gen. William Howe's massive invasion failed to capture Washington's Continental army in 1776, the new year brought a radical shift in Britain's imperial policy toward their rebellious American colonies. From the perspective of the Court of St. James, the revolutionaries needed to be stamped out as quickly as possible; as seen in previous uprisings, radical ideas of political independence spread like wildfire if left unchecked, and once entrenched they were nearly impossible to remove. Guided by this urgent principle, British administrators anxiously announced an entirely new strategy for ending the war. It was wildly different than anything yet attempted, and served as a necessary reboot in their failing attempts at making peace in North America.

Only two years into the war, the British still viewed the Patriot movement as a uniquely New England phenomenon. While the war would eventually engulf the whole of the continent east of the Mississippi, officials believed that if the northeastern colonies could be physically separated from their colonial neighbors, the rebellion could be contained and eventually destroyed. The 315-mile-long Hudson River Valley served as the primary border separating New England from New York, and its total military occupation would achieve Britain's overall objective. As the empire retained control of Canada and fully occupied New York City, the most critical components were already in place for

2. Speech of the Oneida Chiefs, January, 19, 1777 as quoted in Barbara Graymont, *The Iroquois in the American Revolution* (Syracuse: Syracuse University Press, 1972), 113.
3. Colin G. Calloway, *The American Revolution in Indian Country* (Cambridge: Cambridge University Press, 1995), 129.

launching such an expedition, and many in London felt that success was within reach.

In what would come to be known as the Saratoga Campaign, Gen. John Burgoyne would lead 8500 troops southward out of Quebec along the Lake Champlain-Lake George corridor and follow the Hudson all the way to Albany. Once there, Burgoyne hoped to cooperate with forces under the command of Sir William Howe in New York City. Finally, a third army would land on the shores of Lake Ontario led by recently-breveted Brig. Gen. Barrimore St. Leger. This final force would snake its way eastward through the Mohawk Valley capturing noted Patriot strongholds en route to their great union at Albany. It was an ambitious plan and timing was its most critical element.

The Mohawk Valley was a warzone. Since the Iroquois warriors declared for the Crown, local Patriots had regularly come under attack from raiding war parties and Loyalist rangers. Homes and farmsteads were destroyed, families were split, and the region disintegrated into a terrible civil war. While Redcoats and Continentals toiled in the Pennsylvania countryside, partisans on both sides arrested, harassed, and murdered their enemies in New York making it the most terrifying theater of the entire war. In the midst of the madness, Patriot forces maintained a series of forts along the Mohawk River, and these outposts became bastions of safety for the battered populace seeking refuge from the conflict. As Barry St. Leger's Loyalists, Germans, and Indian allies descended upon the region, they were given the specific task of razing these fortifications before finally connecting with Burgoyne at Albany.

Upon St. Leger's arrival on the shores of Lake Ontario, the whole of the Mohawk Valley was put on notice. Shortly after their landing, some 800 Iroquois warriors led by Joseph Brant, known amongst the Mohawk as Thayendanagea, greeted the British commander in a show of support. Brant had proven to be a loyal ally and vital asset to the royal war effort on the frontier, and his cooperation would be equally vital during the Saratoga campaign. Joined by other sachems from across Iroquoia including Cornplanter, Guyasuta and Sayenqueraghta, the expedition was a microcosm of the British Empire's overall imperial vision. To the romantic onlooker, St. Leger's column was precisely the multicultural, multiethnic response force desired to suppress the rebels that menaced their American colonies. While Albany was always the final rallying point, the post of Fort Stanwix was squarely in St. Leger's proverbial crosshairs; recently captured by New York Patriots and presumptuously renamed "Fort Schuyler" after the commander of the Northern Department of the Continental army, the British were anxious to reclaim the site. By July 14 St. Leger began to assemble his column at Oswego, and on July 26 his awesome force began their march eastward.

The Patriots of Tryon County, New York had grown accustomed to defending their own territory, and were more than comfortable taking their defense into their own hands. Led by Nicholas Herkimer, the Tryon County militiamen had received warnings of a potential British attack on Fort Stanwix from their Oneida allied scouts; on July 30 the spies discovered that St. Leger's men were indeed marching on the post. With this vital intelligence the Oneida nation and sachems like Han Yerry cemented their place as a loyal partner in the cause of freedom. By August 2 St. Leger's column had reached Fort Stanwix near modern Rome, New York, and by nightfall it was fully under siege. With these developments, the men of Tryon County and the warriors of the Oneida rallied 800 men to liberate the fort. For the Americans inside their only hope was the joint Patriot-Oneida force under Herkimer and Han Yerry.

THE BATTLE OF ORISKANY

From the nearby Oneida village of Oriska, Herkimer attempted to reach out to the besieged Fort Stanwix. Now the head of a major relief column, Herkimer instructed three runners to deliver a message to the commandant of the post, Peter Gansevoort, informing him of his movements. According to Herkimer's wishes, Gansevoort was to fire his cannons in three successive bursts upon receipt of the message, and promptly sortie his men out from the post to join with the approaching militiamen. It was a bold maneuver designed to break St. Leger's siege of the fort, but Herkimer's instructions did not reach Gansevoort in time. Instead his scouts were delayed while sneaking through the British lines, and Herkimer's message remained undelivered. Overcome with urgency, on the morning of August 6 the Tryon County militiamen and their Oneida allies elected to liberate the post, with or without the cooperation of the men inside.

Although he was in a foreign land and deep in the American frontier, Brig. Gen. Barry St. Leger remained one step ahead of his opponents. The warriors allied with the British were the eyes and ears of the forests, and Molly Brant, the sister of the Mohawk war chief Joseph Brant, played a crucial role in St. Leger's intelligence gathering operation. With Fort Stanwix surrounded, the commander received valuable intelligence from Molly Brant that a Patriot force was marching westward presumably to rescue the garrison inside the post. With the news of Herkimer's advancing column, the commander ordered the Loyalists of the King's Royal Regiment of New York and Butler's Rangers to intercept the Tryon County militia; Joseph Brant and 400 Iroquois warriors joined in anticipation of the fight to come.

On the morning of August 6, Herkimer's Tryon County militiamen and Han Yerry's Oneida warriors trekked westward toward their target. As per the commander's orders, the militia marched in two separate columns. The Oneida warriors marched alongside the columns as flankers, and another party served as the vanguard marching ahead to gather any actionable intelligence that could serve the New Yorkers. Herkimer strode near the front of his men on a white horse, and his status was clear as the overall leader of the Patriots; less so his Oneida counterpart. In the strictest sense Han Yerry had no authority to order his fellow warriors into battle—he was merely a first among equals. The respect afforded him was garnered from past bravery, not an awarded commission or inherited title. Instead of fighting *for* Han Yerry, the Oneida merely followed his example and fought *with* him. As such he made no effort to distinguish himself amongst his peers as their marched, a contrast that was only one of the many seen in a war that brought so many alternative worldviews onto the same battlefield. At his side was his wife Tyonajanegen (meaning "Two Kettles Together") and his son Cornelius. As the joint Patriot-Oneida force marched within six miles of the besieged Fort Stanwix, the rough road and dense forests provided ample cover for any would-be attackers waiting in ambush, and the potential for danger awaited around every bend.

Unbeknownst to the approaching force, they were walking into a trap. Earlier that day Joseph Brant and his Iroquoian warriors positioned themselves on a deep ravine that bisected the Albany-Oswego Road. Using his previous knowledge of the ground, Brant relied on the ancient methods of tactical ambush to surprise his enemies, and with any luck, destroy them before a general battle could begin. According to his plan Brant would arrange his Seneca and Cayuga warriors along both sides of the main road in a silent position allowing the Patriots to march past them. As the unsuspecting column climbed out of the ravine, they would discover Sir John Johnson's Royal Yorkers positioned across the main road. When Herkimer's men engaged the Loyalists, Brant would spring his trap in the ravine and sever the marching column, creating utter chaos on the road and swarming their enemies. With the right combination of patience and fury, the great showdown in the wilderness would be no contest. Although he could not control all of the warriors on hand, Brant relied on other prominent war chiefs to keep the younger, more rambunctious warriors under control until the time was right. Seneca warriors such as Guyasuta (sometimes Ki-

asutha), Cornplanter, and Sayenqueraghta were instrumental in selecting the ambush location, and Brant trusted that they could manage the
oncoming assault as well.[4]

At 10 AM the Patriots had reached the ambush site. As planned,
the warriors remained silently hidden as the front of the column passed
by along the Albany-Oswego Road. Eyewitness accounts place
Nicholas Herkimer near the front of his men, so much so that he was
able to guide his horse fifteen feet into the ravine and climb back out
the other side without ever noticing the enemy war party that quietly
surrounded him. With only the head of the column through the ravine,
the sachems were undoubtedly surprised to hear shots ringing out from
the rear. With the Patriots in their grasp it appeared that some of the
overzealous warriors fired on Herkimer's men too soon, and the battle
began in earnest with nearly three quarters of the Patriot column yet
to enter the kill zone.

By the time that Herkimer was able to turn to investigate the nature
of the popping muskets, the ambush was already taking effect. Despite
its premature initiation, Col. Ebeneezer Cox, the head of the first regiment of the Tryon County militia, was dead. Soon after, Herkimer was
struck through the thigh and his horse killed. Herkimer was badly
wounded but refused to leave the battlefield; his men sat him against a
tree and he directed the battle from that spot, even managing to smoke
his pipe in the process. As was the case in most frontier battles, the engagement was chaotic. Rather than armies aligned in traditional formation, the fighting appeared more like a series of independent duels
and brawls. When Brant's warriors left Fort Stanwix quickly, many
failed to bring muskets and powder. Instead, they settled the matter
with hand to hand combat. One of the war chiefs on hand was Governor Blacksnake of the Seneca, who recalled: "they had 3 cannon and
we have none, But Tomehawks and a few guns amongst us, But agreed
to fight with Tomehawk Skulling Knife."[5]

The fighting was hotly contested, and the Patriots were reeling. As
the battle progressed, the British-allied Iroquois took full advantage of
their enemies' weaknesses. After the Tryon County militiamen fired
their muskets, the warriors would spring from cover to attack with knife
and tomahawk. By 1777 the Iroquois were well-versed in traditional,
European-style battlefield tactics, and they knew to wait for the flash-
ing muzzle as a signal to attack. As the frontiersmen tried in vain to

4. Michael O. Logusz, *With Musket and Tomahawk* (Philadelphia: Casemate, 2012), 2: 123.
5. Blacksnake to Benjamin Williams, as quoted in Thomas S. Abler, *Chainbreaker: The
Revolutionary War Memories of Governor Blacksnake* (Lincoln: University of Nebraska,
2005), 128.

reload their firearm, they were struck down by a pouncing Iroquoian warrior. Despite these deficiencies the Patriots still fared better than their colleagues from Virginia and New England; a life on the frontier had schooled them in Indian warfare, and they comfortably discarded their muskets to fight with blades of their own.

Mother Nature cares little for the politics of man, but on August 6 she intervened on the Patriots' behalf. At midday, a thunderstorm suddenly appeared and soaked the battlefield. The combat stopped for an hour, and afterwards both sides tried to capitalize on the break. After the rains subsided, Herkimer was able to rally his men out of the ravine and position them on the high ground. Likewise, the British commander Johnson instructed his men to turn their jackets inside out as a means of confusing the Patriots. The ruse nearly worked, but due to the intensely localized nature of the battle neighbors soon recognized one another and alerted their superiors as to the apparent scheme.

To fend off the attack in the second phase of the battle, the wounded Herkimer instructed his men to fight in pairs. As one man loaded and reloaded his musket, the other would fire on the charging enemy. This tactic meant that no soldier would ever be without a loaded weapon, and served to negate the Indian strategy of attacking during the reloading process. One of the most spectacular scenes of the battle was of the Oneida sachem Han Yerry and his wife Tyonajanegen—as he fired alongside his Patriot allies, Two Kettles Together made sure that he had a fully charged musket at the ready to fend off the next wave of Seneca, Cayuga, and Mohawk attackers. As the day wore on, tradition holds that she joined the fight as well.

Ironically, the turning point of the battle did not occur on the field itself. Six miles away at Fort Stanwix, the commandant Peter Gansevoort finally received Herkimer's lost intelligence from the previous day. Gansevoort ordered the sortie that was requested, but not to the battle site. With most of the warriors now fighting at the ravine, Gansevoort's troops immediately began to plunder the vacant camp of the British-allied Indians. When the warriors sparring with Herkimer caught wind of the raid, they immediately fled from the battlefield to save their valuable winter stores that had been left unattended. When the British-allied Iroquois fled, Johnson and Brant lost most of their manpower, and gave the Patriots a timely window to flee from the battle. As Blacksnake recollected years later, "the Blood Shed a Stream Running Down on the Decending ground."[6]

6. Ibid.

BLOODY CREEK

War is not a game. It does not play by the traditional rules of a game, and therefore cannot be evaluated as such. One of the most challenging aspects of the Battle of Oriskany remains the determination of a "winner." Body counts are a means of "keeping score," but not a good one. Holding the field remains another traditional axiom of victory, but it alone does not tell the whole story. Frontier warfare was brutal in its suddenness and often ended in indecisive stalemates. For this reason, the frontier battles of the war are often overlooked, but in doing so a critically important part of the Revolutionary drama is missed.

The British and Iroquois warriors fled the battlefield first, but the damage that they inflicted was far greater than that of their opponents. While the Patriots retreated on their own terms, their original goal of liberating Fort Stanwix was a failure. Instead of continuing westward, Herkimer ordered his men to return east toward Fort Dayton. He died from his wounds ten days later. As the British and allied warriors stopped the Tryon County militiamen and the Oneidas from reaching their destination, the battle known as "Bloody Creek" has tentatively been labeled a victory for the Crown.

In frontier warfare the traditional battle lines are blurred in more ways than one, and in most cases engagements rarely have "winners" that are readily identifiable. Considering the terrible costs of the Battle of Oriskany, it is truly difficult for either side to appear triumphant. Estimates state that the Patriots suffered nearly fifty percent casualties during the battle, while the British lost roughly fifteen percent.[7]

The losses on the Native side will likely never be known, but the carnage was undeniable. Accounts vary, but most tally Indian losses at sixty-eight warriors, and a staggering twenty-three war chiefs. Blacksnake recalled "There I have Seen the most Dead Bodies all it over that I never Did see, and never will again." Another witness, Continental scout Frederick Sammons, wrote: "I befell the most shocking sight I had ever witnessed. The Indians and white men were mingled with one another, just as they had been when death had first completed his work. Many bodies had also been torn to pieces by wild beasts." Many speculate that the engagement was one of the single bloodiest days of the entire war.[8]

The war in the Mohawk Valley continued. In response to the siege of Fort Stanwix and the loss at Oriskany, Maj. Gen. Benedict Arnold led a force of 700 men to liberate the post. He never arrived, but mis-

7. Isabel Kelsay, *Joseph Brant* (Syracuse: Syracuse University Press, 1984), 205-209.
8. Ibid. and Frederick Sammons as quoted in Logusz, *With Musket and Tomahawk*, 2: 171.

leading intelligence spread by allied warriors thoroughly convinced General St. Leger that Arnold was on his way with 3,000 men. By the time Arnold began his march, he received word from a joyous Gansevoort that the British had abandoned their assault on Fort Stanwix. In one of the master strokes of the war, the Patriot parties would all meet once more at Saratoga. By October, Gen. John Burgoyne's great invasion came to a screeching halt.

A PLACE OF GREAT SADNESS

The Battle of Oriskany plays a terrible role in the oral traditions of the Haudenosaunee. Known amongst them as "a place of great sadness," the fight in Upstate New York stands as watershed moment in the history of the Iroquois. With the council fire extinguished, the six member nations of the Iroquois Confederacy acted on their own during the American Revolution. When they met on the battlefield at Oriskany, it marked the end of a centuries-old system that had ruled the American Northeast. In the wake of the battle, British-allied sachems delivered a tomahawk to their Oneida brethren. Unthinkable only a year earlier, the reception of the now infamous weapon represented a formal declaration of war.[9]

As the traditional story of the American Revolution played out between the Continentals and Redcoats, the forgotten Iroquois civil war ravaged the frontiers. In the wake of Oriskany Jospeh Brant's warriors raided and destroyed the Oneida village of Oriska. In retaliation, the Patriot-allied Oneida razed Tiononderoge, Canajoharie, and eventually Fort Hunter Mohawk. The inter-tribal conflict would go on until 1779, when George Washington ordered the joint forces of James Clinton, John Sullivan, and Daniel Brodhead to march their armies into Iroquoia. The 1779 campaign burned villages, fields, and stores leaving the region utterly devastated.

By 1783 the world witnessed the foundation of a new American nation, as well as the destruction of another.

9. Recollections of Iroquois Visitors as quoted in Joy Bilharz, *Oriskany: A Place of Great Sadness* (Boston: Northeast Region Ethnography Program, National Park Service, 2009), 93.

A Demographic View of North Carolina Militia and State Troops, 1775–1783

🌺 DOUGLAS R. DORNEY, JR. 🌺

After nearly a quarter of a millennium, what do we really know about the militia and state troops that served during the Revolutionary War? Historians and researchers over the past century have dedicated entire volumes to addressing this question with numerous publications of militia rosters. While this research has proven invaluable, what does it really tell us about the men and their units beyond their service in a particular unit or battle? For instance, how old was the typical militiaman (if there was a "typical" militiaman)? How long did he serve and in how many battles did he fight? Was he a volunteer or a reluctant draftee? Where did he serve? Was he literate? Where did he live after the war? And perhaps most importantly, what was his personal experience? What unique circumstances or events did he have a part in that is not covered in already written histories of the war?

Information contained within pension applications provides at least some answers. In the past fifteen years, most of the 150,000 known Revolutionary War pension documents have been digitally scanned.[1] Tens of thousands of these have been transcribed and posted in online databases. The most prominent repository of these transcribed pension documents is the Southern Campaigns Revolutionary War Pension Statements & Rosters website. Researchers Will Graves, C. Leon Harris and several others have, since 2006, meticulously deciphered and transcribed thousands of pension applications. To date there are over 25,000 transcribed documents on the site. All of the known

---

1. J. D. Lewis, *NC Patriots 1775-1783: Their Own Words*, 1: vii.

Federal pension applications from men who served in Georgia, South and North Carolina, and Virginia have been posted there.[2]

This work is a demographic study of the North Carolina militia and state troops utilizing data derived from Federal Pension applications. Included are men of the North Carolina Continental Line who also served in the militia or state troops. In the interest of keeping this piece relatively brief and to avoid confusion, men who served exclusively in the North Carolina Continental Line have been excluded from this work. Clearly, North Carolina Continental soldiers warrant their own dedicated study.

North Carolina fielded between 30,000 and 36,000 soldiers during the war, of which 22,000 to 28,000 were militia and state troops.[3] Between fifteen and twenty percent of these men (or their families) filed pension applications.[4] For this study over 9,000 applications were reviewed pertaining to North Carolina. Of these, data from only 3,721 applications was collected and entered into a simple spreadsheet. The two critical requirements to be included were that the men entered military service in North Carolina *and* also provided details about themselves and their service. Generally, this included date and place of birth, place of enlistment, dates of service, type of enlistment, duration of service, place of pension location and participation in battles or skirmishes. If an application provided little more than a name and only a vague description of a man's service it was not included.

PENSION ACTS

There were numerous laws providing pensions for Revolutionary War soldiers. The first started with the Continental Congress during the Revolution and the last act was passed after the Civil War. Two particular Pension Acts, those of 1818 and 1832, yielded 53,910 pensions of the overall 57,623 awarded.[5] Briefly summarized, the 1818 act provided pensions for Continental soldiers who did not desert, served at least nine months, and who were suffering financial hardship. The 1832 Act extended full pensions to militia, state troops, and Continentals who had served at least twenty-four months, regardless of financial circumstances, and partial pensions to those who had served at least six months.

2. All Virginia state pension applications are also posted there along with some of those from South Carolina.
3. Ibid, iv.
4. Ibid, 2: v.
5. Will Graves, "Pension Acts: An Overview of Revolutionary War Pension and Bounty Land Legislation and the Southern Campaigns Pension Transcription Project", Southern Campaigns Revolutionary War Pension Statements & Rosters, revwarapps.org/

Before venturing into the demographics, readers should be advised that this was not intended to be a definitive study of all North Carolina militia and state troops. Nor is this work intending to capture information from all of the known North Carolina pension applicants. The data herein represents a portion of a small portion of the total number of men who served in the North Carolina militia and state troops who provided details about their time in these units. The analysis, summation, and synthesis here only applies to the data collected from the 3,721 pension applications.

A word of further caution is necessary regarding statistics on dates of birth, length of service and number of terms the men served. Pension applicants almost certainly served more time, more tours of duty, and were younger than those who did not file applications. The minimum length of service requirements for pensions meant that those that served less than the minimum six or nine months and/or only one standard three-month term of service would be highly unlikely to file an application. Likewise, many descendants may have been less likely to file applications, as they may not have known the details of service or have been unable to provide third-party verification of the relative's service. Pension applicants were likely to be younger because many men died before 1832 when most applications were filed. As life expectancy in eighteenth-century America was between forty-one and forty-seven years of age, it certainly seems possible, if not probable, that the men studied here represent the younger range of North Carolina soldiers.[6]

PLACE AND DATE OF BIRTH

Most of the men who filed pension applications for North Carolina militia and state troop service were not born in the former colony. Over fifty-six percent were born in other colonies or other countries. More of these men were born in Virginia, Maryland and Pennsylvania than North Carolina, those colonies accounting for over forty-nine percent of all pension applicant places of birth. Those born in New Jersey and South Carolina account for just over one percent each, respectively. Connecticut, Delaware, Georgia, Massachusetts, New York, and Rhode Island were also noted as birthplaces, comprising a fraction of a percent for each state. Slightly over three percent of North Carolina pension applicants were foreign-born, arriving from six countries. Just over two percent were born in Ireland, less than one percent were born in Scotland. Fewer than a dozen men each were born in Canada, England, France, and Germany (Figure 1).

6. David J. Hacker, "Decennial Life Tables for the White Population of the United States, 1790-1900." *Historical methods* vol. 43 no. 2 (2010): 45-79.

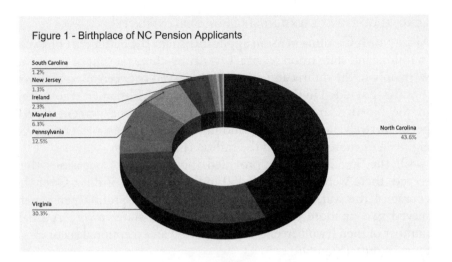

Figure 1 - Birthplace of NC Pension Applicants

South Carolina
1.2%
New Jersey
1.3%
Ireland
2.3%
Maryland
6.3%
Pennsylvania
12.5%

North Carolina
43.6%

Virginia
30.3%

Over sixty-eight percent of those born out of state entered service in counties in the western half of North Carolina. Fairly prevalent in pension applications is a trend of those born out of state congregating in certain counties of North Carolina. For instance, seventy-six percent of those born in Ireland (Ulster) settled in the three counties of Guilford, Rowan, and Mecklenburg. Seventy-seven percent of those born in Scotland settled in the southeastern counties of North Carolina. Over eighty-six percent of those born in Pennsylvania settled in the five western counties of Guilford, Mecklenburg, Orange, Rowan, and Tryon. Just over sixty-two percent of those born in Virginia settled in the northern counties of North Carolina. The three counties with the highest percentages of those born out of state were the western counties of: Surry with seventy-six percent, Burke with seventy-seven percent, Wilkes with eighty-one percent, and Tennessee (then part of North Carolina) with eighty-three percent.

Conversely, most militia and state troop applicants in the eastern counties of the state were born in North Carolina. Over sixty-two percent of those from eastern counties report being born in the state. Very high rates of in-state birth were recorded in several inland eastern counties: Edgecombe with seventy-five percent, Pitt with eighty-two percent, Dobbs with eighty-three percent, Duplin and Hertford with eighty-four percent, Martin with eighty-five percent, and Craven with eighty-eight percent.

The average birth year of the men from the pension applications is 1757. The earliest birth year noted is 1732, the latest recorded is 1767. There is very little variation based on where in the state the man was born, or whether he was born inside or outside of North Carolina.

LENGTH OF SERVICE AND NUMBER OF DEPLOYMENTS

Most North Carolina pension applicants spent the better part of a year in militia and state troop service. Over sixty-three percent of men who were only in the militia and state troops served between six and eleven months. Excluded in this percentage are those Militiamen who served in the North Carolina Line.[7] Another twenty-one percent served between twelve and seventeen months. Over thirteen percent served eighteen or more months in the militia (Figure 2).

Of the 3,652 men that provided the number of occasions they served, there were a total of 9,450 individual tours of duty. Over the course of the war, ninety percent of all North Carolina pensioners served two or more terms in the militia and state troops. A small number of men (two percent) report serving an exceptional six or more tours of duty (Figure 3).

Given the dozens of battles and skirmishes in the South throughout 1780 and 1781 it is not surprising that most North Carolina men served tours and experienced combat during this period. Over seventy-five percent of the total tours of duty by pensioners were during 1780 or 1781. Ninety-one percent of all North Carolina pension applicants served at least one term of military service during 1780-1781. Over sixty-two percent of all men served two or more terms during this time frame (Figure 4).

TERMS OF SERVICE

Pension applicants served a tour of duty in one of three ways: as a volunteer, draftee, or substitute.[8] More than thirty-eight percent served solely as a volunteer, fifteen percent as a draftee, and two percent as a substitute. The remainder of men served in more varied ways as a volunteer and draftee, volunteer and substitute, draftee and substitute or all three. Despite the numerous conditions under which men served, the data is clear that a substantial majority of North Carolina applicants (upwards of eighty-four percent) actively chose to enter military service as a volunteer or substitute at least once during war. However, it is also true that half were drafted on at least one occasion (Figure 5).

There are several interesting anecdotes from substitutes in their applications. Many applicants describe paying money or providing goods to their substitute or receiving them to serve in another's place. One man volunteered in 1777 but afterward coordinated with several other

---

7. As Continental soldiers generally served continuously, some for multiple years, and for much longer terms than those in the Militia, it felt prudent to exclude them from the narrative on length of service.
8. 3,300 men provided the terms of their service.

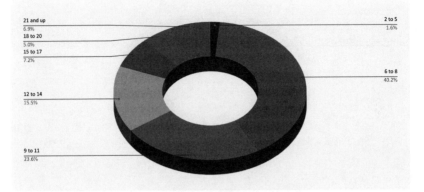

Figure 2 - Total Months of Service by NC Pension Applicants*
* Excludes Continental Soldiers who also served in the NC Militia/ State Troops

21 and up
6.9%
18 to 20
5.0%
15 to 17
7.2%

2 to 5
1.6%

6 to 8
40.2%

12 to 14
15.5%

9 to 11
23.6%

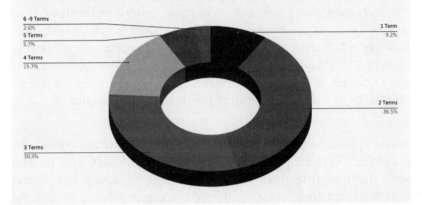

Figure 3 - Total Number of Tours of Duty by NC Pension Applicants

6 -9 Terms
2.6%
5 Terms
5.7%

1 Term
9.2%

4 Terms
15.7%

2 Terms
36.5%

3 Terms
30.3%

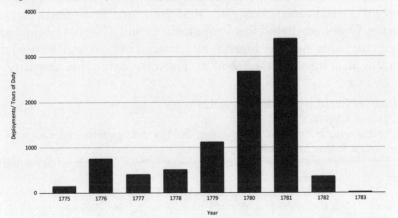

Figure 4 - Tours of Duty of NC Pension Applicants by Year

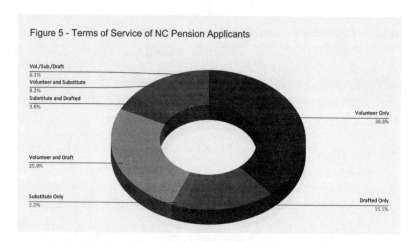

Figure 5 - Terms of Service of NC Pension Applicants

Vol./Sub./Draft
6.1%
Volunteer and Substitute
8.2%
Substitute and Drafted
3.6%

Volunteer Only
38.8%

Volunteer and Draft
25.9%

Substitute Only
2.2%

Drafted Only
15.1%

men to pay substitutes four times from 1777 to 1780.[9] Fairly common among substitutes are men serving in the place of a relative. Almost all these men substituted themselves in their fathers' or brothers' place. Perhaps the most interesting story of a substitute is that of Ishmael Titus. He was a slave who was substituted (it appears illegally) in his master's place. As a reward for his service he was granted his freedom.[10] Titus's example is the only known case in the North Carolina pension applications of a slave manumitted for their military service.[11]

LITERACY

Pension applications were generally either signed by the applicant *or* with a "mark" if the applicant was not literate. Compilation of this data reveals that only fifty-three percent of pension applicants were literate (enough to sign their names).[12] There is some indication though that this percentage may be high as there are instances of court officials signing statements for the applicant. Even at fifty-three percent, the percentage indicates lower rates than indicated in colonial literacy studies. One study found that Perquimans County, North Carolina had a seventy-nine percent literacy rate from 1748-76 and sixty-eight percent in Virginia in 1762-68.[13] The reason for this disparity is

9. Frederick Daniel, pension application R2646.
10. Ishmael Titus (R10623).
11. Several other North Carolina slaves were freed by their wartime service but none of them appear to have filed a pension application.
12. 3,038 of the sample set provided their signature or "mark". Of these, 1,617 provided their own written signature.
13. F.W. Grubb, "Growth of Literacy in Colonial America: Longitudinal Patterns, Economic Models, and the Direction of Future Research," *Social Science History* Vol. 14 No. 4 (Winter, 1990), 451-482.

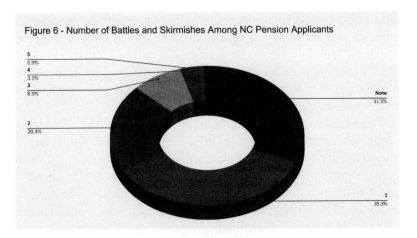

Figure 6 - Number of Battles and Skirmishes Among NC Pension Applicants

unknown but could be due to several factors. Schools in colonial North Carolina were few and widely scattered. The same academic study noted that increased population density generally correlated to higher rates of literacy which was just then occurring in North Carolina. Another study suggests that colonial literacy rates were inflated because the "unlanded poor," who were more likely to be illiterate, were under-represented in legal documents, the primary method in determining literacy. That said, the few counties which seem to have had schools also had relatively high literacy rates. Mecklenburg County had the highest rate at seventy-three percent, New Hanover at sixty-eight percent, and Caswell at sixty-two percent.

BATTLES AND SKIRMISHES

North Carolina militia and state troop pension applicants (including those who also served in the North Carolina Line) reported being in ninety-nine known battles and skirmishes in at least seven different states. At least sixty-eight percent of North Carolina pension applicants were involved in at least one battle or skirmish.[14] The highest proportion of men (thirty-five percent) reported being in one battle followed by those who fought in two battles (twenty percent). A very few, six men, reported being in seven or more battles and skirmishes during the war (Figure 6).

Of the ninety-nine battles, North Carolina pension applicants report themselves most prominently in eleven actions. The Battles of Camden and Guilford Courthouse have the highest number of reported pension applicant participation. Approximately nine percent of all North Carolina

14. 2,536 out of 3,721 men.

militia and state troop pensioners (including those with no previous battle experience) report being engaged in the Battle of Camden. Ten percent of the total sample were in the Battle of Guilford Courthouse. Of the eleven battles, six were fought outside of North Carolina. Three of these eleven battles were fought against primarily Loyalist units with very few if any British regular troops present (Figure 7).

Of the 2,536 men that fought in at least one battle, seventy-eight percent saw combat in the 1780-81 time period. Of those that participated in the battles and skirmishes of 1780-81 only 381 (fifteen percent) report previous battle experience prior to 1780. About nine percent of men report being in unnamed skirmishes. Most of these were against British-aligned Native Americans on the western frontiers of North and South Carolina, Virginia, and Georgia. A smaller proportion of these unnamed skirmishes were with unnamed Tory units across both Carolinas between 1775 and 1781.

A few personal battle accounts of pensioners' military actions stand out. As militia companies were formed locally, many men served with family members. Two separate men report relatives killed at the Battle of Ramsour's Mill, one man's father and another's brother.[15] One man reported that his brother was killed by his side at the Battle of Guilford Courthouse.[16] Another man reported that both his brother and father were killed at the Battle of Kings Mountain.[17] A man who was on his way to the Kings Mountain but missed the action encountered captured Loyalist prisoners on his return home. Among the prisoners was his brother who was captured in the battle.[18]

CONTINENTAL ARMY SERVICE

Approximately twelve percent of North Carolina pension applicants served in the North Carolina Continental Line as well as in the militia and state troops.[19] Analysis of these pension applications support the two distinct periods in the history of the North Carolina Line. From May 1780 when over 800 of them were captured at Charleston, to April 1781 when new regiments were raised, the North Carolina Continental Line had essentially ceased to exist. The vast majority of those who served in both the line and militia had either completed their Continental service before 1780, serving in the militia later *or* served

---

15. Joseph Dobson (W19187), William Falls (S6834).
16. Jeremiah Gurley (S13231).
17. Enoch Berry (W8128).
18. Lewis Carlton (R1692).
19. 448 men were identified as having served in the North Carolina Continental Line and a North Carolina militia or state troop unit.

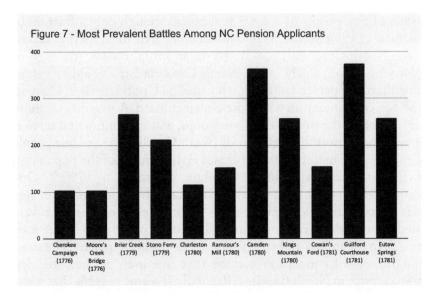

Figure 7 - Most Prevalent Battles Among NC Pension Applicants

in the militia before April 1781 and served in the Continental Line sometime afterward. Their places of enlistment reveal that most of them came from one portion of the state. Nearly two-thirds of them enlisted in the northeast quadrant of North Carolina from the eastern boundary of Guilford County in a line directly eastwards towards the coast.[20]

Among the most interesting stories of men who served in both the line and militia are those of two men during the siege of Charleston. These men, with the knowledge that militia units were to be quickly paroled, assumed the role of militiamen. One man's term ended in late 1779 but he chose to stay in service only to be captured. He changed from his Continental uniform and attached himself to an Orange County militia unit. Another man's term ran out during the siege and he joined an unidentified militia unit. While both were subsequently paroled, only one served a militia term afterward.[21]

"OTHER FREE" PERSONS

Pension applications are mostly devoid of an applicant's race or ethnicity, but free people of color did indeed serve in the militia and state troops during the war. Less than two percent of North Carolina militia pension applicants cross reference with "Other Free" or "Free Colored" persons listed in Federal Census data and contemporary

20. Of the 448, 408 identified their place of residence when starting military service.
21. Thomas Hale (S37975) and Jesse Rickertson (W27382).

rosters of free people of color.[22] It seems as though only a fraction of free men of color served in the militia compared to those that served in the North Carolina Line. Based on an initial review, free men of color who served solely in the North Carolina Line could represent more than five percent of all North Carolina Continentals.[23] There is, however, consistency on where these men enlisted. A majority of those who served in the militia and state troops, and in Continental service, entered in the northeastern part of North Carolina, where free people of color represented between four and eight percent of the population of five northeastern North Carolina counties in 1790.[24] One northeastern county (Granville) had a relatively high number of free men of color in a local militia unit—almost seventeen percent were listed as non-white in complexion.[25] The lower percentage of free men of color in the militia and state troops is not readily apparent. The most straightforward conclusion may be that free men of color avoided militia service in North Carolina. Relatedly, it seems possible that many of these free men of color saw Continental service as more appealing and joined those units early in the war.

PRISONERS OF WAR

Over ten and a half percent of militia and state troop pension applicants noted being held prisoner at some point in the war. This figure is not surprising given that North Carolina soldiers were present at many actions such as Brier Creek, Charleston, Camden, Fishing Creek and other engagements where American prisoners were taken. There are clear indications in pension applications of British soldiers recruiting American prisoners. One man, a prisoner at Charleston, was offered "$50 cash, a suit of Regimentals and a share of the Spoils or booty of the City" to join the British army.[26] Several American prisoners appear to have joined British units to better their conditions. These prisoners

22. Eric Grundset, ed., *Forgotten Patriots: African American and American Indian Patriots in the Revolutionary War* (National Society Daughters of the American Revolution, 2008), 560-566. Fifty-nine total men identified, two were noted as being part or "full blood" Native American, four were noted as "mulatto". The remaining were mostly identified in Census records as "Other Free".
23. If ten to fifteen percent of 8,800 North Carolina Continentals filed applications and seventy-two "free persons of color" have been identified this would amount to between five and eight percent of the total.
24. Paul Heinegg, *List of Free African Americans in the Revolution: Virginia, North Carolina, South Carolina, Maryland and Delaware*, www.freeafricanamericans.com/introduction.htm
25. Size Roll taken by Capt. Ralph Williams of Men enrolled in Granville County May 25th 1778 to fill the North Carolina quota of Continental Soldiers, revwarapps.org/ b250.pdf.
26. John Davis (S3259).

noted being "with" British units and then "deserting" them when the opportunity arose.[27] Two men recorded that they joined British service to be released from prison ships but later noted "escaping" from them.[28] There is at least one instance in pension applications of a British soldier deserting and joining the North Carolina militia. He later received a bayonet wound in action near Wilmington in 1781.[29]

Numerous pensioners reported guarding British and Loyalist prisoners. For some unknown reason, a few of these men felt it proper to note in their applications witnessing violence against enemy prisoners or perpetrating it themselves. One pension applicant initially felt remorse after witnessing the killing of Loyalist prisoners after the Battle of Pyle's Defeat but changed his sentiments the next day when confronted by a young man lying on the road who had suffered a bayonet wound and was left for dead by the enemy.[30] Two brothers, serving together, noted in their applications capturing and killing the same Tory prisoner.[31] Another two men in separate incidents reported hanging a group of three and four Tories after capturing them.[32] One man was guarding a prisoner of the British Legion when another band of militia arrived, took the prisoner and executed him on the side of the road.[33] In perhaps the strangest incident in the reviewed pension applications, one man led his militia unit to his brother who was a Tory. His fellow militiamen were originally planning to kill the Tory brother but instead devised a plan of exchanging him for American prisoners. The Tory was successfully exchanged for American prisoners. The pension applicant recalled his brother was "absent one or two years."[34]

LOCATION OF PENSION APPLICATIONS

Just as most pension applicants were not born in North Carolina an even higher percentage chose to leave the state in the years after the war ended. Over sixty percent of the pension applicants who served North Carolina during the war filed their claims outside the state.[35] The three states of Tennessee, Georgia, and Kentucky account for nearly forty percent of locations where applications were filed and about

27. John Sims (W10252), Michael Nash (W4042), Joseph McPeters (W1303).
28. William Poplin (W10231), John Hancock (R4551 & W10086).
29. John Gaspenson (S1818).
30. Moses Hall (W10105).
31. Amos Church (S8191), John Church (W3943).
32. John Sawel (S4657), George Parks (W27457).
33. Allen Howard (S8730).
34. David Erwin (R3369).
35. 3,696 applications note where the pensions were filed. 2,252 Pensions were filed outside of North Carolina.

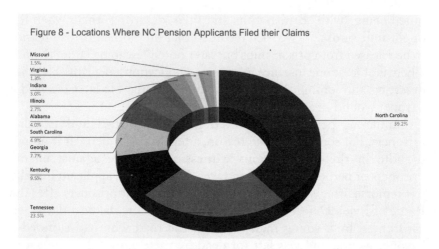

Figure 8 - Locations Where NC Pension Applicants Filed their Claims

two-thirds of the all locations filed outside of North Carolina. Only two percent of applications were filed west of the Mississippi River. Just five men filed applications in northeastern states (Figure 8). The highest out of state application rates were of those that entered service in the western and northern counties of North Carolina. Conversely, relatively high portions of those who remained in the state after the war were in the southeastern counties of the state.

CONCLUSION

The men studied here represent only thirteen to sixteen percent of the men who served in the North Carolina militia or state troops during the war. It seems unlikely that we may ever know as much about the remainder, over eighty percent, and their war exploits as we know about the men studied here. However, coming away from this study it is apparent that there is much more to be known about how these North Carolina men compare with the militia of other states. For instance, were most of the men that served in the Maryland militia born outside the state like those of North Carolina? Or how many tours of duty did the men of the Massachusetts militia serve in comparison to North Carolina? These and many more questions present themselves when considering the data here in comparison to other states. Fortunately, the pension application data to answer these questions have been transcribed and made available online (or will be soon). The pension applications are there; their personal and collective stories are waiting to be told.

The author would like to thank Will Graves and C. Leon Harris for their insights on Federal Pension applications which form the basis of this work.

Minorcans, New Smyrna, and the American Revolution in East Florida

GEORGE KOTLIK

Beyond Florida's state boundaries the history of New Smyrna is seldom mentioned.[1] Well known to the locals of New Smyrna Beach, the region's settlement by European colonists dates to 1768 when Scottish physician Andrew Turnbull led a colonization effort to Britain's far flung outpost in North America. After a trip to Asia Minor and the Mediterranean, Turnbull married Maria Gracia Dura Bin from Greece. While in the Mediterranean, Turnbull hatched the idea of colonizing Florida with Mediterranean folk, people from a climate similar to that of Florida and skilled in the raising of semitropical products.[2] Turnbull immediately recruited colonists after securing financial backing for his vision and acquiring 20,000 acres of land on the Florida frontier.[3] Most settlers who agreed to go with him were from the island of Minorca. In total, 1,403 people sailed under Turnbull's patronage in the spring of 1768.[4] After arriving at St. Augustine, Turnbull made the decision to settle Mosquito Inlet,[5] establishing New Smyrna in early August.[6]

---

1. For further reading on the New Smyrna colony see Carita Doggett Corse, *Dr. Andrew Turnbull and The New Smyrna Colony of Florida* (Florida: The Drew Press, 1919); Charles Loch Mowat, *East Florida as a British Province, 1763-1784* (Berkeley: University of California Press, 1943); Kenneth H. Beeson Jr., *Fromajadas and Indigo: The Minorcan Colony in Florida* (Charleston: The History Press, 2006); Epaminodas P. Panagopoulos, *New Smyrna: An Eighteenth Century Greek Odyssey* (Gainesville: University of Florida Press, 1966); Wilbur Henry Siebert, "Slavery and White Servitude in East Florida, 1726-1776," *The Florida Historical Quarterly* 10, no. 1 (July 1931): 3-23.

2. Mowat, *East Florida*, 71-72.

3. Corse, *Dr. Andrew Turnbull and The New Smyrna Colony of Florida*, 19.

4. Mowat, *East* Florida, 72.

5. Corse, *Dr. Andrew Turnbull and The New Smyrna Colony of Florida*, 24-28.

6. Mowat, *East Florida*, 72.

According to eighteenth century naturalist William Bartram, New Smyrna was established on a "high shelly bluff, on the West bank of the South branch of Musquito river." During the time of Bartram's visit, the area was a large orange grove containing "oaks, magnolias, palms, [and] red bays."[7] Upon the colonists arrival , they were under contractual obligation to work for Turnbull for a number of years until they were granted their freedom; in the meantime, they were allowed to retain half of the crops they raised.[8] Life at the plantation was not what the colonists had expected. New Smyrna had to literally be carved out of the wilderness. To give perspective on how deep into the frontier this settlement was, St. Augustine was seventy miles north of the colony. The need, then, to establish a working settlement was of the utmost importance. Until the cultivation of crops became a reality, the land would not support the settlers. The work of carving out civilization in the Florida tropics demanded hard work. Turnbull employed over-seers, former British army noncommissioned officers, to keep the set-tlers (his investment) working. Hard days were met with a scarcity of available food. Sure, there were plenty of fish in the lagoons, but the settlers were not permitted to divert time and energy away from con-structing a plantation, which was worked on seven days a week—the workers often receiving no days for rest. Those poor colonists who dared lag behind optimal productivity endured harsh punishments in-cluding floggings.[9]

As they found out soon after their arrival, settlers suffered brutal working conditions which contributed to a high death rate.[10] Other factors that caused numerous deaths were starvation, scurvy, dropsy, lack of sanitation, yellow fever, typhoid fever, and pneumonia.[11] After a long day's work in the hot summer heat with the sun beating down their necks, mosquitos visited the settlement at night, sometimes car-rying malaria. Settlers wore rags and slept on bedding found to be in poor condition. For the first couple of years, New Smyrna settlers were forced to live in huts with sand floors, but by 1777 the colony boasted 145 houses. Conditions at the colony were so bad that the settlers, who felt imprisoned, led an unsuccessful revolt before their first year was over. By 1777, 964 deaths were recorded at New Smyrna from the

7. William Bartram, *Travels Through North and South Carolina, Georgia, East and West Florida, the Cherokee Country, the Extensive Territories of the Muscogulges, or Creek Confed-eracy, and the Country of the Chactaws* (Philadelphia: James and Johnson, 1791), 142.
8. Siebert, "Slavery and White Servitude in East Florida, 1726-1776," 18.
9. Panagopoulos, *New Smyrna*, 58, 87.
10. Beeson Jr., *Fromajadas and Indigo*, 63.
11. Panagopoulos, *New Smyrna*, 85; Beeson Jr., *Fromajadas and Indigo*, 82-83.

roughly 1,400 who came with Turnbull in 1768.[12] To make matters worse, New Smyrna colonists reported that Turnbull refused to honor their contracts after they expired, forcing them to work despite the end of their indentures.[13] Notwithstanding their slave-like treatment, Minorcans were not an enslaved work force, nor were they servants. They were a temporary work force of free people—at least from a legal perspective.[14] Regardless of their status, life for Minorcans at New Smyrna was deprived, primitive, and characterized by constant struggle.

As unrest gripped the northern colonies, Parliament was determined to keep Florida under British control. In March 1774, Col. Patrick Tonyn was named governor of East Florida.[15] In 1775, East Florida became a designated loyalist haven for refugees fleeing violence from colonies enveloped in the anti-British movement.[16] The following year, on February 27, 1776, East Florida's inhabitants drafted an address to the king affirming their loyalty to him. They wrote that they were "deeply deploring and disavowing the present unhappy and unnatural Rebellion, which prevails through most of Your Majesty's other Colonies on this Continent." East Florida's inhabitants also promised to avoid any "connection and Correspondence with, or Support of [the rebels] . . . we shall be always ready, and willing to the utmost of our weak abilities to manifest our Loyalty to Your Majesty's Person, and a due Submission to Your Majesty's Government, and the Legislature of Great Britain."[17] Tonyn held no doubts about the loyalty of East Florida. His did have concerns, however, about the ability of East Florida to defend against attack.[18] As far as Tonyn was concerned, the colony was nearly indefensible.[19]

To counter the colony's weakness, Tonyn organized a militia battalion made up of loyalist refugees from the northern colonies.[20] "Attested

12. Panagopoulos, *New Smyrna*, 59, 83, 86, 91-92.
13. Patrick Tonyn to George Germain, May 8, 1777, in *The Turnbull Papers* (Jacksonville, 1940), 211.
14. Beeson Jr., *Fromajadas and Indigo*, 82.
15. Corse, *Dr. Andrew Turnbull and The New Smyrna Colony of Florida*, 106.
16. Wilbur Henry Siebert, *Loyalists in East Florida, 1774-1785*, Vol. 1, *The Narrative* (Reprint, Greenville: Southern Historical Press, 1972), 23-24.
17. "The humble Address of the Inhabitants of the Providence of East Florida," February 27, 1776, in *The Turnbull Papers*, 124.
18. Jim Piecuch, "Patrick Tonyn: Britain's Most Effective Revolutionary-Era Royal Governor," *Journal of the American Revolution*, March 22, 2018, allthingsliberty.com/2018/03/patrick-tonyn-britains-most-effective-revolutionary-era-royal-governor/#_edn11.
19. Ibid.
20. Patrick Tonyn to George Germain, August 21, 1776, from *The On-Line Institute for Advanced Loyalist Studies*, transcribed by Todd Braisted, www.royalprovincial.com/military/rhist/eastflmil/eflmillet1.htm.

to serve three Years or during the Rebellious Troubles," they would bolster East Florida's defenses.[21] Tonyn sought to raise four companies of
men from among the people of African descent in the colony, plus two
companies from the Saint John's River, four from St. Augustine, and
one from New Smyrna.[22] Tonyn considered raising a company of Minorcans as well, but he and Andrew Turnbull were suspicious of the
Minorcans' loyalties to the Crown. In a letter to Lord George Germain,
Secretary of State for America in Lord North's Cabinet, Tonyn stated,
"I am credibly informed, that they have invited the Rebels in Georgia,
to come to their relief, and deliverance, and have promised their assistance."[23] Andrew Turnbull Jr. even expressed his concern in a private
letter, saying "there is a good number of them [New Smyrna colonists]
at present a little discontented, and I am fully perswaded would Join
the Rebels immediately on their landing at Smyrna."[24] Turnbull Jr. was
so concerned he requested an additional eight to ten British regulars
to bolster the garrison already stationed at New Smyrna.[25] Tonyn complained to Germain about sending additional soldiers to the settlement;
after all, soldiers were much needed farther north to defend the
Florida-Georgia border.[26] Colonel Robert Bisset, a British officer stationed in East Florida, attested to the indefensibility of New Smyrna
which was largely due to the settlement's lack of arms and ammunition.
According to Bisset, the situation in New Smyrna was "very alarming
especially with regard to Dr. Turnbull's people, a great many of whom
would certainly Join them [the rebels]." Bisset assured Tonyn that he
would go to New Smyrna and arm trustworthy settlers and disarm suspected rebel sympathizers.[27]

Ambitious to tap into the manpower residing in New Smyrna,
Tonyn tempted the settlers to join his militia with offers of land, freedom, and protection if they abandoned their lot with Turnbull.[28] Of

21. Patrick Tonyn to Augustine Prevost, December 24, 1777, from *The On-Line Institute
for Advanced Loyalist Studies*, transcribed by Todd Braisted, www.royalprovincial.com/mil-
itary/facts/ofrlet8.htm#:~:text=Other%20Facts%2FRecords%20Tonyn%20to%20Pre-
vost%3A%20St.%20Augustine%2024th,always%20ready%20to%20give%20you%20Sir%2
0every%20Satisfaction.
22. Patrick Tonyn to George Germain, August 21, 1776.
23. Patrick Tonyn to George Germain, May 8, 1777, in *The Turnbull Papers*, 211.
24. Andrew Turnbull Jr. to Arthur Gordon, September 1, 1776, in *The Turnbull Papers*, 157.
25. Andrew Turnbull Jr. to Arthur Gordon, September 1, 1776, in *The Turnbull Papers*,
157; Corse, *Dr. Andrew Turnbull and The New Smyrna Colony of Florida*, 103.
26. Patrick Tonyn to George Germain, September 8, 1776, in *The Turnbull Papers*, 159.
27. Bisset to Patrick Tonyn, September 1, 1776, in *The Turnbull Papers*, 158.
28. Corse, *Dr. Andrew Turnbull and The New Smyrna Colony of Florida*, 157.

course, in letters to Germain, Tonyn played innocent against his true intentions of bolstering his militia ranks.[29] In March 1777, a few settlers escaped New Smyrna while Turnbull was away in England, and arrived at St. Augustine seeking an audience with Governor Tonyn to confess their grievances about life under Turnbull at the New Smyrna settlement. What followed was a months-long process of processing complaints issued by the settlers against Turnbull and his overseers. Some of the accusations detailed the horrid sufferings endured by the colonists which included "cruelties and murders." What followed was a rapid succession of events that ultimately contributed to the demise of New Smyrna. The East Florida courts ruled in favor of Dr. Turnbull and ordered the settlers to return to their indentures.[30] In July 1777, Tonyn told Germain that the New Smyrna settlers were liberated on account of "conditional" and "shocking" circumstances. He informed the Secretary of State that small lots of land would be given to families of the freed settlers.[31] In reality, Tonyn disregarded the court's decision to return the indentured New Smyrna workers back to their master's plantation, and instead encouraged the colonists to settle in St. Augustine where he assured them that he would protect them. As a result of Tonyn's murky treatment of the law, the entire New Smyrna settlement up and left for St. Augustine. During their time in the colony's capital, they were almost forgotten. Land was never doled out and many were forced to beg in the streets or find sustenance in fishing—they were wholly ignored by Tonyn.[32] Desperate for coin, many joined the East Florida Rangers.[33] Some were dispatched to the Florida-Georgia border where they helped Indians scalp American settlers.[34] Turnbull was furious, charging Tonyn as the reason for his plantation's collapse.[35] In the end, Tonyn got what he wanted out of Turnbull's colonists: men for his loyalist militia.

Even after the Minorcan exodus, not all the settlers had left; New Smyrna was still in operation and produce continued to be exported from the plantation.[36] To this day, the city of New Smyrna Beach in

29. Patrick Tonyn to George Germain, May 8, 1777, in *The Turnbull Papers*, 211-212.

30. Corse, *Dr. Andrew Turnbull and The New Smyrna Colony of Florida*, 157-159, 163.

31. Patrick Tonyn to George Germain, July 26, 1777, in *The Turnbull Papers*, 220.

32. Corse, *Dr. Andrew Turnbull and The New Smyrna Colony of Florida*, 164-165.

33. Andrew Turnbull to Earl of Shelburne, November 10, 1777, in *The Turnbull Papers*, 221.

34. Corse, *Dr. Andrew Turnbull and The New Smyrna Colony of Florida*, 170.

35. Andrew Turnbull to Earl of Shelburne, November 10, 1777, in *The Turnbull Papers*, 221. This aspect of East Florida/New Smyrna history, which I will not go into detail here due to a lack of space, covers a prominent episode in the colony's histories. The feud between Tonyn and Turnbull was a long, drawn-out battle that often became personal.

36. Beeson Jr., *Fromajadas and Indigo*, 83.

Florida stands on the former settlement founded by Turnbull. Turnbull later left Florida after it was ceded to the Spanish and went on to petition a compensation claim Parliament had offered to former British Florida colonists who had lost land in the Spanish secession. He won 916 pounds. After the evacuation of East Florida, Turnbull moved to Charleston, South Carolina where he was permitted to remain a British subject after the former colony officially became a state. He died on March 13, 1792 in Charleston.[37] As for the Minorcans, some fled with the loyalists and resettled in the Bahamas, Dominica, and Europe.[38] Most of them, however, stayed behind, choosing to convert to the Catholic religion and become Spanish subjects.[39]

Although their story is not well-known, the Minorcans lived out the drama that unfolded between East Florida's leaders during the American Revolution. Put in a precarious situation and far from their native home, some Minorcans served the British during the war, but not out of true loyalty. Most served the Crown out of desperation and to avoid a bitter death in a harsh, war-torn, scarcely populated frontier colony that rested on the far-flung fringes of the British Empire. The reluctance of many Minorcans to evacuate with the British speaks volumes about not only their lack of commitment to the British government, but also the loyalty they had for each other and their community. For many Minorcans, most of what they did, they did together. They endured the brutality of New Smyrna's overseers together, they petitioned Tonyn against their injustices suffered at Turnbull's plantation together, most abandoned New Smyrna together to live under Tonyn's protection, and many remained in Spanish Florida together after the British departure in the 1780s. The rest is history. Minorcan descendants still live in St. Augustine to this day where they continue to represent a large portion of the city's population.[40]

---

37. Corse, *Dr. Andrew Turnbull and The New Smyrna Colony of Florida*, 186, 192-194.
38. Patrick Tonyn to Thomas Townshend (Lord Sydney), April 4, 1785, in *The Turnbull Papers*, 359.
39. Patrick Tonyn to Thomas Townshend (Lord Sydney), April 4, 1785, in *The Turnbull Papers*, 359-360. In June 1784, when Spanish governor de Zespedes arrived in Florida, he promoted the Minorcan priest, Pietro Campo who influenced many Minorcans to remain behind (Corse, 191).
40. Beeson Jr., *Fromajadas and Indigo*, 83.

The American Revolution Sees the First Efforts to Limit the African Slave Trade

❀ CHRISTIAN M. MCBURNEY ❀

The American Revolution changed the way Americans viewed one of the world's great tragedies: the African slave trade. The long march to end the slave trade and then slavery itself had to start somewhere, and it arguably started with the American Revolution.

Typically, with great movements, there is no direct line of progress. More often, progress is like a wave, moving forward, but then receding somewhat. That describes the progress on the antislavery front in the United States—during the years of the Revolution, there was definite progress, progress that receded somewhat in the years after the end of the Revolutionary War. Still, when the dust had settled in the early 1800s, clear progress had been achieved: each Northern state had either prohibited slavery or provided for gradual emancipation, and American participation in the African slave trade was formally banned in all states by 1808. Tragically, the American Revolution did not end slavery in the South. It would take a Civil War and hundreds of thousands of deaths to end the institution in 1865.

In the first three quarters of the eighteenth century, prior to the American Revolution, Great Britain was the leading slave trading country in the world. By the 1770s, each year, on average, British merchants from Liverpool, Bristol, London and smaller ports sent ships to the coast of West Africa, purchased more than 45,000 captives, and transported them across the Atlantic Ocean, mostly to the West Indies, British island possessions in the Caribbean such as Jamaica and Barbados. There, the African captives worked in horrible conditions on sugar cane plantations, suffering a high death rate; white planters de-manded more replacements from Africa, creating an annual cycle of tragedy.[1]

In the course of four centuries British merchants carried an astound-ing number of Africans across the Atlantic, approximately 3,250,000. Taking into account the years 1501 to 1867, merchants sailing from Great Britain outfitted an estimated thirty-one percent of all slave voy-ages even though their participation in the trade stopped in 1807.[2] Still, that placed them second to the Portuguese, who carried more than 5,800,000 African captives in the Middle Passage, mostly to Brazil. They had a head start, beginning a few hundred years earlier than the British, in the 1400s, and ending decades after Britain's 1807 prohibi-tion of the slave trade.

The merchants of what would become the United States played a comparatively small role in the African slave trade. From 1501 to 1867, North American colonial mainland and, later, United States merchants carried about 305,000 captives across the Atlantic and outfitted about two and a half percent of the slaving voyages.[3] In the twenty-five-year period from 1751 to 1775, however, North American ships accounted for between four and five percent of the slaving voyages. The colony of Rhode Island sent more than one-half of the slave trade voyages from North America, with New York and Boston also sending ships on long voyages to the West Africa coast.[4]

Comparatively few of the captive Africans carried across the At-lantic Ocean were landed on North American mainland shores. Of the approximately 12,500,000 slaves forced across the Atlantic, fewer than 400,000 were disembarked in what would become the United States,

---

1. David Eltis and David Richardson, *Atlas of the Transatlantic Slave Trade* (New Haven, CT: Yale University Press, 2010), 13. The leading online source of information on African slave trading voyages concludes that British ships carried twenty-six percent of all African captives. Voyages, The Trans-Atlantic Slave Trade Database, www.slavevoyages.org/assess-ment/estimates (using search terms "Flag" and "Only Embarked").

2. Eltis and Richardson, *Atlas*, 25-27.

3. Ibid., 23, 26-27. The leading online source of information on African slave trading voy-ages concludes that North American ships carried 2.4 percent of all African captives. Voy-ages, The Trans-Atlantic Slave Trade Database, at www.slavevoyages.org/assessment/estimates (using search terms "Flag" and "Only Embarked"); see also Stephen D. Behrendt, "The Transatlantic Slave Trade," in Robert L. Paquette and Mark M. Smith, eds., *Slavery in the Americas* (Oxford, UK: Oxford University Press, 2010), Table 11.1, 263 (same, 2.4 percent).

4. For more on Rhode Island's dominance in the North American slave trade (particularly Newport), see Jay Coughtry, *The Notorious Triangle: Rhode Island and the African Slave Trade, 1700-1807* (Philadelphia, PA: Temple University Press, 1981).

just over three percent of the total. The Caribbean, where sugar cane plantations created an insatiable demand, and South America (mostly Brazil) accounted for ninety-five percent of the captives brought from Africa.[5]

The half-decade leading up to April 1775, when armed hostilities broke out at Lexington and Concord, was a particularly idealistic time in what would become the United States. Whig supporters spouted the rhetoric of freedom from Great Britain and personal liberty for themselves. This strong passion for freedom and liberty spilled over to result in the first organized national movement to end the slave trade in American history and possibly the first in world history. But before that happened, disparate protests in various colonies had to arise. The conviction that the slave trade and slavery itself were completely wrong took time for most white Americans to realize. African slavery had existed in the Western world since the mid-fifteenth century, and national movements to achieve humanitarian ends were not yet known in the Western countries. Slowly, some voices became louder and more strident in opposing the slave trade and even the institution of slavery itself. This process was unquestionably accelerated by the American Revolution.

As historian David B. Davis has written, "By the eve of the American Revolution there was a remarkable convergence of cultural and intellectual developments which at once undercut traditional rationalizations for slavery and offered new modes of sensibility for identifying with its victims."[6] The process was advanced by increasing capitalism: as free labor became more common, other labor relations—indentured servitude, debt bondage, and slavery—came increasingly to appear antiquated and anomalous. White laborers in particular did not want to compete in the workplace against enslaved persons. Enlightenment ideas about human equality and shared human nature also played an important part in this process, as did the rapid growth of evangelical Christianity.

The American Revolution itself was a key catalyst to antislavery thought. With American colonists declaring their beliefs in "liberty"

5. Eltis and Richardson, *Atlas*, 17-19. The Trans-Atlantic Slave Trade Database concludes that 3.6 percent of all African captives disembarked in the New World were carried to North America. Voyages, The Trans-Atlantic Slave Trade Database, www.slavevoyages.org/assessment/estimates (using search terms "Broad disembarkation regions" and "Only Disembarked"); see also Behrendt, "The Transatlantic Slave Trade," Table 11.1, 263 (3.7 percent).
6. David Brion Davis, *The Problem of Slavery in the Age of Revolution, 1770-1823* (Ithaca, NY: Cornell University Press, 1975), 48.

and "natural rights" and denouncing a British plot to "enslave" them by taxing them without representation, it is not surprising that some were moved to question the plight of those whom the colonists themselves had actually enslaved. After all, at this time around twenty percent of the population of the thirteen colonies consisted of blacks, most of them enslaved persons treated as mere pieces of property. Historian W. E. B. DuBois put it more bluntly: "the new philosophy of 'freedom' and the 'rights of man,' which formed the cornerstone of the Revolution, made even the dullest realize that, at the very least, the slave-trade and a struggle for 'liberty' were not consistent."[7]

In North America, political opposition to slavery began within the Society of Friends, or Quakers. Founded in England in the seventeenth century, Quakerism was a radically egalitarian creed that led many in the Society to question the morality of slave trading and slavery. By the start of the Revolutionary War, most Quaker meetings in the thirteen colonies had prohibited their members from holding enslaved persons.[8]

By 1774 Quakers began trying to persuade others of its immorality, but they hardly represented general public opinion in the colonies. For the dual slave institutions to be attacked successfully, mainstream religious sects and other groups would have to raise their voices in protest. As historian Joanne Pope Melish notes, "it was only in the context of the Revolution that the antislavery movement gained support outside a fringe group of Quakers and other agitators."[9]

The first Congregationalist ministers from New England to come out against slavery did so in the early 1770s. Samuel Hopkins of the First Congregational Church of Newport, Rhode Island, a Connecticut native who had moved to the port town in 1770, began to preach against the slave trade in the very town most implicated in it. He published a pamphlet railing against the slave trade in 1776. Calling the trade "a scene of inhumanity, oppression, and cruelty, exceeding everything of the kind that has ever been perpetrated by the sons of men, " Hopkins painted with words vivid scenes of war, death and destruction along the coast of Africa, on the purchases at the seaports, the brandings, the terrors of the Middle Passage, the uncounted deaths from the

7. W. E. B. DuBois, *The Suppression of the African Slave Trade to the United States of America, 1638-1870* (New York, NY: Longmans, Green, and Co., 1896), 41.

8. Dwight L. Dumond, *Antislavery: The Crusade for Freedom in America* (Ann Arbor, MI: University of Michigan Press, 1961), 19; see also Arthur Zilversmith, *The First Emancipation, The Abolition of Slavery in the North* (Chicago, IL: University of Chicago Press, 1967), 79-81 and 89-93.

9. Joanne Pope Melish, *Disowning Slavery, Gradual Emancipation and "Race" in New England, 1780-1860* (Ithaca, NY: Cornell University Press, 1998), 50.

process of acclimatization, and the brutal whippings.[10] Most of the slave traders in Newport, however, belonged to the Second Congregational Church, the Anglican Church or other religious groups. Still, Hopkins and one other religiously-inspired antislavery leader, the Quaker Moses Brown, became active in trying to persuade the Rhode Island General Assembly to limit the slave trade.

In Connecticut, a few Congregationalist ministers began to publish provocative antislavery pieces. Jonathan Edwards, Jr., the son of the famous minister by the same name and pastor of the New Haven Congregational Church, published several anonymous antislavery pieces in New Haven newspapers in the fall of 1773 and early 1774. In 1774 the Rev. Levi Hart, a trustee of both Yale and Dartmouth Colleges, delivered an important sermon in Connecticut (published the next year) that attacked the slave trade and slavery as a moral evil. "What have the unhappy Africans committed against the inhabitants of the British colonies and islands in the West Indies," Hart asked, "to authorize *us* to seize them, or bribe them to seize one another, and transport them a thousand leagues into a strange land, and enslave them for life?"[11] Hart lamented, "I could never believe that British Americans would be guilty of such a crime, I mean that of the horrible slave trade, carried on by numbers and tolerated by the authority in this country."[12]

In Massachusetts, more Congregationalists spoke out. In 1770, the Reverend Samuel Cooke, a minister in the western village of Menotomy (now Arlington), preached to recently elected members of the General Court. He raised the controversial issue of the legislature assisting enslaved persons in the colony, imploring his listeners "at least, to prevent the future importation of them."[13] Deacon Benjamin Colman of Newbury, Massachusetts, in two pieces published in a Newburyport newspaper, in 1774 called slavery "a God-provoking and wrath-procuring sin," and the next year called the slave trade a "crime . . . more particularly pointed . . . than any other."[14] In 1775, preacher Nathaniel Niles of Newburyport, exclaimed in a sermon, "God gave us

10. Samuel Hopkins, *A Dialogue Concerning the Slavery of the Africans . . .* (Norwich, CT: Judah P. Spooner, 1776), 6 and 17.
11. Quoted in Joseph Conforti, *Samuel Hopkins & the New Divinity Movement* (Grand Rapids, MI: Christian University Press, 1981), 127.
12. Quoted in Stewart M. Robinson, *Political Thought of the Colonial Clergy, Words of the Declaration of Independence Foreseen in the Writings of Clergymen Prior to July 1776* (Privately Printed, 1956), 33.
13. Quoted in J. L. Bell, "I Wish For a Happy Harmony in the Legislature," May 31, 2020, online article at www.boston1775/blogspot.com (search for "Samuel Cooke").
14. Quoted in Joshua Coffin, *A Sketch of the History of Newbury, Newburyport, and West Newbury* (Boston, MA: Samuel G. Drake, 1845), 339-40 (citing *Essex Journal*).

liberty, and we have enslaved our fellow-men. May we not fear that the law of retaliation is about to be executed on us?"[15]

The Rev. Samuel Hopkins expressed disappointment that more of his fellow Congregational clergymen in New England did not speak out opposing the slave trade. He once wrote, "The Friends [Quakers] have set a laudable example in bearing testimony against the slave trade . . . and I must say have acted more like Christians in this important article than any other denomination of Christians among us. To our *shame* be it spoken!"[16] One of the problems for the Congregationalists was that unlike the Quakers with their monthly, quarterly and annual meetings, there was no umbrella organization over the Congregationalist churches that could help to formulate a unified position. Still, the opinions expressed by Hopkins, Edwards and a few others was a start, and they would influence New England town meetings in the 1770s prior to the outbreak of the Revolutionary War.

Baptists were increasing in numbers in New England by the 1770s. One of the most widely-read pamphlets and sermons in the thirteen colonies prior to the outbreak of war in 1775 was an "Oration" titled in part the *Beauties of Liberty*, published in 1772 and thought to have been written by the Rev. John Allen, a Baptist minister in Boston who would die prematurely in 1774 at the age of thirty-three. In his sermon Allen defended American rights, including the burning of the British revenue cutter *Gaspee* in Narragansett Bay in Rhode Island earlier in 1772. But in the published edition he added as an addendum a scorching criticism of the slave trade and slavery. Allen railed, "for mankind to be distressed and kept in slavery by Christians, by those who love the gospel of Christ; for such to buy their brethren (for of one blood he has made all nations) and bind them to be slaves to them and their heirs for life. Be astonished, ye Christians, at this!" Moving on to the horrors of the slave trade, Allen wrote powerfully, "for Christians to encourage this bloody and inhuman trade of man-stealing, or slave-making, oh how shocking it is!"[17]

The 1760s and 1770s were times of great political fervor in the thirteen colonies. By 1774, the political lives of many Americans had been radicalized by the Whig cause. Writing years after the Revolutionary War ended, John Adams penned to Thomas Jefferson:

15. Quoted in Robinson, *Political Thought of the Colonial Clergy*, 33.
16. S. Hopkins to M. Brown, April 29. 1784, in Edwards A. Park, *Memoir of the Life and Character of Samuel Hopkins, D.D.*, 2nd ed. (Boston, MA: Doctrinal Tract and Book Society, 1854), 120.
17. Quoted in Stewart M. Robinson, *Political Thought of the Colonial Clergy, Words of the Declaration of Independence Foreseen in the Writings of Clergymen Prior to July 1776* (Privately Printed, 1956), 36.

What do we mean by the Revolution? The War? That was no part of the Revolution. It was only an effect and consequence of it. The Revolution was in the minds of the people, and this was effected from 1760 to 1775, in the course of fifteen years before a drop of blood was drawn at Lexington.[18]

The increasing politicization and radicalism of Whigs showed itself in other arenas too, including with antislavery efforts. Whigs (also known as Patriots) who favored liberty for all and who opposed slavery realized that before that institution could be ended, importations of enslaved persons first had to cease. They realized it would be too radical for many of their fellow citizens—and for their British rulers—to press for an immediate end to slavery, when the institution had existed for more than a century in their colonies. But they realized the terrible institution could be weakened by halting the importation of enslaved persons into their colonies. The main source of importations was, of course, the African slave trade.

On its face, prohibiting slave imports was not a big step in the North. One report (likely not complete) indicates that from 1769 to 1772, there were no imports of captive Africans by any northern colony, with the exception of New York, which imported sixty-seven in 1770 and nineteen in 1772.[19] Still, as will be seen below in the language used by many Patriots, limiting slave imports was seen as a principled first step in eventually prohibiting slavery itself in the colony. Antislavery advocates even in the North were not yet willing to promote seriously the end of slavery, when so many of their neighbors still owned slaves.[20]

As will be seen, when various colonies attempted to limit the African slave trade within their colonies, they met resistance from royal authorities in London. The thirteen colonies were still colonies ruled by Great Britain. The African slave trade was a financial boon to British manufacturing, shipping, shipbuilding, insurance, banking and other businesses. The "Guinea trade" was so substantial a part of the British economy that a powerful lobby arose in London to protect it. To have control over the African slave trade in the colonies, as in so many other areas, Americans would have to become independent from Britain.

18. J. Adams to T. Jefferson, August 24, 1815, in J. Jefferson Looney, ed., *Jefferson Papers, Retirement Series*, vol. 8 (Princeton, NJ: Princeton University Press, 2011), 682-83.
19. Slave Trade by Origin and Destination, 1768 to 1772, in *Historical Statistics of the United States, Colonial Times to 1970*, Part 2 (Washington, DC: U.S. Department of Commerce, 1975), 1172.
20. See Melish, *Disowning Slavery*, 52-53 and n8.

The effort to limit the importation of enslaved persons started, not surprisingly, in Massachusetts. Massachusetts had been the colony where the slave trade had first taken root in North America in the seventeenth century, but by the 1760s only a few of its merchants were active in the trade. There was an uptick, however, in slave trading by Boston merchants in the 1770s. From 1771 to 1774, Boston and other Massachusetts merchants on the average sent at least six vessels to the African coast.[21] Moreover, while Massachusetts was not a slave society, about one and a half percent of its population still consisted of enslaved persons.

At the time, efforts were not made to prohibit the participation of Massachusetts residents in the slave trade. This was probably because the colonists believed they did not have the authority to take such a step and that only London officials could prohibit the trade. In this, the colonists were correct.

James Otis of Massachusetts, in his influential 1763 pamphlet, *The Rights of the British Colonies*, on the rights of colonists not to be taxed without their consent, asserted that there were laws higher than acts of Parliament. Otis identified natural rights held by all men as divinely inspired. While not necessary to do so to make his main point, he delved into race relations. He exclaimed: "The colonists are by the law of nature free born, as indeed are all men, white or black . . . Does it follow that 'tis right to enslave a man because he is black?" Speaking of the African slave trade, he said, "Nothing better can be said in favor of a trade that is the most shocking violation of the law of nature, has a direct tendency to diminish the idea of the inestimable value of liberty, and makes every dealer in it a tyrant, from the director of an African company to the petty chapman in needles and pins on the unhappy coast. It is clear truth that those who every day barter away other men's liberty will soon care little for their own."[22]

Otis's sentiments were impressive for the time. Perhaps using his influence as a member of the Massachusetts House of Representatives, in early 1764 that legislative body for the first time considered a bill to prohibit the importation of enslaved persons into the colony, but the time was not yet ripe for it to be taken seriously.[23]

21. Custom House Items, 1771-1774, in Elizabeth Donnan, ed., *Documents Illustrative of the History of the Slave Trade to America*, vol. 3 (Washington, DC: Carnegie Institution, 1932), 76.
22. James Otis, "The Rights of the British Colonies Asserted and Proved," in Gordon Wood, ed., *The American Revolution. Writings from the Pamphlet Debate. 1764-1776*, 2 vols. (New York, NY: Library of America, 2015), 1: 69-70.
23. Minutes, January 6 and February 2, 1764, in *Journals of the House of Representatives of Massachusetts*, vols. 37-47 (1760-1771), (Reprint, Boston, 1965-78), 40: 170 and 263.

Samuel Dexter, a local Boston politician, recalled after the Revolutionary War, "about the time of the Stamp Act, what before were only slight scruples in the minds of conscientious persons became serious doubts, and, with a considerable number, ripened into a firm persuasion that the slave trade was *malum in se*" [Latin, "wrong in itself"].[24] Items began appearing in Massachusetts newspapers and pamphlets opposing the slave trade in 1766.[25] In that year, the town meeting of Worcester instructed its representative to the Massachusetts legislature to use his influence "to obtain a law to put an end to the unchristian and impolitic practice of making slaves of the human species in this province."[26] James Swan in 1772 wrote an influential pamphlet, arguing that slavery was contrary to scripture and that the slave trade depopulated Africa, kept it in a constant state of conflict in the effort to acquire captives to sell, and hindered the development of a profitable trade in precious metals, ivory and spices. It was reprinted "at the earnest desire of the Negroes in Boston," in order that a copy might be sent to each Massachusetts town with a view to instructing their legislators.[27] At Harvard College's commencement in 1773, two Newbury graduates debated the morality of "enslaving Africans."[28]

The first serious efforts to end slave importations began ten years before the Declaration of Independence. On May 6, 1766, the Boston town meeting re-elected James Otis, Samuel Adams, and Thomas Cushing, and voted in John Hancock for the first time, to the Massachusetts House of Representatives. That month the Boston town meeting instructed them to push for "a law, to prohibit the importation and purchasing of slaves" in Massachusetts. The town meeting was hopeful it would lead to the "the total abolishing of slavery from among us."[29] In June the House of Representatives appointed a committee that in-

24. S. Dexter to Dr. Belknap, February 23, 1795, in "Queries Relating to Slavery in Massachusetts," *Collections of the Massachusetts Historical Society,* Series 5, vol. 3 (1887), 385.
25. See Donnan, *Documents of the Slave Trade* 3: 73n2.
26. Worcester Town Meeting instructions, May 19, 1766, in William Lincoln, *History of Worcester, Massachusetts . . .* (Worcester, MA: Charles Hersey, 1862), 68.
27. James Swan, *A Dissuasion to Great Britain and the Colonies, from the Slave-Trade to Africa. Showing the Injustice Thereof* (Boston, 1773) (originally published in 1772), ix-x, 18, 43; see also Zilversmith, *First Emancipation,* 99-100.
28. See Coffin, *History of Newburyport,* 339; Donnan, *Documents of the Slave Trade* 3: 73n2.
29. Boston Town Meeting vote for representatives, May 6, 1766, in, *A Report of the Record Commissioners of the City of Boston Containing the Boston Town Records, 1758-1769* (Boston, MA, 1886) 16: 183; Town Meeting instructions to representatives, May 27, 1766, in ibid., 183.

cluded Otis, Adams and Hancock, to "prepare and bring in a bill at the next session to prohibit the importation of slaves for the future."[30]

The next year, in March, the Boston town meeting again expressed its support of such a bill.[31] The Whig firebrand from Boston and one of the leaders of the resistance to British authority, Samuel Adams, then introduced a bill in the House of Representatives that went even further than prohibiting the importation of slaves. It was entitled, "A Bill to prevent the unwarrantable and unusual practice or custom of enslaving Mankind in this Province, and the importation of slaves into the same."[32] The House, not ready for any drastic steps, as an alternative, appointed a committee to provide for taxing the importation of slaves as a measure to discourage slave importations into the colony.[33] But the bill died in the more conservative upper chamber, the Council. According to Dexter, who strongly supported the bill, "Had it passed both houses," the royal governor, Francis Bernard, "would not have signed it. The duty was laid high."[34]

In 1771 antislavery proponents tried again. A representative from the town of Hadley, on April 9, 1771, introduced a bill to "prevent the importation of slaves from Africa."[35] This time the legislation passed both the House of Representatives and the Council, but the royal governor, Thomas Hutchinson, vetoed it.[36] In early 1773, another effort was made to pass a nonimportation of slaves bill; it passed the Council, but the House carried it over to 1774.[37]

The Massachusetts government also began seeing new petitions from the enslaved persons themselves. A self-styled "humble petition of many slaves" submitted in January 1773 was the first public protest

30. Minutes, June 10, 1766, in *Journals of the House of Representatives of Massachusetts*, 40: 110.

31. Boston Town Meeting resolution, March 16, 1767, in, *Boston Town Records*, 16: 200.

32. Minutes, March 13, 1767, in *Journals of the House of Representatives of Massachusetts* 43: 387; see also Douglas R. Egerton, *Death or Liberty, African Americans and Revolutionary America* (Oxford, UK: Oxford University Press, 2009), 56.

33. Minutes, March 14 and 16, 1767, in *Journals of the House of Representatives of Massachusetts* 43: 390, 393.

34. S. Dexter to Dr. Belknap, February 23, 1795, in "Queries Relating to Slavery in Massachusetts," *Collections of the Massachusetts Historical Society*, Series 5, vol. 3 (1887), 384; see also George H. Moore, *Notes on the History of Slavery in Massachusetts* (New York, NY: D. Appleton, 1866), 126-28.

35. Minutes, April 19, 1771, in *Journals of the House of Representatives of Massachusetts* 47: 197.

36. Moore, *Notes on the History of Slavery in Massachusetts*, 130-32.

37. Minutes, January 28, February 2 and March 5, 1773, in *Journals of the House of Representatives of Massachusetts* 49: 195, 204-05, 287.

against slavery made by blacks to a New England legislature.[38] Later in June 1773, four Boston enslaved persons submitted a petition to Governor Hutchinson and the Massachusetts legislature proposing the end of slavery in the colony and making direct analogies to white Patriots seeking to avoid "slavery" imposed on them by far-away powers in Britain.[39] The black men submitting this petition approached Samuel Adams for his assistance, which speaks well of Adams's reputation in the black community.[40] More enslaved persons submitted another petition in 1774, which, like the others, went unaddressed.[41] Massachusetts lawmakers were prepared to address the importation of slaves, but not yet their freedom. Still, the issue had been raised and made public.

In May 1773, when town meetings were typically held, Massachusetts Patriots throughout the colony, engulfed in the rhetoric of liberty and natural rights of all men, again turned their attention to slavery. The Salem town meeting instructed its representatives to the House of Representatives to endeavor to prevent slave importations as "repugnant to the natural rights of mankind, and highly prejudicial to this Province."[42] The town meeting of Leicester instructed its representative as follows:

> And, as we have the highest regard for (so as to even revere the name of) liberty, we cannot behold but with the greatest abhorrence any of our fellow-creatures in a state of slavery. Therefore, we strictly enjoin you to use your utmost influence that a stop may be put to the slave trade by the inhabitants of this Province, which, we apprehend, may be effected by one of two ways: either by laying a heavy duty on every negro imported or brought from Africa or elsewhere into this Province, or by making a law that every negro brought or imported as aforesaid should be a free man or woman as soon as they come within the jurisdiction of it . . . Thus, by enacting such a law, in process of time will blacks become free.[43]

38. Minutes, Jan. 28, 1773, in ibid. 49: 195.
39. Melish, *Disowning Slavery,* 80-81.
40. See S. Adams to J. Pickering, January 8, 1774, in Harry Alonzo, ed., *The Writings of Samuel Adams,* vol. 2 (New York, NY: Putnam, 1907), 78; Ira Stoll, *Samuel Adams. A Life* (New York: Free Press, 2008), 116-17.
41. See Benjamin Quarles, *The Negro in the American Revolution* (New York, NY: W. W. Norton & Co., 1961), 39-40.
42. Salem Town Meeting Resolution, May 18, 1773, in James B. Felt, *Annals of Salem,* 2nd ed., vol. 2 (Salem, MA: W. & S. B. Ives, 1849), 416-7.
43. Leicester Town Meeting Instruction, May 19, 1773, quoted in Emory Washburn, *Historical Sketches of the Town of Leicester, Massachusetts* (Boston, MA: John Wilson and Son, 1860), 442-43.

The town meetings of Sandwich and Medford, and probably more, issued similar instructions to their respective representatives. Medford went even further, directing its representative also to "use his utmost influence to have a final period put to that most cruel, inhuman and unchristian practice, the slave trade."[44]

Finally, in early March 1774, the Massachusetts legislature passed a bill to prohibit slave imports. Governor Hutchinson lumped this bill with others as inconsistent with the "authority of the King and Parliament" and refused to sign it. The Massachusetts legislature enacted the same prohibition again, but the new governor, Gen. Thomas Gage, refused to sign the measure on the ground that he had no authority to do so absent instructions from London, a position that was correct.[45]

Rhode Island and Connecticut lacked a royal governor. Thus, they were relatively unfettered by oversight in London.

Rhode Island's dominant politician in the years leading up to the American Revolution, and the leader of its most popular faction, was Stephen Hopkins, who served as governor numerous times and would sign the Declaration of Independence. One of the oldest of the Founders, he was a long-time friend of Benjamin Franklin. With his Quaker upbringing, he typically donned a plain grey suit and simple broad-rimmed felt hat. Even though he received no formal schooling, he became widely read, and in 1765 he showed off his learning in a respected pamphlet opposing the Sugar Act and trade regulations. Hopkins was a slaveowner who freed his enslaved persons in 1772 and 1773, except for insisting on keeping an enslaved woman to care for his ailing mother and children. For this he was expelled from the Society of Friends in 1773. Hopkins's views on slavery did evolve. By the eve of the American Revolution, he, the Quaker Moses Brown, and the Rev. Samuel Hopkins (no relation) became a powerful triumvirate in Rhode Island opposing both slavery and the slave trade.

On May 17, 1774, the town meeting of Providence, Rhode Island, instructed its representatives to the General Assembly to obtain an act

44. Sandwich Town Meeting Resolution, May 18, 1773, in Frederick Freeman, *The History of Cape Cod. The Annals of The Thirteen Towns of Barnstable County*, vol. 2 (Boston, MA: Privately Printed, 1862), 114-15; Medford Town Meeting Resolution, 1773, quoted in Moore, *Notes on the History of Slavery in Massachusetts*, 133.

45. Minutes, March 2-7, 1774, and June 16, 1774, in *Journals of the House of Representatives of Massachusetts* 50:221, 224, 226, 228, and 237; Message from Governor T. Hutchinson to the Council and House, March 8, 1774, in ibid., 243; Minutes, June 16, 1774, in ibid., 287; S. Dexter to Dr. Belknap, Feb. 26, 1795 and March 19, 1795,, in "Queries Relating to Slavery in Massachusetts," *Collections of the Massachusetts Historical Society*, Series 5, vol. 3 (1887), 388 and 395 and note; see also Moore, *Notes on the History of Slavery in Massachusetts*, 142-43; Egerton, *Death or Liberty*, 56; DuBois, *Suppression of the Slave Trade*, 32.

banning the importation of slaves, and to free all slaves born in the colony after they reached maturity.[46] With Stephen Hopkins and Moses Brown working behind the scenes, the Rhode Island legislature complied with the first request, banishing the importation of enslaved persons in June of that same year.[47]

It is noteworthy to consider the high-sounding preamble to the law Rhode Island passed in 1774 prohibiting the importation of enslaved persons, given Rhode Island's prominence as the leading slave trading colony. Probably penned by Stephen Hopkins, the recital justified the ban on the ground that "the inhabitants of America are generally engaged in the preservation of their own rights and liberties, among which, that of personal freedom must be considered as the greatest; as those who are desirous of enjoying all the advantages of liberty themselves should be willing to extend personal liberty to others."[48] Note that the recital addressed the evils and inconsistencies of slavery as a whole, and not just the slave trade. The radical Patriots, including those opposing slavery, were in ascendancy in the colony that sent out the most ships to Africa each year (about twenty-two annually). Newport slave merchants were not influential leaders in the Patriot cause.

Still, with a higher percentage of enslaved people than any other New England colony, and the one most implicated in the slave trade, Rhode Island legislators were not yet willing to press for an end to slavery in the colony or its participation in the slave trade. In a concession to slave traders, in the nonimportation bill, the legislators allowed them to bring enslaved persons into the colony for no longer than a year if those persons were on board their ships, had been obtained in Africa and had not been sold in the Caribbean, but only after posting a bond of £100 for each such captive.[49]

To the chagrin of the Rev. Samuel Hopkins and Moses Brown, the Rhode Island ban applied only to the importation of slaves and not to participation in the slave trade overall. It did not address Newport merchants sending voyages to the west coast of Africa and bringing captives to the Caribbean for sale there. Still, the ban on importations of enslaved persons by the colony most deeply involved in it represented

---

46. Quoted in William R. Staples, *Annals of Providence* (Providence, RI: Privately Printed, 1843), 235-36.
47. Resolution, June 1774 session, in John R. Bartlett, ed., *Records of the Colony of Rhode Island and Providence Plantations*, vol. 7 (Providence, RI: A. C. Greene, 1862), 251-52; Mack Thompson, *Moses Brown, Reluctant Reformer* (Chapel Hill, NC: University of North Carolina Press,1962), 97.
48. Resolution, June 1774 session, in Bartlett, *Records of Rhode Island* 7:251.
49. Ibid., 252.

progress for the growing antislavery movement. Even the great slave trade historian Elizabeth Donnan, whose work covered the African slave trade from the fifteenth century in vivid detail, called Rhode Island's slave importation ban "a substantial gain. Dr. Hopkins need not have felt so much discouragement."[50]

In Connecticut, the Rev. Levi Hart urged its residents to follow Rhode Island's example on grounds of morality, religion and public spirit. A few weeks later, Connecticut's Assembly also ended slave importations.[51]

* * *

American Patriots in the middle and southern colonies also began raising their voices against the African slave trade. Those who opposed the African slave trade in colonies ruled by royal governors appointed in London focused on what they could realistically accomplish—reducing or limiting imports of African captives by placing high duties on them.

In 1773, the New York Assembly approved a punishing £20 per imported slave duty, but the royal governor and upper council refused to concur.[52] In 1774, a group of New York City rum distillers unanimously voted not to refine molasses intended for the Atlantic slave trade.[53] A strong contingent of Loyalists in the colony apparently prevented Whigs from doing more.

There were no known slave importations into Pennsylvania from Africa, the Caribbean or any other source by sea after 1767 and through the end of the Revolutionary War.[54] Still, in 1773, Pennsylvania doubled its already existing tariff on imported Africans in a move designed to tax importations out of existence, but in 1774 the law was disallowed by the Lords of Trade in London. In reviewing the bill, a British trade official in London advised the Board of Trade members that the proposed increase in duties was "manifestly inconsistent with the policy adopted by your Lordships . . . of encouraging the African trade" especially at a time when "so many of His Majesty's lands in the West Indies remain understocked with negroes."[55]

50. Donnan, *Documents of the Slave Trade* 3:335, n.1.

51. Resolution, Oct. 1774 session, in Charles J. Hoadley, ed., *The Public Records of the Colony of Connecticut*, vol. 14 (Hartford, CT: Case, Lockwood & Brainard, 1887), 329.

52. Zilversmith, *The First Emancipation*, 91.

53. Egerton, *Death or Liberty, African Americans and Revolutionary America*, 62.

54. Gregory E. O'Malley, *Final Passages: The Intercolonial Slave Trade of British North America, 1619-1807* (Chapel Hill, NC: University of North Carolina Press, 2014), 214.

55. Quoted in William R. Riddell, "Pre-Revolutionary Pennsylvania and the Slave Trade," *Pennsylvania Magazine of History and Biography* (1928), 52: 18.

The New Jersey Assembly in 1762 attempted to levy a duty on imports of Africans, on the ground that because its neighbors in New York and Pennsylvania imposed such duties, too many captive Africans were being brought into New Jersey and transshipped to New York and Pennsylvania, or were remaining in the colony. The Board of Trade, however, instructed the royal governor of New Jersey to veto the bill.[56] In 1773, the New Jersey lower house proposed a punishing duty on slave imports, but the upper council, influenced by Loyalists, refused to concur.[57] On March 25, 1775, the Delaware Assembly passed a bill to prohibit the importation of slaves into the colony, but its royal governor refused to sign it.[58]

In the slave-holding Chesapeake Bay region, in Maryland and Virginia, even planters joined in the campaign against importing African captives. In 1771, Maryland imposed a duty of £9 for each enslaved African brought into Maryland. This was an attempt to ban importations indirectly, perhaps in order to avoid a veto from the colony's royal governor.[59]

Admittedly, the effort in Maryland and Virginia was mostly driven by the desire of planters to improve their economic circumstances and not as a first step to end slavery. Due to poor farming practices, depleted tobacco plantations were becoming less productive. In addition, some planters were shifting from tobacco to wheat, which was less labor-intensive. All this resulted in a surplus of enslaved persons. Unlike those enslaved persons brought to the Caribbean and forced to work in incredibly harsh and unhealthy conditions on sugar plantations, Maryland's and Virginia's unfree labor force was treated better and worked in more humane conditions. As a result, they grew in population, with natural births exceeding natural and unnatural deaths. Thus, if African captives could be banned from being imported into the colony in the future, the value of existing enslaved persons might rise. If slave importations ended in all the colonies, the prices of enslaved persons might rise even more, and "excess" stock could be sold into South Carolina and Georgia.

---

56. J. Hardy to Board of Trade, January 20, 1762, in Donnan, *Documents of the Slave Trade* 3: 456 and n2.
57. Quarles, *The Negro in the American Revolution,* 41. In 1769, the New Jersey legislature successfully imposed a duty of £15 on every imported enslaved person, which effectively put an end to the slave trade in the province. Donnan, *Documents of the Slave Trade* 3: 457n2. But the law was apparently either repealed or overruled, requiring another effort in 1773.
58. George Livermore, *An Historical Research Respecting the Opinions of the Founders . . . on Negroes as Slaves, as Citizens, and as Soldiers* (Boston, MA: Massachusetts Historical Society, 1862), 20.
59. DuBois, *Suppression of the African Slave Trade,* 22.

The use of tax policy to limit the slave trade may indicate that Virginians wanted to end slave imports but avoid any discussion of the more contentious issue of the morality of the slave trade or of slavery itself. This is how progress in the moral sphere sometimes works: a non-moral rationale is first applied, and the moral rationale comes later.

Virginia planters made other arguments that were not related to a humanitarian feeling for the enslaved person. Richard Henry Lee, a slave owner and member of one of the most influential families in Virginia, in 1759 supported limiting slave imports into Virginia on the ground that colonies such as Pennsylvania, with its numerous small farms tended by hard-working white farmers and their families, had outstripped Virginia in economic development. Whites who could create such farms from the wilderness tended not to immigrate to colonies where slavery dominated.[60] The prominent Virginia Whig George Mason agreed, adding in a 1765 letter to George Washington that he worried about the adverse consequences of slavery on the "morals and manners of our people." He warned ominously, "the primary cause of the destruction" of Rome had been "the introduction of great numbers of slaves."[61] Furthermore, there was always the fear of slave rebellions. The more enslaved people there were, the higher the security risk.

On occasion moral concern was expressed about the slave trade in particular. In a remarkable speech in the House of Burgesses in 1759, Richard Henry Lee said:

> Nor, sir, are these the only reasons to be urged against the importation. In my opinion, not the cruelties practiced in the conquest of Spanish America, not the savage barbarity of a Saracen, can be more big with atrocity than our cruel trade in Africa . . . There we encourage these poor, ignorant, people to wage eternal war against each other . . . [so] that by war, stealth, or surprise, we Christians may be furnished with our fellow-creatures, who are no longer to be considered as created in the image of God as well as ourselves.[62]

Turning to natural rights theory, Lee, stunningly, said that Africans were "equally entitled to liberty and freedom by the great law of nature."[63]

---

60. Oliver Perry Chitwood, *Richard Henry Lee: Statesman of the Revolution* (Morgantown, WV: West Virginia Library, 1967), 18.
61. G. Mason to G. Washington and G. W. Fairfax, December 23, 1765, in Robert A. Rutland, ed., *The Papers of George Mason, 1725-1792*, vol. 1 (Chapel Hill, NC: North Carolina University Press, 1970), 61-62.
62. Quoted in Chitwood, *Richard Henry Lee*, 18.
63. Ibid.

As early as 1763, Arthur Lee, Richard's brother and also a future Patriot leader, stated emphatically in a pamphlet that "the bondage we have imposed on the Africans is absolutely repugnant to justice" and "is shocking to humanity" and "abhorrent utterly from the Christian religion."[64] Surprisingly, in the heart of slave-holding Virginia, James Horrocks, the rector of the Bruton Parish Church at Williamsburg, Church of England, offered a powerful antislavery sermon, also in 1763.[65]

None of this meant that slavery would be ending in Virginia any time soon. Most Virginia planters supported the effort to limit slave imports for economic reasons and fear of slave rebellions. Indeed, none of the Lees, George Mason, George Washington or any other Virginia Founder would free his enslaved persons during his lifetime (Washington freed his enslaved persons in his will, the only Founder to do so). While they may have individually opposed aspects of slavery, since most other contemporaries did not share their concern they carried on as usual. Economically, they were not willing to give up their plantations run by enslaved labor. But there was a budding realization of the moral and religious wrong of slavery. This was a start. It was hypocrisy for the Lees to take their stands, as it would be for Thomas Jefferson later, but it was also part of a transition period where the realization that slavery was a dreadful wrong began to take root. The easiest target to attack initially was the barbarous slave trade. With the rhetoric of liberty and freedom dominating discourse in Virginia and Maryland in the late 1760s and early 1770s, it was inevitable that the link to the slave trade would be made.

The Virginia Assembly had been trying, with mixed success, to tax imports of Africans since 1759.[66] In late 1769, the House of Burgesses enacted a law to increase the duty on slave imports to fifteen percent, which in Great Britain led to more than seventy petitions from Liverpool and Lancaster slaver and other merchants who argued that the aim of the tax law was to raise the value of those enslaved persons already in the colony and those born in the future. The Board of Trade in London not only disallowed the law, but positively instructed the royal governor of Virginia to "assent to no laws by which the importation of slaves should be in any respect prohibited or obstructed."[67]

---

64. Arthur Lee, *An Essay in Vindication of the Continental Colonies of America . . . With Some reflections on slavery in general* (London, 1764), 42.
65. See Robinson, *Political Thought of the Colonial Clergy*, 35.
66. Chitwood, *Richard Henry Lee,* 17.
67. Quoted in ibid., 20; see also Riddell, "Pre-Revolutionary Pennsylvania and the Slave Trade," 52: 18; Petition of the Merchants of Liverpool to the Board of Trade, 1770, in Donnan, *Documents of the Slave Trade* 4: 151; R. Jackson to the Board of Trade, July 18, 1770, in ibid., 152-53.

In 1772 the House of Burgesses attempted again to increase the tariff on slave imports to a total of twenty-five percent of the purchase price, which if adopted would have reduced importations to a trickle. The Virginia Assembly, in conjunction with enacting the law, submitted a petition to the King arguing that "The importation of slaves into the colonies from the coast of Africa has long been considered as a trade of great inhumanity, and under its present encouragement, we have too much reason to fear [it] will endanger the very existence of your majesty's American dominions."[68] In London the effort was accurately portrayed as an attempt "to operate as an entire prohibition to the importation of slaves into Virginia" and therefore was similarly quashed by the Board of Trade as harmful to the "trade and commerce" of Bristol, Liverpool and Lancaster.[69]

In February 1774, a Virginia Quaker who had freed his slaves, Robert Pleasanton, wrote of the "wicked and destructive trade" to a friend. "It seems the attempts of our Assembly to prohibit the further importation of slaves by an imposition of high duties has been frustrated (as I find is the case in New York)," wrote Pleasanton, adding that "I have been told our Government [meaning royal governors] (and it is not unlikely others also) has instructions to pass no such laws."[70]

In July 1774, as part of the overall rising tide against George III's colonial policies, a nascent movement arose in several Virginia counties opposing further slave importations. In most counties the rationale for supporting a prohibition on slave imports was not framed on moral grounds. In Prince George's County, Patriots resolved that "the African trade is injurious to this Colony" in part on the ground that it led to less immigration "from Europe," meaning white settlers who did not want to compete against unfree workers.[71] Underlying the appeal was the increasing fear that blacks in the colony would soon outnumber whites, raising the specter of slave rebellion. Patriots in Culpeper County, citing similar grounds, resolved, "we will not buy any such slave . . . hereafter to be imported."[72]

---

68. Quoted in Paul Finkelman, "American Suppression of the African Slave Trade, Lessons on Legal Change, Social Policy, and Legislation," *Akron Law Review* (2009) 42: 437.

69. See Lord Dunmore to Earl of Hillsborough, May 1, 1772, in Donnan, *Documents of the Slave Trade*, 4: 153-54; Address of the House of Burgesses to the King, 1772, in ibid., 154-55; Order in Council, 1773, in ibid., 155-56; Egerton, *Death or Liberty*, 57.

70. R. Pleasants to A. Benezet, February 22, 1774, in Donnan, *Documents of the Slave Trade* 4: 161.

71. Resolution, undated [late June 1774], in Peter Force, ed., *American Archives*, 4th Ser., vol. 1 (Washington, DC: M. St. Clair Clark, 1853), 494.

72. Resolution, July 7, 1774, in ibid., 523. See also Princess Anne County Resolution, July 27, 1774, in ibid., 641; Nansemond County Resolution, July 11, 1774, in ibid., 530. Han-

In Fairfax County, at a meeting chaired by George Washington, a series of influential resolves, known as the Fairfax Resolves and penned by George Mason, were adopted. The seventeenth resolve stated in part, "during our present difficulties and distress, no slaves ought to be imported into any of the British colonies on this Continent." The resolve made it clear that the request was at least in part based on moral grounds: "We take this opportunity of declaring our most earnest wishes to see the entire stop forever put to such a wicked, cruel and unnatural trade."[73] Washington was directed to present the resolves to a convention scheduled to gather in Williamsburg in early August, and he also carried them to Philadelphia to present to delegates at the First Continental Congress.[74]

At the Virginia convention held in August 1774, consisting of "a very full meeting of delegates from the different counties in the Colony and Dominion of Virginia," delegates adopted twelve resolutions that amounted to an association or agreement for ceasing to conduct business with Great Britain. The members declared that after November 1, they would not import any articles produced in Great Britain except medicine. They specifically resolved, "We will neither ourselves import, nor purchase any slave or slaves imported by any other person, after the first of November next, either from Africa, the West Indies, or any other place."[75] A North Carolina convention followed suit on August 8, changing the wording only to broaden the importation ban to enslaved persons brought "from any part of the world."[76]

The issue that by far most increased tensions between the thirteen colonies of mainland North America and the British government was taxation without the consent of colonial legislatures. While the issue of slave importations was not one that drove colonists to break with the mother country, it was part of the overall problem the North American mainland colonies had with the British empire: colonial legislatures

---

over County enacted resolutions with reference to moral grounds and concern for slave rebellion. Patriots there resolved, "The African trade for slaves we consider as the most dangerous for virtue and the welfare of this country. We therefore most earnestly wish to see it totally discouraged." Hanover County Resolution, July 20, 1774, in ibid., 616.

73. Fairfax County Resolves, July 18, 1774, in ibid., 600.

74. David Ammerman, *In the Common Cause. American Response to the Coercive Acts of 1774* (Charlottesville, VA: University Press of Virginia, 1974), 86; see also ibid., n44 ("The Fairfax Resolutions were also sent to other towns. There is, for example, a copy of them in the Boston Comm. of Corr. Papers.").

75. Virginia Convention Resolutions, August 1, 1774, in Force, *American Archives*, 4th Ser., 1: 686-87.

76. North Carolina Convention Resolutions, August 24, 1774, in ibid., 735. For enforcement efforts in North Carolina, see Donnan, *Documents of the Slave Trade* 4: 237-39.

could not control their own trade or destinies. The colonies would have to declare their independence from Britain in order to rule themselves. Only then could they address sore points in colonial administration, among them the issue of slave imports.

Ultimately, after breaking from Great Britain, in 1778, the Virginia House of Burgesses banned imports of enslaved persons with £1,000 fines for violators and freedom for any slave brought illegally into the state, and Pennsylvania reinstated its £10 duty on each enslaved person imported into the state, while in 1783, after the end of the Revolutionary War, Maryland prohibited importation of enslaved persons by sea.[77] Virginia and Maryland acted primarily from selfish economic motives, but it meant fewer Africans would be forced across the Atlantic Ocean.

South Carolina had the largest percentage of slaves of any of the thirteen colonies at sixty percent. The driving need to import more captive Africans to work on growing rice and indigo plantations, and on farms in the western lands, led South Carolina to continue to accept more slave imports. Still, during the build-up to the American Revolution, tradesmen supporting the Revolutionary movement began to flex their muscles and briefly seized power from large slave holders.

From 1769 to 1771, in opposition to the Townshend duties, South Carolina prohibited the importation of most products from Great Britain. Importantly, the merchants agreed that no enslaved persons be imported from the Caribbean after October 1, 1769, and none from Africa after January 1, 1770. South Carolina Whigs made a strong effort to enforce the association by backing up its promises with threats of intimidation and economic pressure. As a result, the ban was largely successful.[78] Nonimportation lasted until about early 1771, longer than in other colonies.[79] South Carolina's nonimportation association likely hurt British slave merchants more than any other class in Great Britain. The May 24, 1770 edition of the *South Carolina Gazette* estimated that it caused a loss of £300,000 in British trade. Georgia, the newest colony, never agreed to nonimportation during the Townshend duties crisis.

A few visionary Patriots resident in, or connected to, the largest city in the thirteen colonies, Philadelphia, wanted to go further than merely

---

77. Egerton, *Death or Liberty*, 57; Dumond, *Antislavery*, 28; Riddell, "Pre-Revolutionary Pennsylvania and the Slave Trade," 52: 18; DuBois, *Suppression of the African Slave Trade*, 22.

78. See Leila Sellers, *Charleston Business on the Eve of the American Revolution* (Chapel Hill, NC: University of North Carolina Press, 1934), 201-19; Donnan, *Documents of the Slave Trade* 4: 435.

79. Sellers, *Charleston Business*, 220.

banning the importation of enslaved persons. Heavily influenced by Enlightenment thinking, Dr. Benjamin Rush published a remarkable antislavery tract in 1773. Rush countered all the usual arguments raised by defenders of the institution of slavery. Blacks were not inferior intellectually or morally, he stated; it was simply that slavery was so foreign to the human mind that enslaved persons were "rendered torpid" by it. To those who argued that slavery was necessary to the development of the economy of the South, the Philadelphia physician responded that he had "never observed" an economy "to flourish where those rights of mankind were not firmly established." Showing a creative mind not bound by traditional convention, Rush bravely argued that if the Bible's Old Testament was found to support slavery, then that interpretation should be ignored. Rush explained, "Every prohibition of covetousness-intemperance-pride-uncleanliness-theft-and murder, which he [Jesus] delivered—every lesson of meekness, humility, forbearance, charity, self-denial, and brotherly love which he taught, are levelled against this evil; for slavery, while it includes all the former vices, necessarily excludes the practice of all the latter virtues both from the master and the slave." Rush recommended that as a first step against slavery, enslaved persons should no longer be allowed to be imported. If the colonists wanted to take a stand against political slavery imposed on them by Parliament, the physician concluded, they should also oppose the enslavement of black persons.[80]

Rush's egalitarian arguments were surprisingly modern. Yet most in the United States and the rest of the Western World were unwilling to go so far as the Philadelphia physician. It would take well into the nineteenth century for his views to gain wide acceptance. Still, it was an impressive beginning.

In its March 8, 1775 edition, the *Pennsylvania Journal* published an essay entitled "African Slavery in America." Its opening words revealed a straightforward style: "That some desperate wretches should be willing to steal and enslave men by violence and murder for gain is rather lamentable than strange. But that many civilized, nay, Christianized people, should approve and be concerned in the savage practice is surprising." Maintaining that slavery was "contrary to the light of nature, to every principle of justice and humanity, and even good policy," the author urged that after America achieved its independence, the legislatures should pass laws to stop the importation of captive slaves and

---

80. Benjamin Rush, *An Address to the Inhabitants of the British Settlements in America, Upon Slavekeeping* (Philadelphia, 1773), 2-3, 5-7, 9, 13-14, and 16; see also Zilversmith, *First Emancipation*, 94-95.

"in time" to "procure [the] freedom" of enslaved persons already in America.[81] For more than a century this essay was thought to have been penned by the great secular thinker Thomas Paine, but now experts believe it was written by someone else, probably Samuel Hopkins.[82] Whomever wrote the impassioned piece, the author did not support immediate abolition.

Benjamin Franklin, the most famous American in the world on the eve of the American Revolution, exemplified the evolution of many of the whites' views of slavery, particularly in the middle and northern colonies. Franklin owned several enslaved persons from as early as 1735 until 1781. His Philadelphia newspapers advertised the sale of enslaved persons and for the return of runaways. But as a result of his famous friend, Dr. Samuel Johnson, bringing him to tour a school for black children in London in 1758, and becoming friends and corresponding with the antislavery Quaker leader Anthony Benezet in Philadelphia, Franklin's views on race began to evolve. In 1763 Franklin wrote that African shortcomings and ignorance were not inherently natural but came from lack of education, slavery and negative environments. He also wrote that he saw no difference in learning between African and white children.[83] These were remarkable views for white persons at this time.

In 1770, while in London, Franklin struggled to justify the institutions of slavery in the North American colonies when Whigs were pressing for their own liberty in the contest against the Crown. He made the weak arguments that New England and the middle colonies had "very few slaves, and those are chiefly in the capital towns, not employed in the hardest labor," and that "many thousands" in the North American mainland colonies "abhor the slave trade."[84] By 1772, he published a devastating critique in *The London Chronicle*, alerting readers that "the yearly importation" of British merchants in the slave trade, "is about one hundred thousand, of which number about one-third perish by the ... distemper in passage, and in the sickness called the *seasoning*

---

81. Quoted in Quarles, *The Negro in the American Revolution* (citing *Pennsylvania Journal*, March 8, 1775) and Zilversmith, *First Emancipation*, 96 (citing *Pennsylvania Journal*, March 8 and October 8, 1775).

82. See the website for the Thomas Paine National Historical Association at www.thomaspaine.org (search for: African slavery).

83. For a summary of Franklin's changing attitude on slavery, see headnote to A. Benezet to B. Franklin, April 27, 1772, in Founders Online, www.founders.archive.gov. For some of the Franklin-Benezet correspondence, see ibid; B. Franklin to A. Benezet, August 22, 1772, ibid.; and B. Franklin to A. Benezet, February 10, 1773, in ibid.

84. B. Franklin, A Conversation on Slavery, January 26, 1770, in ibid. (citing *The Public Advertiser* (London), January 30, 1770).

before they are set to labor." He asked readers, "Can sweetening our tea, etc., with sugar be a circumstance of such absolute necessity?"[85]

* * *

In October 1774, in a stunning and radical move, delegates of the First Continental Congress signed a pledge for the thirteen mainland colonies not to participate in the African slave trade. Perhaps equally astounding, Americans largely complied, turning the pledge into an outright ban.

Congress's ban and widespread compliance with it during the Revolutionary War years has been underappreciated even by historians of the American antislavery movement. It should not be. It is true that the primary motivation for the banning slave imports was not moral outrage at the slave trade itself, but instead was a means to punish Great Britain in hopes of changing its colonial tax and trade policies. Even so, given the building opposition to the slave trade in the 1770s on moral grounds, moral outrage likely played a substantial role in the adoption of the ban. Revealingly, Congress went farther than simply prohibiting the slave trade with Britain.

Congress first banned all imports of enslaved persons. Thus, neither American slave ships, British slave ships, nor those from any other country could carry captive Africans into any of the thirteen colonies. If Congress had desired simply to punish Britain, it could have limited its ban to British slave ships.

Even more impressively, Congress prohibited Americans from participating in the slave trade altogether—not just with Great Britain and its Caribbean colonies, but with any country. This slave trade ban was the first nationally organized antislavery effort in American history, and one of the first in world history.

The meeting of the First Continental Congress was a reaction to the punishments Parliament imposed on Boston for the Boston Tea Party. Parliament had attempted to force a tax on tea on the Americans, and in response Boston Whigs in December 1773 had dumped a massive shipload of tea in Boston Harbor rather than having it landed and paying the tax. In response, Parliament quickly pushed through four acts, called the Coercive (or Intolerable) Acts. The port of Boston was closed until the tea was paid for; certain powers were taken away from the Massachusetts legislature and judiciary and given to the royal governor; British officials could be tried only in England for accusations

85. B. Franklin, The Somerset Case and the Slave Trade, June 18-20, 1772, in ibid. (citing *The London Chronicle*, June 18-20, 1772).

made in the colonies; and quartering troops among the people was authorized.

To the surprise of British lawmakers and officials in London, Whigs throughout the thirteen mainland colonies of North America united in their opposition to the Coercive Acts. On September 5, the Continental Congress assembled for the first time. Meeting at Carpenter's Hall in Philadelphia, eventually fifty-five delegates from twelve colonies arrived and pondered what steps to take. Only delegates from Georgia were absent. Exceptionally capable Whigs from different colonies, such as Richard Henry Lee of Virginia and John Adams of Massachusetts, met for the first time, sometimes at the nearby City Tavern.

As was typical in the political discourse of the day among American Whigs, the prospect of giving in to the demands of the British government was likened to becoming enslaved. Samuel Ward, a delegate from Rhode Island, wrote to delegate John Dickinson from Pennsylvania, "We must either become slaves or fly to arms. I shall not (and hope no Americans will) hesitate one moment which to choose." To Ward, "even death itself" was "infinitely preferable to slavery, which in one word comprehends poverty, misery, infamy and every species of ruin and destruction."[86] Ward and other Whigs needed only to look around them to see how badly the descendants of Africans were then being treated.

In the past, nonimportation agreements among merchants, including those in the main ports of Boston, Newport, New York and Philadelphia, had been a promising weapon to persuade the British government to repeal offensive trading laws. Only a lack of a nationally organized effort led to its downfall. Arthur Lee advised Richard Henry Lee, his influential brother from Virginia serving as a delegate to the First Continental Congress, that cutting off all trade with Great Britain was "the only advisable and sure mode of defense" against Britain's wrong-headed colonial policies.[87] Richard Henry Lee agreed that imposing a uniform, continental system of nonimportation that would paralyze Britain's commerce was "the only method that Heaven has left us for the preservation of our most dear, most ancient and constitutional exemption from taxes imposed on us not by the consent of our representatives."[88] Support for nonimportation was building, as well as for nonexportation, but this time it would be backed by a continental as-

86. S. Ward to J. Dickinson, December 14, 1774, in Paul H. Smith, ed., *Letters of Delegates to Congress, 1774-1789,* vol. 1 (Washington, D.C.: Library of Congress, 1976), 269.
87. A. Lee to R. H. Lee, March 18, 1774, in Force, *American Archives,* 4th Ser., 1: 229.
88. R. H. Lee to A. Lee, June 26, 1774, in James Curtis Ballagh, ed., *The Letters of Richard Henry Lee,* 2 vols. (New York, NY: Macmillan, 1911-14), 1: 117.

sembly consisting of delegates from twelve colonies of the North American mainland. Whigs believed that harming the finances of British merchants and manufacturers would lead to their agitating the British government to end the objectionable laws against the thirteen colonies. They had a fixation that economic interests would be more influential in persuading the British government than all other forces.

On September 22, "for the preservation of the liberties of America," delegates recommended merchants to send no more orders for foreign goods.[89] On September 27, upon a motion by Richard Henry Lee, it was unanimously resolved to import no goods from Great Britain after December 1, 1774.[90] The debate on nonimportation also included non-exportation. One delegate pointed out, "The importance of the trade of the West Indies to Great Britain almost exceeds calculation."[91] Sam Adams added that suspending trade with the West Indies would leave planters there short of "provisions to feed their slaves."[92] Adams knew this would in turn hurt the productivity of British Caribbean plantations. On September 30, ordering goods from Britain's colonies of Ireland and in the Caribbean were added to the ban.[93]

Next, Congressional delegates turned to identifying the goods that would be subject to the importation ban. Northern merchants deeply entrenched in the Caribbean trade became concerned. In debates, Isaac Low, a delegate from New York, asked, "Will, can, the people bear a total interruption of the West India trade? Can they live without rum, sugar, and molasses?"[94] Delegates believed the answer was that they could, as a sacrifice to retain their rights as free men that others enjoyed in the mother country.

Virginia's delegates brought with them several items that probably influenced delegates to do something bold about the slave trade and slave importations. Virginia delegates carried resolutions passed at the Virginia convention held in early August 1774. The second clause read, "We will neither ourselves import, nor purchase, any slave, or slaves, imported by any person, after the 1st day of November next, either from Africa, the West Indies, or any other place."[95] George Washington also

89. Resolution, September 22, 1774, in Worthington C. Ford, ed., *The Journals of the Continental Congress*, 34 vols. (Washington, D.C.: Library of Congress, 1905-37), 1: 41.
90. Resolution, September 27, 1774, in ibid., 43; Chitwood, *Richard Henry Lee*, 68.
91. John Adams' Notes of Debates, September 26-27?, 1774, in Smith, *Letters of Delegates* 1: 103.
92. Samuel Adams' Notes on Trade, September 27?, 1774, in ibid., 108.
93. Resolution, September 30, 1774, in ibid, 51-52.
94. John Adams' Notes on Debates, October 6, 1774, in Smith, *Letters of Delegates* 1: 152.
95. Virginia Convention Resolutions, August 8, 1774, in Julian Boyd, ed., *Papers of Thomas Jefferson*, vol. 1 (Princeton, NJ: Princeton University Press, 1950), 138.

probably brought the Fairfax Resolves (or delegates read them in local Philadelphia newspapers), which urged Patriots not to import any slaves and declared "our most earnest wishes to see an entire stop forever to such a wicked, cruel and unnatural trade."[96]

Virginia's delegates too brought with them a then unpublished work penned by a young Thomas Jefferson, who drew up charges against King George III. Jefferson had been too ill to attend Congress, and his friends later published his work as a pamphlet without his permission. In his *A Summary View of the Rights of British America*, Jefferson included the following indictment:

> The abolition of domestic slavery is the great object of desire in these colonies where it was unhappily introduced in their infant state. But previous to the enfranchisement of the slaves we had, it is necessary to exclude all further importations from Africa. Yet our repeated request to effect this by prohibitions and by imposing duties which might amount to a prohibition have been hithero defeated by his Majesty's negative, thus preferring the immediate advantage of a few British corsairs [slave-trading vessels] to the lasting interest of the American states, and to the rights of human nature, deeply wounded by this infamous practice.[97]

Jefferson misstated the facts when he claimed that most colonists desired the abolition of slavery, especially in light of his own fellow planters in Virginia. But many, if not most, did want to end slave importations. Interestingly, Jefferson presented ending the slave trade as a prelude to prohibiting slavery itself.

With all these new ideas floating around, on October 6 the committee appointed by Congress to specify products destined for nonimportation added tea, syrup, brown unpurified sugar—and enslaved persons.[98] If any delegate strongly opposed banning the importation of captives from African or the Caribbean, there is no record of it.[99]

The Continental Association also imposed a ban, to become effective September 10, 1775, giving Parliament time to repeal the objectionable laws, on all American exports to Britain, Ireland, and the

96. Fairfax Resolves, July 18, 1774, in W. W. Abbott and Dorothy Twohig, eds., *Papers of George Washington, Colonial Series*, vol. 10 (Charlottesville, VA: University of Virginia Press, 1995), 125.
97. Jefferson, "A Summary View of the Rights of British America . . . , 1774, in Wood, *The American Revolution*, 2: 101-02.
98. Continental Association, October 20, 1774, in Ford, *Journals of the Continental Congress* 1: 77.
99. See Ammerman, *In the Common Cause*, 81-87.

British West Indies. South Carolina delegates, including John Rutledge and Christopher Gadsden, rather than publicly oppose the prohibition on slave imports, spent their political capital insisting that rice be allowed to be exported to mainland Europe, to which the delegates finally acceded.[100]

It was not surprising that the ban on slave imports was specifically included in the Continental Association. Slaves were expressly referred to in the attempt at nonimportation in 1769 to oppose the Townshend duties. Boston was the initiator of the movement for nonimportation, and it was joined by New York City and later Philadelphia before it swept into other colonies. It appears that the first reference to enslaved persons being included in nonimportation was made by George Mason in Virginia's nonimportation resolutions signed by most members of the House of Burgesses on May 18, 1769. The fifth resolution read, "That they will not import any slaves, or purchase any (hereafter) imported until the said Acts of Parliament are repealed."[101] After Parliament repealed all the duties except for tea, there was another attempt at nonimportation. A nonimportation association entered into by most members of the House of Burgesses on June 22, 1770, may have been authored by Richard Henry Lee. Its fourth clause stated that "we will not import or bring into the colony, or cause to be imported or brought into the colony, either by sea or land, any slaves, or make sale of any upon commission, or purchase any slave or slaves that may be imported by others after the 1st day of November next, unless the same have been twelve months upon the continent."[102] This last formulation, with its one year exception, was weaker than the 1769 ban. Nonimportation was relatively short-lived, especially after merchants from Newport, Rhode Island, hesitated to abide by it.[103]

Stunningly, four years later, the Continental Association that contained the nonimportation pledge and was signed by the delegates of the twelve colonies starting on October 20, 1774, went much further than the pledge not to import African captives. The second article stated: "We will neither import nor purchase, any slave imported after

100. Samuel Ward Diary Entry, October 20, 1774, in Smith, *Letters of Delegates* 1: 221 and n1, 222; Chitwood, *Richard Henry Lee*, 68-69.
101. Virginia Nonimportation Resolutions, May 18, 1769, in Rutland, *Papers of George Mason*, 1: 110; see also Draft of Nonimportation Association, April 23, 1769, in ibid., that George Mason shared with George Washington.
102. Virginia Nonimportation Association, June 22, 1770, in ibid., 1: 122; for Richard Henry Lee's authorship, see also ibid., 120, note and 125, note.
103. See Elaine Forman Crane, *A Dependent People, Newport, Rhode Island in the Revolutionary Era* (New York, NY: Fordham University Press, 1985), 117-18.

the first day of December next; after which time, we will wholly discontinue the slave trade, and will neither be concerned in it ourselves, nor will we hire our vessels, nor sell our commodities or manufactures to those who are concerned in it."[104]

This was indeed a shocking development, ending all participation by American merchants in the slave trade. Much of the Continental Association is based on the approach taken in the August resolves passed by the Virginia convention in early August 1774. But while those resolves included a strong stand against importing any enslaved persons from any source, they did not even hint at ending participation in the slave trade.

The slave trade clause went much further than prior efforts at nonimportation. Slave traders from the thirteen colonies could not, without violating the Association, buy captives in Africa and sell them anywhere, not just in their own colonies. Indeed, by the terms of the last part of the clause, they could not even trade with slave merchants in transactions having nothing to do with enslaved persons. The fact that the ban was contained in the second paragraph of the Continental Association reveals how strongly Congress felt about the matter.

Henry Laurens, a prominent Patriot and notorious slave trader from Charleston, succinctly summarized the economic argument for ending slave imports from Britain. He wrote, "Men-of-war, forts, castles, governors, companies and committees are employed [in Africa] and authorized by . . . Parliament to protect, regulate, and extend the slave trade . . . Bristol, Liverpool, Manchester, Birmingham, etc., live upon the slave trade."[105] But Congress had gone much further, banning any American participation in the slave trade by itself or with any country, including France, Spain and Portugal.

Who was behind the insertion of the broad slave trade clause in the final Continental Association agreement is not known. Members of the committee assigned to draft the nonimportation provisions were Richard Henry Lee of Virginia, Thomas Cushing of Massachusetts, Isaac Low of New York, Thomas Mifflin of Pennsylvania, and Thomas Johnson of Maryland.[106] Richard Henry Lee, who had previously given a speech against the evils of the slave trade, likely played an important role in the insertion of the broad slave trade clause.

104. Continental Association, October 20, 1774, in Ford, *Journals of the Continental Congress* 1: 77.
105. H. Laurens to J. Laurens, August 14, 1776, in David R. Chesnutt, et al., eds., *The Papers of Henry Laurens*, vol. 11 (Columbia, SC: University of South Carolina Press, 1989), 224.
106. Resolution, September 28, 1774, in Ford, *Journals of the Continental Congress* 1: 53.

No doubt Lee found a sympathetic ear in Cushing, who was part of many efforts in Massachusetts to ban importation of enslaved Africans into his colony. Samuel Adams, another influential delegate who had a history of pressing for antislavery legislation in Massachusetts, could have pushed for his friend Cushing to press for the broad ban. And in this environment swirled the recent polemics against the slave trade in Jefferson's recent writings and in the Fairfax Resolves brought by George Washington. Crucially, none of the committee members hailed from South Carolina or Georgia, the only two colonies where slave importations had been substantial in prior years and which would tenaciously defend slavery at the Constitutional Convention in 1787. More likely, all of these forces combined at the right time to lead to the insertion of the slave trade clause.

It is also not clear whether the ban on all slave importations and all participation in the slave trade was based on moral grounds, the desire to harm Britain economically, or both. It was probably both. The slave importation and slave trade bans are often described as primarily motivated by the desire to harm Britain economically rather than a recognition of the evils of slavery. Yet such a view ignores the fact that at the time the Continental Association was adopted, opposition to the slave trade on moral grounds was at a high point. Accordingly, moral and humanitarian opposition to the slave trade was likely a key factor.

Revealingly, Congress went further than mere nonimportation to prohibit any participation by North American merchants and sea captains in the slave trade. This by itself indicates that moral and humanitarian factors played a substantial role. If the committee had just wanted to increase the values of enslaved people currently held in their colonies and to protect against the risk of slave insurrections, they could have simply banned slave imports.

Based on the makeup of the committee that drafted the Continental Association, it appears that moral and humanitarian grounds played an important role. Only two southerners were on the committee, and one of them was the influential Richard Henry Lee, who held ideological antislavery feelings. Thomas Johnson of Maryland was on the committee too. A substantial slaveholder, he came from a state that wanted to ban imports of enslaved persons.

Why did Congress decide to ban all slave importations? After all, merchants in Charleston and Savannah could have worked with French, Spanish or Portuguese slave traders, and the wartime disruption of commerce with Britain forced the states to develop direct trade with European powers. There were likely a number of factors at play. First, in the North there was rising opposition to the slave trade on moral grounds. Second, mostly out of economic interest, and on moral grounds at least with a few leaders such as Thomas Jefferson and George Mason, Virginia and Maryland had long tried to limit slave importations. Third, at this time, the power of the slave interests in South Carolina and Georgia was at a nadir. Slave merchants and planters who opposed nonimportation had tried to stack the delegates South Carolina sent to Philadelphia with their allies, but instead a general meeting of Patriots voted in delegates with full authority to agree to nonimportation.[107] Georgia was not even represented in the Congress.

It is possible that committee members considered that an outright ban on all slave importations would be easier to enforce than a partial ban directed solely at Great Britain. They may have thought that Patriot local committees would face difficulties trying to identify what slave had been purchased from Africa by an English trader and what slave had not. At this time, British merchants in Liverpool, Bristol and London dominated the Atlantic slave trade. If imports from, say, Spain were permitted, it might be easy for a Spanish merchant to purchase a captive taken from the African coast by a Bristol merchant and resold to the Spanish merchant in Cuba, and then sell the enslaved person to a Charleston merchant. Accordingly, ease of enforcement may have been an important factor in banning all slave importations.

Even more interesting is the question of why Congress banned all participation in the slave trade by American merchants. After all, a Newport merchant could purchase captives on the Gold Coast of Africa directly from a local chieftain and resell them to, say, a Spanish or French buyer, without importing the slave into any of the thirteen colonies or having any involvement with British factors or merchants. While it is true that at this time, North American slave merchants had not yet developed business relationships with Spanish or French buyers, they could have tried to do so. Here, moral objections to the slave trade may have been paramount. Still, delegates might have been concerned that it would have been easy for North American slave merchants to disguise their purchases from British factories (holding pens for enslaved persons) and forts on the African coast. Again, ease of enforcement may have been a key factor in banning all participation in the slave trade by mainland colonial merchants. In addition, slave merchants did not then have much power in the Continental Congress. Rhode Island's delegates, Samuel Ward and Stephen Hopkins, supported Congress's ban.

107. See Donnan, *Documents of the Slave Trade* 4: 470n1.

Surprisingly, the slave trade ban resulted in little comment outside of Philadelphia. Patriots had other matters to attend to in the growing crisis. The Danbury, Connecticut, town meeting in December 1774 was an exception. It noted "with singular pleasure . . . the second Article of Association, in which it is agreed to import no more Negro Slaves." Calling slavery "one of the crying sins of our land," the town meeting gave as its rationale that it was "palpably absurd to loudly complain of attempts to enslave us, while we are actually enslaving others."[108]

Two Philadelphia merchants must not have known of the deep involvement in the slave trade by one of the Newport merchants they dealt with, Christopher Champlin. In an October 25, 1774 letter, they informed Champlin of the various nonimportation and nonexportation resolutions just passed by Congress, adding, "the slave trade to be discontinued after the first of December . . . which is a most excellent resolve."[109]

The Continental Association contained terms for its own enforcement. Delegates knew that Congress had no power to enforce the association. It was recommended that in every county, city and town a committee be chosen to "observe the conduct of all persons touching this association," publish in local newspapers all violations, and "break all dealings" with any person who violated the association. Delegates were aware that every colony and many localities had formed extralegal committees of correspondence in 1773. Members of committees of correspondence were encouraged even to look at custom house records to seek out violators. Delegates also promised not to trade with "any colony or province, in North America," that would not accede to or did "hereafter violate this Association."[110]

A few days before it adjourned, Congress voted on October 22 to hold another Congress at Philadelphia on May 10, 1775, unless Parliament resolved their grievances in the colonies' favor. Among the first of Congress's achievements, the Continental Association stands out as an important development that ultimately led to war between the thirteen colonies (not just Massachusetts) against Great Britain, and eventually to all of the colonies declaring their independence. But only a few envisioned that development in October 1774. John Dickinson, a Pennsylvania delegate, wrote to Arthur Lee that "the colonists have

108. Resolution, December 12, 1774, in Force, *American Archives*, 4th Ser., 1: 1038-39.
109. Stocker & Wharton to C. Champlin, October 25, 1774, in "Commerce of Rhode Island," *Collections of the Massachusetts Historical Society*, 7th Ser., 10: 517 (1914).
110. Continental Association, October 20, 1774, in Ford, *Journals of the Continental Congress* 1: 79.

now taken such ground that Great Britain must relax [her laws against the colonies], or inevitably involve herself in a civil war."[111]

The delegates at the First Continental Congress, expecting the British government would respond to economic pressure from their boycott, were overly optimistic. British merchants and West Indian planters did petition Parliament to press for compromise, pointing out the drastic economic impact the boycott or war would have on their fortunes. But the appeal failed to consider other factors taken into account by British government decision makers, such as the emotions of pride and stubbornness, parochial attitudes towards colonists, and concern that compromising too much would jeopardize the British empire. Parliament refused to budge.

Enforcement of the Continental Association passed to local Patriot committees. Even the slave-holding colonies of Virginia and South Carolina enforced the ban on importation of African captives. Patriotism trumped the desire to continue to allow slave importations, at least for the time being.

Two early enforcement actions set precedents. On March 6, 1775, the Committee of Correspondence of Norfolk, Virginia, determined that John Brown, a Norfolk merchant, had conspired to import enslaved people into Virginia and therefore had "willfully and perversely violated the Continental Association." Pursuant to the eleventh paragraph of the Continental Association, the Committee ordered that the transgression be publicized, that Brown be identified as one of "the enemies of American Liberty, and that every person may henceforth break off all dealings with him."[112]

The March 6, 1775 edition of the *South Carolina Gazette* announced that the ship *Katherine*, out of Bristol, England, had arrived in Charleston harbor, sailing from the West Coast of Africa from Angola, with 300 enslaved persons on board, consigned to Charleston slave trader John Neufville. Readers must have wondered if the human cargo would be permitted to land in Charleston, since the Bristol captain had not had any notice of the nonimportation ban when he purchased the captives in Angola. In a follow-up, the March 27 edition of the same newspaper informed readers that the 300 captives "according to the Continental Association could not be imported or purchased here," with the result that the vessel "sailed for the West Indies with her whole cargo."

---

111. J. Dickinson to A. Lee, October 27, 1774, in Smith, *Letters of Delegates* 1: 250.
112. Proceedings of the Committee of Correspondence, March 6, 1775, in Force, *American Archives*, 4th Ser., 2: 33-34.

What about Rhode Island, the leading slave trading colony in North America? After all, it had beaten back an attempt to prohibit entirely the colony's participation in the slave trade in June 1774. Samuel Ward and Stephen Hopkins, Rhode Island's two delegates to the Continental Congress, both signed the Continental Association. Shortly after returning to their respective homes in Rhode Island, they travelled to Providence in early December to report to the General Assembly on the developments in Philadelphia. After listening to the presentation, the General Assembly voted to adopt the Continental Association.[113] The colony's small number of slave merchants were overwhelmed by the patriotic surge to support the struggle of Boston's Whigs against British oppression. In this charged atmosphere, Rhode Islanders hardly considered rejecting the Whig cause just to keep the slave trade open.

In mid-December, the respected and well-liked Samuel Ward of Westerly, in a letter to fellow-delegate John Dickinson of Pennsylvania, exulted that Rhode Islanders were "universally satisfied with the proceedings of Congress, and determined to adhere to the Association." Ward added, as if in disbelief, "Even the merchants who suffer the most by discontinuing the slave trade assure me they will most punctually conform to that Resolve and the country in general is vastly pleased with it."[114] Ward, a former three-time governor of Rhode Island whose support came mostly from Newport, was well positioned to know whether or not the colony's slave traders were willing to abide by the ban. Rhode Island's other delegate who signed the Continental Association, Stephen Hopkins, had recently pressed for the Rhode Island General Assembly to end slave importations; Newport slavers could not count on him for support. The General Assembly, satisfied with work of both Ward and Hopkins, appointed them to serve as delegates to the Second Continental Congress.[115]

Whether Newport slavers would really abide by the ban, given the well-deserved reputation of all Rhode Island merchants for evading British trade laws, remained an open question. An initial indication that Newport merchants would abide by the ban was the scramble to send out ships to Africa before the ban took effect on December 1, 1774. In the first ten months of 1774, thirteen slave ships cleared out of Newport for Africa and two sailed from nearby Bristol, Rhode Island. In the single month of November, after learning of the ban shortly to take effect, five ships sailed out of Newport, and one out of Bristol,

113. See Bartlett, *Records of Rhode Island* 7: 263; *Providence Gazette*, December 3, 1774.
114. S. Ward to J. Dickinson, December 14, 1774, in Smith, *Letters of Delegates* 1: 269.
115. Bartlett, *Records of Rhode Island* 7: 264-65.

bound for Africa, with three of them departing with just two days to spare. Several Newport slaving vessels that could not be made ready to sail by December 1 were reportedly kept in port.[116]

Two prominent Newport slave merchants, Christopher and George Champlin, informed their English joint venturer that their brother, Robert Champlin, had sailed their sloop out of Newport bound for Africa nine days prior to the December 1 deadline. But they also warned their London partners, "By the resolves of the Continental Congress, all trade is stopped from this continent to Africa [starting] 1st December last, since which no vessel has sailed for thence, nor will any till our troubles are settled."[117]

The Association's ban on American participation in the slave trade was surprisingly successful. Jay Coughtry, who has studied the slave voyages of Rhode Island merchants most closely, reported no slave voyages departing from a Rhode Island port after December 1, 1774 and before 1784.[118] He further observed that impact of the American Revolution on the Atlantic slave trade exceeded that of the impact of prior wars between Great Britain and France: "the American Revolution finally accomplished what three colonial wars had been unable to do; and from 1776 to 1783, the Rhode Island slave trade ceased."[119] A search of an incredibly detailed online resource, which attempts to record every trans-Atlantic slave trading voyage that ever occurred, reveals no clear evidence of a slave ship owned by an American merchant departing from a North American port for Africa after December 1, 1774 and before 1783, when the Revolutionary War ended.[120] My own investigation reveals that while American slave merchants almost unanimously abided by the slave trade ban, not all slave ship captains did. But that is another story.

On April 6, 1776, the Continental Congress stepped back from its total ban prohibiting Americans from participating in the slave trade. The main thrust of the resolution was a momentous one—to permit American merchants to export goods and merchandise to any foreign country, and to import goods and merchandise from any foreign country "not subject to the King of Great Britain."[121] The resolution added

116. Trans-Atlantic Slave Trade Database, www.slavevoyages.org/voyage/search (search voyages beginning in 1774).
117. C. and G. Champlin to Threlfal and Anderson, January 17, 1775, in Donnan, *Documents of the Slave Trade* 3: 301.
118. Rhode Island Slave Trading Voyages, 1709-1807, in Coughtry, *Notorious Triangle*, 260.
119. Coughtry, *Notorious Triangle*, 31.
120. Trans-Atlantic Slave Trade Database, www.slavevoyages.org/voyage/search (search voyages from 1774 to 1783).
121. Resolution, April 6, 1776, in Ford, *Journals of the Continental Congress* 4: 257-58.

that "no slave be imported into any of the thirteen United Colonies" (they were not states yet). No mention was made of the ability of Americans to participate in the slave trade with other countries. A fair reading of the two resolutions is that American merchants could not deal in enslaved persons with Britain or any of its colonies, but could purchase captives in Africa from non-British interests and sell them to French, Spanish, or Portuguese slave buyers in the New World. They still could not, however, import any African captives into North America.

Congress's total ban on Americans participating in the slave trade was short-lived. With South Carolina and Georgia paying more attention in the Second Continental Congress, the ban was difficult to continue. The need for unanimity in the face of a difficult war against the mother country was paramount. But for a short time, Congress did have in place a total ban that a decade earlier no one thought was possible. And its prohibition on imports of African captives lasted throughout the war. These were steps, albeit relatively small ones, towards the formal end of the African slave trade and abolition of slavery in the North. Of course, stopping violations of the slave trade ban and ending slavery in the South were more intractable problems that would take longer to resolve.

What Killed Prisoners of War?: A Medical Investigation

⚔ BRIAN PATRICK O'MALLEY ⚔

Throughout the Revolutionary War, prisoners learned that dysentery accompanied starvation. Confined to the prison ship *Jersey* in 1781, Christopher Hawkins described rations "not sufficient to satisfy the calls of hunger." In the next two sentences, Hawkins mentioned that "the bloody flux or dyssenterry" prevailed on the *Jersey*, from which "many died on board her." Like other prisoners of war, Hawkins was certain he witnessed epidemic dysentery. Caused either by the ameba *Entamoeba histolytica* or by several species of bacteria, dysentery is characterized by diarrheal expulsions mixed with blood and mucus. Like many victims of starvation, however, prisoners probably had the non-contagious condition known as "hunger diarrhea" or "famine diarrhea." Famine diarrhea figured in two major scandals of prisoner neglect in the Revolutionary War, New York in 1776 and Charles Town (present-day Charleston), South Carolina in 1780.[1]

In a succession of hunger crises in the nineteenth and twentieth centuries, medical professionals gradually distinguished famine diarrhea from dysentery. During the Irish Potato Famine (1845-1850), Dr. Daniel Donovan distinguished "famine dysentery" from "ordinary

---

1. Christopher Hawkins, *The Adventures of Christopher Hawkins*, ed. Charles I. Bushnell (New York: Privately Printed, 1864), 66; Carl P. Borick, *Relieve Us of This Burthen: American Prisoners of War in the Revolutionary South, 1780-1782* (Columbia: The University of South Carolina Press, 2012), 4-5, 15-26; K. David Patterson, "Bacillary Dysentery," Kenneth F. Kiple, *The Cambridge World History of Human Disease* (Cambridge: Cambridge University Press, 1993), 605; K. David Patterson, "Amebic Dysentery," *Cambridge World History*, 570; K. David Patterson, "Dysentery," *Cambridge World History*, 696; Brian Patrick O'Malley, "1776—The Horror Show," *Journal of the American Revolution*, January 29, 2019, allthingsliberty.com/2019/01/1776-the-horror-show/.

dysentery." Donovan, however, still mistook the ailment for a contagion. Doctors in the Finnish Famine of 1866-1868 realized famine diarrhea was noninfectious. In the Madras Famine of 1877-1878, British physicians in Madras, India identified "famine diarrhoea" as a noncontagious affliction, a result of prolonged starvation, and a sign that the patient was near death. Serving as Assistant Director of Medical Services for the 6th (Poona) Division of the Indian Army, Maj. Gen. Sir Patrick Hehir observed famine diarrhea during the Turkish Army's 148-day siege of British and Indian troops at Kut, in modern Iraq (1915-1916).[2]

During World War II, healthcare professionals documented three stages to death from starvation. Danish healthcare workers, arrested by German forces for resistance activity, contributed to a collection of postwar studies of "famine disease" in concentration camps. In the Warsaw Ghetto, established by Nazis in occupied Poland, Polish doctors arrested for their Jewish heritage conducted a series of clandestine studies of "hunger disease," a collection of essays smuggled from the Warsaw Ghetto in 1942. Danish and Polish researchers documented famine diarrhea as an ordeal of the third stage of starvation, the terminal stage.[3]

In the first stage of famine disease, people experienced rapid weight loss. The transformation reminded Polish doctors of prewar "reducing cures" at vacation spas. The second stage of hunger disease reminded one Polish research team of animal hibernation. To avoid burning its own tissues for fuel, the body slowed metabolism, reduced exertion to a minimum and increased the demand for rest. In this quasi-hibernation, weight loss slowed or even halted, but sufferers looked prematurely

2. Daniel Donovan, "Observations on the Diseases to which the Famine of 1847 Gave Origin, and on the Morbid Effects of Insufficient Nourishment: Dysentery," *Dublin Medical Press*, Vol. 19 (May 3, 1848): 275; E. Hess Thaysen and J. Hess Thaysen, "Hunger Diarrhoea," in Per Helweg-Larsen, Henrik Hoffmeyer, Jorgen Kieler, Eigil Hess Thaysen, Jørn Hess Thaysen, Paul Thygesen, Munke Hertel Wulff, "Famine Disease in German Concentration Camps: Complications and Sequels," *Acta Medica Scandinavica*, Supplement 274 (1952), Wiley Online Library, onlinelibrary.wiley.com/toc/16000447/1953/28/s83 (*Famine Disease*), 125-126; Leela Sami, "The Epidemiological, Health and Medical Aspects of Famine: Views from the Madras Presidency (1876-78)," in *Society, Medicine and Politics in Colonial India*, ed. Biswamoy Pati and Mark Harrison (New York: Routledge, 2018), 156-159, 167.
3. Israel Milejkowski, "Introduction," 3-5, in *Hunger Disease: Studies by the Jewish Physicians in the Warsaw Ghetto*, ed. Myron Winick, trans. Martha Osnos (New York: John Wiley & Sons, Inc., 1979), 3-5 (*Hunger Disease*); Joseph Stein and Henry Fenigstein, "Pathology Anatomy of Hunger Disease," *Hunger Disease*, 222-224; Julian Fliederbaum, Ari Heller, Kazimierz Zweibaum, Jeanne Zarchi, "Clinical Aspects of Hunger Disease in Adults," *Hunger Disease*, 15-16; Helweg-Larsen, et al., *Famine Disease*.

aged. The third phase of famine disease was terminal "hunger cachexia" (severe emaciation and muscle atrophy), often accelerated by famine diarrhea. In this terminal phase of starvation, diarrhea killed people in just a few weeks or even a few days.[4]

In the landmark Minnesota Starvation Experiment (1944-1945) researchers at the University of Minnesota subjected volunteers to twenty-four weeks of semistarvation, anticipating the need for famine relief in postwar Europe, and compiled data from historic famines. The humanitarian research had support from three pacifist denominations prominent in the Founding Generation, the Church of the Brethren (popularly known as "Dunkards" or German Baptists during the American Revolution), Mennonites, and the Society of Friends (Quakers). Based on historic famines, Minnesota researchers confirmed diarrhea can typify end-stage starvation, but sufferers can also die with diarrhea in abeyance and edema predominating, with patients swollen from retained fluid.[5]

Hunger disease stems from a severe, long-term caloric deficiency. A healthy person needs 50 calories daily for every kilogram of body weight. Polish researchers estimated a healthy person of average weight and stature needed about 3,000 calories per day. Subjects in the Minnesota Starvation Experiment received an average of 1,570 calories per day for twenty-four weeks (six months) and lost an average of twenty-five percent of their pre-hunger body weight. Ancel Keys of the Minnesota experiment warned that forty percent was usually fatal, though some individuals can survive losing fifty percent of their initial weight. In the Warsaw Ghetto, a research team headed by Dr. Julian Fliederbaum estimated their patients got about 1,100 calories per day; a team headed by Dr. Emil Apfelbaum-Kowalski estimated their patients, for many months, only got 600 to 800 calories per day. For Danish political

4. E. Hess Thaysen, J. Hess Thaysen, J. Kieler, P. Thygesen, "Hunger Cachexia," *Famine Disease*, 81, 83, 84, 86, 90-91; Fliederbaum et al., "Clinical Aspects," 15-16, 36; Emil Apfelbaum-Kowalski, Ryszard, Jeanne Zarchi (medical student), Ari Heller, Zdzislaw Askanas, "Pathophysiology of the Circulatory System in Hunger Disease," in *Hunger Disease*, 127, 149-150; P. Thygesen and J. Kieler, "The Mussulman," *Famine Disease*, 251-254; Stein and Fenigstein, "Pathological Anatomy," 223; Patrick Hehir, "Effects of Chronic Starvation During the Siege of Kut," *The British Medical Journal* 1 (1922): 867, www.jstor.org/stable/20420147.
5. Ancel Keys, Josef Brožek, Austin Henschel, Olaf Mickelsen, Henry Longstreet Taylor, *Biology of Human Starvation*, 2 vols. (Minneapolis: The University of Minnesota Press, 1950), 1:xxvii; 63-64, 70; 2:955; Todd Tucker, *The Great Starvation Experiment: Ancel Keys and the Men Who Starved for Science* (Minneapolis: The University of Minnesota Press, 2007 [2006]), 37.

prisoners, the daily caloric intake from concentration camp rations ranged from 700 to 1,100 calories. Food parcels from the Danish or Swedish Red Cross could give Danish prisoners an additional 1,000 to 1,500 calories per day.[6]

Historians can only guess the daily caloric intake of prisoners during the American Revolution. Historian Edwin G. Burrows estimated prisoners of the British Army received no more than 1,640 calories per day and prisoners of the British Navy received about 1,556 calories per day. Burrows cautioned his nutritional assessment of official rations was generous, and prisoners often received less than their official allotment. Privates Thomas Boyd and William Darlington of Chester County, Pennsylvania, for instance, described rations more meagre than British claims of what was provided.[7]

Gen. Sir William Howe probably held over 3,000 captive Continental soldiers by December 1776. From August 27, 1776 to November 20, 1776, the British and Hessian forces under Howe brought 4,114 American soldiers and 305 American officers as captives to New York City. While the military officers enjoyed parole within the occupied city, the British warehoused the privates on prison ships and confiscated buildings like sugarhouses and non-Anglican churches. Joshua Loring, a Loyalist who served the British as Commissary General of Prisoners, indicated over 700 of 4,114 captive soldiers offered to enlist with British recruiters. The recruitment of 700 to 800 soldiers left Howe with about 3,300 to 3,400 Continental soldiers. The naval forces under Howe's brother, Adm. Richard, Viscount Howe, took prisoner perhaps

---

6. Julian Fliederbaum, Ari Heller, Kazimierz Zweibaum, Suzanne Szejnfinkel, Regina Elbinger, Fajga Ferszt, "Metabolic Changes in Hunger Disease," *Hunger Disease*, 86; Apfelbaum-Kowalski, "Pathophysiology of the Circulatory Systerm," 127; J. Kieler, "Deportation," *Famine Disease*, 45-48, 50-51, 53; Thaysen, et al., "Hunger Cachexia," 87-89; Thygesen and Kieler, "Avitaminoses Incident to Semistarvation," 226-227; E. Hess Thaysen and J. Hess Thaysen, "Hunger Oedema," *Famine Disease*, 98; Tucker, *Great Starvation Experiment*, 96; David Baker and Natacha Keramidas, "The Psychology of Hunger," *APA Monitor on Psychology* 44 (October 2013): 66, www.apa.org/monitor/2013/10/hunger; W. W. Abbot, editorial note 5, at Peter Hog to George Washington, January 27, 1756, *Founders Online*, founders.archives.gov/documents/Washington/02-02-02-0304.

7. Edwin G. Burrows, *Forgotten Patriots: The Untold Story of American Prisoners During the Revolutionary War* (New York: Basic Books, 2008), 251-253; "Quantity of Provisions. . .," January 19, 1778, enclosed in William Howe to George Washington, January 19, 1778, *Founders Online*, founders.archives.gov/documents/Washington/03-13-02-0238; Affidavit of Thomas Boyd, February 27, 1777, *Pennsylvania Evening Post*, May 3, 1777 (Boyd Affidavit); Affidavit of William Darlington, February 27, 1777, *Pennsylvania Evening Post*, May 3, 1777 (Darlington Affidavit).

a few hundred sailors from the Continental Navy, several state navies and privateer crews.[8]

The experience of American prisoners epitomized the progression of hunger disease. For several months, British and Loyalist observers associated American prisoners with "filthiness" and "laziness." Writing for the British press and claiming informants in British-occupied New York City, "Politicus" blamed the unhealthiness of the prisoners on "their own Listlessness and Sluggishness," "their own Laziness and Filth." Admiral Howe mentioned "the indolence of the Prisoners." In his diary for November 12, 1776, British staff officer Maj. Frederick Mackenzie described the prisoners as "low spirited creatures" whose "dirty, unhealthy, and desponding appearance" was "enough to shock one." The November 25, 1776 issue of Loyalist newspaper *The New-York Gazette; and the Weekly Mercury* likewise noted the "Filthiness" of the prisoners.[9]

British and Loyalist commentary captured the quasi-hibernation phase of hunger disease. The first symptom of hunger is not emaciation but laziness. After witnessing semistarvation in London with mass unemployment in 1837-1838, Dr. Richard Baron Howard wrote, "The first indications of a deficiency of food . . . are languor, exhaustion, and general debility." According to one research team in the Warsaw Ghetto, "The hungry person becomes lazy . . . hoarding the last of his vital energy." According to another Polish medical team, starvation transformed "busy, energetic people" into "apathetic, sleepy beings."[10]

---

8. Joshua Loring, "Return of Prisoners taken during the Campaign, 1776" December 1, 1776, enclosed in Sir William Howe to Lord George Germaine, December 3, 1776, *The New-York Gazette; and the Weekly Mercury*, March 17, 1777; Joshua Loring, "State of the Prisoners," undated, Elias Boudinot Papers, Library of Congress; Edwin G. Burrows, *Forgotten Patriot*, 276-277n15; Timothy Parker and Others to Governor Jonathan Trumbull, December 9, 1776, *Naval Documents of the American Revolution*, ed. Michael J. Crawford, vol. 13 (Naval History and Heritage Command, Department of the Navy, 1964-2019), 7: 421, www.history.navy.mil/research/publications/publications-by-subject/naval-documents-of-the-american-revolution.html (*Naval Documents*); Affidavit of William Gamble, February 8, 1777, *Pennsylvania Evening Post*, April 29, 1777.

9. *Politicus*, "Case of the Rebel Prisoners Truly Stated," *The Public Advertiser* (London), August 13, 1777, Newspapers.com, www.newspapers.com/clip/25390612/sluggish-prisoners/; Richard Howe to George Washington, January 17, 1777, *Founders Online*, founders.archives.gov/documents/Washington/03-08-02-0095; Frederick Mackenzie, *The Diary of Frederick Mackenzie*, 2 vols. (New York: New York Times, 1968 [1930]), 1:103; "New-York, November 25," *The New-York Gazette; and the Weekly Mercury*, November 25, 1776.

10. Richard Baron Howard, *An Inquiry into the Morbid Effects of Deficiency of Food . . .* (London: Simpkin, Marshall, & Co., 1839), 19; Apfelbaum-Kowalski, et al., "Pathophysiology of the Circulatory System," 127; Fliederbaum, et al., "Clinical Aspects," 34.

In November 1776, neither Major Mackenzie nor the anonymous contributor to the *New-York Gazette* mentioned gauntness among captive Americans. Of course, publicly acknowledging weight loss among prisoners was politically damaging. Even in the privacy of his diary, however, Mackenzie did not mention emaciation. Mackenzie even rejected the claim that American prisoners were starving. Two major factors might account for Mackenzie's failure to see emaciation among the prisoners. First, even clinical researchers who see starving people every day, or at regular intervals, will fail to notice gradual weight loss. Secondly, as researchers in the Warsaw Ghetto learned from patient interviews, severe emaciation might take several months to develop.[11]

The "filthiness" of American prisoners was probably another misunderstood symptom of starvation. During the Potato Famine, Donovan found that the skin released a foul odor "and was covered with a brownish, filthy-looking coating, almost as indelible as varnish." At first, Donovan mistook the discoloration for "encrusted filth." In Madras, Alexander Porter wrote of "Famine skin," "It had the general appearance of dirt, as if the person had not washed for some time, but soap and water would not remove it; nothing short of scraping would do this." Researchers in the Warsaw Ghetto and the Minnesota experiment associated semistarvation with pale, grayish skin, sometimes cyanotic, but also vulnerable to splotches of "dirty," "brownish" pigmentation. Danish resistance members collapsed the discoloration into a single spectrum of "'dirty,' greyish-brown complexion." In 492 autopsies of people who died from starvation in the Warsaw Ghetto, doctors Joseph Stein and Henryk Fenigstein found skin discoloration in 466 (almost 95 percent) of the cases. Stein and Fenigstein classed 385 instances (82.5 percent) of discoloration as "pale, almost cadaverlike" and 81 cases (17.5 percent) as "dark brown." Of the 81 autopsy subjects

11. Richard Howe to George Washington, January 17, 1777; William Howe to George Washington, April 21, 1777, *Founders Online* , founders.archives.gov/documents/Washington/03-09-02-0211; Mackenzie, *Diary*, 103-104; Keys, et al., *Biology of Human Starvation*, 1: 132-133; Apfelbaum-Kowalski, et al., "Pathophysiology of the Circulatory System," 127; Thygesen and Kieler, "The Mussulman," 254.

12. Daniel Donovan, "Observations on the Peculiar Diseases to which the Famine of Last Year Gave Origin, and on the Morbid Effects of Insufficient Nourishment," *Dublin Medical Press* 19 (February 2, 1848): 67; Alexander Porter, *The Diseases of the Madras Famine of 1877-78* (London: H. K. Lewis, 1889), 207-208; Russell M. Wilder, "Forward," *Biology of Human Starvation*, 1: xx; Keys, et al., *Biology of Human Starvation*, 1: 237-238; Ancel Keys, "Caloric Undernutrition and Starvation, with Notes on Protein Deficiency," *Journal of the American Medical Association* 138 (1948): 505; Fliederbaum, et al., summarizing a lost paper by Dr. B. Raszkes, "Clinical Aspects," 16; Stein and Fenigstein, "Pathological Anatomy,"

with brownish pigmentation, only 20 had edema and 61 had "dry" cachexia, the dehydrated emaciation often associated with diarrhea.[12]

Of the 4,114 rank and file held by General Howe, the largest contingent (about 63 percent) were the 2,607 privates who surrendered after the Battle of Fort Washington (November 16, 1776). If conditions and food were bad enough, it was possible for prisoners taken as late as November 16 to develop hunger diarrhea by the end of December. Danish police, arrested by German forces to forestall possible armed revolt, experienced better conditions and received better food than members of the Danish resistance. Among Danish police who developed hunger diarrhea in Nazi custody, 56 percent developed diarrhea after about two months. For members of the resistance who developed hunger diarrhea, 84 percent developed it after about two months. The average was about one and three-quarter months. Danish political prisoners who received no relief parcels, living only on camp rations, lost between twenty and thirty percent of their initial weight before the onset of diarrhea.[13]

Diarrhea started as intermittent and, in the fatal stage of starvation, became constant. Eigil Hess Thaysen and Jørn Hess Thaysen described a "vicious circle:" weight loss intensified diarrhea, diarrhea intensified weight loss, "and most of the patients died in extreme cachexia." Irish doctors noticed the same vicious cycle during the Potato Famine. Donovan wrote, "The discharges continued unabated; the body wastes to a skeleton." Dr. F. J. Lynch described famine victims who survived fever only to reach an interval, "from one to three weeks," during which "the patients became living skeletons, uncontrollable diarrhea returned, and quickly carried them off."[14]

Perhaps surviving a contagion cost starving bodies the last of their strength. Patrick Hehir wrote that men starving in Kut "could stand little in the shape of illness." Significantly, many of the prisoners preemptively released by Howe from New York in the winter of 1776-1777 had smallpox. Caring for American prisoners in a Charles Town, South Carolina hospital in September and October 1780, Dr. Peter Fayssoux witnessed famine diarrhea kill undernourished prisoners as

218-219, 227; Michal Szejnman, "Changes in Peripheral Blood and Bone Marrow in Hunger Disease," *Hunger Disease*, 165; Thaysen, et al., "Hunger Cachexia," 83.

13. J, Kieler, "Deportation," 64; Thaysen and Thaysen, "Hunger Diarrhoea," 137; Thaysen, et al., "Hunger Cachexia," 86, 141-142.

14. Thygesen and Kieler, "The Mussulman," 254; Donovan, "Observations on the Disease," 276; "Report upon the Recent Epidemic Fever in Ireland," *The Dublin Quarterly of Medical Science* Vol. 7 (February and May 1849), 401; Thaysen and Thaysen, "Hunger Diarrhoea," 133.

they recovered from smallpox. Fayssoux recalled that British officers permitted American surgeons to inoculate captives on prison ships but let doctors provide no further care. The prisoners, Fayssoux lamented, were "fed on salt provisions, without . . . any proper kind of nourishment." Ideally, inoculation resulted in a case of smallpox milder than naturally contracted smallpox. Instead, starvation and neglect led to "a small-pox with a fever of the putrid type; and to such as survived the small-pox, a putrid dysentery." British officers only let prisoners go ashore for treatment after the smallpox pustules erupted. Tending to prisoners onshore, Fayssoux found that putrid fever and "dysentery" caused "the death of at least one hundred and fifty of the unhappy victims." Fayssoux's 1785 recollection did not indicate what proportion of his patients 150 represented, but he considered the losses catastrophic.[15]

Accounts of prisoners in late-1776 associated diarrhea with terminal starvation. A captured Continental officer on parole in New York City, Col. Ethan Allen, visited captive soldiers warehoused in confiscated churches. Allen wrote, "The filth in these churches (in consequence of the fluxes) was almost beyond description. The floors were covered with excrements." Pvt. Thomas Boyd mentioned expulsions becoming problematic after he described the onset of starvation, implying fluxes became worse after prolonged hunger. Ethan Allen more explicitly associated the fluxes with death from starvation. Allen recalled, "I have seen in one of these churches several dead . . . lying among the excrements of their bodies."[16]

Famine diarrhea killed quickly. Danish researchers explained the terminal phase of starvation was epitomized by any prisoner who reached a state known as "the Mussulman" (Muslim). The Mussulman was stooped from weakness like a humble penitent. With a slow metabolism, without insulating fat, the Mussulman was sensitive to cold and liable to drape his blanket over his shaven head, accentuating his supposed resemblance to a religious pilgrim. Horrifically, Thaysen and Thaysen observed, "The duration of the Mussulman phase . . . usually only extends over a couple of weeks."[17]

15. Hehir, "Effects of Chronic Starvation," 867; Jonathan Trumbull, Sr. to George Washington, February 7, 1777, *Founders Online*, founders.archives.gov/documents/Washington/03-08-02-0289; Borick, *Relieve Us of This Burthern*, 18; Peter Fayssoux to David Ramsay, March 26, 1785, in William Moultrie, *Memoirs of the American Revolution. . .*, Vol. 2 (New York: David Longworth, 1802), 2: 399.

16. Boyd Affidavit; Ethan Allen, *A Narrative of Colonel Ethan Allen's Captivity* (Philadelphia: Robert Bell, 1779), 29-30.

17. Thaysen, et al., "Hunger Cachexia," 83; Thygesen and Kieler, "The Mussulman," 253; Jørn Kieler, *Resistance Fighter: A Personal History of the Danish Resistance Movement 1940-1945*, trans. Eric Dickens (New York: Gefen Publishing House, 2007), 275.

Sadly, hunger diarrhea might kill in even less than a week. Hehir noted that most soldiers at Kut recovered from diarrhea, "but many of them became intensely collapsed and died on the second, third or fourth day." For Stein and Fenigstein, the brevity of famine diarrhea was a critical difference from dysentery. Bacillary or amebic, dysentery was a long-term illness. In autopsies of famine victims, however, Stein and Fenigstein found that diarrhea inflicted damage "probably in the last days or weeks of life." Famine diarrhea most resembled dysentery in the final days of starvation.[18]

Famine diarrhea killed quickly in 1776. Although some prisoners died in November, Pvt. John Adlum recalled that prisoners "began to die very fast in the month of December," namely, "the latter part of December." Confined to a prison ship, Pvt. John Caryl implied prisoner deaths increased after December 25, 1776. Caryl associated the increased mortality with a change in prisoner rations and the introduction of a "very bitter" burgoo (oatmeal gruel). Caryl did not specify diarrhea, but Danish researchers confirmed a change of diet could cause fatal famine diarrhea among people already poorly nourished.[19]

By the end of 1776, American prisoners exhibited several symptoms of terminal starvation, including the reduction of the voice to a whisper. Ethan Allen witnessed several prisoners "speechless, and near death." Another Continental officer on parole, Lt. Jonathan Gillet, also visited the prison-churches and found "want of food" among prisoners meant "some almost loose their voices." Describing prisoners returning to Connecticut, Col. John Chester wrote, "They are mere skeletons, unable to creep or speak in many instances." In Pennsylvania, Rev. Hugh Henry Brackenridge indicated the typical returnee was an emaciated man with a voice "shrill, feeble, and not to be distinctly heard."[20]

During the Siege of Kut, Hehir specifically noted the absence of "the change in the voice met with in cholera." Other doctors, however, compared starvation's reduction of the human voice to *vox cholerica* (Latin for "cholera voice"), the debilitating effect of cholera on speech.

---

19. John Adlum, *Memoirs of the Life of John Adlum in the Revolutionary War*, ed. Howard H. Peckham (Chicago: The Coxton Club, 1968), 98, 125 (*Adlum Memoirs*); Affidavit of John Caryl, February 17, 1777, *Pennsylvania Evening Post*, May 3, 1777; Thaysen and Thaysen, "Hunger Diarrhoea," 133, 143-144; Boyd Affidavit; Darlington Affidavit.

20. John Chester to Samuel Blachley Webb, January 17, 1777, in *Correspondence and Journals of Samuel Blachley Webb*, ed. Worthington Chancey Ford (Lancaster, PA: Wickersham Press, 1893), 184; Hugh Henry Brackenridge, "The Bloody Vestiges of Tyranny," in Hugh Henry Brackenridge, *A Hugh Henry Brackenridge Reader, 1770-1815*, ed. Daniel Marder (Pittsburgh: University of Pittsburgh Press, 1970), 66; Allen, *Narrative*, 29; Jonathan Gillet to Elizabeth Gillet, December 2, 1776, in *Letters from the Prisons and Prison-Ships of the Revolution*, ed. Henry R. Stiles (New York: Privately Printed, 1865), 11.

In the Warsaw Ghetto, a research team headed by Julian Fliederbaum wrote, "In the terminal stage of cachexia . . . the voice becomes hoarse, like *vox cholerica*." With the onset of emaciation and debility, Donovan noted, "the voice is so weak as to resemble the cholera whine." Lynch wrote that when diarrhea became constant (that is, with the onset of end-stage famine diarrhea), victims suffered "increasing debility," a "remarkable tendency to emaciation," and an "altered, whispering, whining voice."[21]

In his portrait of the typical returnee, Brackenridge mentioned "legs swollen, and from the ankle to the knee of an equal shape." In many starvation deaths, edema subsided as hunger diarrhea dehydrated and emaciated the victim. Edema in the lower extremities, however, could persist. Paul Thygesen and Jørn Kieler found the emaciated Mussulmans rarely had edema, except for those with swelling in the lower legs. Thygesen and Kieler were shocked by the contrast between skeletal thighs and swollen calves. In the Warsaw Ghetto, edema appeared randomly around the body throughout the course of hunger disease. In the terminal stage, however, edema concentrated in the lower legs. In 492 autopsies of starvation victims in the Warsaw Ghetto, 164 (33.3 percent) had edema. Of 164 starving people who died with edema, 160 (97.6 percent) had edema in the lower extremities. Only 21 (12.8 percent) showed edema in the upper extremities and only 18 (about 11 percent) in the torso.[22]

Curiously, during the Madras Famine, Alexander Porter found edema concentrated in the feet. The principal of Madras College, Porter operated a famine relief camp. Conducting autopsies on a sampling of famine victims, Porter noted a high incidence of "Oedema of the feet" in "emaciated cases." Porter found edema of the feet in 139 (44.8 percent) of 310 emaciated men, women and children. In his later book, Porter recorded the figure as 140 of 310 (about 45 percent). Edema rarely occurred elsewhere. Edema of the hands, for instance,

21. Hehir, "Effects of Chronic Starvation," 867; Donovan, "Observations on the Peculiar Diseases," 67; Donovan, "Observations on the Diseases," 267; "Report upon the Recent Epidemic Fever," 400; Fliederbaum, et al., "Clinical Aspects," 19; Howard, *Inquiry*, 19.
22. Fliederbaum, et al., "Clinical Aspects," 17-18; Stein and Fenigstein, "Pathology Anatomy," 218, 219 (Table 5), 227. This paper slightly adjusts the figures of Martha Osnos's English translation of Stein and Fenigstein (the original Polish manuscript was consulted for this paper). Column C in Table 5 transposes the total number of edema cases (95) for the specific number of edema cases in the lower extremities (91) in Period C (July 1, 1941-December 31, 1941). The changes are slight, the preponderance of lower-extremity edema remains. Where this paper finds lower-extremity edema in 160 of 164 cases (97.6 percent), Stein and Fenigstein find it in 157 of 160 cases (98.1 percent); Stein and Fenigstein, "Pathological Anatomy," 217, 219, 227.

was only present in six men and three women (2.9 percent of overall emaciated cases, or 3.6 percent of emaciated adults).[23]

End-stage starvation also exposed American prisoners to the macabre risk of premature burial. During the Potato Famine, Donovan wrote, "Great attention should . . . be paid to the subject of interments, as from the influence of cold on those suffering from starvation, many may be buried alive whilst in a state of asphyxia." Donovan knew two cases of children mistakenly put on the dead cart only to show signs of life before or just after landing in a mass grave. In 1777 depositions, privates Thomas Boyd and James Stuart recalled several prisoners in New York were mistakenly thrown into mass graves while still alive. Stuart, "on his oath declares," that one sick man, "reviving after being thrown with the dead in the pit," "with help got out."[24]

Death from starvation, even with famine diarrhea, was so quiet and uneventful that the dead were mistaken for living and the living for dead. Patrick Hehir wrote of semistarvation, "In fatal cases so imperceptibly does life ebb away that it is sometimes not easy to say whether the man is really dead or not." Dropped with other prisoners at South Amboy, New Jersey, Pvt. John Adlum helped a stumbling fellow-returnee step from the boat. Adlum spotted his new friend a moment later, at the fireplace of a household that opened its door to prisoners. "I went to ask him how he was when to my astonishment he was dead. The crowd about the fire I presume kept him from falling for none of those at it knew at the time that he was dead."[25]

Several avitaminoses (diseases of vitamin deficiency) can cause symptoms akin to hunger disease. Pellagra (niacin deficiency) can cause diarrhea. Scurvy (Vitamin C deficiency) can cause swelling of the legs. Vitamin requirements, however, are proportional to caloric intake. Typically, a severe calorie deficit precludes vitamin deficiencies. Danish researchers considered protein deficiency the primary deficiency of

23. Alexander Porter, "Notes on Famine Diseases," *The Dublin Journal of Medical Science*, 83 (January-June 1887): 135-136; Porter, *Diseases of the Madras Famine*, 72, 73
24. Donovan, "Observations on the Peculiar Diseases," 68; Boyd Affidavit; Affidavit of James Stuart, February 27, 1777, *Pennsylvania Evening Post*, May 3, 1777.
25. Hehir, "Effects of Chronic Starvation," 867; Fliederbaum, et al., "Clinical Aspects," 36; *Adlum Memoirs*, 137.
26. William Clowes, *A Profitable and Necessarie Books of Observations*, 3rd ed. (London: M. Dawson, 1637 [1596]), 40, Crawford Historical Books, University of Maryland, Baltimore, http://hdl.handle.net/2027/uc1.31378008343157; Stewart R. Roberts, *Pellagra: History, Distribution, Diagnosis, Prognosis, Treatment, Etiology* (St. Louis, Missouri: C. V. Mosby Company, 1913), 128; Fliederbaum, et al., "Metabolic Changes," 101-105; P. Thygesen and J. Kieler, "Avitaminoses Incident to Semistarvation," *Famine Disease*, 215, 226-227,

hunger disease. However paradoxically, American prisoners probably suffered no vitamin deficiency while starving to death.[26]

General Howe witnessed perhaps the most shocking aspect of hunger diarrhea, its lethality. Howe started December with about 3,300 Continental soldiers, leverage to demand an exchange of 3,300 British rank and file from American custody. In a December 3, 1776 letter to Lord George Germain, Britain's Secretary of State for the colonies, Howe complained of the "great expense and inconvenience" of accommodating prisoners, implying most of the prisoners were still very much alive. In the last days of December 1776 and the first days of January 1777, Howe suddenly learned he held about 1,100 corpses and about 2,200 stumbling, whispering skeletons.[27]

From about December 21, 1776 to January 27, 1777, Howe shipped surviving prisoners to American-held territory. He tried to get living prisoners into American hands. In their stage of starvation, however, recovery was unlikely. As Hehir learned at Kut, "there is a stage . . . in chronic starvation from which recuperation cannot take place." Indeed, several of Howe's prisoners died on the transport ships taking them from New York to Connecticut or New Jersey. Most of the returnees probably died before the end of February 1777. George Washington complained that Howe released prisoners "in so emaciated and languished a State," as to render their death "almost certain and inevitable." As one Connecticut resident lamented, "Their constitutions are broken . . . they cannot recover, they die."[28]

229-230, 233-234; Thaysen and Thaysen, "Hunger Diarrhoea," 134, 149; Thaysen and Thaysen, "Hunger Oedema," 99-100.

27. William Howe to George Germain, December 3, 1776, Peter Force, *American Archives*, Series 3, Vol. 3 (Washington, DC: St. Clair Clarke and Peter Force, 1853), 1055, Northern Illinois University Digital Library, digital.lib.niu.edu/islandora/object/niu-amarch%3A8 8768; Thygesen and Kieler, "The Mussulman," 253.

28. Jabez Fitch, *The New-York Diary of Lieutenant Jabez Fitch*, ed. William H. Waldon Sabine (New York: The New York Times & Arno Press, 1971 [1954]), 92; James McHenry to George Washington, January 31, 1777, *Founders Online*, founders.archives.gov/documents/Washington/03-08-02-0214; *Connecticut Journal*, January 8, 1777; *Adlum Memoirs*, 124; Thomas Hartley to Washington, February 12, 1777, *Founders Online*, founders.archives.gov/documents/Washington/03-08-02-0341; Samuel Holden Parsons to Washington, February 19, 1777, *Founders Online*, founders.archives.gov/documents/ Washington/03-08-02-0406; "A Madras Correspondent. . .," February 24, 1877, *The Times* (London), March 28, 1877, Newspapers.com, www.newspapers.com/clip/55083644/famine-diarrhea-madras/; Thaysen and Thaysen, "Hunger Diarrhoea," 134, Hehir, "Effects of Chronic Starvation," 868; Thygesen and Kieler, "The Mussulman," 253; George Washington to William Howe, April 9, 1777, *Founders Online* , National Archives, founders.archives.gov/documents/Washington/03-09-02-0103; Miserecors (pseud.), "Messieurs Greens," *The Connecticut Journal* (New Haven), January 30, 1777.

Washington agonized that the prisoners might have survived, if only Howe released them sooner, "before these ill fated men were reduced to such extremity." Howe could not have recognized the necessity of the mass release any sooner. Like Major Mackenzie, Howe could not believe sluggish American prisoners were really dying of starvation. Alas, by the time Howe's prisoners *looked* like they were starving, it was too late to save them.[29]

29. Washington to Howe, April 9, 1777.

Tapping America's Wealth to Fund the Revolution: Two Good Ideas That Went Awry

❄ TOM SHACHTMAN ❄

"Unless some great and capital change suddenly takes place," Gen. George Washington wrote from Valley Forge on December 23, 1777,[1] to Henry Laurens, the recently-appointed president of the Continental Congress, "the Army must inevitably be reduced to one or the other of these three things. Starve—dissolve—or disperse, in order to obtain subsistence." A week later, in letters sent to the state governors,[2] Washington reported that more than 2,898 soldiers at Valley Forge were "unfit for duty" because they lacked clothes; the troops at the camp had not been fed in three days, but he pledged to continue to "conceal the true state of the army from public view" to prevent the British learning of its condition and attacking while it was so weak.

The estimated amount of money required to supply the army for the coming year and to operate the new country's central government was three million British pounds. During that terrible winter of 1777-1778, Henry Laurens and his son, John Laurens, a Washington aide-de-camp, independently hatched two interesting ideas for tapping the country's wealth to underwrite the war.

Even a friendly biographer[3] faulted Henry Laurens for being too "cocksure about the rightness of his contentions," a man whose "ego-

---

1. George Washington to Henry Laurens, December 23, 1777, founders.archives.gov/documents/Washington/03-12-02-0628.

2. Washington "circular letter" to governors, December 29, 1777, www.loc.gov/resource/mgw3c.002/?sp=212&st=text.

3. Leila Sellers, *Charleston Business on the Eve of the American Revolution* (Chapel Hill: University of North Carolina Press, 1934), viii.

tism was something a little too much in evidence." Laurens had come to the Revolution reluctantly but steadily. One of the wealthiest colonists in South Carolina, he was a major importer-exporter and the owner of four plantations that utilized slave labor. His fellow delegates to the Continental Congress thought so highly of him that less than six months after his arrival in their midst they selected him to succeed John Hancock as president of Congress.

He took the job and its responsibilities very seriously.[4] When Congress moved to York, Pennsylvania to continue its work after having to leave Philadelphia ahead of the British capture of that city, many delegates just went home for the winter. Laurens stayed with the Congress in York, living in a boarding house and, as the troops were doing, dining on bread, cheese, and grog—while suffering from gout to the point that he could hardly walk, yet putting in eighteen-hour work days.

Laurens wanted to cut back on government spending and find new ways to bolster the treasury. He advocated new "taxation in each colony," to "sell vacant and forfeited estates," and to "do a thousand other things which . . . we would do, if luxury and avarice were discountenanced."[5] He pushed these ideas in Congress, but to little avail.

His specific idea for marshaling the wealth of the country was detailed in a letter to his son, then at Valley Forge. It was to lobby 500 wealthy families to buy new government-issued bonds. Each of those families would purchase £3,000 worth, and their willingness to buy in would serve as an inducement to the rest of the population to purchase the remainder. He wrote that he would "subscribe to morrow five or Ten Thousand Pounds Sterling & if these were found insufficient all my Estate shall be given for saving the public."[6]

Laurens' idea was statistically not a wild stab. The population of the United States of America just then numbered more than three million. Thus the top one percent consisted of 30,000 people, or, given the average family size of five, about 6,000 fairly wealthy households.[7] A plan to get money from less than one out of ten of these wealthy families was quite reasonable. Moreover, governmental bond sales were usual in Europe as a way of raising money to fight wars.

4. Daniel J. McDonough, *Christopher Gadsden and Henry Laurens: The Parallel Lives of Two American Patriots* (Sellinsgrove, PA: Susquehanna University Press, 2000). See also Gabriel Neville, "The Tragedy of Henry Laurens," allthingsliberty.com/2019/08/the-tragedy-of-henry-laurens/.
5. Henry Laurens to Isaac Motte, January 26, 1778, in Laurens, *Papers of Henry Laurens*, vol. 12 (Columbia: University of South Carolina Press, 1980), 343-350.
6. Henry Laurens to John Laurens, March 15, 1778, *Papers*, 12: 558-561.
7. Peter H. Lindert and Jeffrey G. Williamson, *Unequal Gains: American Growth and Inequality Since 1700* (Princeton: Princeton University Press, 2016), 1-39.

John Laurens was a hotshot, everyone at Valley Forge agreed. His family's roots were among the Huguenots, and he spoke French well. After training as a lawyer in London and in Geneva, he returned home to take part in the war. His talents and potential would be recognized by two good judges of character, George Washington, who advanced him to a field command and sent him on important missions, and Benjamin Franklin, with whom he would later deal in Paris.

The plan that John Laurens put forth for mobilizing the country's wealth was constructed with the enthusiastic participation of his twenty-something pals at Valley Forge, the Marquis de Lafayette, Alexander Hamilton, and Pierre L'Enfant. (Washington had asked Laurens and Hamilton, who both spoke French, to assist in integrating the French officers into the American command.)[8] John's idea was to mobilize that portion of the country's wealth that was held in slaves. He would double the size of the Continental army by inducing slaves to enlist in exchange for their eventual freedom. L'Enfant and Laurens each offered to lead one of these new army units themselves.[9]

Currently, Rhode Island was trying to put that idea into practice at the behest of Gen. James Varnum, enlisting slaves in the 1st Rhode Island regiment in exchange for their later freedom. As we now know, this regiment would be among the finest in the country, distinguished for valor and bravery in every encounter throughout a long war, from 1778 through to Yorktown.[10]

Back in 1776, Henry Laurens had made a speech denouncing slavery, and had recently clarified his position on it to John: he abhorred slavery as an institution but was resigned to its current economic necessity.[11] He now said he would agree to the young officers' plan for enlisting slaves, with the caveat that slave-owners would have to be compensated so that they could hire replacement workers. Washington echoed that formulation. But if these two older slave owners thought that the compensation objection might kill the young men's idea, they were wrong, because the junior officers had anticipated and budgeted for paying the slave owners to allow their slaves to go to the front lines. And to further assuage their elders, they added a new condition, that

8. Thomas Fleming, *Washington Secret War: The Hidden History of Valley Forge* (New York: HarperCollins, 2005).

9. Gregory D. Massey, *John Laurens and the American Revolution* (Columbia: University of South Carolina Press, 2000).

10. Robert A. Geake, *From Slaves to Soldiers: The 1st Rhode Island Regiment in the American Revolution* (Yardley, PA: Westholme, 2016).

11. Neville, "The Tragedy of Henry Laurens."

the slaves would only be freed at the successful conclusion of their military service, as attested to by their commanding officers.

The British were already freeing slaves in the territories they conquered, and were inducing them to join the redcoats. By war's end, some 20,000 would have done so. Could the American army do less than the British for and with America's slaves?

Washington agreed to have the John Laurens plan sent on to the Congress for approval and funding.

Both plans, that of Henry Laurens and that of John Laurens, came to naught.

The wealthy did not rush to participate in Henry Laurens' bond plan, for several reasons. First and foremost, many of the one-percenters were Loyalists, and had chosen to sit out the war; some were emerging from the woodwork just then in Philadelphia and fawning over Gen. William Howe and the British occupiers. Estimates of how many Loyalists there were in America range from twenty-five to forty percent; one solid figure shows that of 1,100 Loyalists who chose to abandon Boston with the British in the spring of 1776, 213 were merchants and their families—seventy percent of all the merchants in the Boston area.[12]

The more Revolutionary-minded of America's wealthy had a justifiable fear of an eventual American loss of the war, and with it, their fortunes. Then too, not all American merchants were profiting from the war: historian Thomas Doerflinger's study of the records of Philadelphia merchants found that there was no "general prosperity" among them, and "despite the rise of a few great fortunes, the capitals of many merchants shrank or stagnated."[13]

Even such proven patriots as Jeremiah Wadsworth of Hartford, an experienced commissary officer who would soon be appointed as chief of that service, were wary. He had already advanced $50,000 for the cause and had not been reimbursed, in Continental dollars or in any other currency, and so was not inclined to risk more. "The want of this money much retards my accounts," he wrote, "as it is in vain for me to call on People [to purchase new supplies for the Army] when I can't pay them."[14] A Wadsworth friend, an officer at Valley Forge, similarly advised that he had lost "two or three thousand pounds" advanced for

12. Lorenzo Sabine, *Biographical Sketches of Loyalists of the American Revolution* (Boston: C. C. Little and J. Brown, 1864), 12-13.
13. Thomas M. Doerflinger, *A Vigorous Spirit of Enterprise: Merchants and Economic Development in Revolutionary Philadelphia* (New York: W. W. Norton, 1987), 198.
14. Jeremiah Wadsworth to Thomas Mifflin, January 11, 1778, Wadsworth Papers box 4 file 1, Connecticut Historical Society.

the public interest, "and I think I have done my part that way."[15] Robert Morris, who a year earlier had sent Washington $50,000 of his own money to distribute to the troops after the daring Christmas crossing of the Delaware River,[16] had retired from Congress to pay more attention to his business, which was falling apart.

So Henry Laurens' idea fizzled out. The effort to sell it to the wealthy was soon overtaken by the news that France was to become the United States' ally, and the hope that King Louis XVI would grant loans to the United States of America to carry on the joint war against Great Britain.[17]

As fate would have it, Henry Laurens would later be captured at sea while sailing to Europe to negotiate more funding for the Revolution. He would spend the remainder of the war in the Tower of London.

As for John Laurens' idea of giving slaves their freedom in exchange for front-line military service, the Continental Congress had too many slave owners in it for that idea to pass in early 1778.

Until the arrival of funds from France, and even after it, America's armies were supplied largely by means of the personal credit of middle-rank commissaries and provisioners, who expressed their patriotism by putting their own money and credit at considerable risk. Many were never repaid.[18]

Two years later, in the spring of 1780, Charleston, South Carolina—John Laurens' home town—was being threatened by a British invasion, and John took this crisis as reason to convince Congress to do what it had refused to do in 1778, pass a resolution allowing the states of South Carolina and Georgia to enlist 3,000 slaves each in their army units, in exchange for promises of freedom at the end of their enlistment, and to authorize cash payments to those slaves' current owners at the rate of $1,000 for each new enlistee.

Savannah had already fallen and Charleston was on the brink. More manpower was needed to save Charleston. Nonetheless, South Carolina refused to go along with the enlisting-slaves plan. Weeks later, Charleston did fall; one of the reasons why was that there had not been enough American troops outside of the city to harry the British, who

15. Jedediah Huntington to Wadsworth, Janaury 18, 1777, ibid.
16. Robert Morris to Washington, January 1, 1777, alfounders.archives.gov/documents/Washington/03-07-02-0402.
17. Tom Shachtman, *How the French Saved America* (New York: Saint Martins Press, 2017).
18. E. Wayne Carp, *To Starve the Army at Pleasure: Continental Army Administration and American Political Culture, 1775-1783* (Chapel Hill: University of North Carolina Press, 1984); Erna Risch, *Supplying Washington's Army* (Washington, D.C.: United States Army Center of Military History, 1981).

were thus able to throw at Charleston their entire force, producing the surrender of 5,000 American and French defenders.

John Laurens was among them. Then, released on parole, John was sent to France by Congress to complete his jailed father's mission of obtaining new loans. In Paris, he and Franklin played good-cop, bad-cop with the Versailles government. As Franklin wrote to John Jay, "Mr. Lawrens is worrying the minister for more money and we shall I believe obtain a farther sum."[19] Franklin was so impressed with Laurens that he thought the young man would be an admirable successor to him as emissary in Paris. The amount granted to the U.S. through Laurens's efforts was double what Franklin had first been promised. That money underwrote the Washington campaign that in 1781 took his main army from the Hudson River to Yorktown alongside Rochambeau's.

John Laurens served with distinction at Yorktown, and continued with the southern army thereafter. In 1782, in a militarily insignificant battle with the British in South Carolina, he was killed.

His idea for mobilizing the wealth of the country by freeing some of its slaves for duty on the front lines never came to pass, and after his death it had an unfortunate codicil. When Henry Laurens was released from the Tower of London, in exchange for Gen. Charles, Earl Cornwallis, to take part in the Paris Peace talks, one of the treaty clauses under consideration dealt with the return of stolen, confiscated, and seized property. Although he was still in mourning for his idealistic son John, and although he continued to abhor slavery, his sense of the planters' economic interests guided his actions. Henry Laurens' sole contribution to the peace process was to insist that the list of property to be returned to Americans include improperly-freed slaves. The effect of this clause was to embed slavery into the fabric of the American economy for the next eighty years.

19. Benjamin Franklin to John Jay, April 12, 1781, founders.archives.gov/documents/Franklin/01-34-02-0417.

The Outlaw Cornelius Hatfield: Loyalist Partisan of the American Revolution

❦ ERIC WISER ❦

The war for all practical purposes was over when hostilities ended with a cease fire negotiated by the Americans, British, French, and Spanish in January 1783.[1] In New York, on June 19, British Brig. Gen. Samuel Birch wrote Commander-in-Chief Sir Guy Carleton that he had failed in his mission to locate and apprehend Capt. Cornelius Hatfield.[2] Carleton promised to comply with New Jersey Gov. William Livingston's request that an "immediate search to be made for Cornelius Hatfield, that effectual justice may be done."[3] Hatfield was usually seen around Gen. Cortlandt Skinner's headquarters on Staten Island, a place that served as an island fortress garrisoned by Loyalist battalions.[4] General Birch had "taken much pains to discover if Hatfield was in the garrison and the only information I have been able to obtain, is, that he embarked privately on a schooner, and sailed two or three days before the last fleet for Nova Scotia."[5]

The man being sought was the Loyalist partisan Cornelius Hatfield, an articulate and intelligent young man with boundless energy, and skill

1. Treaty of Paris, 1783, *U.S. Department of State Archive*, 2001-2009.state.gov/r/pa/ho/time/ar/14313.htm.

2. Samuel Birch to Sir Guy Carleton, June 23, 1783, Joanna McKinnon, *Cornelius HAT-FIELD, American Loyalist, Some of his story and an outline of his descendants* (Blurb.com, 2016), 72, www.blurb.com/ebooks/pc62960b2818cd883ae0b.

3. Guy Carleton to William Livingston, June 20, 1783, ibid., 71.

4. Certificate of Brig. Gen. Cortlandt Skinner, November 19, 1785. Treasury, Class 1, Volume 634, folios, 182-183, Great Britain, The National Archives (TNA).

5. Samuel Birch to Carleton, June 23, 1783, McKinnon, *Cornelius HATFIELD*, 72.

in violence. The only description of Hatfield's appearance that exists is from an unsourced nineteenth century history that says, "he was fine looking man, with dark hair, fair skin, and fine, ivory-like teeth," and that he received a "fine education. He was very active and strong."[6] A Loyalist who knew him said that "Hatfield was a very zealous Loyalist . . . but a loose, drinking sort of man and not of the coolest sense."[7] Hatfield's bravery was never in question, as demonstrated when he and about a dozen men under his leadership captured a twelve-gun sloop while under a hail of musket and artillery fire from a Rebel picket.[8] The captain's valor was buttressed with bitter resolve—a Patriot spy in New York witnessed Hatfield's promise to "hang every one of those committeeman and others that have sworn the King and Congress and then taken arms against the King."[9]

The highest levels of the American Revolutionary government grew to fear Cornelius Hatfield. When it was learned that Hatfield left New York in a small schooner to bring dispatches to Lord Cornwallis at Yorktown in September 1781, Continental Congress President Thomas McKean warned Delaware President Caesar Rodney that if "Cornelius Hatfield should be apprehended, I am to request that he may be securely confined and guarded."[10]

A native of Elizabethtown, New Jersey, Cornelius Hatfield was commissioned a captain of an independent company of Loyalists by Gen. Henry Clinton on February 19, 1779.[11] At the time of Hatfield's commission, New York was still the command center of British military operations in North America despite the conflict's shift to the Southern colonies and West Indies. Hatfield's career was most prolific in "an odd sort of battleground, on which vengeful partisans warred while their respectful armies remained essentially above the fray" according to historian Thomas Allen. Hatfield was considered a "Refugee" whom Allen defines as a displaced class of Tories that occasionally returned to their homelands as raiders.[12]

6. Richard Bayles, *History of Richmond County, (Staten Island) New York, From is Discovery to the Present* (New York: L.E. Preston & Co., 1887), 244.

7. E. Alfred Jones, *The Fighting Loyalists of New Jersey: Their Memorials, Petitions, and Claims, Etc. from English Records* (Westminster, MD: Heritage Books, 2008), 162.

8. Certificate of Brig. Gen. Cortlandt Skinner, T 1/V634.

9. William Maxwell to George Washington, April 27 1779, Founders Online, National Archives, *Papers of George Washington*.

10. Thomas McKean to Caesar Rodney, September 19, 1781, Letter Books of the President of Congress, 1775-1787, Roll 24, M247, 78-79.

11. Memorial of Cornelius Hatfield to the Lord Sidney, London, January 2, 1786. T 1/634 folio 180, TNA.

12. Thomas B. Allen, *Tories: Fighting for the King in America's First Civil War* (New York: Harper, 2010), 301, 309, 311.

The officers who employed Hatfield swore on their reputations that he was courageous and "zealous" in all his missions. Loyalist Gen. Cortlandt Skinner said of Hatfield, "I have a very high sense of his merit and services as a brave partisan . . .and steady Loyalist."[13] Hatfield was content if only afforded the opportunity to perform his duty as a loyal British subject. Lt. Gen. James Robertson declared that Hatfield "asked for no office, or solicited any reward."[14] Skinner said, "I have several times offered him money for his services but he always refused it, declaring he wished for nothing more that the restoration of government."[15] General Clinton endorsed his subordinates' opinions of Hatfield.[16]

Hatfield was from Elizabethtown, New Jersey, the strategically important "gateway to New Jersey and Philadelphia." The town was fortified and garrisoned by the Patriots early in the war. Staten Island, occupied by British forces in the summer of 1776, was only several hundred feet across the Arthur Kill from Elizabethtown's main landing.[17] That December, Hatfield started providing the Loyalists on Staten Island with information during the British invasion of Northern New Jersey.[18]

Staten Island remained under armed-Loyalist occupation after Northern New Jersey was vacated by the British Army. General Skinner, the island's preeminent Loyalist-Commander and last Royal Attorney-General of New Jersey, received intelligence from Hatfield in interviews and written correspondence during 1777. The messaging became more sophisticated as Hatfield and Skinner worked out a signal system. Skinner said that Hatfield provided him with "the movements of the Rebel Army in the Jerseys and settled signals with me to be made from his Father's house, in sight of Staten Island that I might know of the arrival of Troops in Elizabeth Town, their movements towards Sandy Hook, or attempts on Staten Island."[19] Hatfield had his own parcel but also farmed the land of his father Cornelius Hatfield, Sr. which was in close proximity to the shore at Halstead's Point.[20]

13. Certificate of Brig. Gen. Cortlandt Skinner, T 1/V634.
14. Certificate of Lt. Gen. James Robertson, London, November 25 1785. T 1/634 folio 183, TNA.
15. Certificate of Brig. Gen. Cortlandt Skinner, T 1/V634.
16. Certificate of Lt. Gen. James Robertson, T 1/V634.
17. Ernest L. Meyer, *Map of Elizabeth Town, N.J. at the Time of the Revolutionary War, 1775-1783: Showing That Part of the Free Borough and Town of Elizabeth, Which is now the site of the City of Elizabeth* (New York: J. Schedler, 1879).
18. Memorial of Cornelius Hatfield to the Lord Sidney, T 1/634.
19. Certificate of Brig. Gen. Cortlandt Skinner, T 1/V634.
20. Meyer, *Map of Elizabethtown*.

The Patriots of Elizabethtown started to suspect that Cornelius Hatfield was assisting the British.[21] The tipping point for the Patriots came when Hatfield journeyed south to Middletown (present-day Mattawan) and "was apprehended under suspicion that he was going to the enemy with a vessel he was loading at Middle Town." Hatfield was arrested while loading a boat with substantial quantities of provisions including Iron. Patriots concurrently intercepted a letter directing a "C.H." to liaise with a "J.H." of an armed escort ship off Sandy Hook for the purposes of transporting the cargo to Virginia.[22]

Gen. William Maxwell, the military authority in Elizabethtown during the winter of 1778-1779, was instructed by Gen. George Washington that "the principal object of your position is to prevent the Enemy stationed upon Staten Island from making incursions upon the main and also to prevent any traffic between them and the inhabitants."[23] Maxwell was determined to fulfill his mission and therefore placed Hatfield in the Elizabethtown provost.

A writ of habeas corpus dated December 17, 1778 from the New Jersey Supreme Court had been obtained by advocates for Hatfield, but was refused on several occasions by Maxwell.[24] An effort to turn Cornelius Hatfield over to the civilian authorities was persistent and most likely driven by Hatfield's father Cornelius, Sr., a very well respected, wealthy, and influential gentleman.[25] Elizabethtown during the Revolution was populated with 1,200 people mostly descended from the original town "Associates" who had carved-out the first English-speaking settlement of New Jersey.[26] A late eighteenth century map of the town and environs reveals a quilt of properties owned by descendants of the Associates.[27] Decades of the cementing influences of intermarriage bound the community together. The timing of the cargo shipment and the "C.H." letter implicating Hatfield were considered by his advocates to be "circumstantial."

The relationship between civilian and military authorities in Elizabethtown deteriorated when Maxwell refused several attempts to

21. Certificate of Brig. Gen. Cortlandt Skinner, T 1/V634.
22. Abraham Clark to John Jay, December 21, 1778, *Papers of the Continental Congress*, Letters Addressed to Congress 1775-1789, Roll 93, M247, p. 287-289 (POTCC).
23. Washington to Maxwell, December 21, 1778, *Founders Online*, National Archives, *Papers of George Washington*.
24. The Writ of Habeas Corpus, December 17, 1778, McKinnon. *Cornelius HATFIELD*, 26; Clark to Jay, December 21, 1778.
25. Abraham Hatfield, *Descendants of Matthias Hatfield* (New York: New York Genealogical and Bibliographical Society, 1954), 21.
26. Jean Rae Turner and Robert T. Koles, Elizabeth: The First Capital of New Jersey (Charleston: Arcadia Publishing, 2003), 7.
27. Meyer, Map of Elizabethtown.

honor Hatfield's writ of habeas corpus. The general hurled "several undeserved insults" at one advocate serving the writ, while another received "reproachful language" and was grabbed by "his neck or hair and shoved" out of his quarters.[28] Abraham Clark, a native of Elizabethtown and signer of the Declaration of Independence, argued to the Continental Congress that the "young man expectant of a large fortune in this place" deserved a civilian trial. True to his convictions as an ardent 'Whig' mistrustful of military authority, Clark requested a reprimand of Maxwell.[29]

Clark and the civilian authorities won the argument over ownership of Hatfield's justice, and General Washington subsequently ordered Hatfield be released. But it was too late.[30] On January 9, 1779, Governor Livingston informed Washington that Cornelius Hatfield had escaped. Livingston expressed good riddance and tried to provide a silver lining: "While the Magistrates had the charges against Hetfield under consideration, he made his escape from the guard; and unless his treason (of which I have no doubt) could be more clearly proved than I imagine it would have been upon his trial, it is perhaps best for the public, that he has been thus driven to take sanctuary with the enemy where I believe he can do us less mischief."[31] General Skinner was on Staten Island waiting with open arms and said that as soon as Hatfield escaped "he joined me and immediately commenced an active partisan."[32]

Hatfield's first large scale raid serving as a guide for the British occurred a few weeks after he received his commission in January 1779. With 1,000 British troops he landed a short distance northeast of Elizabethtown at DeHart's Point.[33] General Clinton ordered the raid because "I was tempted by the uncommon mildness of the season to beat up the enemy's quarters" and "surprise one of their brigades that

28. Deposition of William Barnot, December 21, 1778, POTCC, Letters Addressed to Congress 1775-1789, Roll 93, M247, V5, 291-292. 297-298; Deposition of Garret Rapalje, Elizabethtown, December 21, 1778, POTCC, Letters Addressed to Congress 1775-1789, Roll 93, M247, V5, 293.
29. Clark to Jay, Dec 21, 1778; Bogin, Ruth, *Abraham Clark and the Quest for Equality in the Revolutionary Era*, (East Brunswick, NJ: Associated University Presses, 1982), 29-31.
30. Washington to Maxwell, December 20, 1778, *Founders Online*, National Archives, *Papers of George Washington*.
31. Livingston to Washington, January 9, 1779, *Founders Online*, National Archives, *Papers of George Washington*.
32. Certificate of Brig. Gen. Cortlandt Skinner, T 1/V634.
33. Extract of a Letter from an officer at Elizabeth-Town, dated March 1, 1779, *The New Jersey Gazette*, in William Nelson ed., *Archives of the State of New Jersey* Second Series, vol. 3 (Trenton, NJ: John L. Murphy Publishing Co., 1906), 106-109 (ASNJ).

lay at Elizabeth Town."[34] Between 2 and 3am the alarm sounded, and the "Whig"-leaning townsfolk hid on the far western outskirts of town. Some of the British troops split from the main group and headed toward Governor Livingston's home a mile west of town, but the governor was away on business and his family had received warning and fled.

When it was all over, three plumes of smoke billowed into the night sky marking the locations of a flaming blacksmith shop, soldier's barracks, and academy. Maxwell's militia did not respond until the British were marching eastward to their waiting craft which were accompanied by a handful of gunboats lobbing ordinance at the pursuing militia.[35] General Clinton denied that the purpose of the raid was the capture Livingston in a reply to a letter sent by the governor complaining of what he deemed "dark proceedings."[36]

The summer after Hatfield's commission in 1779 started off on a high note for the partisan captain. On an evening in June, Hatfield with five of his men crossed over to Elizabethtown and proceeded to the residence of Lt. John Haviland of the Essex County militia. Haviland was captured in the dead of night, transported to New York, and imprisoned on Long Island.[37] The Loyalist newspapers reported these types of captures with jollity. *The New York Gazette* commented on a different headhunting raid: "Yesterday Capt. Cornelius Hatfield, with adroitness peculiar to himself, after an incursion upon the Jonathans in Jersey, brought off a lieutenant and 5 or 6 others, of which we shall give more particulars, when our sprightly partisan arrives in town, and makes his report."[38]

Hatfield claimed two years after the war that he "captured nearly three hundred officers of rank and soldiers, the chief part of which were at different times exchanged for British of the same rank."[39] The capture of Col. Matthias Ogden and Capt. Jonathan Dayton in November 1780 was his most significant haul. Hatfield learned from one his contacts in Elizabethtown that Ogden and Dayton were staying the evening in Connecticut Farms, about four miles away. This was too

34. Maxwell to Washington, Feb 27, 1779, FN 5, *Founders Online*, National Archives, *Papers of George Washington*.
35. ASNJ S2 V3: 106-109.
36. Maxwell to Washington, Feb 27, 1779.
37. *The New York Gazette: and the Weekly Mercury*, June 14, 1779, ASNJ S2 V3: 441.; Lt. John Haviland, New Jersey. Complied Service Records of Soldiers Who Served in the American Army During the Revolutionary War 1775-1785, M881, Roll 0645, National Archives and Records Administration (NARA).
38. *The New York Gazette: and the Weekly Mercury*, November 27, 1780, ASNJ S2 V5: 127.
39. Memorial of Cornelius Hatfield to the Lord Sidney, T 1/634.

great an opportunity to pass up—both Ogden and Dayton were high-ranking officers and influential citizens of Elizabethtown. Hatfield was related to Ogden through the Colonel's mother Phebe Hatfield (an example of the American Revolution's many localized inter-family political differences). "With only two or three of his party, he made a circuit of many miles and brought off a rebel Colonel and Captain."[40] The Refugees found the officers in Connecticut Farms "horizontal, Cheek by Jowl" as a Loyalist newspaper gloated.[41]

No fish was too big for Hatfield to attempt to catch, not even the enemy's commander-in-chief. General Skinner testified that Hatfield conceived a plan to capture General Washington who was staying at a mansion away from the main Continental Army encampment at Morristown, and the British army staged a major expedition to effect his plan. Skinner wrote that the "troops marched to make the attempt but were prevented by a severe fall of snow, otherwise in all probability he would have succeeded."[42]

General Skinner said of Hatfield's value to the Staten Island Loyalist-headquarters: "he was well acquainted with the creeks and inlets into New Jersey and kept a good correspondence with his friends" and "always procured of the enemy's strength and situation, and almost every day informed me of the placing of their sentinels and by that means he has often gone at my request into Elizabeth Town and brought off particular people."[43] Hatfield had miles of tall marsh-grassed coastline to conceal his landings. Elizabethtown had three major landing points on the coast facing Staten Island: DeHart's Point to the North; Elizabethtown Point in the Center (one mile from town, the main road ran there to the west); and the Refugee's favorite Halstead's Point to the south, that was the entrance to a river and creeks snaking through salt meadows into the interior.[44]

Hatfield and his partisans using the cover of darkness attacked small Rebel patrols on the roads, and sentinels at the landings and homes of the inhabitants. Tory sympathizers provided Hatfield with intelligence and their homes served as sanctuaries. The sense of surveillance was so apparent to the locals that one of Hatfield's neighbors cautioned a Continental soldier guarding Halstead's Point, "they know your situation

40. Certificate of Brig. Gen. Cortlandt Skinner, T 1/634; Edwin F. Hatfield, *History of Elizabeth, New Jersey; including The Early History of Union County* (New York: Carlton and Lanahan, 1868), 325.
41. *The Royal Gazette*, November 8, 1780, ASNJ S2 V5: 104-106.
42. Certificate of Brig. Gen. Cortland Skinner, T 1/634.
43. Ibid.
44. Meyer, *Map of Elizabethtown.*

better than you do yourselves." The Continental remembered that "with all the vigilance we could exercise, we could hardly escape being surprised and cut-off by the enemy. They exerted themselves more than common to take some of our guards, because we had challenged them to do it."[45] A New Jersey militiaman recalled "skirmishes with small parties of the enemy . . . were very frequent, and occasionally men were killed on both sides. Cornelius Hatfield, a noted Tory and Refugee, gave us much trouble by taking off our sentries at night, and often killed our scouts, by intercepting them, knowing the ground."[46]

In accordance with Gen. Guy Carleton's promise to Governor Livingston in 1783, Hatfield was finally tracked down and incarcerated in New York's Provost on August 15.[47] Hatfield's arrest had nothing to do with his escape from rebel captivity or the raids he led. Back in June, Livingston wrote Carleton requesting "Hatfield to be apprehended and secured" in order to be brought into New Jersey to be tried for petty robbery.[48]

An affidavit including sworn testimony of the victim of Hatfield's alleged crime landed on Carleton's desk. An elderly Elizabethtown man named Joseph DeHart, testified to an Essex County judge that Cornelius Hatfield and a group came into his home on the evening May 6, 1783, "seized the Deponent, one of who presented a Pistol at his Breast and ordered him to deliver up all he had in Money and swore by his maker that if he did not deliver up all his Silver and Gold, he would blow him through." According to DeHart's testimony, his wife Elizabeth retrieved a pocketbook, but the contents were considered wholly immaterial to the intruders and they tossed it aside. One of the intruders told DeHart "they knew he was to have received of his Uncle Samuel, Twenty Pounds the day before, and said they were come for it, and ordered him to deliver it up." DeHart claimed ignorance of the money's existence and was unable to produce it, at which point the intruders left his home.[49]

On August 24, 1783, nine days into his imprisonment in New York, Hatfield wrote a letter to General Carleton presenting his version of the events that had taken place at Joseph DeHart's home:

45. Joseph Plumb Martin, *Private Yankee Doodle: Being a Narrative of Some of the Adventures, Dangers and Sufferings of a Revolutionary War Soldier*, ed. George F. Scheer (Eastern Acorn Press, 1998), 176, 178.

46. Pension Affidavit of Morris Aber, State of New Jersey, Morris County July 31, 1832. Revolutionary War Pension and Bounty-Land Warrant Application Files, M804, Roll 0005, Pension File S.2525, NARA.

47. *The Royal Gazette*, September 3, 1783, McKinnon, *Cornelius HATFIELD*, 68.

48. Livingston to Carleton, June 12, 1783, McKinnon, *Cornelius HATFIELD*, 70.

49. Affidavit of Joseph DeHart, June 5, 1783, ibid., 69.

My former residence, and that of my Friends is near the Complainant at Elizabeth town, and on the Night he charges me to have been at his House . . . I was in the country on a visit to see these Friends and on my return Home hearing a Noise at the House of the Complainant, I went to it from the Road and found that some Persons had been there and endeavored to frighten the Complainant who is a poor weak illiterate Man, easily imposed on. On my entering the House I made myself known the Complainant and advised him to go to Bed, and make himself easy as no Injury was intended him . . . He accordingly went to his Bed, and appeared happy that I interfered for his Relief. This is simply all the circumstances I am acquainted with relative to this Transaction.

Hatfield reasoned in his defense that it took a full month for the incident to be reported and escalated. The length of time allowed DeHart to be "urged to it by Persons who are inimical to me for my uniform opposition to Congressional Measure." Hatfield called Joseph DeHart "of all men the most ignorant and does not understand the simplest English Term," making him ripe for manipulation. He argued that it was not logical that Hatfield did not conceal his identity from DeHart, and he believed he was entitled to have DeHart testify in person. The letter to Carleton included an impassioned assessment of his own character:

During the whole progress of the late War I have been an active and zealous assertor of the King's Cause and as such, been frequently employed in the most important enterprises . . . My character as a man of probity and no plunderer much less a robber is too firmly established.[50]

Hatfield's detractors in Elizabethtown could refute him by pulling court records related to an incident in June 1778. Hatfield was indicted by the New Jersey Supreme Court for trespassing, assault, and theft of a sword in Elizabethtown. Also, though on the record long after the trial, a Newark man spying for the British named Zopher Lyon claimed Hatfield robbed him of goods in 1780. Hatfield and his cousin John Smith Hatfield, were hired by Lyon to pilot a large craft to New York to purchase "wares & merchandise." Later, when Lyon and another man were moving the procured goods in a small boat along the Bergen Shore, they were boarded by "three men in disguise having their faces covered in black handkerchiefs." One of the men put a pistol to Lyon's chest and demanded the cargo. Lyon "verily believes the voice to have been the aforesaid Cornelius Hatfield." Cornelius Hatfield's masked

50. The Answer of Cornelius Hatfield, August 24, 1783, *Cornelius HATFIELD*, McKinnon, 78.

robbery of Lyon was corroborated in 1786 by Newark Loyalist-soldier Isaac Ogden.[51]

In addition to his own personal plea Hatfield had witnesses, mostly from his own family and relatives, provide sworn statements for his defense. The Revolutionary War participants of the Hatfields in Elizabethtown were the fourth and fifth generation grandchildren of Elizabethtown settlers Matthias and Maria Hatfield.[52] Joseph Plumb Martin said of the family: "There was a large number in this place and its vicinity by the name of Hetfield who were notorious rascals."[53] When General Washington was asked permission that a Hatfield be allowed to come through the lines to visit his brother in Elizabethtown, the commander-in-chief replied: "From the information I have had of the character of this family of people—I am by no means satisfied that they would answer any valuable purposes if they were employed—and therefore I wish it to be declined."[54]

A trio of Loyalist brothers, Abraham, Jacob, and James Hatfield, settled in Canada when the war ended.[55] There were the Tory brothers Job and John Smith Hatfield, the latter at Cornelius' side more than any of his other cousins.[56] Cousin Abel Hatfield was suspected by members of the Rebel intelligence apparatus as being a part of the "perfidious treachery of that family" in the form of manipulating Patriot military officers with misinformation provided by General Skinner.[57]

The Hatfields also sent soldiers into the field for the cause of American Independence who fought with fervor and earned distinction. However, one of them was suspected of straddling both sides of the fence: Moses Hatfield—a major in the New York Militia who as a commissary for the army, was investigated for mismanagement and graft.[58] Treasonous suppositions from the highest levels including General Washington strengthened when Moses was arrested for going into the British lines without a pass.[59]

51. Ibid., 20, 119-120; Evidence on the foregoing Memorial of Isaac Ogden, March 27, 1786. American Loyalist Claims Series I, Class AO13, Piece 14, TNA.
52. Hatfield, *Descendants of Matthias Hatfield*, 43, 76.
53. Martin, *Private Yankee Doodle*, 180.
54. Washington to Samuel Holden Parsons, December 23, 1779, *Founders Online*, National Archives, *Papers of George Washington*.
55. Hatfield, *Descendants of Matthias Hatfield*, 90-98.
56. Ibid., 76-84.
57. John Vanderhovan to Washington, November 6, 1780, Founders Online, National Archives, *Papers of George Washington*.
58. Board of War to Washington, January 5, 1780, Founders Online, National Archives, *Papers of George Washington*.
59. William Burnet, Sr. to Washington, April 12, 1782, *Founders Online*, National Archives, *Papers of George Washington*.

Cornelius Hatfield was born around 1755, the middle-son of Cornelius Hatfield Senior and Abigail Price.[60] Cornelius' older brother Abner was recommended for a quartermaster's position in December 1775 but there is scant evidence that this went through.[61] His younger brother Caleb appears to have not been actively involved in the war. Cornelius had twin sisters named Abigail and Joanna, the latter married to Patriot light horse captain John Blanchard.[62]

Appearing on Cornelius Hatfield's behalf in 1783 were his sister Abigail, his cousins James, Job, John Smith Hatfield, and an unrelated partisan named Abraham Jones. All five simply reinforced Hatfield's version of events—all were with him that night with the exception of Abigail who testified to overhearing DeHart's wife Elizabeth state that her brother visited the couple's home that evening but that Cornelius was courteous and that legal authorities of Essex County were exaggerating events.[63] Separately, a lawyer named George Ross certified that "I have never heard or do I believe that Cornelius Hatfield junior ever made the practice of entering houses of people with a design to plunder, on the contrary . . . he has protected houses of individuals from robbery and plunder, several instances of which I was a witness."[64] Cornelius Hatfield's combined defense to General Carleton rested on the idea that Joseph DeHart was not intellectually sound and had been manipulated by leading Patriots. Hatfield's exoneration, as he most likely saw it, rested on whether he would be brought to a civil trial in New Jersey or a court martial in New York.

Two events involving Cornelius Hatfield guaranteed that he would never receive a fair trial in New Jersey. In January 1780, Hatfield guided an expedition in-force over the iced-over Arthur Kill from Staten Island.[65] Lt. Col. Abraham Van Buskirk's force consisted of 120 Royal Provincials supplemented by twelve dragoons and Hatfield's partisans. The Loyalists crossed the ice at night and split into two divisions before entering Elizabethtown. What General Washington called "the late misfortune and disgrace at Elizabethtown" unfolded in the last few hours before midnight.

60. Will of Cornelius Hatfield, Jr., Prerogative Court of Canterbury and Related Probate Jurisdictions: Will Registers; Class: Prob 11, Piece: 1674, TNA.

61. Lord Stirling to the President of Congress, December 3, 1775, *American Archives: Consisting of a Collection Authentick Records, State Papers, Debates, and Letters, and Other Notices of Publick Affairs* (Washington: Peter Force M. St. Clair Clarke, 1843), 4: 165.

62. *Descendants of Matthias Hatfield*, 23, 48-50.

63. Affidavit of Abigail Vergereau, August 30, 1783, *Cornelius HATFIELD*, McKinnon, 82.

64. Ibid., Affidavit of George Ross, August 24, 1783.

65. *The Royal Gazette*, February 9, 1780, ASNJ S2 V4: 178-179.

Van Buskirk's raid achieved total surprise. [66] Before the raid, Captain Hatfield learned the positions of the Continentals and militia and formulated the plan of attack. General Skinner said "he pointed out to me the manner in which the Maryland Troops under Major Eccles, posted at Elizabeth Town could be surprised . . . Mr. Hatfield conducted with so much secrecy the post was completely surprised, the Major and all his officers made prisoner with about 80 of his troops and 40 militia without the loss of one life or even a shot being fired."[67] The beautiful Presbyterian church "ornamented by a steeple" and the structure where "their pilgrim fathers had worshipped God" was put to the torch by Van Buskirk's men. Cornelius Hatfield's father was a member of the board of trustees of the church—and the land for which the church was built, a donation to the village by Hatfield's great-grandfather Matthias.[68]

Cornelius Hatfield and his cousins were also mutually involved in a brutal incident that stirred passions in New Jersey long after the war. A Rahway man named Stephen Ball, a "London Trader," was committing illicit commerce with the British when he brought his goods to Staten Island in February 1781. Refugees including the Hatfields seized Ball, brought him to Bergen Point and hung him. Sources primarily attribute the murder to John Smith Hatfield, though all the partisan Hatfields were placed there. The hanging was in retaliation for the execution of a Refugee by the Patriots. General Skinner refused to endorse the hanging.[69]

Fortunately for Hatfield, Carleton rebuffed Livingston and ordered a court martial in New York. Joseph DeHart was invited to testify under protection but failed to appear. British Lt. Col. James Gordon, president of the court, summarized the decision: "The Court having considered the charge brought against the prisoner in Cornelius Hatfield together with the several exhibits produced before them, no Viva Voce [oral] evidence, for or against him having appeared, is of the opinion that he is not guilty . . . that the prosecution is not only groundless but insidious and malicious in the utmost extreme."[70]

During the war, Hatfield and his cousins had been divested of their property via formal inquisition and seizure by Essex County "for joining the army of the king of Great Britain, and other treasonable prac-

66. W. Woodford Clayton, *History of Union and Middlesex County, New Jersey* (Philadelphia: Everts and Peck, 1882), 85-86.
67. Certificate of Brig. Gen. Cortlandt Skinner, T 1/634.
68. Hatfield, *History of Elizabeth*, 77-78, 482.
69. Hartford Courant, March 6, 1781, www.newspapers.com/image/233716974.
70. McKinnon, *Cornelius HATFIELD*, 89.

tices."[71] Following the Treaty of Paris, the Hatfield Loyalists along with thousands of Americans headed north to New Brunswick, Canada to start a new life. On November 21, 1784, Cornelius Hatfield experienced the only thing resembling a victory celebration. The former Partisan had the honor of piloting the sloop *Ranger* bringing the first lieutenant governor of New Brunswick across St. John's Bay to his new province. The celebration of Gov. Thomas Carleton's arrival "received an enthusiastic welcome from the Loyalists. A salute of seventeen guns was fired from the Lower Cove battery as the Ranger entered the harbor, and as he landed a similar salute was thundered from Fort Howe. A great concourse of the inhabitants received him with shouts of welcome. The crowd gave him three cheers, and cries of '"Long live our King and Governor.'"[72]

Unlike his cousins, Cornelius Hatfield chose the imperial capital as his new home, arriving in London in 1785. He immediately applied for relief from the Loyalist Claims Commission. Hatfield was living on the outskirts of London near the Marylebone Tollgate when he was granted a backdated temporary pension "for his uniform Loyalty and spirited exertions in favor of Government during the American War," and was subsequently granted a military pension. The colonial immigrant carved out a life in metropolitan London, and at forty years of age married forty-two-year-old Briton Joan Hinkley in December 1797 at the Old Church, St. Pancras, London. Curiously, the couple had three children by the time they married, and two more born "legitimately."[73]

Cornelius Hatfield never gave up on his inheritance in his father's will and his own son Sidney was named heir to the farm in Elizabethtown. Hatfield's father Cornelius, Sr. passed away in 1795 and Hatfield made the first of two trips to the United States in 1796.[74] His journey in 1807 resulted in a media sensation when the headline "A Tory caught" appeared in print throughout the United States.[75] Hatfield, who was called "an obnoxious refugee character" by *The Vermont Journal*, was in Newark when he was recognized and arrested for the hanging of the "London Trader" Stephen Ball. Hatfield had a team of three

71. ASNJ S2 V3: 384; ASNJ S2 V3: 508.

72. D.R Jack, *History of the City and County of St. John* (St. John, NB: J&A McMillan, 1883), 70-71.

73. McKinnon, *Cornelius HATFIELD*, 109; Joanna McKinnon, "Cornelius Hatfield, Jr., Loyalist, of Elizabeth Town and London, and Some of His Descendants," *The Genealogical Magazine of New Jersey* vol. 91 no. 3 (2016), 142, 144, 147-151.

74. McKinnon, *Cornelius HATFIELD*, 119.

75. *Lancaster Intelligencer*, October 20, 1807, www.newspapers.com/image/556417383.

lawyers for his defense including cousin Aaron Ogden—the younger brother of his cousin Col. Matthias Ogden whom he captured at Connecticut Farms.[76] Hatfield was lucky the charges were dropped because the terms of the Treaty of Paris stipulated that British or American citizens could not be tried for actions committed during the war.[77]

During this 1807 visit, Essex County deed books show that "Captain Cornelius Hatfield of Great Britain (but at present in America)" sold fifteen and half acres of land to Caleb Halstead. Hatfield retained rights to a substantial portion of his father's land as evidenced in 1829, when his son and heir Sidney, sold the "farm formerly belonging formerly belonging to Cornelius Hetfield." Sidney Hatfield, a painter, moved to the United States after Cornelius' death in 1823. The son and heir of one of the most zealous Loyalist-Refugees of the Revolutionary War lived in New York for a time, then moved to Augusta, Georgia where he died in 1840.

Cornelius's wife Joan passed away in March 1818 and was buried in St. James, Piccadilly.[78] His will, written on February 24, 1823, began, "I Cornelius Hatfield late of the borough of Elizabeth Town State of New Jersey America but now residing at No. 4 Great George Street Hempstead Road Parish of St. Pancras County of Middlesex Great Britain being sound in mind to make this my last Will & Testament."[79] Capt. Cornelius Hatfield, Jr. passed away at sixty-eight years of age on August 13, 1823. He was buried four days later in the same cemetery as his wife in St. James, Piccadilly.[80]

76. *The Vermont Journal*, October 26, 1807, www.newspapers.com/image/489003666.
77. *Virginia Argus*, October 30, 1807, www.newspapers.com/image/605064605.
78. McKinnon, *Cornelius HATFIELD*, 122-123, 135.
79. Will of Cornelius Hatfield, Jr., C: P11, P: 1674, TNA
80. McKinnon, *Cornelius HATFIELD*, 123.

General Isaac Gregory's Fictitious Treason

❦ MICHAEL CECERE ❦

Col. Josiah Parker of Virginia was at a loss at what to do. He had just arrived outside the British outpost at Great Bridge in early March 1781 with 300 Virginia militia hoping to take the enemy garrison of 120 men, but upon an inspection of the works he determined that an assault would be "too dangerous, and would be attended with no views of success."[1] His disappointment at this realization was not what troubled Colonel Parker, however. While he inspected the enemy works, he had noticed a gun-boat making its way downriver from the fort and ordered a party of his militia to attack it. They successfully did so, sinking the craft and capturing its occupants and most of their baggage.[2] Although he was not aboard the gunboat, Capt. Francis Stevenson of the Queen's Rangers had sent his baggage, including a number of letters, with the vessel. It was the contents of two of these letters that alarmed Colonel Parker.

> G.G.
> Your well-formed plan of delivering those people now under your command into the hands of the British General at Portsmouth gives me much pleasure. Your next [letter] I hope will mention the place of ambuscade, and the manner you wish to fall into my hands.
> General Gregory,
> A Mr. Ventress was last night made prisoner by three or four of your people. I only wish to inform you that Ventress could not help doing

---

1. Henry A. Muhlenberg, "Colonel Parker to General Muhlenberg, 2 March, 1781," *The Life of Major-General Peter Muhlenberg* (Philadelphia: Cary and Hart, 1849), 394.
2. Ibid.

what he did in his helping to destroy the logs. I myself delivered the orders to him from Colonel Simcoe.

I have the honour of your acqua—[the letter ended abruptly].[3]

Just months after the shocking treason of Gen. Benedict Arnold in New York, it appeared to Colonel Parker that yet another American officer, Gen. Isaac Gregory of North Carolina, was plotting to join the enemy. Prior to the discovery of the letters there had been no hint of treason from General Gregory, in fact, quite the contrary. An experienced militia officer from North Carolina, Gregory fought bravely at the Battle of Camden while most of the militia around him fled. Pinned under his horse, Gregory suffered two life-threatening bayonet wounds at the hands of Gen. Charles Cornwallis's troops. Convinced that his wounds were mortal, Gregory was paroled by the British and allowed to return home to northeastern North Carolina where he surprisingly recovered and returned to the field in November 1780.[4]

General Gregory had only recently arrived outside Great Bridge in early March 1781 to reinforce Gen. Peter Muhlenberg's Virginia militia in southeastern Virginia and was in fact, with Colonel Parker when Parker read the incriminating letters.[5]

General Gregory forcefully declared his innocence, denying a correspondence with Captain Stevenson or any enemy officer, but Colonel Parker was rattled by what he read and confessed to his superior, General Muhlenberg, that the contents of the letters, "embarrassed me amazingly, the more so as General Gregory had furnished the guards for the night."[6] Parker expressed his hope to Muhlenberg of General Gregory's innocence, but felt compelled to quietly post his own guard detachments to guard General Gregory's guards.[7]

Gen. Peter Muhlenberg, who was in Suffolk and commanded all of the troops in southeast Virginia, was also disturbed by the contents of the letters and wrote to his superior in Richmond, Gen. Frederick von Steuben, that, "I really do not know what to think of General Gregory; appearances are much against him."[8]

---

3. Muhlenberg, "Colonel Parker to General Muhlenberg, 2 March, 1781," *The Life of Major-General Peter Muhlenberg*, 394.
4. William S. Powell, ed., *Dictionary of North Carolina Biography*, Vol. 2 (University of North Carolina Press, 2000), 367.
5. Muhlenberg, "Colonel Parker to General Muhlenberg, 2 March, 1781," *The Life of Major-General Peter Muhlenberg*, 394.
6. Ibid.
7. Ibid.
8. Muhlenberg, "General Muhlenberg to General Steuben, 10 a.m., March 4, 1781," *The Life of Major-General Peter Muhlenberg*, 395.

Just five hours later, upon the return of Colonel Parker to Suffolk, General Muhlenberg was more resolved on the matter and wrote again to Steuben, declaring that, "From [Colonel Parker's] report, as well as from other circumstances, I am fully convinced that some treasonable practices have been carried on by General Gregory."[9] Muhlenberg added that, "the officers and men with General Gregory are so much dissatisfied that I was afraid the whole would disperse unless Gregory was removed."[10] Even General Gregory recognized the angst the letters had caused among the Virginia and North Carolina troops at Great Bridge and pressed Colonel Parker to assume command until the matter could be cleared up, but Parker had orders to return to Suffolk, so one of Gregory's subordinates likely took command.[11]

General Muhlenberg wanted Col. Richard Meade, an experienced continental officer who had been ordered by General Steuben to join the troops at Great Bridge, to take command of General Gregory's troops, some 700 strong, but Meade deferred to Colonel Parker and both marched for Great Bridge with additional troops on March 9.[12] What transpired in General Gregory's camp in the five days prior to Parker's return is uncertain. It appears that General Muhlenberg's wishes that, "Gregory must give up his command until the matter is cleared up," were implemented and that he was placed under arrest pending a court martial.[13]

In the British camp, Capt. Francis Stevenson, the author of the letters, and his fellow officers initially found amusing the turmoil they assumed the letters had caused in the American camp.[14] However, upon learning that General Gregory had been placed under arrest, 'Capt. Stevenson's humanity was alarmed," and he asked his commander, Lt. Col. John Simcoe, to intervene.[15] Simcoe wrote to Colonel Parker explaining that the captured correspondence between Stevenson and Gregory was fictitious, composed by Captain Stevenson by way of

9. Muhlenberg, "General Muhlenberg to General Steuben, 3 p.m., March 4, 1781," ibid., 396-397.

10. Ibid.

11. Ibid.

12. Muhlenberg, "General Muhlenberg to General Steuben, March 11, 1781," *The Life of Major-General Peter Muhlenberg*, 398-399.

12. Muhlenberg, "General Muhlenberg to General Steuben, 3 p.m., March 4, 1781," ibid., 396-397.

13. John Graves Simcoe, *Simcoe's Military Journal: A History of the Operations of a Partisan Corps, The Queen's Rangers*, (New York: Bartlett & Welford, 1844), 171.

14. Ibid.

15. Simcoe, *Simcoe's Military Journal*, 288 and 171.

amusement and boredom.[16] Simcoe added with a bit of sarcasm that, "Upon the sacred honour of a soldier and a gentleman, that I have no reason to believe or suspect that Mr. Gregory is otherwise than a firm adherent of the French King, and of Congress."[17]

Simcoe's letter eventually reached General Muhlenberg, who admitted to General Steuben on March 11 that he was now unsure of Gregory's guilt. "I confess myself at a loss to judge," wrote Muhlenberg, "He may be innocent, and I hope he may prove himself so."[18]

With no further evidence against General Gregory and Lieutenant Colonel Simcoe's letter of assurance that the entire affair had been in jest, the question of General Gregory's patriotism was resolved in his favor. Events soon drew everyone's attention back to Portsmouth, where General Muhlenberg hoped to strike with the assistance of reinforcements under General LaFayette. Although General Gregory was deeply resentful at the doubt expressed of his patriotism, it did not seem to adversely impact his reputation in North Carolina, for upon his return to the Tar Heel state he served in the state legislature until 1795.[19]

16. Simcoe, *Simcoe's Military Journal*, 288.
17. Ibid.
18. Muhlenberg, "General Muhlenberg to General Steuben, March 11, 1781," *The Life of Major-General Peter Muhlenberg*, 398-399.
19. Powell, ed., *Dictionary of North Carolina Biography*, Vol. 2, 367.

Stony Point: The Second Occupation, July–October 1779

💢 MICHAEL J. F. SHEEHAN 💢

George Washington, commander-in-chief of the Continental Army, arrived at the American defenses at West Point "very much fatigued."[1] He had ridden one his two beloved mounts, either Nelson or Blueskin, nearly fourteen miles over rugged hills. It was late afternoon on July 19, 1779, and Washington was just getting settled after "returning from Stony Point," as he informed Gen. (and Governor of New York) George Clinton. The previous day, the Americans had "dismantled the works at Stony Point . . . and last night destroyed them as far as circumstances would permit;" days earlier, the Continental Army had taken possession of Stony Point, a rocky peninsula jutting out from the west shore of the Hudson River. The British had landed there and directly across the river at Verplanck Point on June 1 and fortified both points. After nearly three weeks of deliberation and planning, Washington and one of his fightingest officers, Brig. Gen. Anthony Wayne, came up with and brilliantly executed an assault on Stony Point in the wee hours of July 16. From the assault to Washington's departure (he had arrived on July 17), the dead were buried, the prisoners marched off, and goods carried away, while the developing assault on Verplanck crumbled in the face of advancing British forces. Col. Richard Butler, third in command of the Corps of Light Infantry, the unit that as-

---

1. Sources in this paragraph: George Washington to George Clinton, July 19, 1779, Founders Online (FO), founders.archives.gov/documents/Washington/03-21-02-0462; Michael J. F. Sheehan, "The Unsuccessful American Attempt on Verplanck Point, July 16-19, 1779," *Journal of the American Revolution*, September 10, 2014, allthingsliberty.com/2014/09/the-unsuccessful-american-attempt-on-verplanck-point-july-16-19-1779/; Richard Butler to George Washington, July 19, 1779, Founders Online, founders.archives.gov/documents/Washington/03-21-02-0461.

saulted Stony Point, reported to Washington that hours after the commander-in-chief had departed, the Americans also left, only to see right
behind them the British land on Stony Point after a brief bombardment
to "Cover their landing . . . they took immediate possession of the Point
. . . & Confined themselves within their Sentries."

British Brig. Gen. Thomas Sterling landed his brigade, consisting
of the 42nd Royal Highland, the 63rd, and 64th Regiments of Foot,
for the night of the July 19. In the next few weeks, they would begin
construction of a new fort on the point with a very different design
from the original. The Americans, however, did not let this go unnoticed. From headquarters at West Point, Washington wrote to two of
his officers on July 25. He asked Col. Richard Butler to gather information on the British, to be as "particular & critical" as he could in "as-
certaining the several Works the Enemy are carrying on- their number
and nature—whether inclosed or otherwise." Numbers of tents were
important too, he directed, as that would help form "an estimate of their
force." He asked twenty-three-year-old Maj. "Light Horse" Henry Lee,
who commanded his own legion, to "obtain the most precise ideas of
the situation at Stony Point . . . I wish to know upon what plan the
enemy are now constructing their works . . . what is the strength of the
garrison, the corps that compose that strength the number and sizes of
cannon, [and who] commands." Gathering detailed intelligence was
not something new to Washington, and in this case he had pressing
reasons for it, for on the following day, he summoned a council of his
general officers. The commander-in-chief requested that his generals
reply to him in writing with their opinions on the following question:
Do we attack the British at Stony Point again?[2]

Sixteen of Washington's generals returned written replies. Following
are the core answers from each letter. The generals who answered in
the affirmative:

Brig. Gen. Anthony Wayne: "I have fully Considered & am of
Opinion that something ought to be attempted in order to draw Genl
[Henry] Clinton's attention towards *King's Ferry*, which will not only
give great Security to the Adjacent States-but leave it in your power to
cover [West Point]."

2. Sir Henry Clinton to Lord George Germain, July 25. 1779, in Henry P. Johnston, *The
Storming of Stony Point on the Hudson, Midnight Jul 15, 1779* (New York: James T. White
& Co., 1900), 123-5; Washington to Butler, July 25 1779, FO, founders.archives.gov/doc-
uments/Washington/03-21-02-0530; Washington to Henry Lee, July 25, 1779, FO,
founders.archives.gov/documents/Washington/03-21-02-0563 Note 2;, Alexander Hamilton to Nathanael Greene, July 25, 1779, FO, founders.archive.gov/documents/Hamilton/
01-02-02-0339.

Brig. Gen. William Irvine: "My Opinion is that we should not lose any opportunity—(where there is a rational prospect of success) of Attacking them by Detachments . . . the infant state of their works on Stony Point renders it in my Opinion practicable—I am for Attacking it."

Maj. Gen. Arthur St. Clair: "[It] may . . . be carried by Surprize, which seems to me the only eligible Method all things considered."

Maj. Gen. Robert Howe: "To attack, or if that is not eligible, to hover about their favourite Posts might oblige them to k eep a large Body of Troops in and about their Works, to the Dimunation of their Main Body . . . if it can be done without too much risque."

Maj. Gen. William Heath: "Stony and ver planks points are Vulnerable, the works at the former being as yet incomplete maybe attacked by assault & perhaps carried, tho' it is to be supposed that the Enemy from his late misfortune . . . will make an Obstinate resistance . . . [it] should not be purchased at too dear a rate."

Brig. Gen. Mordecai Gist: "I am of Opinion that a Movement of part of our Army on each side of the River within supporting distance of this post to show a disposition of attack on their Works, may in some measure counteract their scheme of plundering."

Brig. Gen. Samuel Parsons: "If we can procure a Sufficiency of Military Stores for the Purpose . . . an attempt to dispossess the Enemy of Verplank's and Stony Points ought to be attempted . . . if this Enterprize Should be undertaken both Sides of the River should be attempted at the same Time because the Post on the east side cannot be carried whilst the Enemy remain posses'd of Stony Point."

Maj. Gen. Baron de Kalb: "As to Stony Point . . . we Should interrupt and retard their Works and Strike a Blow there—if it can be done with any prospect of Success."[3]

The following generals urged caution and voiced a preference to not attack.

3. Anthony Wayne to Washington, July 27, 1779, FO, founders.archives.gov/documents/Washington/03-21-02-0571; William Irvine to Washington, July 27, 1779, FO, founders.archives.gov/doucments/Washington/03-21-02-0557; Arthur St. Clair to Washington, July 27, 1779, FO, founders.archives.gov/documents/Washington/03-21-02-0564; Robert Howe to Washington, July 27, 1779, FO, founders.archives.gov/documents/Washington/03-21-02-0555; William Heath to Washington, July 27, 1779, FO, founders.archives.gov/documents/Washington/03-21-02-0554; Mordecai Gist to Washington, July 27, 1779, FO, founders.archives.gov/documents/Washington/03-21-02-0552; Samuel Parsons to Washington, July 27, 1779, FO, founders.archives.gov/documents/Washington/03-21-02-0563; Johann de Kalb to Washington, July 27, 1779, FO, founders.archives.gov/documents/Washington/03-21-02-0559.

Maj. Gen. Baron von Steuben: "I am not of opinion to hazard a second attempt upon the same point . . . [yet] the more of their force we can keep at bay here, the less they can employ in operations elsewhere."

Brig. Gen. William Smallwood: "At present I should judge it more expedient to hold out appearances of attacking or annoying their Garrisons."

Brig. Gen. John Nixon: "Considering the Great Effusion of Blood in taking Stony Point, it might more than Countervail the advantage we Should Gain thereby . . . unless upon both [points] at the same time."

Maj. Gen. Nathanael Greene: "I cannot think a second attack upon Stony Point would be crowned with the same success as before; and our Army is not in force to make a great sacrifice of men by way of experiment, or for the purpose of giving Military glory to individuals."

Maj. Gen. Alexander McDougall: "The present Strength of thee Garrisons and works at Kings ferry are such, as renders a Second attack by Storm on either of them very Hazardous, and would in all Probabil[ity] . . . cost us more men, than the acquisition."

Brig. Gen. Henry Knox: "An Attempt on Verplanks or Stony point has been mention'd as an elig[i]ble circumstance. I confess I do not see the Advantage of such an attempt . . . Stony Point from its peculiar situation appears to be out of the question."

Brig. Gen. Louis Duportail: "I think that we ought to not attack them, because we should be likely to lose a good many men and perhaps without success—Besides, . . . we should not have any great advantage by gaining possession of Stony Point, because we must also be masters of Verplanks . . . if we should attack Stony Point . . . we must not believe, that we should succeed in the same manner a second time."

Brig. Gen. Jedediah Huntington: "That an attack . . . [on] the Posts at Kings ferry would occasion too great an Expenditure."[4]

The council was split down the middle. Privately, Washington wrote to Anthony Wayne. He wrote that he wished for his "opinion as a

4. Friedrich von Steuben to George Washington, July 27, 1779, FO, founders.archives.gov/documents/Washington/03-21-02-0567; William Smallwood to Washington, July 27, 1779, FO, founders.archives.gov/documents/Washington/03-21-02-0566; John Nixon to Washington, July 27, 1779, FO, founders.archives.gov/documents/ Washington/03-21-02-0562; Greene to Washington, July 27, 1779, FO, founders.archives.gov/documents/Washington/03-21-02-0553; Alexander McDougall to Washington, July 27, 1779, FO, founders.archives.gov/documents/Washington/03-21-02-0561; Henry Knox to Washington, July 27, 1779, FO, founders.archives.gov/documents/Washington/03-21-02-0560; Louis Duportail to Washington, July 27, 1779, FO, founders.archives.gov/documents/ Washington/03-21-02-0551; Jedediah Huntington to Washington, July 27, 1779, FO, founders.archives.gov/documents/Washington/03-21-02-0556.

friend, not as commanding officer of the light Troops—whether an attempt on Stony Point by way of surprize is eligible." The following day, Wayne replied, noting that the "Enemy will certainly profit so far by their late misfortune . . . as to provide for, or against a Surprize." The British "were at this time Industriously employed" in strengthening their defenses. However, Wayne thought that his "Light Corps with the addition of One Thousand more picked men & Officers properly Appointed would cary that post by Assault in the night with the loss of between four & five Hundred men . . . supposing the Enemy to be but One Thousand strong." If Washington agreed, Wayne offered himself "with the greatest chearfulness [to] under-take the charge, altho' I am not quite Recovered of my former hurt," referring to his wound from July 16. Wayne would not get his second chance; Washington erred on the side of caution and instead of making an assault, continued to monitor activity at King's Ferry.[5]

While the Americans deliberated on attacking again, the British kept on working. Once reestablished at Stony Point, it was evident a new system of defensive works were necessary. To that end, Capt. Patrick Ferguson of the 70th Regiment of Foot, inventor of the Ferguson rifle, who had been stationed at Verplanck Point since June, was handed the job. As Capt. Archibald Robinson recalled, at a meeting with Gen. Sir Henry Clinton and other officers, "Capt. Ferguson undertook to finish [the works] in 14 days then got 8 more added, then the General sent him up from Camp." This was not Ferguson's first time thinking of ways to redesign Stony Point. At some time in late June or early July, Capt. Robert Douglas of the Royal Artillery recalled a meeting in which Ferguson "from the first Moment disapproved of the Mode, in which Stony Point was fortified; it was his almost constant conversation in my hearing."[6]

Apart from some gunboat activity in August, the Stony Point side of the Hudson River remained fairly quiet. On September 6, with British defenses well under way, Wayne reconnoitered the post. He reported to Washington that the British had "nearly Completed their works—which Consist of One Advanced Redoubt on the Hill Com-

5. Washington to Wayne, July 30, 1779, FO, founders.archives.gov/documents/Washington/03-21-02-0596. Wayne to Washington, July 31, 1779, FO, founders.archives.gov/documents/Washington/03-21-02-0. With the addition of 1,000 men, Wayne's strength would grow to near 2,300 men and officers.

6. Archibald Robertson *His Diaries and Sketches in America*, ed. Harry Miller Lydenberg, (New York: New York Public Library, 1930), 200; Testimony of Capt. Robert Douglas in the Court Martial of Lt. Col. Henry Johnson in Don Loprieno, *The Enterprise in Contemplation: The Midnight Assault of Stony Point* (Westminster, MD: Heritage Books, 2004), 297.

manding the ferry, way encloses & finished with a good Abbatis & Block House." Their main work, confined to the higher ground on the point, was also

> Enclosed the parapet raised much higher than usual & fraised in the most Capital manner & surrounded with a wide & formidable Abbatis—within this is a Citadel Independent of the Other work with a Strong high parapet (with fraised) and a Block House which (fires) in Barbett the top of all the parapets neatly & almost Completely (sodded). They have about Eight Guns mounted.

Wayne was impressed: "They have appearantly done more work . . . than all our Army have Effected the whole Campaign." Ferguson himself was pleased with his work, and wrote to General Clinton saying, "at Stony Point it has been our Endeavour to Secure the Post against a surprize or *Coup de Main* by Multiplying the Obstacles on the Grounds by which the works are to be approach'd." He further reassured the British commander-in-chief that, "I flatter myself you need not apprehend any Danger . . . & if your Excellency will allow the Thirty Pioneers now here to remain another fortnight we shall be so bury'd in abatti, that the Garrison will not be obliged to be harass'd upon every alarm." Days later, another of the aforementioned alarms took place. On September 22, Sgt. Henry Nase of the King's American Regiment noted that "a large Body of rebells appeared Before the Lines." Maj. Charles Graham of the 42nd Regiment, who had commanded Stony Point during its reoccupation, that same day wrote to Clinton that at about ten in the morning, "a very large body of Rebells . . . appeared drawn up on the Rising grounds about three Quarters in our front," not doing much until night, when they "kept up a popping [firing muskets] from the Woods." The most likely candidate for this force of Americans was Wayne's Corps of Light Infantry, as they were the only sizeable unit in the vicinity of Stony Point.[7]

Just four days later, Washington wrote to Wayne that "General Knox and du Portail are to go down to night, or early to-morrow to reconnoitre the enemy's post at Stony Point," and that they would expect

7. Anthony Wayne to George Washington, September 7, 1779, FO, founders.archives.gov/documents/Washington/03-22-01-0303 ; Patrick Ferguson to Henry Clinton, September 18, 1779, "An Officer Out of His Time: Patrick Ferguson," in Howard Peckham, ed, *Sources of American Independence: Selected Manuscripts from the Collections of the William L. Clements Library*, Vol II, (Chicago: University of Chicago Press, 1975), 329; Diary of Henry Nase, King's American Regiment, Nase Family Papers, New Brunswick Museum, 7, transcribed by Todd W. Braisted, kiltsandcourage.com; Charles Graham to Henry Clinton, September 22, 1779, Sir Henry Clinton Papers, Vol. 68: 45, William L. Clements Library, University of Michigan, transcribed by Paul Pace, kiltsandcourage.com.

him to join them. General Knox, commander of the Continental Army's artillery, reported their adventure to Washington on September 30. After initially taking a "general view . . . from the Donderburgh [Dunderberg Mountain]," they then got dangerously close, at a "piece of Ground which we estimated at about 800 yards distance," barely out of range for a light cannon. Knox noted that there were a few eligible places north and west of Stony Point to open batteries, but to really pummel the post into submission, "it would be necessary to have 15 or 16 heavy Cannon and eight or ten mortars and howitzers," and that it would take at least a "ten days Siege." Luckily though, the Enemy [had] demolished a number of their Works on Verplanks point."[8]

On September 27, just as the Hudson Valley began to shake off the summer heat, Captain Ferguson was handed a devastating letter to which he immediately replied, pouring out his frustrations. To his commander-in-chief, he wrote that,

> Your letter was put into my hand by Major Graham an hour ago . . .
> After having so long exerted myself to the utmost & been a witness of
> the zeal & perseverance with which the Troops have labor'd to put this
> Post out of reach of Insult, it is with the Greatest Pain I read . . . that
> Circumstances may oblige us to abandon our Works to the rebels.

Ferguson's harangue went on for another seven paragraphs before closing with the wish that his recipient would "pardon the warmth with which I have express'd myself." In a postscript, he wrote "May I beg to know your Determination [on maintaining the post] soon, to prevent unnecessary labor." The demolition of the out works at Verplanck that Knox noted was the first stage of Clinton's reduction of the posts at King's Ferry. Despite the shrinking of forces, Stony Point was still sufficiently strong, at least to Ferguson. In a letter to Capt. John André, he boasted that Stony Point had a "Compliment of iron Ordinance to two 18's & six 4's, Exclusive of the Rebel 32 [pounder] & a 24 [pounder] still here which wants . . . a Carriage." On October 3, Washington wrote Wayne that "General Du Portail proposes tomorrow to reconnoitre a second time the post of Stony Point," and to meet him at eleven in the morning with a "Regiment ready," or one fourth Wayne's force to cover them, and also to take special care to see if the enemy had any "bomb proofs in Stony Point, what number, extent and thickness." Washington was once again seriously considering an attack on Stony Point; he wrote to Gen. Arthur St. Clair that "if the Posts on the

8. Washington to Wayne, September 26, 1779, FO, founders.archives.gov/documents/ Washington/03-22-02-0435; Knox to Washington, September 30, 1779, FO, founders. archives.gov/documents/Washington/03-22-02-0471.

North [Hudson] River are not drawn in, I suppose two thousand Men, with proper Artillery might, in a Week reduce Stony Point without .. . much upon the greater Operations of the Army." On the same day, Washington wrote to Gen. William Alexander, known to the Americans as Lord Stirling, that the "prospect of preventing the retreat of the garrisons at Stony- and Verplanks (so far as it is to be effected by a Land operation) again revives upon probable ground."[9]

On October 9, Wayne reported on the second reconnoitering of Stony Point, "Enclosed is a plan of the Enemies works . . . taken by Colo [Rufus] Putnam with the points of attack in case of Investiture." The enemy,

> Have neither Bomb proofs- nor a Magazine, their Ammunition is kept on Board a Sloop in the rear of the point except a few rounds . . . Covered by two tents-they have a 32 pounder mounted on their Right . . . one 18 on their left . . . a few fives [and] Sixes [actually 4 pounders] & four 5 [1/] 2 & 42 inch [?] Howitz at Intermediate distances between the two extremes where the 32 & 18 pounders are & in Block Houses.

Wayne then described his thoughts on how any type of siege might progress. He thought that "two 18 & two or three 12 pounders on travelling Carriages with two 8 inch Howitz[ers] would be a sufficiency of Artillery to reduce this post." A "Combined attack on verplanks point ought to take place at the same time . . . I think we should- carry the Works by storm with great care."

Generals Wayne and Duportail's snooping about did not go unnoticed. It alarmed Captain Ferguson, who wrote to Clinton on October 9, "Since . . . I did myself the honour of writing on the 6th we have passed some anxious moments. The rebel movements . . . [indicate] a Design of Attacking these Posts." Despite the earlier order to withdraw defenses, Ferguson was still genuinely concerned with the security of the posts. Desertions, he maintained, were a problem but siege worried him more. Correctly, he estimated that the Continental Army would utilize a "design of distressing by Shells & not withstanding that I have done my utmost to secure us," for "the Proximity of the rebel army &

9. Patrick Ferguson to Henry Clinton, September 27, 1779, in Peckham, *Sources of American Independence*, 330-2; Ferguson to John André, undated October 1779, ibid, 332-3; Washington to Wayne, October 3, 1779, FO, founders.archives.gov/documents/Washington/03-22-01-0506. Bomb proofs are generally blockhouses sunk into the ground and covered with sod to absorb the shock of exploding mortar and howitzer shells; Washington to St. Clair, October 4, 1779, FO, founders.archives.gov/documents/Washington/03-22-02-0502-0006; Washington to Lord Stirling, October 4, 1779, FO, founders.archives.gov/documents/Washington/03-22-02-0502-0008.

Labour of procuring . . . heavy trees has prevented our being as yet in great degree defended." The next day, Washington acknowledged Wayne's letter, but urged caution. "It is not to our Interest to disturb the enemy," but that they should be "lulled into security, rather then alarmed." The usually decisive Washington could not make up his mind.[10]

Down towards headquarters in New York, Capt. John Peebles of the 42nd Regiment's grenadier company noted in his diary, "Tuesday 12 Octr: strong [Southerly] wind. The Com[mander] in chief gone up to Stoney Pt. with the [HMS] *Fanny* & some small craft." Wayne noticed the arrival of these new vessels. A few "Ships & other Vessels made their Appearance . . . I have sent down to try to Discover whether they have brought a Reinforcement . . . or [are] preparing for an evacuation." The next day, October 14, Washington replied to Wayne that "a deserter from the [HMS] *Vulture* sloop the day before yesterday informs that Sir Henry Clinton . . . and several other officers came up the River." A week passed with little to report on either side. Suddenly, on October 21, Wayne fired off to Washington that the previous evening he gained "Intelligence that a number of flat Bottomd boats & Several vessels were moving up Haverstraw Bay—the troops were Ordered to lay on their arms," for "some Capital move was in agitation," but whether coming or going Wayne could not decipher. All was quiet until daylight, when Wayne "could observe them busily employed in Imbarking their Baggage & Cannon—About 10 O Clock they began to Demolish their parapets & fraise on Verplanks."

On Stony Point, however, they had not yet begun, and Wayne was determined to "prevent them from Demolishing the face of their works . . . [although] they will probably burn or blow up their Block Houses." He then waxed triumphant, assuring his commander that he'd only "keep a Captains guard at Stony Point . . . for be assured the [works] will be in our possession this Night—the moment we enter them I shall Announce it by the firing of five Cannon—observing the time of half a Minute between each gun." Washington, already composing a letter

10. Wayne to Washington, October 9, 1779, FO, founders.archives.gov/documents/Washington/03-22-02-0561. Wayne's reference to a forty-two inch howitzer is either his or an editorial mistake, as the largest shell throwing weapon of the war was a thirteen inch, and even they were traditionally mounted on a boat, and so he must mean a 4 ½, sometimes written 4 2/5, inch mortar, known as a cohorn. His reference to a fifty-two inch should likewise read 5 2/5 inch, or a Royal mortar/howitzer. Since the cohorns are usually mounted at an angle as mortars, perhaps they were mounted as howitzers, at a straighter angle, which may have confused him; Ferguson to Clinton, October 9, 1779, in Peckham, ibid, 334-6; Washington to Wayne, October 10, 1779, FO, founders.archives.gov/documents/Washington/03-22-02-0573.

to his favorite aide, Lt. Col. Alexander Hamilton, who was on a mission with General Duportail in New Jersey, told them he had just received a line from Major General Heath, and that "the Enemy have left both points having burnt & destroyed their Works;" with that, the British peacefully departed their works at King's Ferry which, except for Stony Point for under four days, had been theirs for almost five months. Washington told his two closest commanders, Wayne at Stony Point and Heath near Verplanck, to be ready for his arrival at eight in the morning on October 23. Crossing in the mail was Wayne's brief report to Washington that at Stony Point, "all the *Block houses* are Destroyed with some of the fraizing & parapets, but the far greater part is perfect, & very little of the Abbatis Injured." Until he heard otherwise, Wayne kept his promise that he'd "Keep a Captains Guard at Stony Point in the day time." By now, news of the change in possession of King's Ferry had reached the British, specifically Hessian Jäger officer Capt. Johann Ewald, who commented, "We have again abandoned the posts of Stony and Verplank's Point . . . [the Americans] already taken possession of them . . . Once more, we are no further than we were at the beginning of the campaign." Frustrated at Lt. Col. Henry Johnson's loss of Stony Point back in July, he said, "How easily can the plan of an entire campaign be upset by the negligence of an officer to whom a post is entrusted!"

After his inspection of the points of King's Ferry, Washington returned to West Point where he told General Heath that to "protect the communication by Kings Ferry, I think the Connecticut Division may as well move down as low as . . . Pecks Kill [Peekskill]." He would "direct Colo [Jean-Baptiste] Gouvion to lay out two small Works at Verplanks and Stoney points," and ordered that the Connecticut men would supply the work parties on the eastern shore. On the west side, Wayne was given similar instructions, and to "furnish a party from the [Light] infantry," and to coordinate with Gen. William Woodford who would "furnish a party from the Virginia line also." As the "Work will be trifling," Washington said, he wished that "the parties may be as such as will finish it out of hand."[11]

11. John Peebles, *John Peebles' American War: The Diary of a Scottish Grenadier, 1776-1782*, Ira D. Gruber, ed. (Mechanicsburg, PA: Stackpole Books, 1998), 299; Wayne to Washington, October 13, 1779, FO, founders.archives.gov/documents/Washington/03-22-02-0592; Washington to Wayne, October 13, 1779, FO, founders.archives.gov/documents/Washington/03-22-02-0600; Wayne to Washington, October 21, 1779, FO, founders.archives.gov/documents/Washington/03-22-02-0652; Washington to Louis Duportail and Alexander Hamilton, October 21, 1779, FO, founders.archives.gov/documents/Hamilton/01-022-02-0508; Washington to Wayne, October 22, 1779, FO, founders.archives.gov/

The following day, Washington received intelligence that the British had landed troops near Amboy in New Jersey, and consequently, the Light Corps and Woodford's Brigade were sent off to shift towards that area. Because of this shift, Washington asked Heath to send some of his Connecticut troops to Stony Point to pick up the slack. With the British gone for a week now, it was time to reestablish the normalcy at King's Ferry that had been absent since June. From his headquarters at Peekskill, Heath issued a series of orders regarding Stony and Verplanck Points. Heath ordered "two Sentinels," on each of the points "as will best facilitate observation. They are to . . . keep a Watchful Eye down the river & Should they perceive any Vessell . . . to give notice" immediately. In addition, "two men will patrole in the Neighboorhood of each point," and a "Sentinel . . . is to be posted at each Ferry ways to examine passengers & prevent any unknown persons from passing without passports from proper Authority." Such persons as did not pass muster would be "detained & report made without Delay to a General Officer. No stranger is to be suffer'd to enter the works unless known & attended by a Commissioned Officer." The Continental Army wasn't sure at the time, but Stony and Verplanck Points would never be contested again. The Americans would have full control of King's Ferry until relinquished at some point in late 1783. King's Ferry would go on to play roles in the Arnold-André affair, host the Grand Encampment of Autumn 1782, and see Count Rochambeau's Expeditionary Force cross the river twice.[12]

documents/Washington/03-23-02-0011; Washington to Heath, October 22, 1779, FO, founders.archives.gov/documents/Washington/03-23-02-0003; Wayne to Washington, October 22, 1779, FO, founders.archives.gov/documents/Washington/03-23-02-0012; Johann Ewald, *Diary of the American War: A Hessian Journal,* Joseph P. Tustin, ed. (New Haven, CT: Yale University Press, 1979), 179; Washington to Heath, October 24, 1779, FO, founders.archives.gov/documents/Washington/03-23-02-0024; Washington to Wayne, October 26, 1779, FO, founders.archives.gov/documents/Washington/03-23-02-0054.

12. George Washington to Heath, October 27, 1779, FO, founders.archives.gov/documents/Washington/03-23-02-0058; Note 1, General Orders, October 29, 1779, FO, founders.archives.gov/doucments/Washington/03-23-02-0079; Michael J. F. Sheehan, "Top 10 Events at King's Ferry," *Journal of the American Revolution,* August 24, 2015, allthingsliberty.com/2015/08/top-10-events-at-kings-ferry/.

Outbreak! New York, 1779

DON N. HAGIST

"The number of sick increasing every day, in all the different Camps of the army," wrote Capt. John Peebles in his diary on September 5, 1779.[1] Encamped on Manhattan Island eight miles north of the city of New York, at the time rural farmland, the army was beginning to suffer from the consequences of an unusually rainy and windless summer. On August 24 Peebles, who commanded the grenadier company of the 42nd Regiment of Foot, part of the army's grenadier battalion, noted that the light infantry battalion was moving to Long Island from the "wet swampy ground" they had been camped upon because men were getting sick.[2] Seven days later he wrote, "The Men growing very sickly within these few days, a general complaint over the whole army, they are mostly taken with headache & universal pain a chill & feverishness, which for the most part turns into a quotidian or tertian intermittent, & some few are rather with the flux." Twelve men in his one-hundred-man company had fallen ill, six within the last twenty-four hours.[3] It was only the beginning.

Techniques for keeping an army healthy were well-known to the British army in America. A century of corporate knowledge was reinforced by a host of textbooks that aggregated experience from Europe's professional armies. For the most part, officers knew how to choose ground for encampments and cantonments based on prevailing winds and sunlight as well as tactical considerations, and the importance of things like drainage, refreshing the straw used for tent and barrack bed-

1. John Peebles, *John Peebles American War: the Diary of a Scottish Grenadier, 1776-1782,* Ira Gruber, ed. (Mechanicsburg, PA: Stackpole Books, for the Army Records Society, 1998), 291.
2. Ibid., 288.
3. Ibid., 289.

ding, burying offal and waste well away from habitations, frequently relocating "necessary houses" (latrines), and providing adequate ventilation in hospitals and barracks, was well known. When the weather and location permitted, soldiers bathed regularly in rivers or the sea. It was rare for sickness to ravage the British armies in Canada and New York, but the autumn of 1779 was different.

The "quotidian or tertian intermittent" fevers that Captain Peebles wrote of were familiar in a general sense. British army surgeon Thomas Reide divided fevers into two categories, remitting and inflammatory, noting that some fevers showed characteristics of both. As the name suggests, remitting fevers recurred every day or two. Many writers used the term "ague," meaning malarial fever, for any remitting fever regardless of whether malaria was known to have been the cause. Reide called remitting fever "the most common disease that mankind is attacked with."[4] He described an assortment of symptoms. The fever's onset was characterized by "chilliness, lassitude, yawning; pains of the head, back and bones, vertigo, anxiety, nausea, and oppression of the stomach." Next came "heat, dry skin, thirst, parched tongue, though sometimes white and moist; violent head-ache, difficulty of breathing, delirium, restlessness, frequent hard pulse, bilious vomiting and loose stools, sometimes with worms; often costiveness, with a hardness of the belly, and flatulency; high-coloured urine, yellowness of the eyes, and frequently of the whole body." These fevers were remitting because "generally in a short time a copious perspiration" occurred, followed by some relief of symptoms. But the symptoms came back, sometimes every day, sometimes every other day, "sometimes it is quite irregular. The exacerbation is generally at night, and the remission in the morning."[5]

Captain Peebles observed on September 5 that the army's sick men had "nearly the same complaint vizt a fever from Accumulated Bile more or less continued, according to the load or treatment of the patient & terminates in remissions, or intermissions with an ague."[6] The next day he observed that some 200 men of the grenadier battalion, about a quarter of its strength, were hospitalized.[7] By the end of the month, when a fresh breeze arose, he observed with concern, "I hope this weather will be of service to the sick & check the progress of the disease, which is still seizing on new subjects & but very few of the old

4. Thomas Dickson Reide, *A View of the Diseases of the Army* (London: J. Johnson, 1793), 39-40.
5. Ibid., 41-42.
6. Peebles, *John Peebles American War*, 291.
7. Ibid., 291. At that time there were fifteen grenadier companies organized into a single battalion

recovering."[8] On October 1, "The number of sick still increases, some few fluxes which has carried off some men, but the general complaint is an undistinct remitting & intermitting fever, with & without more or less of an ague which proves more lasting & obstinate as their great numbers does not admit of that care, treatment & attention that is necessary." The numbers of stricken men put a strain on the army's medical personnel. The grenadier battalion had, on October 1, "Only one Hospital Mate to attend 130 or 40 Sick, & few comforts."[9]

It wasn't until mid-November that Peebles was able to report, "The Sick recovering but slowly," a phrase he repeated a week later (November 21), adding, "29 in the Doctors lists, & 12 convalescents many relapses."[10] His last mention of the outbreak was on December 3, when he wrote that "the no. of sick decreasing."[11]

Captain Peebles' grenadier company fared well in the long run, with only three deaths during the time of fever.[12] The 37th Regiment, in which nearly every man in its eight battalion companies had been sick, lost thirty-five men from August through December including fifteen newly-arrived recruits and drafts.[13] The 54th Regiment, encamped on Long Island, fared even worse, with sixty-six deaths in the seven battalion companies for which muster rolls survive, almost fifteen percent of its strength.[14]

What was the cause of this outbreak, the likes of which had not occurred during the war in this region, and did not occur again, even though the army occupied much the same ground from the autumn of 1776 through the autumn of 1783? Army surgeon Robert Jackson recognized that some camps on the northern end of Manhattan were situated too close to unhealthy locations. "The situation of the encampment which the 71st regiment occupied at King's-bridge, in the year 1778, affords a curious and direct" example, he remembered. "About two hundred paces to the right of the spot, on which the tents were pitched, was a tract of low and swampy ground; but the immediate situation was dry, and of considerable elevation. The right was particularly so; yet it was principally on the right, where the disease raged

8. Peebles, *John Peebles American War*, 296.
9. Ibid.
10. Ibid., 309-310.
11. Ibid., 313.
12. Muster rolls, 42nd Regiment of Foot, WO 12/5553, British National Archives.
13. Muster rolls, 37th Regiment of Foot, WO 12/5101, British National Archives.
14. Muster rolls, 54th Regiment of Foot, WO 12/6399, British National Archives. The regiment consisted of ten companies, but two of them, the grenadiers and light infantry, were detached and not camped at the same location as the remaining eight companies.

with violence. The left, though on low ground, over which fogs frequently hung till late in the day, suffered a much smaller proportion." He also recognized that "the great degree of sickness, which happened to those people, who not being confined by the nature of their duty to one particular spot, pitched their tents on a hill in the rear of the encampment" proved that it was not elevation and dryness alone that made the difference. "The ground, which those persons made choice of was directly in the tracts of air, which blew over the swamp. It was dry and scarcely ever covered with fogs; yet there was not an individual among them who encamped upon it, who did not suffer from this raging epidemic."[15] Jackson understood the connection between the swamp and the sickness, even though he didn't know the vector—probably mosquitoes—that connected the two.

When the 1779 outbreak began, Captain Peebles, noticing that it was afflicting soldiers and civilians alike on Manhattan and Long Island, thought it was "owing probably to the great deal of rainy weather we had lately, more than any body remembers, with little or no thunder."[16] There was, however, another factor that may have been at play. In late March, just over 1,300 recruits had embarked in Portsmouth, England, along with four British regiments and number of recruits for German regiments.[17] They sailed in April, but the transports soon dropped anchor in Torbay while their escorting warships went to help fend off a French attempt to seize the islands of Jersey and Guernsey. It was a month before the convoy was under way again, finally arriving in New York in late August.[18] The troops had been on ships for nearly five months, and eight hundred were sick, including almost three hundred British recruits; forty-three more recruits had died during the passage.[19] The admiral commanding the convoy was confident that the malady was "principally scurvy" and that most would "soon recover," but they did not. Of sixty-three recruits for the 22nd Regiment, twenty-six died within a year, as did thirty-four out of one hundred and six for the 38th Regiment. They may have brought pestilence with them, or been vulnerable after their long sea voyage.

15. Robert Jackson, *Treatise on the Fevers of Jamaica* (London: J. Murray, 1791), 86-87.
16. Peebles, *John Peebles American War*, 289-290.
17. "State of the Troops which arrived in the fleet from England under the Command of Vice admiral Arbuthnot, New York 1st. Septr. 1779," CO 5/98, p493, British National Archives.
18. Mariot Arbuthnot to George Germain, May 2, 1779, *Report on the Manuscripts of Mrs. Stopford-Sackville* (Hereford: Hereford Times Co., 1910), 2: 127.
19. "State of the Troops which arrived in the fleet from England."

Gen. Henry Clinton, commanding the afflicted garrison, called the outbreak a "malignant jail fever,"[20] suggesting a belief that it was brought by the recruits. A board of army doctors convened to examine "the present extraordinary unhealthy state of the Army," on the other hand, recognized that the first cases of fever had occurred before the convoy from Britain arrived. Commencing "about the middle of July, & has continued to increase ever since," it had "attacked the Natives of all Conditions, & Ages, on the Islands of New-York, Staaten & Long Islands,—previous to the unhealthy State of the Military." The board concluded that the "Intermittent, Bilious Fever, & Dysenteries" that swept through the army and civilian population were caused by "the frequent heavy rains, succeeded by unusual, calm, sultry Weather, with the defect of Thunder, and Lightning Common to the Climate," but also noted that "the chief Mortality in the Hospitals has been amongst the Troops which arriv'd from England on the 25th August owing to a contagious Fever that they brought with them."[21]

20. William B. Willcox, *The American Rebellion: Sir Henry Clinton's Narrative of his Campaigns, 1775-1782* (New Haven: Yale University Press, 1954), 140.
21. Minutes of an Hospital Board held at the College Hospital at New York 27th Sepr. 1779. Henry Clinton Papers V69: 27, William L. Clements Library.

The Mysterious March of Horatio Gates

✻ ANDREW WATERS ✻

Following the American surrender at Charleston on May 12, 1780, the Continental Army's "Southern Department" was in disarray. Taken prisoner that day were 245 officers and 2,326 enlisted, including Maj. Gen. Benjamin Lincoln, the Southern Department's commander-in-chief. Along with perhaps as many as three thousand militia and armed citizens also taken captive (based on British accounts), it was the most American prisoners surrendered at one time during the American Revolution.[1]

That summer, scattered elements of the Continental Army regrouped in central North Carolina under command of Johann Kalb, the European officer and self-proclaimed "Baron de Kalb." Earlier that spring, Kalb had been placed in charge of the first and second Maryland brigades, along with the Delaware Regiment and the 1st Artillery with eighteen field pieces, about 1,400 soldiers in all. Marching from Morristown, New Jersey, in mid-April, their mission was to relieve Charleston and serve as a nucleus for Southern militia. But arriving in central North Carolina in late June, Kalb found Charleston already surrendered and provisions and militia reinforcements scarce throughout the south.[2]

Meanwhile, the Continental Congress named Lincoln's successor on June 13, picking Horatio Gates, the hero of Saratoga. By 1780, Gates was well-known for personality conflicts with his fellow officers,

---

1. Mark M. Boatner, *Encyclopedia of the American Revolution* (New York: David McKay Company), 213
2. Christopher Ward, *War of the Revolution* (New York: Skyhorse Publishing, 2011), 714.

prominently Benedict Arnold and George Washington. But Gates's political reputation, at least, had survived his conflict with Washington, and he was still well regarded for his rapport with the enlisted and volunteer militia. "Unlike most American generals," Gates "had great confidence in short-term soldiers and showed a keen understanding of their temper," writes his biographer. "It was his announced policy never to call up the militia until almost the very moment they were needed. Once they had finished their tour of duty, he was quick to thank them and to send them packing off to home."

By June 1780, the now fifty-three-year-old Gates was on furlough from the Continental Army, convalescing at his Virginia estate. Washington had wanted Nathanael Greene for the southern command, but Congress wanted Gates, who was, after all, available and not far away. So Gates got the job.[3]

He joined Kalb on July 25, 1780, at Cox's Mill on Deep River, in modern-day Randolph County, North Carolina, south of today's Ramseur community. What happened next is perhaps a familiar tale, certainly one of the war's most curious, with a narrative that goes something like this: Eager to repeat his heroics at Saratoga, Gates demanded an immediate and ill-conceived march directly toward the British Army stronghold at Camden, South Carolina, on a direct route through the Carolina's infamously inhospitable "Pine Barrens." In this haste, he ignored his cavalry and the assistance of Francis Marion, the famous South Carolina "Swamp Fox," choosing to rely instead on untested militia, leading to a defeat of disastrous proportions at Camden on August 16, 1781, where Gates fled the field in eternal disgrace.

The framework of this version originates mostly from Otho Holland Williams, colonel of the 6th Maryland Regiment and Gates's adjutant general, who provided many of its tenets in his "Narrative" of the 1780 campaign. Born to Welsh immigrants, Williams had joined the Frederick County rifle corps early in the war and steadily rose through the ranks. Henry Lee described him as "elegant in form . . . his countenance was expressive and the faithful index of his warm and honest heart." But he did have his severe side. "He was cordial to his friends, but cold to all whose correctness in moral principle became questionable in his mind," wrote Lee. Taken prisoner at Fort Washington in November 1776, he was promoted to colonel while still a prisoner at New York, then exchanged and served with distinction at Monmouth Courthouse.

---

3. George A. Billias, "Horatio Gates: Professional Soldier," from *George Washington's Generals and Opponents* (New York: Da Capo Press edition, 1994), 88-100.

Prior to his service with Kalb, Williams had served briefly as Washington's adjutant general, from December 1779 to April 1780.[4]

Williams' narrative, at times, reads almost as a litany of Gates's reckless and inscrutable behavior, including his orders "*to march at a moment's warning*" (italics original) immediately upon taking command of the approximately 1,500 starving and ragged Continental soldiers assembled at Cox's Mill (including elements of the Continental army who had escaped capture at Charleston and joined Kalb in North Carolina). Also, from Williams' narrative we have a negative characterization of Gates's decision to march toward Camden at night with militias and regulars that "had never been once exercised in arms together." Gates, Williams reported, believed this ramshackle force consisted of seven thousand soldiers, though a field return revealed only 3,052. "These are enough for our purposes," replied Gates cryptically, at least according to Williams' account.[5]

Unpublished until 1822, when it appeared in William Johnson's *Sketches of the Life and Correspondence of Nathanael Greene*, Williams' version of Gates's march frequently finds its way into contemporary American Revolution accounts, including the influential *War of the Revolution* by Christopher Ward and *The Road to Guilford Courthouse* by John Buchanan. But many of Williams' aspersions were subsequently disputed by Thomas Pinckney, who served as Gates's aide-de-camp during the Camden campaign. Pinckney's narrative was written in response to Williams, and must be read in the context of a critical response, written over forty years after the events it described. Still, the two accounts differ sharply, with Williams' version perhaps making for better storytelling, a tale of pride goeth before the fall at the expense of George Washington's arch rival. But read in combination, they provide a more nuanced depiction of Gates's strategy, especially when combined with other letters, documents, and critical analysis from the campaign.[6]

Prior to his arrival at Kalb's camp, Gates had spent weeks in Virginia pleading for supplies and reinforcement from state and federal officials,

4. Boatner, *Encyclopedia*, 1208-1209; Henry Lee, *The Revolutionary War Memoir of General Henry Lee* (New York: Da Capo Press edition, 1998), 593, and John Beakes, *Otho Holland Williams in the American Revolution* (Charleston, SC: Nautical & Aviation Publishing Co., 2015), 59-60.

5. Otho Holland Williams, "A Narrative of the Campaign of 1780," in William Johnson, *Sketches of the Life and Correspondence of Nathanael Greene: Major General of the Armies of the United States*, Vol. 1 (Charleston, SC: A.E. Miller, 1822), 485-510.

6. According to Pinckney's editor, Robert Scott Davis, Jr., Pinckney's narrative was first published in *Historical Magazine* in 1866, and not reprinted in its entirety until Davis's edited version in 1985.

including North Carolina governor Abner Nash and Virginia governor Thomas Jefferson. True, Kalb warned him, "I have struggled with a good many difficulties for Provisions" ever since arriving in North Carolina, but Gates apparently believed at least some of the assurances he had received from these officials, including one that "Articles of salt, rum, & c.," would soon follow from the Continental magazines in Hillsboro. And Gates also anticipated supplies and reinforcements from North Carolina militia general. Gen. Griffith Rutherford, waiting for him at a forward position near Cheraw, on South Carolina's Pee Dee River. Also marching toward Cheraw with 1,200 militia and "a plentiful supply of provisions" was former North Carolina governor Richard Caswell.[7]

According to Williams, Gates's orders "*to march at a moment's warning . . .* was a matter of great astonishment to those who knew the real situation of the troops." By now wary of false promises, Kalb intended to march south on a westerly route, through the pro-Whig region around Salisbury and Charlotte, if he intended to march at all. To Williams fell the task of convincing Gates the countryside toward Cheraw was "by nature barren, abounding with sandy plains, intersected by swamps, and very thinly inhabited," with a population hostile to the American cause, while the route through Charlotte was "in the midst of a fertile country and inhabited by a people zealous in the cause of America."[8]

But this route would have taken Gates away from Cheraw, where the North Carolinians had promised him provisions. Pinckney suggested Gates's route was chosen, essentially, due to the blackmail of Caswell and Rutherford, whose safety (and provisions) at Cheraw were threatened by nearby British forces. The only means of preserving Caswell and Rutherford "from defeat & destruction, was to form a junction as rapidly as possible," wrote Pinckney. "Could Genl. Gates under these circumstances have retired to refresh his Army in summer quarters at Charlotte or Salisbury, leaving this body of Militia, the only hope of immediate support from the State in which he was acting, to be sacrificed by the imprudence or misconduct of their commanding Officer? Sound policy forbade it."[9]

7. Baron De Kalb to Horatio Gates, July 16, 1780; Millett & Estis to Gates, July 22, 1780; Griffith Rutherford to Gates, July 30, 1780; Richard Caswell to Gates, July 30, 1780, all in *The State Records of North Carolina* (Goldsboro, NC: Nash brothers, 1886-1907), 14: 503, 508, 514, 515-516 respectively. Quote about Caswell's "plentiful supply of provisions" is from Williams, "Narrative," 486.
8. Williams, "Narrative," 486-487.
9. Thomas Pinckney, "General Gates's Southern Campaign," July 27, 1822, appearing in Robert Scott Davis, Jr., "Thomas Pinckney and the Last Campaign of Horatio Gates," *The South Carolina Historical Magazine*, Vol. 86, No. 2 (April 1985), 94-96.

Also here is evidence of Gates's militia strategy—that once embodied, militia must be used quickly, and toward expedient purpose. Historian Paul David Nelson believes Gates was stung by criticisms of the Saratoga campaign, where he had established a defensive position and won largely by capitalizing on British mistakes. "In the Carolinas he apparently intended to prove to his critics that he could be aggressive if he chose." And probably also true was a Pinckney's assertion that Gates believed the Continentals "may as well march on and starve, as starve lying" at Cox's Mill.[10]

Whatever his rationale, Gates was resolute, assuring Williams "plentiful supplies of rum and rations were on the route, and would overtake them in a day or two," probably referring to the Continental stores he'd been promised from Hillsboro. Williams deemed these assertions "fallacious" and "never . . . verified."[11] Nevertheless, Gates set out for the Pee Dee River on July 27, just two days after his arrival, where starvation and deprivation soon followed. "At this time we were so much distressed for want of provisions, that we were fourteen days and drew but one half pound of flour," recalled William Seymour, a Delaware sergeant, of his trip through the Pine Barrens. "Sometimes we drew half a pound of beef per man, and that so miserably poor that scarce any mortal could make use of it."[12]

Gates had left most of his cavalry behind, a decision Continental officer Henry Lee described as his "Fatal Mistake," for the "plains of Carolina," with their wide fields and mature forests, were perfectly suited to cavalry operations.[13] When Gates arrived at Deep River, his only cavalry at camp were the remnants of Casimir Pulaski's dragoons, now under command of the French officer Charles Armand. The Southern Department's other cavalry regiments, under command of Anthony White and William Washington, had been decimated at Charleston and were refitting near Halifax, Virginia.

Lee's criticisms, however, overlook the fact Gates did order White to join him in a letter dated July 20. But when White responded on July 26 that he had "only twenty horses fit for duty,"[14] Gates rescinded his orders, requesting instead that White join him only when his cavalry

---

10. Paul David Nelson, *General Horatio Gates: A Biography* (Baton Rouge, LA: Louisiana State University Press, 1976), 222; Pinckney, "General Gates's Southern Command," 94.
11. Williams, "Narrative," 486-487.
12. William Seymour, *A Journal of the Southern Expedition, 1780-1783* (Wilmington, DE: The Historical Society of Delaware, 1896), 4.
13. Henry Lee, *Revolutionary War Memoirs*, 171-172.
14. Gates to Anthony White, July 20, 1780, Nelson, *General Horatio Gates*, 226; White to Gates, July 26, 1780, *State Records of North Carolina*, 14: 510-512.

"are equipp'd for Service."[15] Still, Williams' assertion that "General Gates did not conceal his opinion, that he held cavalry in no estimation in the southern field," suggests Gates did underestimate the cavalry's role, which hadn't been of much consequence in the fighting at Saratoga.[16]

More easily defensible is Williams' insinuation that Gates ignored the assistance of Francis Marion. In Williams' account, Marion joined Gates and his Continentals on their march south "attended by a very few followers, distinguished by small black leather caps and the wretchedness of their attire; there number did not exceed twenty men and boys." This appearance, Williams wrote, "was in fact so burlesque, that it was with much difficulty the diversion of the regular soldiery was restrained by the officers."

Williams reports Gates was "glad of an opportunity of detaching Colonel Marion" after receiving a request from the Williamsburg District in eastern South Carolina for a Continental officer to command their militia.[17] Indeed, Marion was the perfect man for the job, but at the least, Williams distorts the timeline of these circumstances, if not their broader implications. Marion biographer Hugh Rankin reports Marion joined Gates sometime around July 27 and did not leave him until August 14 or 15, right before the battle at Camden. Williams admits Gates ordered Marion to "watch the motions of the enemy, and furnish intelligence," but clearly he implies Gates saw little value in Marion or his men.[18]

After arriving at Masks Ferry on the Pee Dee River on August 3, Gates was reinforced by one hundred Virginia state troops under Lt. Col. Charles Porterfield. But Gates was furious to discover Caswell had left Cheraw and was now marching toward the British position on Lynch's Creek. To Williams, Gates declared "it appeared to him, that Caswell's vanity was gratified by having a separate command—that probably he contemplated some enterprise to distinguish himself, and gratify his ambition." But anticipating Williams's opinion they should now turn west toward Charlotte, Gates argued it was now "more necessary to counteract the indiscretion of Caswell, and save him from disaster." Surely, the provisions Caswell possessed were part of this necessity.[19]

---

15. Gates to White, August 4, 1780, Nelson, *General Horatio Gates*, 227.
16. Williams, "Narrative," 506.
17. Ibid, 488.
18. Ibid., 482; Hugh Rankin, *Francis Marion: The Swamp Fox* (New York: Thomas Y. Crowell Co., 1973), 56-58.
19. Williams, "Narrative," 488-489.

Gates also argued "having marched thus far directly towards the enemy, a retrograde or indirect movement, would not only dispirit the troops, but intimidate the people of the country." Indeed, the propaganda effect of Gates's march throughout the eastern South Carolina is widely overlooked in latter histories. Though he failed to find Caswell at the Pee Dee, Gates did issue there on August 4 a proclamation announcing to the people of the region the approach of his "numerous, well-appointed, and formidable army," which would soon "compel our late triumphant and insulting foes to retreat from the most advantageous posts with precipitation and dismay."[20]

Pure propaganda, but the proclamation electrified the countryside—evidence the hero of Saratoga still possessed his common touch. After it, "the spirit of revolt, which had been hitherto restrained by the distance of the continental force now advancing to the southward, burst forth into action," reported Loyalist officer Charles Stedman, Cornwallis's commissary officer. "Almost all the inhabitants between Black River and Pedee had openly revolted and joined the Americans." Similarly, Banastre Tarleton reported Gates's "name and former good fortune re-animated the exertions of the country."[21]

Meanwhile, British Lt. Col. Francis, Lord Rawdon, commanding northern South Carolina from his headquarters at Camden, had ordered the 71st Highlanders to evacuate their outpost at Cheraw and retreat to a defensive position on Lynches Creek at Caswell's approach, sending forward Lt. Col. James Webster and the 33rd Regiment to support their withdrawal.[22] "This the active incendiaries of the enemy represented as an act of fear and so encouraged the disaffected and terrified the wavering that the whole country between Pedee and Black River openly avowed the principles of rebellion," Rawdon admitted in a letter to Cornwallis.[23]

Sensing opportunity in this disruption, Patriot partisans Thomas Sumter and William R. Davie attempted a coordinated attack against the British outposts at Hanging Rock and Rocky Mount on August 1.

20. "Proclamation Issued by Horatio Gates at Pedee, the 4th of August 1780," in Banastre Tarleton, *A History of the Campaigns of 178 and 1781, in the Southern Provinces of America* (London: T. Cadell, 1787), 140-141.

21. Charles Stedman, *The History of the Origin, Progress, and Termination of the American War* (London, 1794), 2: 200 and 205; Tarleton, *Campaigns*, 97.

22. Francis Rawdon to Charles Cornwallis, July 31, 1780, *The Cornwallis Papers: The Campaigns of 1780 and 1781 in the Southern Theatre of the American Revolutionary War*, Ian Saberton, ed. (Uckfield, UK: The Naval & Military Press Ltd, 2010) Volume 1, 223 (CP).

23. Cornwallis to Lord George Germain, August 20, 1780, in Jim Piecuch, ed., *The Battle of Camden: A Documentary History* (Charleston, SC: The History Press, 2006), 52; Rawdon to Cornwallis, July 31, 1780, CP, 1: 223.

Rocky Mount was a heavily fortified outpost on the west side of the Catawba River. Hanging Rock, however, was an open camp, guarding the strategic road connecting Camden to Charlotte and the Waxhaw settlements to the north.

Though Sumter's primary attack against Rocky Mount was repulsed, Davie's diversionary attack on Hanging Rock was a sparkling success. Surprising a Loyalist regiment on the outskirts of camp, Davie routed them with his dragoons, then vanished into the countryside with sixty horses and "one hundred muskets and rifles" before the remainder of the British camp could even beat to arms.[24]

Nothing in the historical record suggests Sumter and Davie were coordinating strategy with Gates at this time. Indeed, Rawdon reported to Cornwallis on August 2 "the enemy are moving about me but, as far as I can see, not with any combined plan."[25] But Sumter, in particular, was a gifted intelligence officer, who actively sought strategic advantage in the turmoil caused by Gates's approach.

And Sumter's intelligence reports were already impacting Gates. Back on July 17, Sumter sent a letter to Kalb proposing an attack on the Santee River crossings at Nelson's and Manigault's ferries, suggesting it would require not more than "one thousand or fifteen hundred Troops." This rearguard action, Sumter argued, would not only cut off Camden's supply lines from the south, but also potential reinforcements, leaving Rawdon isolated and vulnerable to attack. It was a bold plan, uniquely suited to Sumter's expertise, the hit-and-run militia raid. After Kalb handed the letter to Gates upon his arrival at Deep River on July 25, it clearly influenced Gates's later strategies.[26]

On August 6, Gates was still at the Pee Dee when he received correspondence that Caswell "had every reason to apprehend an attack" by the British forces at Lynches Creek.[27] Ordering his troops forward as soon as possible, Gates and Otho Holland Williams raced ahead to Caswell's camp, where they found evidence of the provisions Gates had long believed Caswell possessed. After arriving, they were "regaled with wine and other novelties," recalled Williams, though he found the camp strangely disorganized, a condition he attributed to Caswell's efforts to "divest himself then, of his heavy baggage," forced by the death of several

24. William R. Davie, *The Revolutionary War Sketches of William R. Davie* (Raleigh, NC: N.C. Dept. of Cultural Resources), 11-12.
25. Rawdon to Cornwallis, August 2, 1780, CP, 1: 228.
26. Thomas Sumter to Johann Kalb, July 17, 1780, in Michael C. Scoggins, *The Day It Rained Militia* (Charleston, SC: The History Press, 2005), 134-135; George A. Billias, "Horatio Gates: Professional Soldier," 82.
27. Williams, "Narrative," 489.

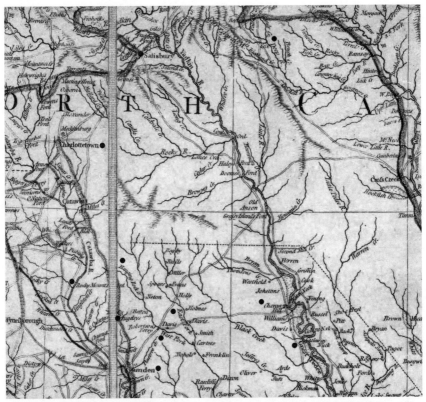

Detail from a 1782 map of Cornwallis's movements through the Carolinas shows the general locations of many places described in this article, marked with black dots: the Deep River, Salisbury, Charlotte[town], Cheraw, Rocky Mount, Hanging Rock, Rugeley's, Lynches Creek (unnamed but an East and West Fork are noted), the Pee Dee River, and Camden.

horses and the "breaking down of carriages" on his march. Still, the long-delayed junction with Caswell "enlivened the countenances of all parties," though the Continental troops "still subsisted upon precarious supplies of corn meal and lean beef, of which they often did not receive half a ration per day, and no possibility existed of doing better."[28]

Meanwhile, Rawdon also raced toward Lynches Creek to reinforce the 33rd and 71st regiments, his object "to retard the progress of Gates . . . or to reduce the enemy to hazard an action where my peculiar advantages of situation would compensate for my disparity in numbers." In all, his collected force totaled 1,100 men, "all regulars and provincials."[29]

28. Ibid, 490.
29. Francis Rawdon, "Account of the Battle of Camden," January 19, 1801, in Piecuch, ed., *Battle of Camden*, 58.

But Sumter "still menaced that road to Camden with a corps of militia," and soon after arriving at Lynches Creek, Rawdon received word the enterprising Sumter and Davie had made another surprise attack on Hanging Rock on August 6. British Provincial and militia casualties were estimated at two hundred, while the American casualties were only fifty-three. But the camp was saved after American looting allowed the British forces to reorganize.[30]

Rarely depicted in the context of Gates's march toward Camden, Sumter and Davie's assault on Hanging Rock had the effect of a coordinated attack to Rawdon and his junior officers. "It appeared a clear consequence that Sumpter, whose men were all mounted, would lose no time in pushing for Camden," Rawdon later recalled. "I addressed the Officers around me, who seemed struck with the obvious magnitude of evil. I told them . . . that we were in a scrape from which nothing but courage could extricate us, & that we must march instantly to crush Sumpter before he could further co-operate with Gates."[31]

Rawdon retreated toward Camden, but learned the following morning Hanging Rock had been saved, diminishing his fears of a Sumter raid. Rawdon now ordered his men to establish a defensive position at a strategic causeway on Little Lynches Creek, a location he later described as "impenetrable" due to the surrounding swamp, "except where a causeway has been made at the passing-places on the great road."[32]

Meanwhile, Gates and Caswell now marched toward Camden, finding Rawdon's position at the Little Lynches Creek causeway too strong to attack when they arrived there on August 11. Gates now turned his army north, marching around the swamps of Lynches River toward Hanging Rock, where he could approach Camden from the main road. Williams suggested he should have detoured even farther north, to the Waxhaws, where he could feed and rest his army, though even he admitted such a "movement would look like retreating from the enemy."[33] As Gates marched north, Rawdon withdrew toward Camden, where he collected most of his detachments and awaited reinforcement from four companies of light infantry sent from the British garrison at Ninety Six.[34]

30. William R. Davie, *Revolutionary War Sketches*, 13-14; John Buchanan, *The Road to Guilford Courthouse* (New York: John Wiley & Sons, Inc., 1997), 133-137.
31. Rawdon, "Account of the Battle of Camden," 58.
32. Ibid, 59.
33. Williams, "Narrative," 490.
34. Charles Stedman, *History*, 2: 204.

Ever industrious, and with his forces swelling after the successful attack on Hanging Rock, on August 12 Sumter sent Gates a detailed report of British troop movements and assured him that Camden was "altogether defenseless . . . if Gen'l Gates, thenk proper to Send a Party over pinetree Creek to fall in their Rear . . . it Woud Totally Ruen them, and Nothing is more Certain then that their Retreat woud be Rendered exceedingly precareous." This was another version of the plan Sumter had sent to Kalb in July—to cut off Camden from the south and west, rendering it vulnerable to siege or attack by a superior force, forcing Rawdon to either retreat or attack under unfavorable circumstances.[35]

After a detour of thirty-four miles, Gates and his army arrived on August 14 at Rugeley's Mill, a small settlement about twelve miles north of Camden. That same day he was joined by approximately seven hundred soldiers under Gen. Edward Stevens, a former Continental Army officer now commanding Virginia militia.[36]

Likely at this time, after arriving on the outskirts of Camden, assessing the situation, and hearing from his informants, Gates began to finalize strategies contemplated on his march. Many histories now jump ahead to Gates's decision to march toward Camden on the night of August 15, his decision supposedly bolstered by "a rough estimate of the forces under his command, marking them upwards of seven thousand men," according to Williams's narrative. Astounded by Gates's exaggerated estimate, Williams requested an immediate field return, reporting only 3,052 present and fit for duty. "These are enough for our purpose," answered Gates, a response that, according to Williams, astonished the American officers, who "could not imagine how it could be conceived, that an army, consisting of more than two-thirds militia, and which had never been once exercised in arms together, could form columns, and perform other maneuvers in the night, and in the face of the enemy."[37]

Gates's bogus belief in his numerical superiority, therefore, became motivation for his foolish expedience in marching toward Camden in the dark, at least according to canon narrative influenced by Williams. "On August 15, Gates ordered a night march which he expected would

---

35. Sumter to Thomas Pinckney, August 12, 1780, *The State Records of North Carolina*, 14: 553-554; Williams, "Narrative," 492, and Joseph Graham, *General Joseph Graham and His Papers*, William A. Graham, ed. (Raleigh, NC: Edwards & Broughton, 1904), 241.
36. Ward, *War of the Revolution*, 721.
37. Williams, "Narrative," 492-493.

bring his army into position to trap a much smaller British force," wrote historian Robert Middlekauff in *The Glorious Cause*. "Gates's haste for battle had led him into a deadly predicament, a snare that he only began to comprehend on August 15," agrees historian John Ferling in *Almost a Miracle*.[38]

Many of these histories further castigate Gates for his decision to send Sumter a hundred of his precious Maryland Continentals, along with three hundred North Carolina militia and two artillery pieces, with orders to intercept all stores and troops at the Wateree River headed for Camden. These precious resources would have been invaluable in the battle to come, argues historian John Buchanan, who calls it yet "another foolish decision."[39]

But these criticisms are based on an assumption that it was Gates's intention to attack, as Williams insinuated. From Thomas Pinckney's narrative, we have a conflicting account, indicating the purpose of the nighttime march was only to establish a strong position seven miles north of the town. From this location, Gates would be "so near him [Rawdon] as to confine his operations, to cut off his supplies of Provisions . . . to harass him with detachments of light troops & to oblige him either to retreat or to come out & attack us upon our own ground, in a situation where the Militia . . . might act to the best advantage."

Pinckney recalled Gates sent forward two officers, one an engineer, likely on August 14, "to select a position in front," and upon their return, they reported "they had found a position . . . with a thick swamp on the right, a deep Creek in front & thick low ground also on the left" that could be fortified well enough "with a Redoubt or two & an Abbatis."[40]

Supporting Pinckney's version is an account from European officer John Christian Senf, who claimed he attended a council of Gates's officers the afternoon of August 15 to discuss "taking another position for the Army, as the Ground where they were upon was by no means tenable. On reconnoitering, a Deep Creek,[41] 7 miles in front, was found impassable 7 miles to the Right, & about the same distance to the left, except only in the place where the Ford intersects the great road." By marching there, Senf recounted, Gates's army "would get a more secure

38. Robert Middlekauff, *The Glorious Cause: The American Revolution, 1763–1789* (New York: Oxford University Press, 1982), 455; John Ferling, *Almost a Miracle: The American Victory in the War of Independence* (New York: Oxford University Press, 2007), 441.
39. Buchanan, *The Road to Guilford Courthouse*, 155.
40. Pinckney, "General Gates's Southern Campaign," 84–86.
41. Reported as Sanders Creek in Piecuch but Granny's Creek elsewhere.

Encampment, come nearer Genl. Sumpter, occupy the road on the East side of the Wateree river, and would be able to get nearer intelligence of the Enemy."[42]

From this perspective, Sumter's rearguard attack becomes part of a coordinated strategy to isolate Rawdon, not a foolish diversion of indispensable troops and artillery. And Francis Marion also may have played an important role in this plan. Despite Williams's assertions Gates was "glad of an opportunity of detaching" the "burlesque" Marion into the South Carolina interior, it was only on August 14 or 15 that Gates sent Marion south, with orders to "go Down the Country to Destroy all boats & Craft of any kind" in order to prevent British troops from escaping Camden.[43]

With Sumter and Marion menacing British supply lines from behind, Rawdon would be forced to either attack Gates at his defensive position or retreat. Though his defenses at Camden were stout, Rawdon's force was inferior to Gates, with about "1,400 fighting men of regulars and Provincials," along with four to five hundred militia and North Carolina refugees. Also inside Camden were almost eight hundred sick or invalid soldiers deemed unfit for combat.[44] Indeed, Rawdon would later admit his plan was to "wait till my spies should apprize me of Gates's being approached within an easy march, when I meant to move forward & attack him."[45]

But if Gates's plan was to set up a defensive position tempting Rawdon into attack, why wasn't Williams notified? "It is possible that Col. Williams, who does not mention it, may not have known the transactions," reported Pinckney, "but I have the most perfect recollection of it." A perfect recollection shared by Senf and also Gates's aide, Maj. Charles Magill, who recalled discussing the movement of the Army "to an advantageous post with a swamp in our front, fordable only at the Road" at a council of officers on the evening of August 15.[46] Referring to Williams' quote that Gates deemed the number of troops "enough for our purpose," Pinckney believed this was in reference only to the effort to establish a strong defensive position north of town, not in reference to a nighttime attack, as Williams insinuated.[47]

42. John Christian Senf, "Extract of a Journal concerning the Action of the 16th of August," in Piecuch, ed., *The Battle of Camden*, 22-23.

43. Hugh F. Rankin, *Francis Marion*, 58. Quote is from, Peter Horry to Nathanael Greene, April 20, 1781.

44. Cornwallis to Germain, August 21, 1780, CP: 2: 12.

45. Rawdon, "Account of the Battle of Camden," 60.

46. Charles Magill to his father, n.d., in Piecuch, ed., *The Battle of Camden*, 43.

47. Pinckney, "General Gates's Southern Campaign," 86-87.

Here, then is perhaps the true mystery of the mysterious march of Horatio Gates, for Williams' clearly depicts an officer corps afflicted with "animadversion" by Gates's plans, his narrative describing men who "could not imagine how it could be conceived" the American forces "could form columns, and perform other maneuvers in the night, and in the face of an enemy."[48]

Was Williams referring only to Gates's decision to march at night? Gates's biographer attributes that decision to Gates's "need to reach his expected area of fortification hastily and secretly." Senf reported that, at the council of officers, "It was Unanimously agreed upon to march that Night the Army to that Creek, by which means they would get a more secure Encampment."[49] William R. Davie attributed Gates's primary mistake not to the nighttime march, but to his failure to secure the forward position earlier in the day with "2 or 3 pieces of artillery" and light troops, who could scout British movements.[50] Pinckney's editor, Robert Scott Davis, suggests Williams was not present at the meeting he recounted so vividly in his "Narrative," but only reported the accounts of others.[51] If so, it seems odd Williams was not included, or not informed of the council's assent to Gates's plan.

Like any organization, the Continental Army had its factions. Having served on George Washington's general staff almost five months as adjutant general, Williams was well aware of Gates's feud with Washington. Were these rivalries the inspiration for the critical nature of Williams' "Narrative"? Impossible to say. Certainly, among Gates's many shortcomings during the Camden campaign, his failure to effectively communicate was one of them, though it is not hard to imagine Williams was predisposed to a bias against Washington's arch rival. But here is one mystery about the mysterious march of Horatio Gates we can never solve, only attempt to put in context.

And though Rawdon was outnumbered, his position at Camden threatened by Sumter and Marion on his flanks and rear, he had an ace up his sleeve in the form of Charles Cornwallis. Becoming more and more concerned about the dispatches he was receiving from Rawdon and his northern outposts, Cornwallis decided to assume command of the Camden forces himself, and set out for the town from his Charleston headquarters early in the morning of August 14. "The British General approached rapidly, & I believe with only his personal

---

48. Williams, "Narrative," 493; Senf, "Extract of a Journal," 23.
49. Nelson, *General Horatio Gates*, 230; Senf, "Extract of a Journal," 23.
50. Davie, *Revolutionary War Sketches*, 17.
51. Robert Scott Davis, "Thomas Pinckney and the Last Campaign of Horatio Gates," 78.

escort," recalled Pinckney, somehow escaping the reconnaissance of Marion, "expressly instructed for that purpose."[52]

Arriving at Camden the next day, Cornwallis agreed with Rawdon's assessment to either attack or retreat, though in retreat he "clearly saw the loss of the whole province, except Charlestown, and of all Georgia except Savannah." With Sumpter advancing down the Wateree, Cornwallis feared his "supplies must have failed me in a few days." And so, "seeing little to lose by defeat and much to gain by a victory," he serendipitously ordered his army to "march at 10 o'clock on the night of the 15th" toward Gates's position, his plan "to attack at day break."[53]

For Gates, it was a devastating stroke of bad luck. By sheer coincidence, both armies marched toward one another at almost the same time, around ten o'clock the evening of August 15, Gates marching south, presumably toward the position identified in Senf's memoir, Cornwallis on the same road heading north toward Rugeley's Mill. "If the American Army had marched from Rugeley's two hours earlier, or Cornwallis had moved from Camden two hours later, the event of the contest would probably have been very different," conjectured Pinckney. "But the meeting in the night was one of those incidents frequently occurring in War, which so often defeats the best combined arrangements."[54]

Destiny, it seems, was leading Horatio Gates and his impoverished, hungry army toward conflict with a foe not superior in number, but superior in discipline and experience. The Battle of Camden would be fought the following morning, on August 16, 1781, after the two armies collided in the night, skirmished, then formed for combat. And it was a destiny that would lead not only to the demise of Gates's military career, but also the eternal destruction of his historic legacy, for the adversities of Gates's "mysterious" march foreshadowed a fate even worse in the battle to come.

---

52. Pinckney, "General Gates's Southern Campaign," 91.
53. Cornwallis to Germain, August 20, 1780," CP, 2: 11-12.
54. Pinckney, "General Gates's Southern Campaign," 91.

"Mad Anthony": The Reality Behind the Nickname

❋❖ MICHAEL J. F. SHEEHAN ❖❋

It is often a tradition amongst soldiers and sailors to give monikers to their commanders. American military history resounds with names like Gen. Thomas "Stonewall" Jackson, Gen. Lewis "Chesty" Puller, Gen. Andrew "Old Hickory" Jackson, and so on. One such sobriquet, "Mad Anthony" for Gen. Anthony Wayne, has stuck on and off in the American consciousness for near two centuries. Its origin is not precisely known nor is it totally clear through which veins it most enduringly entered the public mindset, though there are clues. There is, however, one unifying theme to nearly each documentable time Wayne is referred to as "mad" prior to the era of the Mexican-American War: it is not endearing, and it generally carries harsh criticism.

There is a brewery in Fort Wayne, Indiana called Mad Anthony. Erie Brewing in Pennsylvania has a Mad Anthony Pale Ale, and there is an artist in New York City who goes by the name Mad Anthony. In Ohio there is a band called Mad Anthony, and at Waynesboro, Virginia there is a Mad Anthony Mud Run. There are even two books on Wayne which include the name in their title: *Mad Anthony Wayne and the New Republic* by Glenn Tucker and *Unlikely General: 'Mad' Anthony Wayne and the Battle for America* by Mary Stockwell. So what do we know about the supposed origin of this name?[1]

---

1. Mad Anthony Brewing Company, www.madbrew.com; Erie Brewing Company, www.eriebrewingco.com/pages/our-brews; Mad Anthony, www.madanthonynyc.com; Mad Anthony Band, www.madanthonyband.com; Mad Anthony Mud Run, adventuresignup. com/race/VA/Waynesboro/MAMR; Glenn Tucker, *Mad Anthony Wayne and the New Nation: The Story of Washington's Front-Line General* (Harrisburg, PA: Stackpole Books, 1973);

A number of Wayne's biographers attribute the start of the "mad" nickname to a mysterious soldier under Wayne's command called Jemmy the Drover/Rover, or sometimes the "Commodore." Ultimately traced back through printed records to the earliest documentable version of this tale, we find that it appears in 1829 in a Philadelphia magazine called *The Casket*. Essentially, the story goes that in 1781 Jemmy, upon being sent to the guardhouse and threatened with flogging for disorderly conduct, was upset to find that these orders and threats were handed down from Wayne himself. An angry Jemmy exclaimed "Anthony is mad—farewell to you—clear the coast for the commodore, mad Anthony's friend!" The story is difficult to take seriously for a number of reasons. Firstly, the publisher failed to mention where they themselves had heard the tale. Secondly, the publisher says "Jem[m]y, the rover['s] . . . real name is not recollected," so it is nearly impossible to identify who this soldier may have been through muster or pension records. He may have been a real soldier, but it is also questionable as to why the story only comes to light nearly fifty years after the supposed incident took place, and thirty years after Wayne's death.[2]

The publication of the "mad" moniker in *The Casket* was not the first historical reference to it. It shows up during Wayne's lifetime, in a 1781 London pamphlet one year after originally being written. On July 20, 1780, Wayne led a disastrous attack on a blockhouse in New Jersey at Bull's Ferry. After some time and the loss of too many men, the British and Loyalists stood their ground in the blockhouse, and Wayne opted to retreat with some captured cattle and a defeat on his hands. To make fun of Wayne and the whole affair, British adjutant general Maj. John Andre wrote a long, mocking poem entitled "The Cow Chace." One passage that fictionally portrays a nymph or young woman fleeing the battle goes:

> A nymph, the Refugees had drove, Far from her native tree
> Just happen'd to be on the move, when up came Wayne and Lee
> She in mad Anthony's fierce eye, the hero saw pourtray'd
> And all in tears, she took him by the bridle of his Jade

Wayne, it is implied, then went on to seduce her, so in this case, the term "mad" is associated with Wayne's shortcomings as a gentleman and as an officer, his failing to take the blockhouse.

Mary Stockwell, *Unlikely General: "Mad" Anthony Wayne and the Battle for America* (New Haven, CT: Yale University Press, 2018).
2. "Biography of General Wayne," *The Casket, or Flowers of Literature, Wit & Sentiment*, Volume 4 (1829):498-9, Hathi Trust, babel.hathitrust.org/cgi/pt?id=uc1.b3007583&view= 1up&seq=557.

The following year, Wayne was in Virginia with General Lafayette. On July 6, 1781, he fought in the Battle of Green Springs, a fight in which the Americans were seriously outnumbered, yet Wayne did not order a retreat. One of the physicians with his troops, Dr. Robert Wharry, wrote to a colleague, Dr. Reading Beatty, sending him an account of the action. In his letter, he wrote that the battle was "another Blockhouse affair—Madness—Mad A[nthon]y, by G[od] I never such a piece of work heard of—about eight hundred troops opposed to five or six thousand Veterans upon their own ground." Clearly Wharry, in using the term "mad," was not saying anything kind about Wayne but was in fact sharply criticizing him of being impetuous, as evident by his continuing that "one hundred Rank & file" were killed and wounded in the action.[3]

Such critical references to Wayne do not readily appear again until 1793, a full twelve years later. At this point, the American Revolution had concluded favorably for the Americans, and as the 1780s rolled in to the 1790s, hungry eyes looked west to the lands of the Ohio River Valley and the Northwest Territory. After two military expeditions into the territory were crushed by the Miami Confederacy and their leader Little Turtle, the army was reorganized into the Legion of the United States. President George Washington and Secretary of War Henry Knox selected Wayne to lead this new force. While Wayne headed west and began constructing a series of small posts that ensured a proper line of communication with Philadelphia (at the time the capital), the newspapers kept a watchful eye. In March 1793, someone wrote a song called the "Parnassian Chronicle" for the *Vermont Gazette*. Supposed to be to the tune of the then-popular song "Derry Down," one verse reads:

> In the system of war we are rising apace, Mad Anthony's keeping the Indians in place
> With the pomp and parade of a nabob . . . a Knox, While he stall feeds his men he's avoiding hard knocks

While not particularly critical, it does poke some fun at Wayne's love of pomp and ceremony, which at times during his career wasn't far off the mark.[4]

3. John Andre, *The Cow Chace* (London: John Fielding, 1781), 25, google.com/books/edition/The_Cow_Chace/oRIvAAAAYAAJ?hl=en&gbpv=1&printsec=frontcover; Robert Wharry to Reading Beatty, July 27, 1781, in John U. Rees, *A Smart firing commenc'd from both parties: Brig. Gen. Anthony Wayne's Pennsylvania Battalions in Virginia, June to November 1781*, www.scribd.com/document/125429123/Appendix-!-A-Smart-firing-commenc-d-from-from-both-parties-Brig-Gen-Anthony-Wayne-s-Pennsylvania-Battalions-in-Virginia-June-to-November-1781.
4. "Parnassian Chronicle," *The Vermont Gazette*, Vol X, No 41 (March 8, 1793), www.nespapers.com/images/51961319.

The following year proved to be more discriminating towards Wayne in the papers. The *Gazette of the United States* published a scathing editorial against Wayne, the author of which was only identified as a "gentleman from Gen. Wayne's camp, who may be depended upon." In the piece, a number of anecdotes and accusations are delivered, one of them being about a group of native people who met with the Americans to request peace, where "Wayne expressed his sorrow at the arrival of the peace applicants . . . being as mad and sanguinary as ever; and very much bloated with the ideas of his military prowess, wants to be dealing in blood." A little while later, the gentleman claimed, "mad Anthony began to be alarmed at the prospect of peace," and so ordered the construction of a new road, ostensibly to coax the Miami into a fight. After the pioneering of the road, which was very much impassable due to the wetness of the season, "mad Anthony discovered . . . [the road] was improper . . . [as] the country was under water." The Legion itself was a mess, he went on, due to the "discontent, the drinking, gambling, quarrelling, fighting, and licentiousness of almost all ranks." He continued on that

> These melancholy truths have been produced in a great measure by the conduct and example of the general, whose manners are despotic, whose judgement is feeble, infirm, and full of prejudice, whose temper is irascible and violent, whose language is indecent and abusive, and whose conduct to his officers is capricious and irregular, being at one time childishly familiar and at another tyrannical and overbearing.

As if that wasn't excoriating enough, Wayne is further accused of favoring his "tools, spies, and toad-eaters," assigning work on the Sabbath, "substituting domination for law, and resentment for justice," and protecting his "pimps and parasites." Every interpretation of this piece will conclude that the use of "mad" is not an endearing title, but a burning criticism. As there was a bit of an open rivalry between Wayne and his second in command, Gen. James Wilkinson, with some officers supporting each general, it would seem likely that is where these accusations originated, but alas, the "gentleman's" name who wrote the editorial is lost to history, while Wilkinson's less than clean service to the United States is a matter of historical fact.[5]

General Wayne died at Presque Isle (present Erie), Pennsylvania on December 15, 1796, and so passed from the realm of current events. The "mad" nickname, however, continued to appear. During the War

---

5. "Stubborn Facts!," *The Gazette of the United States and Daily Evening Advertiser.* June 25, 1794, Vol. VI, No. 12, 2-3. www.newspapers.com/image/466184409. Wilkinson was found to be working as an agent for the Spanish government.

of 1812, the British captured the USS *Chesapeake*. In a London paper, it was pointed out that all the guns on the *Chesapeake* had little copper plates on them bearing names; one of them was "Mad Anthony," among a mix of others like "Putnam," "Washington," and "Bunker Hill." There are a few other mentions, like in the *Long-Island Star* in 1821: "Gen. Wayne, often called mad Anthony from the impetuosity of his attacks," and in *The Democrat* in 1832, where a tale of "the dare devil Wayne—'old mad Anthony' as they called him," is told. There are other references, each telling a military tale of his, and some that aren't stories at all, like the challenge issued by Joseph Jarvis in 1822 to enter his rooster "Mad Anthony" into a fight against any challenger, and in 1838, a horse being entered into a race near New Orleans was named Mad Anthony. In 1845, Horatio N. Moore published the first official biography of Wayne with the help of the general's son Isaac, at the time in his seventies. The book includes the Jemmy the Drover tale (much of the book is taken from the pieces on Wayne in *The Casket*), and so perhaps for the first time the "mad" moniker reached a national audience, as opposed to local newspapers, though it is evident that the name was already associated with Wayne.[6]

What conclusion can we draw from the available information? Should we continue to call General Wayne "Mad"? The closer the document is to his lifetime, the answer would be no, because in each case printed or written during his lifetime the name was accusative or mocking. Yet, we can see that as time went on, likely because nineteenth century people did not have extensive access to information, the meaning of "mad" began to change towards "bold and daring," but always with the shadow of impetuosity. Still, because of Wayne's attacks at Monmouth, Stony Point, Green Spring, and Fallen Timbers the name certainly may feel appropriate. Permit the author to pose a question. With all the evidence against the use of the name, and the absolute dearth of evidence that anyone ever addressed him as "Mad Anthony," would you still call him that?

6. "Yankee Wit," *The Morning Chronicle*. August 16, 1813, No. 19,824, www.news papers.com/image/393100192; *The Long-Island Star*, May 24, 1821, Vol. XII, No. 620, www.nespapers.com/image/118243108; *The Democrat*, August 30, 1832, Vol IX, No 464, www.newspapers.com/image/348716937; "Elegant Amusement," *The Charleston Courier*, June 14, 1822, Vol XX, No. 6973, www.newspapers.com/image/604364433; "Races," *The Daily Picayune*, March 22, 1838, Vol II, No. 49. www.newspapers.com/image/29011576; H. N. Moore, *Life and Services of Gen. Anthony Wayne: Founded on Documentary and Other Evidence, Furnished by his son Col. Isaac Wayne* (Philadelphia: Leary & Getz, 1845), 133.

The British Invade Nicaragua

❀❧ GEORGE KOTLIK ❧❀

According to Andrew Jackson O' Shaughnessy, the San Juan Expedition was among "the most ambitious enterprises of the American Revolutionary War."[1] In 1779, after Spain's formal entry into the war, the British aimed at striking Spanish interests in Central America. They would invade by first securing control of the San Juan River in present-day Nicaragua. Their operation sought to protect against attack the most popular overland route through Central America to the Pacific Ocean. The San Juan River was conveniently situated in the middle of New Spain, the Spanish Empire in the Americas. The British plan, if successful, would split the Spanish Empire in two. The construction of forts along this route would be used to invade surrounding territory and plunder the wealth of the Spanish empire.[2] British invasions into Central and South America would eventually, Whitehall hoped, put pressure on Spain to make peace and exit the war.[3]

The conflict in the Caribbean produced an entirely different war than the American Revolution's northern and southern theaters and the conflict west of the Appalachian Mountains, albeit one that is still part of the overall American War for Independence. Fighting in the West Indies was not between dissatisfied, rebellious provincials pitted against their former King and country. The revolution in the West Indies was fought between empires.[4] And yet there is far less literature

1. Andrew Jackson O'Shaughnessy, *The Men Who Lost America: British Leadership, the American Revolution, and the Fate of the Empire* (New Haven: Yale University Press, 2013), 178.
2. Ibid., 179. Terry Coleman, *The Nelson Touch: The Life and Legend of Horatio Nelson* (London: Oxford University Press, 2002), 28. During this time, unrest within the dominions of New Spain arose from dissatisfied subjects in Popayan, Nuevo Reyno, and Peru .Robert Southey, *The Life of Horatio Lord Nelson* (New York: E. P. Dutton & Co., 1906), 15.
3. O'Shaughnessy, *The Men Who Lost America*, 182.
4. Kathleen DuVal, *Independence Lost: Lives on the Edge of the American Revolution* (New York: Random House, 2015), xv.

about the conflict in the West Indies compared to other aspects of the American Revolution, and the San Juan Expedition is barely mentioned.[5]

In Whitehall, the British secretary at war, Lord George Germain, was aware of the strengths of Britain's enemies in the Americas. Spain was weaker than France. The San Juan River campaign would, ideally, force Spain out of the fight. Germain wanted to take New Orleans, but after learning of Don Bernardo de Galvez's preparations and his amassment of troops and supplies aimed at capturing British West Florida, Germain realized that Central America proved to be a promising opportunity to surprise Spain by attacking a region that did not boast a heavy concentration of troops bent on invasion.[6]

The plan of invading Spain's possessions in Central America was hatched by Maj. Gen. John Dalling. A veteran of the French and Indian War, Dalling was governor of Jamaica from 1777 through 1782.[7] Dalling fancied ideas of conquering Honduras after a successful plundering of Spanish-controlled Omoa situated in the Bay of Honduras in October 1779.[8] The treasure captured from the Spanish garrison was valued at over two million dollars.[9] His interest piqued, Dalling leafed through Thomas Jeffrey's *West-India Atlas*, published in 1775, which contributed even more to his already whetted appetite.[10] Among its contents, Jeffrey's atlas outlined the riches of New Spain: "the Spanish mines [in the Americas] have sent into the metropolis, from 1492 to 1740, that is, in the space of 248 years, more than nine millions of millions of piastres . . . We ought to add to these riches those which are not registered, in order to avoid paying the duty, and which may amount to be a fourth more." In addition to astounding gold and silver reserves, Spanish America boasted a wealth of valuable trade goods

---

5. For further reading on the San Juan Expedition see: O'Shaughnessy, *The Men Who Lost America*, 178-185; Coleman, *The Nelson Touch*, 28-35; Southey, *The Life of Horatio Lord Nelson*, 15-20; John Sugden, *Nelson: A Dream of Glory, 1758-1797* (New York: Holt, 2004), 150-175; Roger Knight, *The Pursuit of Victory: The Life and Achievement of Horatio Nelson* (New York: Basic Books, 2007), 55-59, 61; David F. Marley, *Wars of the Americas: A Chronology of Armed Conflict in the New World, 1492 to Present* (Denver: ABC-CLIO, 1998), 325-326; Thomas E. Chavez, *Spain and the Independence of the United States: An Intrinsic Gift* (Albuquerque: University of New Mexico Press, 2002), 150-157; David R. Radell, "Exploration and Commerce on Lake Nicaragua and the Rio San Juan – 1524-1800," *Journal of Interamerican Studies and World Affairs* 12, no. 1 (January 1970): 123-125.
6. O'Shaughnessy, *The Men Who Lost America*, 179.
7. Ibid., 179, 181.
8. Chavez, *Spain and the Independence of the United States*, 152-153; Sugden, *Nelson*, 150.
9. Sugden, *Nelson*, 150.
10. Coleman, *The Nelson Touch*, 28.

such as cochineal, indigo, logwood, cacao, and sugar.[11] Dalling's decision to invade New Spain was no doubt influenced by the wondrous riches described in his personal copy of *West India Atlas*.

Reports from Maj. James Lawrie, superintendent of British settlers on the Mosquito Shore,[12] assured Dalling that he could raise thousands of volunteers, including negroes and Indians, in addition to furnishing plenty of small boats for an expedition up the San Juan River.[13] Encouraged by Lawrie's reports, Dalling arrogantly wrote to London claiming that if he was given a force of "no great extent," he would be answerable to give the entire Dominion of Spain in the Americas to the home government.[14] Dalling truly believed that with a force of fifteen hundred troops supplemented by Indian and volunteer forces, he could conquer the Yucatan Peninsula.[15] The plan was simple: a force would ascend the San Juan River and capture the Immaculate Conception, a fort located near the mouth of Lake Nicaragua.[16] After that, one or more vessels patrolling Lake Nicaragua coupled with the capture of the city of Granada on the north end of the lake would grant Britain control of the entire region. Garrisoned outposts could receive supplies from the San Juan, Bluefields, and Matina rivers. From Lake Nicaragua, an invasion force would secure the towns of Leon and Relaejo on the western coast of the isthmus before the establishment of a naval squadron would grant Britain access to the Pacific Ocean. With New Spain cut in two, the British would utilize the western squadron to plunder New Spain's west coast possessions. Simultaneously, British agents would destabilize Spanish colonies by fomenting rebellion among the local populace before invading with ground troops. The result would provide Britain access to the resources of Central and South America which would then be open to exploitation and British trade.[17]

11. Thomas Jeffreys, *The West-India Atlas* (London, 1775), 7, www.loc.gov/resource/g4900 m.gar00006/?sp=1. Cochineal was used for making the colors purple and scarlet
12. British settlers occupied the coast of the Bay of Honduras, later known as the coast of Nicaragua, since the late seventeenth century. They established a logging trade, exporting logwood and mahogany. Informal logging communities stretched along the coast at Black River, Rattan (Roatoan), St. George's Key, and Cape Gracias a Dios. These settlers were not recognized by Spain. They were considered squatters and Spain attempted to discourage their presence through military force. Despite Spain's hostility, these communities "thrived and became informal colonies complete with a local superintendent general who reported to the governor of Jamaica." O'Shaughnessy, *The Men Who Lost America*, 181.
13. Sugden, *Nelson*, 151.
14. John Dalling Report, February 4, 1780, *The On-Line Institute for Advanced Loyalist Studies*, www.royalprovincial.com/history/battles/jamalet1.shtml.
15. O'Shaughnessy, *The Men Who Lost America*, 181.
16. Coleman, *The Nelson Touch*, 29.
17. Sugden, *Nelson*, 151.

Back in Whitehall, Germain was initially apprehensive of supporting Dalling's plan, but after some deliberation he changed his mind
and in January 1780 he informed Dalling that he not only supported
the venture but was also sending 3,000 additional soldiers to defend
Jamaica and partake in the expedition.[18] Eager to get on with the campaign, Dalling did not wait for Germain's reinforcements.

As early as 1779, Dalling sent a small expeditionary force to "capture
control of the San Juan River."[19] On November 19, Major Lawrie wrote
to Dalling from Black River on the Mosquito Shore requesting arms
and ammunition for not only the defense of the shore but also to use
as presents for local Indian tribes who conducted open negotiations
with the Spanish.[20] Presents would help prevent and deter Native
friendship with the Spaniards and entice the locals to join British efforts. Lawrie also informed Dalling of his attempts at recruiting volunteers consisting of Mosquito men, Indians, and "Trusty Negroes."[21]

Dalling, in preparation for an expedition up the San Juan River,
placed Capt. John Polson of the 60th (Royal American) Regiment in
command. Polson was instructed to bring with him ship-carpenters
with materials needed to assemble a vessel on Lake Nicaragua for the
purposes of "securing command of the Lake."[22] The vessel went with
the expedition, in pieces, to be assembled on site. Horatio Nelson was
placed in charge of the naval force that escorted the expedition's troop
transports.[23] Nelson's orders were to safely deliver the expedition ships
to Mosquito shore and the mouth of the San Juan River, then to protect
the expedition's back and maintain secure supply lines.[24] To recruit more
men, Dalling, in 1779, published a proclamation by the English king
calling on Jamaica volunteers. Anyone who signed up would "easily Acquire Riches and Honor, and be of Essential Service to their Country."[25] They would be outfitted, formed into companies, paid the same
wages as soldiers, receive rations, and divide plunder equally.[26]

The expedition set out to sea at six in the morning on February 3,
1780. Several transports, approximately six vessels, set out from Jamaica

---

18. O'Shaughnessy, *The Men Who Lost America*, 181.
19. Ibid., 181.
20. James Lawrie to John Dalling, November 19, 1779, *The On-Line Institute for Advanced Loyalist Studies*, www.royalprovincial.com/history/battles/moslet1.shtml.
21. Ibid.
22. John Dalling Report, February 4, 1780.
23. Coleman, *The Nelson Touch*, 29.
24. Sugden, *Nelson*, 153.
25. John Dalling, Jamaica Volunteers: Proclamation by the King, 1779, *The On-Line Institute for Advanced Loyalist Studies*, www.royalprovincial.com/military/rhist/jvol/jvrcrt.htm.
26. Ibid.

carrying 300 to 400 regulars from the 60th and 79th regiments, a Loyalist unit called the Loyal Irish Corps, sixty sailors, roughly two hundred Jamaican volunteers, sixty to seventy Irish, and a mix of foreigners, blacks, and Indians. Provided with six months worth of provisions, the force first landed on the British-held island of Providence off the coast of Nicaragua before sailing on for Cape Gracias a Dios on the Honduran coast. The expedition planned on meeting up with Lawrie at the cape, who promised to provide the campaign with significant local support, pick up his force of volunteers, and sail south along the coast of the Yucatan Peninsula before making for the mouth of the San Juan River and proceeding inland.[27]

On February 14, the expedition arrived at Cape Gracias a Dios—and Lawrie was nowhere to be found. Instead, a lone officer offered news that Lawrie was still recruiting somewhere on the Black River. This setback, while minor, was the first of many difficulties to come. Unwilling to proceed without Lawrie and his "considerable force," the expedition set up camp on the marshy wetlands known as Wank's Savannah. While there, they reached out to local Indian groups bearing presents in an attempt to enlist their manpower. The vessel that was brought in pieces was assembled and called the *Lord Germain*. On February 22, Lawrie finally arrived with 200 or so men, in poor health, and thirteen Black River craft. This was hardly the promised "sizeable" force, and the expedition lingered at Wank's Savannah for another week before setting sail for San Juan on March 7. Between March 7 and 24, local Indians were recruited along the Yucatan coast.[28]

On March 24, the fleet arrived at the mouth of the San Juan River to a shanty village called Greytown. A base was immediately set up on shore while men and cargo were unloaded from the ships. The boats ferrying soldiers and supplies to the shore were overloaded and many capsized. Consequently, badly needed supplies were lost and one man drowned. Eventually, the British had set up a defensible base at Greytown and, in no time, preparations were made to advance up the San

27. Sugden, *Nelson*, 154-155. The British were confident in enlisting Native support. The Spaniards had a history in the region of enslaving locals. This knowledge helped guide British expectations for amassing a large body of local support in Nicaragua.

28. Sugden, *Nelson*, 155-158. For further reading on local assistance to the British expedition see Matthew P. Dziennik, "Miskitu, Military Labour, and the San Juan Expedition Of 1780," *The Historical Journal* 61 no. 1 (March 2018): 155-179. The soldiers who arrived with Lawrie had fevers and dysentery. In total, Lawrie recruited 12 whites, 60 African American slaves, and 220 Mosquito Men. His results did not match the expectations of substantial local support counted on by British leadership.

Juan. Polson, accompanied by Horatio Nelson, split his forces in two. The advance force was composed of disciplined regulars while the second force followed behind. Prior to setting out, a letter from Dalling in Jamaica dated March 17 informed Polson that reinforcements of 300 regulars and 300 volunteers were on their way from Kingston under the command of forty-six-year-old Lt. Col. Stephen Kemble of the 60th Regiment. According to the letter, Kemble would assume command of the expedition.[29]

The following morning Polson advanced up the half-mile wide river. Initially, the forward party advanced only six miles a day; shallow water grounded boats, causing crippling delays.[30] Mosquitos, heat, and humidity tortured the expedition members as they waded deeper and deeper into the unforgiving jungle. Eventually, the advance force reached an outpost manned by fifteen to eighteen Spanish regulars and guarded by anywhere from four to nine or even ten swivel guns.[31] The outpost was called "Platalorma," and was situated on Bartola Island in the middle of the river.[32] Careful not to raise an alarm, the British encircled the outpost. Nelson led a naval assault while ground forces under the command of Lt. James Mounsey of the 79th Regiment attacked by land, blocking a Spanish retreat through the jungle.[33]

On April 9, the British advance force descended upon the outpost. In no time, the Spanish were defeated. Some prisoners were taken and one Spaniard escaped. Only one British soldier was injured when a snake fell from a branch and bit him in the eye. He died shortly after his eye dissolved, his body swelled up, and his skin turned a deep yellow. Following its capture, the outpost was converted to a British base. According to Spanish prisoners, they were only five miles from El Castillo de la Immaculada Concepcion. The castle was spotted by a British scouting party on April 10.[34]

El Castillo de la Immaculada Concepcion proved to be a formidable obstacle for the British. Situated on a hill, its walls were four feet thick and fourteen feet high. Bastions rested on each corner of the castle and the Spanish flag flew above a fifty-foot keep. A ditch enclosed it. Tim-

---

29. Sugden, *Nelson*, 158-160. Nelson refused to remain behind at camp and face boredom. Instead, he decided to leave the boats and head up river with Polson and his ground forces. Polson needed the help and Nelson offered to command the vessels heading up the river.
30. Sugden, *Nelson*, 160-162. Once they reached deeper water, they advanced ten miles a day.
31. Radell, "Exploration and Commerce on Lake Nicaragua and the Rio San Juan," 124; Sugden, *Nelson*, 163.
32. Chavez, *Spain and the Independence of the United States*, 154.
33. Sugden, *Nelson*, 163.
34. Ibid., 163-164.

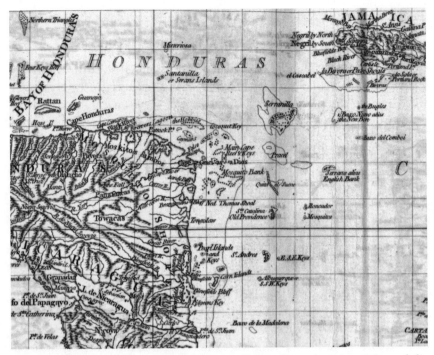

Detail from a 1775 map of the West Indies, with Jamaica at the upper right, and the San Juan River, at bottom center, with Lake Nicaragua to the left.

ber was cleared around its perimeter providing a field of vision for defenders. It was commanded by Don Juan de Ayssa and garrisoned by a force of twenty cannons, twelve swivels, a mortar, and 149 armed defenders (half of which were regulars and the rest a collection of unprofessional fighters). In order to proceed up the San Juan River, the British needed to take control of this fortress. Unfortunately for them, de Ayssa had been notified of their advance from the Spaniard who escaped the assault on Platalorma. The Spaniards were ready. In preparation for a siege, de Ayssa hoarded freshwater, stockpiled food, brought in cattle from the fields, and sent two messengers, accompanied by his wife, away to Granada to get help.[35]

On April 11, British troops made camp along a bend in the river, hidden from view a few miles below the fort. Four 4-pounders accompanied them. Late at night on April 12, cannon were placed on a ridge overlooking the fort. On the morning of April 13, British bombardment of the castle began, commencing the siege which lasted much

---

35. Ibid., 163-165; Chavez, *Spain and the Independence of the United States*, 154.

longer than the British had expected or wanted. Despite their superior numbers, they did not easily conquer the Spanish castle. Throughout the entire siege, ammunition for the artillery was constantly in short supply. Boats bearing supplies and ammunition capsized in the river, losing much-needed provisions. Sometimes British resupply ships would go up the wrong river and fail to deliver their cargo on time.[36] At one point a Spanish sally, armed with machetes, engaged in fierce hand-to-hand combat against British bayonets.[37]

Ever since the siege started, rain poured down on the attackers almost every day. Tempests were a common occurrence in the region. The British camp became muddy and miserable. Soldiers fell ill from malaria, dysentery, and typhoid fever. In an attempt to bring down the wall, a mine was dug at the foot of the hill.[38] It was for naught; after seventeen yards they hit rock and the mine was abandoned.[39] Eventually, after sixteen days, the castle surrendered.[40] The Spaniards had run out of water, ammunition, and space to put their wounded.[41]

On May 15, Colonel Kemble arrived at El Castillo de la Immaculada Concepcion and took command of the surviving British forces.[42] He brought reinforcements with him, intending to proceed up the river to secure the mouth of Lake Nicaragua.[43] Kemble immediately noticed the poor state of the expedition. Everything was in disorder, the soldiers were weak, and there was no relief for men standing guard. The Indians deserted, angry for not being allowed to plunder the castle and take slaves. Without the assistance of local Indians, the British were further weakened despite the arrival of Kemble's reinforcements. Sickness plagued the men, tents failed to keep out water, and supplies were constantly in want. Some of the more unfortunate men went without blankets, shoes, or stockings. Heavy rains continued to pour down, and supplies sent from the San Juan River Harbor were regularly late, lost, or destroyed from rain or eaten by worms. Survivors were forced to eat

36. Sugden, *Nelson*, 165-167. Cannonfire had to stop on multiple occasions because they ran out of ammunition. More ammunition would arrive by boat, but sometimes they did not bring enough for any long-term cannonading of the castle.

37. Chavez, *Spain and the Independence of the United States*, 155.

38. Sugden, *Nelson*, 166-168.

39. "Kemble's Journal 1780," *Kemble Papers* (New York: New-York Historical Society, 1885), 2: 6.

40. Sugden, *Nelson*, 168-169. Horatio Nelson left to Jamaica due to illness on the same day the fort surrendered.

41. Chavez, *Spain and the Independence of the United States*, 155.

42. "Kemble's Journal 1780," *Kemble Papers*, 2: 10.

43. Sugden, *Nelson*, 164. Kemble brought 250 British troops and 270 men from the Jamaica Legion. O'Shaughnessy, *The Men Who Lost America*, 183.

bananas and monkeys.[44] The men were convalescent and, as a result, progress in all departments was slow, if they progressed at all.[45] Despite these setbacks, Kemble had to surge on.

On Friday, July 7, 250 soldiers finally advanced up the river after delays by heavy rain. On July 8, Kemble made his way up the river to join the advance party, leaving behind Sir Alexander Leigh in command of the castle. Progress up the river was slow. Boats were regularly grounded, violent rain prevented the expedition from lighting fires at night, soldiers were left without tents, and supplies were always badly needed. A corporal drowned attempting to deliver supplies upriver.[46] All of this contributed to the general fatigue of the force. Eventually, the expedition arrived at the mouth of Lake Nicaragua where the Spaniards, anticipating the British invasion, had fortified the lake entrance.[47] According to a report issued by Edward Marcus Despard, a fort called Fort St. Carlos[48] offered views of the lake and river and was capable of containing 200 to 300 men; two armed vessels, a sloop and a schooner, protected the lake's entrance.[49] During his reconnoitering, Despard was discovered by the Spanish who raised an alarm. This, coupled with the fatigue of his troops, poor supplies, and general sickliness of the men forced Kemble to turn back and avoid any assault on the mouth of the lake.[50] Kemble realized he was not prepared well enough for an assault, especially an extended one, on a fortified Spanish position. Instead of realizing his ambitions in capturing control of Lake Nicaragua, Kemble withdrew back down the river to the castle.

Kemble still sought to take Fort St. Carlos, but found himself busy managing the affairs of the campaign with no moves made to assault the mouth of the river. In the meantime, he gathered intelligence of the Spanish and even entertained alternative invasion routes other than the San Juan River from which an expedition, ideally, could launch an assault upon the Spanish country. In August, Francisco Yore, a Spanish

44. Chavez, *Spain and the Independence of the United States*, 156.
45. "Kemble's Journal 1780," *Kemble Papers*, 2: 7, 10, 14-16, 19-21, 24.
46. "Kemble's Journal 1780," *Kemble Papers*, 2: 21-25.
47. Don Francisco Saavedra de Sangronis, *The Journal of Don Francisco Saavedra de Sangronis, 1780-1783*, ed. Francisco Morales Padron, trans. Aileen Moore Topping (Gainesville: University of Florida Press, 1989), 40. Messengers from El Castillo de la Immaculada Concepcion warned Spanish officials in Granada who moved to fortify the mouth of the river.
48. "Kemble's Journal 1780," *Kemble Papers*, 2: 41.
49. "Edward Marcus Despard Report, 27 July, 1780," *Kemble Papers*, 2: 29-30.
50. "Kemble's Journal 1780," *Kemble Papers*, 2: 31-32.

Negro, brought information that the fort boasted twelve cannon, an abatis around its exterior, 50 regular soldiers, and 15 artillerymen with more reinforcements expected daily; the vessels on the lake each boasted two cannons and swivel guns; the sloop was maintained by 30 men and the schooner 50; two more vessels were being assembled on-site[51] (in reality, the Spaniards boasted a 500-troop garrison at the fort which was defended by double walls).[52] Intelligence continued to arrive, but no feasible alternative routes were discovered. Back in Jamaica, Dalling's commitment to the expedition waned. Ever promising fresh reinforcements, of which none ever came, British leadership became anxious at rumors of a pending attack on Jamaica (a direct result of gains made in North America against Crown forces). Orders to prepare to withdraw were given to Kemble on August, 1780.[53]

On November 24, Kemble received a letter from Dalling ordering him to blow up and abandon El Castillo de la Immaculada Concepcion. The fort was abandoned by the end of the year and the Spanish regained control of what remained in early January, 1781 with a force of 150 men under the command of Capt. Thomas de Julia.[54] Between November and late January, the British made preparations to evacuate Central America. Kemble arrived at Port Royal, Jamaica on Tuesday, February 27, 1781.[55] By April 1781 the Spanish had pushed all British forces to the mouth of the San Juan River, effectively ending the British threat up the river.[56]

In all, Britain lost roughly 2,500 men in its San Juan campaign. Of around 1,800 soldiers dispatched on the campaign, only 380 returned. In addition, 1,000 sailors who accompanied the expedition lost their lives.[57] The campaign not only ended in failure, it was a complete disaster. It was poorly supplied, lacked sufficient manpower, and failed to consider the impact the tropical environment would have on expedition members. Had British leaders such as Governor Dalling acquainted themselves with the British attempt at capturing Cartagena de Indias in 1741 during the War of Jenkins Ear, they would have been better informed and armed with the knowledge of the effects tropical disease and tempests would have on an invasion force. Careful preparation cou-

---

51. Ibid., 2:41-42, 50-51.

52. Chavez, *Spain and the Independence of the United States*, 156.

53. Ibid., 156-157.

54. "Kemble's Journal 1780," *Kemble Papers*, 2: 51-52, 56-57; Chavez, *Spain and the Independence of the United States*, 157.

55. "Kemble's Journal 1780," *Kemble Papers*, 2: 62-63.

56. Chavez, *Spain and the Independence of the United States*, 157.

57. O'Shaughnessy, *The Men Who Lost America*, 185.

pled with more manpower would have produced a much different result in Nicaragua in 1780.

In Whitehall, Germain groaned at the expedition's failure, especially considering how it diverted much-needed men and supplies from the war effort on the North American mainland.[58] Had the campaign been successful, it would have produced dramatic results. If Spain wanted to keep its possessions in the Americas, the Spanish crown would have had to resources from aiding the American revolutionaries and instead focus on fighting British invasion forces in Central and South America, possibly aided by disgruntled Indians, throughout the North American South West, Central America, and South America. Britain, if they ended up losing the war in North America, would have gained territory in Latin America rich in natural resources that they could colonize with loyalist refugees. Indeed, Dalling had planned on using loyalists to settle the lands conquered by Britain in the territories acquired from New Spain.[59] He even sent a young officer to New York to encourage poor people to settle Nicaragua.[60] In an ideal situation, a successful British invasion up the San Juan River could have prevented the Spanish capture of Pensacola in 1781, by diverting Spanish attention away from British West Florida. Assuming a successful British defense of West Florida, Britain could then use the province as a bargaining tool in peace negotiations.

As Thomas Chavez points out, the Central American theatre of the American Revolution was significant not only for the mere fact that both sides, Spain and Britain, had committed large amounts of troops in the fighting; if the region was not important, "both sides . . . would have quit the area. Instead, after defeats, each side regrouped to counterattack or to take the offensive."[61] In the end, the Union Jack almost dominated Latin America and the American Southwest during the 1780s, but their Nicaragua campaign was a failure, but the ambitions it attempted never produced an alternate historical narrative.

58. Ibid.
59. Sugden, *Nelson*, 151.
60. John Dalling, *John Dalling Report, May 21, 1780*, from *The On-Line Institute for Advanced Loyalist Studies*, transcribed by Todd Braisted, www.royalprovincial.com/history/battles/jamalet2.shtml.
61. Chavez, *Spain and the Independence of the United States*, 150-151.

Mapping the Battle of Eutaw Springs: Modern GIS Solves a Historic Mystery

❀ STEPHEN J. KATZBERG ❀

When dealing with available sources to investigate questions related to historical events, the researcher has at his disposal a limited set from which to choose. Contemporaneous accounts, reports, maps, plats, legal filings, and location evidence exist in a more or less complete record. Nevertheless, linking the elements bearing witness to one event or another is limited by the fact that quantitative analysis, across multiple data sets, is a modern invention. Navigation based on known, regularized coordinates only became available in the middle 1700s. Instrumentation to measure location and distance is also of modern origin.

Creating maps with accurate local detail has made plats or land resurveys great resources, but very difficult to "sew" together since they generally contain very few identifiable topographic features and are at various scales. The advent of geographical information systems (GIS) has caused major improvements in quantitative mapping. The ability to relate maps done on known scales has made for a whole host of applications when coupled with modern remote sensing from sources such as aircraft cameras, spacecraft imagery, surveyed maps, GPS mapping and laser scanning LIDAR. These applications include county property mapping, road routing, commercial company siting, business locating, and the like. Using GIS to corroborate the historical record compared to quantitative maps is an obvious potential application.

The Battle of Eutaw Springs has associated with it an historical mystery concerning the details of the distribution of troops and their actions. What follows is an illustration of applying GIS to the historical record. The result is a proposed resolution of that mystery that allows the historical narrative to be reconciled with a correct geographical interpretation. A venerated map passed down in time from 1822 until today will need to be redone.

BACKGROUND

(The following description is adapted from Henry Lee, 1812.) Early on the morning of September 8, 1781 groups of British soldiers camped near Eutaw Springs were awakened in preparation for a morning chore. These soldiers had been detailed to foraging and were drawn from the major units under Lt. Col. Alexander Stewart's command. These men represented the last large-scale Royal Army command left in the Carolinas. Lord Cornwallis, after having been staggered at Guilford Court House, had refitted at Wilmington and moved his army north and, a month later, would meet his undoing at Yorktown in Virginia.

The foragers moved up the Congaree River Road turning down one or another of the various paths that led down to the Santee River plantations. Waiting for the commissary wagons coming from Charlestown was a matter of irritation, since the deliveries were fraught with peril and delay. Partisan rangers were likely to swoop down and capture food and escort. Adequate provisions were always in short supply.

September is the month for harvesting sweet potatoes in South Carolina and this little army of a couple thousand regulars and American tory volunteers intended to supplement their meager provisions while waiting for the promised wagons coming from Charlestown. No intelligence of Rebel forces had been gained from the various patrols and scouts sent out by Lt. Colonel Stewart. Ominously others had failed to report back. Nevertheless, Lt. Colonel Stewart had taken the precaution of sending an escort of cavalry under Major John Coffin to shepherd the little band, just in case.

As the foragers had gotten about four miles from the British army camp, a group of unidentified horsemen appeared in the road. Immediately Major Coffin charged and just as quickly his troopers were shattered: He had run straight into the vanguard of three thousand troops of the massed patriot army in South Carolina.

Gen. Nathanael Greene had marched his army from Burdell's plantation, seven miles from the British camp down the Congaree River Road, to attack Stewart. Now aware of their danger, the foragers reacted with confusion and panic. Some had been armed and fought back. Others, troops Stewart would soon sorely need, hid in the forest only returning after the battle.

Panicked horsemen, remnants of Coffin's command, came rushing back into Stewart's camp raising the alarm. It was full morning now and the British Army, although caught unaware, quickly formed for battle. Lieutenant Colonel Stewart formed one line stretching from the creek formed by the Eutaw Springs that leads to the Santee River, then athwart the Congaree River Road and continuing into the open woods to the south. He placed a pair of his three pounder cannon in each of two batteries along his line as the Americans approached. He waited.

Thus began one of the most obstinate, bloody and chapter ending battles of the Revolution. In the aftermath, never again would a British Army venture into the interior of the Carolinas or Georgia. The disasters of the year before such as the fall of Charlestown and Gate's defeat at Camden, had somewhat been set right. The much-maligned southern militia had grown into now-seasoned troops who fought volley-to-volley and bayonet-to-bayonet against trained British troops. The day after the battle, the British Army scurried to Charlestown, in near panic, leaving behind their most seriously wounded, their abandoned weapons and their reputation. Patriots now controlled the liberated colony except for a small enclave around Charlestown.

The importance of this battle fought a month before Cornwallis's surrender at Yorktown has been very much overshadowed by the great events in Virginia. Lately, however, more attention has been shown to this great battle along the Santee, engendering a re-examination of the events of September 8, 1781.

A MAP APPEARS AND A MYSTERY DEVELOPS

Beginning shortly after the Revolution, histories began to be written that offered records, critiques, and points of view related to the war. One of the earliest publications came from Lt. Col. Banastre Tarleton in 1787, *A History of the Campaigns of 1780 and 1781, in the Southern Provinces of North America*. Tarleton was not in the battle himself but was engaged in a running dispute with some fellow officers primarily over who was at fault in his disaster at the Cowpens. Nevertheless, he included in his history correspondence from Lieutenant Colonel Stewart to General Cornwallis.

In 1812 Henry "Light Horse Harry" Lee published his *Memoirs of the War in the Southern Department of the United States* which contains a detailed account of the Battle of Eutaw Springs. He was a participant as colonel of the Virginia Legion.

In 1822 Dr. William Johnson published *Sketches of the Life and Correspondence of Nathanael Greene, Major General of the Armies of the United States in the Revolution In Two Volumes*. Johnson was a physician who

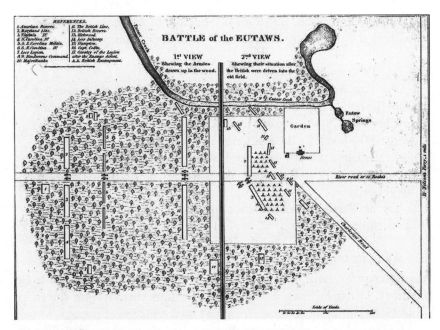

Figure 1. Battle of Eutaw Springs, from *Sketches of the Life and Correspondence of Nathanael Greene, Major General of the Armies of the United States in the Revolution* by Dr. William Johnson, 1822.

lived from 1771 to 1834, served in the House of Representatives and was an Associate Justice of the Supreme Court. Johnson and his brother Dr. Joseph Johnson actually slept in the so-much fought over Eutaw Springs brick house the year after the battle when they were youngsters.

Dr. Johnson's 1822 book has in it the first map of the Battle of Eutaw Springs, presented in two-stage panels. There is no attribution to this map, but careful inspection of the map border shows the inscription, "H.S. Tanner, Sc" which indicates *Sculptor* or the engraver of the map. H.S. Tanner was a well-known publishing house in Philadelphia and was used by the Supreme Court for publications. The map was likely commissioned for the book by Dr. Johnson who was a member of the Supreme Court at the time and would have most certainly been familiar with H.S. Tanner.

Shown in Figure 1 is the two stage map from Dr. Johnson's book. While the sources that led to the creation of the map are unknown, it is well discussed in the book:

> At about two hundred yards west of the Eutaw Springs, Stewart had drawn up his troops in one line, extending from the Eutaw Creek beyond the main Congaree road. The Eutaw Creek effectually covered

his right, and his left, which was in the military language, in air, was supported by Coffin's cavalry, and a respectable detachment of infantry, held in reserve at a convenient distance in the rear of the left, under cover of the wood...

The American approach was from the west; and at a short distance from the house, in that direction, the road forks, the right-hand leading to Charleston, by the way of Monk's Corner, the left running along the front of the house by the plantation of Mr. Patrick Roche, and therefore called, by the British officers, Roche's road; being that which leads down the river, and through the parishes of St. Johns and St. Stephens...

The artillery of the enemy was also posted in the main road... [Authors emphasis]

THE MAP IS EASILY SHOWN TO BE SEVERELY FLAWED

The descriptions and the associated map are easily demonstrated to be incorrect. What follows outlines the questions surrounding the map. Objections can be raised concerning at least four major areas.

The first objection relates to the map depiction of the distribution of the artillery and military units. Referring to the two primary eye-witness sources, Stewart and Lee, we have from the report of Stewart in his September 19 letter to Cornwallis:

> I immediately formed the line of battle with the right of the army to the Eutaw branch and its left crossing the **road leading to Roche's Plantation,** leaving a corps on a commanding situation to cover the Charleston road and to act occasionally as a reserve

And again from Stewart in the same report:

> the action was renewed with great spirit; but I was sorry to find that **a three pounder, posted on the road leading to Roche's,** had been disabled, and could not be brought off when the left of the line retired.

While Lee wrote:

> The artillery was distributed along the line, a part on the Charleston road and another part on a road leading to Roache's plantation, which passed through the enemy's left wing.

Both officers, Lieutenant Colonel Stewart who directed the deployment of the single British line and Lieutenant Colonel Lee commanding the right of the American advance, refer to the existence of two batteries of artillery, one of which was along a road to Roche's, or Roache's. Moreover, both men refer to the deployment of the British line as extending from the springs on the north in a southerly direction with the left posted on or crossing the road to Roche's.

The Johnson map cannot possibly be an accurate rendition of the battlefield as described by these independent observers, since it does not show either the British troops extending from the springs, posted on or crossing both the Congaree River road, and a "Road to Roche's."

The second battery of artillery which was posted on the described road is missing from Dr. Johnson's map. It was, in fact, one gun from this battery which remained in the possession of the American Army after it had lost the other pieces of artillery in the attack on the brick house British headquarters during the battle.

The second objection is that Dr. Johnson's map with a road to Roche's as shown would represent illogical posting of a battery of artillery to the east of the battle and firing through his own men and camp. This piece was lost to the west of the springs and house. In no description of the battle is it stated that Americans went around the British, gaining their rear to offer such a target from that location.

A third objection concerns the River Road depicted on the map. Was there actually a "River road" during the time of the battle? The roads in the area of the battlefield were at various times "established" by the South Carolina Assembly and as such became public roads. The development of these roads can be followed through the Acts of the General Assembly Related to Roads, Ferries (hereafter, "the Acts.")

The Congaree River road, (oddly, also known as the Road to the Congarees when headed inland and the Monck's Corner Road, or the road to Charlestown when headed to the coast), certainly existed as a public road established by the General Assembly but it was not until the early 1800s that the General Assembly authorized a road along the Santee from St. Stephens and then later to the Eutaw Springs itself. This can be seen from early maps of the period as well as state establishment of public roads as found in entries in the Acts.

In 1786, after the battle and much before the publication of Dr. Johnson's book, the General Assembly authorized the completion of a "River Road":

> Be it enacted, by the Honorable the Senate and House of Representatives, now meet and sitting in General Assembly, and by the authority of the same, that a public road shall be laid out in Saint John's Parish, Marion County, from the Saint Stephen's road, along Santee River, to the Congaree road near the Eutaws

A fourth objection arises from a search of recorded plats. While the Roche family is well represented in the history of property owners in the low country until the early 1800s, a search of the registered plats from the colonial period do not show any evidence that the road to the east went by any property owned by Patrick Roache or Roche.

We are led to the conclusion that the "Road to Roche's" is misidentified on the Johnson Map. Nevertheless, a road must have existed since all the eyewitness accounts are in agreement in this regard. But if the road to Roacheswas not as shown on the map, a rational alternative supported by evidence needs to be found.

SEARCH FOR THE "ROAD TO ROCHES"

What has been established from the narratives is that a road existed in 1781 and that it was positioned to accommodate the British left-wing and simultaneously host two pieces of artillery. Because the British had to generally face perpendicular to the Americans coming from a westerly direction, and the road passed through the left of the British line, the road must have extended in a somewhat southerly direction. Furthermore, the road had to be at least two hundred yards or "a few hundred paces" from the British camp. Given the objections to the Johnson map, the battle narratives show that there was a road to Roche's. Where was it, if it was not the one referred to by Johnson?

Finding such a road could be simple enough if it had come into common use and been established as a public road, but searches for a public or much-used road have proved fruitless. Maps from the period are generally large scale and rarely capture roads of secondary, let alone tertiary, importance. County maps are nonexistent until much later. Plats do capture small road or paths, but are rarely easy to locate on a large scale map due to the lack of geophysical features. One hope in finding the mystery road lay in the possibility that the road retained some use until modern times when more advanced mapping techniques came into use.

A major stumbling block to the search for the mystery road lay in the damming of the Santee River to form Lakes Marion and Moultrie, done by the Corps of Engineers in the late 1930s to early 1940s. Accurate maps created after that time are readily available, but have on them the effects of Lake Marion flooding of Eutaw Creek. Nevertheless, many of the Santee River plantations, drowned roads and relocated roads still carry with them original names. Thus, accurate maps with which to begin a road search are limited to those created before the 1930s.

A good source for well-referenced map information comes from the United States Army which produced maps that showed roads, topography, schools, towns, and land marks (cartographic information).

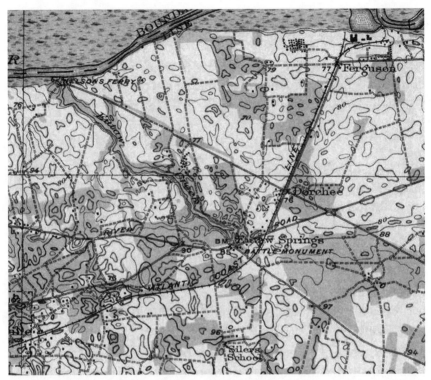

Figure 2. 1921 Eutawville Quadrangle topographic map zoomed in to show the battlefield area, with the actual site marked as Battle Monument. This was done before the creation of Lake Marion. The scale is approximately 1 mile from the last "R" of "RIVER ROAD" on the left to "B" in "BATTLE MONUMENT."

These maps were first generated from field surveys and printed on paper. Some maps exist for the Eutaw Springs area as early as 1921 and have been archived by the University of South Carolina Digital Collections, Topographical Maps of South Carolina 1888-1975 (www.sc.edu/library/digital/collections/topomaps.html) among others. One map, Eutawville Quadrangle, is fifteen minutes of longitude by fifteen minutes of latitude and has been used as a high resolution base map that can bridge historical maps with modern, surveyed maps.

Examining the area around Eutaw Springs can be done by zooming in to the specific area of the battle as has been done in Figure 2.

The "modern" River Road (with slight modifications from the 1786 General Assembly authorization) can be found passing through the area of the battle and forking to the north-east on the right side of the Battle Monument. The Monck's Corner road can be seen passing to the south-east from the Battle Monument. Note that the River Road in this 1921 map was numbered as State Route 45 before Lake Marion was formed. Some of the road disappeared under the newly formed lake.

A number of dotted roads, indicating unimproved or dirt roads, are on the map as well as paved or otherwise improved roads. To the west of the Battlefield Monument, only one appears to travel in a southerly direction. The distance from the battlefield fits the descriptions from Lee and others of a couple hundred or so paces (one pace is approximately two and a half feet), or about five hundred feet from the monument.

The suggested "Road to Roches" has been called "Brigade" (modern historical, South Carolina Department of Natural Resources Orangeburg County GIS Roads, "rds75") or, as of 2019, "Yahoo Road" plus "Oilers Road" and a section of "Cartoon Circle" (for a modern detail of the segments in this area see, Orange County South Carolina GIS gis2.orangeburgcounty.org/maps/.) This road represented a possibility that met many subjective criteria but without corroborating support. An onsite inspection shows that there are currently driveways and one or two subdivision entrances along Route 6 as it changes course and heads to Monck's Corner from the monument.

THE CONNECTION TO THE ROCHES: EVIDENCE OF THE PLATS

Plats contain information to provide testing for the suspected Roches Road location. The role of the plats now takes center stage.

Guided by the reasoning that the Johnson map was in error and that the comments by Lieutenant Colonel Stewart and Lieutenant Colonel Lee of their observations as to which direction the "Road to Roche's" must have gone, a search for possible plantations associated with the Roche family was begun. The evidence of residual roads heading south from the battlefield also suggested the possibility.

A "Map of Santee Cooper Project" (May 1951 version of an older map) depicts plantations expected to be flooded by the Santee Cooper Project. Many times old plantations acquired a name that was passed down year-to-year and became property tracts. Referring to this map, it can be seen that there were plantations to the south of the battlefield in the direction of Sandy Creek. The origins and title history of the plantations were investigated to find likely matches.

Examination of one of the tracts of land on the Corps of Engineers map of land to be flooded, a 700-acre tract named Wampee, led to the name Francis Roche. The Roche family appears early and prominently in the colony, beginning with Patrick Roche's property in St. Thomas and St. Denis Parish around 1710. By the 1770s-1780s the family included four brothers, Ebenezer, Francis, Thomas, and Patrick, and two

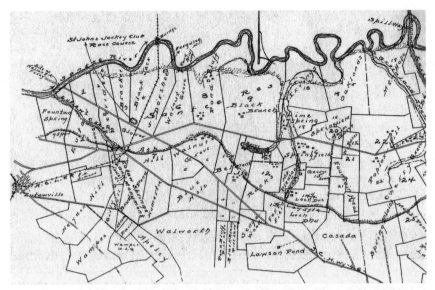

Figure 3. Section of the surveyor's plat from the Corps of Engineers prior to the flooding of the Santee River area to produce Lake Marion and Lake Moultrie (note the plantations named Wampee in the bottom left map area).

sisters, Elizabeth Motte and Mary Miller. After the early 1800s the male line no longer appears in property records.

FOUR THOUSAND ACRES GRANTED TO WILLIAM THOMSON IN 1786

A 4,000-acre tract was surveyed and granted in 1786 to Col. William Thomson. The tract is in Charleston District "on a Creek called Sandy Run, Waters of four holes." The 1786 plat shows Thomson's 4,000-acre tract: Bounding northwestward on the "District Line" between Charleston and Orangeburgh districts and bounding northeastward on "Francis Roach's Land." The plat implies that "Francis Roach's Land" adjoins most of the Thomson tract's northeastern property line.

This District Line was defined at various times by the Assembly, while the surveyors depicted it on various plats consistently as "The District Line terminates at Nelson's ferry, and with the bearing Northeast at an angle of 54 degrees" (although there were indicated some minor adjustments as to the exact bearing). (See, for example, 1786 August 20 SCDAH, State Plats, Charleston Series S213190, Vol. 20, page 132 and 1786 December 4 SCDAH, State Land Grants, Series S213022, Vol. 16, page 342.)

THOMSON TRACT PARTIALLY RESURVEYED IN 1829

The South Carolina Historical Society houses a May 1829 plat with the somewhat misleading title "Plat of Eutaw Springs" and misleading summary "Plat (resurvey) of the Eutaw Springs Plantation." Actually, the plat is an 1829 resurvey of the above-described 4,000-acre tract granted in 1786 to William Thomson and completed in 1830:

> This plat represents a tract of Land situate in the Neighbourhood of the Eutaw Springs, Charleston District and State of So Carolina, originally granted to Col William Thompson (sic) for 4000 Acres on 4th December 1786. But found by this resurvey to contain about Eight thousand, four hundred and fifty / 8450 / Acres. I say about, because not having closed the survey I cannot be certain of the true content. Done at the request of William Thompson [sic] and James Smith Esquires in May 1829 ——— Charles Parker

Inside the northeastern corner of William Thomson's 8,450-acre tract, the 1829 resurvey plat delineates part of "Frances [sic] Roche's grant dated 4th Decr 1786." Also inside the northeastern corner, the resurvey plat delineates part of "Farr Grant now Capt Gaillard," including "Capt Gaillard's House." The tract was resurveyed in 1829 at the request of William Thompson (actually William Sabb Thomson, a grandson of Col. William Thomson) the original grantee in 1786. The 1829 plat is South Carolina Historical Society Call No. 32-55-06.

A more detailed version of this plat was completed in 1832 (Charleston District, Court of Common Pleas, Judgment Roll, 1832 #109A (L 10018 Box 315), South Carolina Department of Archives and History). While the 1832 plat is well worth examining for the artistically excellent rendering, it does not add any additional identifiable geographical landmarks.

GEOREFERENCING

One of the capabilities typically included in Geographical Information Systems is the ability to convert a properly-organized depiction of mapped objects without a geographical basis into one that has a geographical basis. This process is called *georeferencing*. The map to be processed must have objects plotted in proper relationship to one-another and with identifiable geographical features. For mapping, the identifiable features might be crossroads, rivers, topography, etc., features that can be given known locations in some coordinate system.

The unknown depiction can be georeferenced to another map that is properly surveyed in a coordinate system or by assigning coordinates to the un-georeferenced map. The conversion is done mathematically to assign coordinates to the map, making it viewable and useable as a

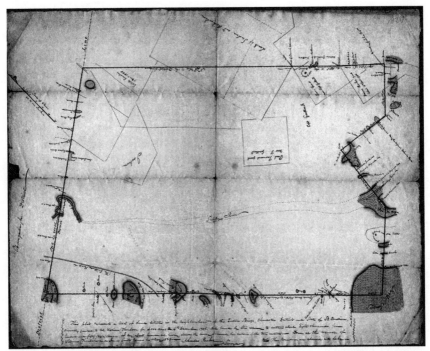

Figure 4. The "Rosetta Stone Plat" showing a property owned in 1786 by Francis Roche known as "Wampee Pond" (South Carolina Historical Society Call No. 32-55-06). A more detailed plat was completed in 1832 (Charleston District, Court of Common Pleas, Judgment Roll, 1832 #109A [L 10018 Box 315], South Carolina Department of Archives and History).

quantitative object. This identification is done by matching objects to the same objects on the reference map. The mathematical operations can be simple rotation and scaling or much more complex algorithms. The quality of the georeferencing is determined from reports on residual errors incurred during the mathematical processing. In this fashion poor conversions can be rejected. The new map can be used along with other map-like data sources for a virtually limitless set of quantitative cross assessments and analyses.

HOW THE GEOREFERENCING WAS INFORMED BY THE PLATS: EVIDENCE FROM THE GIS

Once the identification of a property belonging, at one time or another, to a person named Francis Roche was made in the grand plat the question was, what is the hope that it can be geo-referenced? Typically this is not possible for small plats since they include no features relatable to some more or less immutable feature like a creek, river, road, canal, etc.,

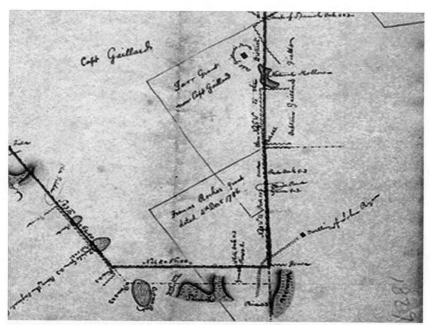

Figure 5. Magnification of the 1829 plat corner area showing the existence of a property ascribed to Francis Roche. The bottom right inset reads "Frances Roches grant dated 4th Dec 1786."

which lasted long enough to be surveyed in some quantitative coordinate system.

One feature that does stand out on the plat is Toney Bay. Bays appear to be sinks, low areas of terrain that suggest a shallow pond holding water after suitable periods of rain. If the bay is impressive enough, it may be identified with a name. Such is the case of Toney Bay, which is still found on maps.

The plats have dimensions and angles on them, so in principle it is possible, if not easy, to orient the plat and then stretch it or compress it until the sides match the scale of the map on which it is being geo-referenced. For this "Rosetta Stone" plat, however, there is the additional clue as to its location. One edge of the grand plat is identifiable as the "District Boundary," discussed earlier between the relatively newly created County of Berkeley and Orangeburg County. Aligning of the plat then becomes a simpler geo-referencing problem amenable to GIS software.

This "Rosetta Stone" plat was imported into an open-source GIS system called Quantum Geographical Information System (Qgis), and georeferenced on the 1921 Eutawville Quadrangle introduced earlier

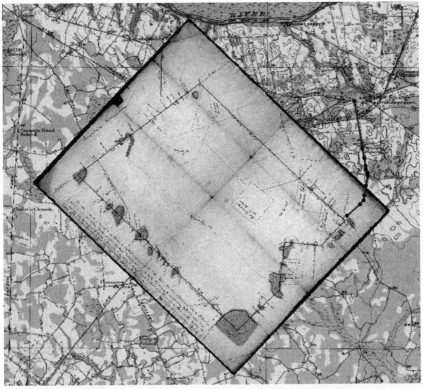

Figure 7. The final overlay of the historical plat georeferenced to the topographic map utilizing the "District Line," Toney bay (a hydrological feature), and extant roads.

as Figure 2 (which itself had been georeferenced onto a map canvas using the NAD 27 UTM Zone 17N projection) Modern road and hydrological features were also georeferenced. The very surprising result is shown in Figure 6.

SYNTHESIS OF THE GIS AND PLATS

After the plat was georeferenced, it was clear that the area identified with Francis Roche was apparently connected to the Congaree road by the suggested road identified earlier. On the GIS "canvas," a line was traced along the suspected road until it reached the area of the Francis Roche property as shown on Figure 7.

With this identification made, further support was found in a letter from Francis Marion to General Greene on September 21, 1781 that the British had reoccupied some of the abandoned ground around Eutaw Springs, twelve days after the battle:

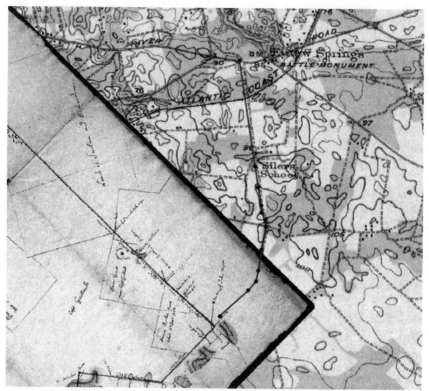

Figure 7. The suggested "road to Roche's" made from road segments proceeding southward from an area a couple hundred meters west of the Eutaw Springs Battlefield
Monument.

> Majr Doyle Commands the main body at Mrs Fludds (within three
> miles of Eutaw) they are Collecting Negroes to Intrench, but give out
> they Intend to pass the river. Their Army is much Sctterd, a part is at
> Majr Olivers at Eutaw, & Mr Roches, Either of them is three miles
> from the main body at Mrs Fludds.

An examination of the area around the likely road on the GIS map
shows that the distance from the battlefield area is 2.4 miles.

To show how the Battle of Eutaw Springs could be better illustrated,
Figure 8 shows a notional modification of Dr. Johnson's 1922 map to
reflect the modern interpretation of the facts. In this map, the Road to
Roches is shown headed approximately due south. Along this road
Lieutenant Colonel Stewart placed two of his three pounders, one of
which he lost during the battle. The River Road or "to Roches" is now
removed in agreement with the historical record of established roads
of South Carolina in this area.

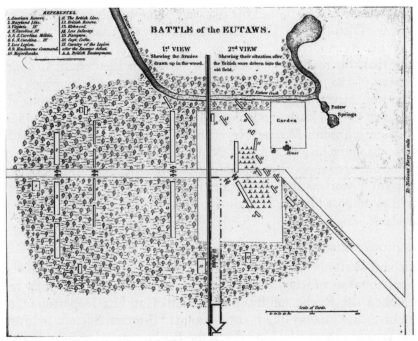

Figure 9. A notional redrawing of Dr. Johnson's 1822 battle map consistent with the identification of Mr. Roche's Plantation and consistent with the established roads as of 1781.

DISCUSSION AND CONCLUSION

The use of topographic and hydrological features makes it possible to extend the process of describing history correctly in geographical terms even before the existence of maps with widely known coordinates. The application of GIS to historical studies is particularly useful when geographical questions arise concerning the historical record. After the mid-1700s well-known coordinate systems began to be incorporated into maps that make it possible to relate features, and events to modern locations.

The example presented here has demonstrated the power of reviewing history subject to the physical strictures of a quantitative representation of the local environment. The map produced by William Johnson in 1822 has been shown to be unrepresentative of the events of this famous battle. This map used, copied and reused in histories as far as modern times has been shown to be fanciful in some respects.

Applying Geographic Information Systems techniques coupled with archived plats has been shown to offer a solution to an historical mystery. The search for the missing road has been shown to have benefitted greatly from a lucky find in the plats: a geographically referenced feature, the District Line. This is, however, rarely the case.

While it cannot be more than proposed from the evidence presented here that this road is in fact the one on which Lieutenant Colonel Stewart placed two of his cannon, the independent paths by which the proposed correct "Road to Roches" was identified makes it a strong alternative to the clearly inadequate depiction and description found in William Johnson's *Sketches*. Nevertheless, a clear case has been made for revising the historical record. More corroborating information may yet be found to support or possibly refute what has been found. Going forward, historians should consider the alternative view of the battlefield as proposed here in addition to the only other one that has been available.

ACKNOWLEDGMENTS

Richard Watkins of Saint Matthews, South Carolina, provided the foundation on which this work is grounded. Dick has rigorously researched the Roche family in the South Carolina Department of Archives and History, the South Carolina Historical Society archives, and various others. Tracking down the Roche family led to plats (the one referred to as "the Rosetta Stone Plat") containing Wampee Plantation and with it, the road from the battlefield to Roche's. Without Dick's contribution, this work could never have been successful.

REFERENCES

Dennis M. Conrad, Ed., *Papers of General Nathanael Greene*, Volume IX 11 July 1781–2 December 1781, The University of North Carolina Press, Chapel Hill and London, Published for the Rhode Island Historical Society, 1997.

Joseph Johnson, *Traditions and Reminiscences, Chiefly of the American Revolution in the South: Including Biographical Sketches, Incidents, and Anecdotes, Few of which Have Been Published, Particularly of Residents in the Upper Country*, Walker and James, Charleston, SC, 1851.

William Johnson, *Sketches of the Life and Correspondence of Nathanael Greene, Major General of the Armies of the United States in the Revolution In Two Volumes*, Printed by A.E. Miller, Charleston, SC, 1822.

Last Will & Testament of Ebenezer Roche, Probated June 4, 1784. From Abstracts of Wills of Charleston District 1783-1800, compiled and edited by Caroline T. Moore.

Henry Lee, *The American Revolution in the South*, Edited by Robert E. Lee, University Publishing Company, New York, 1869.

Henry Lee, *Memoirs of the War in the Southern Department in the United States, In Two Volumes*, Bradford and Inskeep, Philadelphia, 1812.

W. Gilmore Simms, ed. *The Life of Nathanael Greene, Major-General in the Army of the Revolution*, George F. Cooledge & Bro., New York, c. 1849.

The Statutes at Large of South Carolina; Edited Under the Authority of the Legislature by David J. McCord. Volume the Ninth, Containing the Acts Relating to roads, Bridges and Ferries, with an Appendix Containing the Militia Acts Prior to 1794, A.S. Johnston, Columbia, SC, 1841.

Banastre Tarleton, *A History of the Campaigns of 1780 and 1781 in the Southern Provinces of North America*, Dublin, 1787.

University of South Carolina Digital Collections, Topographical Maps of South Carolina 1888-1975 (www.sc.edu/library/digital/collections/topomaps.html), Eutawville Quadrangle.

1829 plat from South Carolina Historical Society, Call No. 32-55-06

1832 finished plat from Charleston Deeds, Volume Z-4, page 260 Charleston District, Court of Common Pleas, Judgment Roll, 1832 #109A (L 10018 Box 315), South Carolina Department of Archives and History.

Attack Up the Connecticut River: The First British Raid on Essex

MATTHEW REARDON

By April 1782, the war in America was supposed to be over. It had been nearly six months since Lord Cornwallis surrendered his army to Generals Washington and Rochambeau at Yorktown. The previous February, the British Parliament had voted to stop funding the war. Peace negotiations between British and American representatives had begun in Paris. But almost 4,000 miles away, along the Connecticut coastline, the war continued unabated.

For the previous six years, the Connecticut militia had been constantly engaged with the Associated Loyalists and their counterparts, the Loyal Refugees, based on British-occupied Long Island.[1] These loyalists were irregular forces which operated independently of the regular British army in New York City. Their ranks on Long Island were made up of displaced New England loyalists, many of whom were from Connecticut. They armed and equipped themselves and even had their own small naval vessels. Starting in 1776, the two sides routinely launched raids against each other's coastal towns and shipping in what came to be known throughout the war as the "Whaleboat Wars."

Early in the first week of April 1782, the Refugees did something they had not done before: they proceeded into and then up the Connecticut River. Up until then, they had never ventured very far from the coastline.[2] This attack would have been completely lost to history

---

1. Though the two were separate organizations, most American reports and correspondence refer to them only as the Refugees.
2. *Connecticut Gazette*, April 5, 1782. The exact date of the attack is not known, nor was it given, but the *Connecticut Gazette* stated the attack occurred "a few nights ago," placing the raid on April 1, 2 or 3.

had it not been for a brief mention in two local newspapers and a single letter found in the Governor Jonathan Trumbull Papers at the Connecticut State Library. The letter to the governor was drafted by the three selectmen of Saybrook: Samuel Field, Richard Dickinson, and William Hart Jr., on April 26, 1782. Its main purpose was in response to the raid, to lobby the governor for additional resources which could be used to more adequately protect their coastline as well as the lower part of the Connecticut River.³

Saybrook was a coastal town just over thirty miles east of New Haven, which traced its history back to the seventeenth century. Today, the oldest part of the town is known as Old Saybrook. In 1782, the town was much larger and also included the modern-day towns of Westbrook, Deep River, Chester, and Essex. During the Revolutionary War, two of the town's boundaries ran along the waterfront. The southern boundary rested on Long Island Sound, while the eastern boundary ran along the Connecticut River. An earthen fort, equipped with six guns, garrisoned by a small company of state troops, protected the mouth of the river. The fort, erected at Saybrook Point, stood at the western entrance of the river, a few miles east of the main part of town.⁴ The garrison, under the command of Lt. Martin Kirtland, was responsible for not only the protection of the fort, but also for patrolling the adjacent coastline and riverfront in order to counter the illicit trade. In 1782, the company was understrength and "wholley destitute" and not entirely prepared to resist any attack, much less a raid up the river. The armed boat *Success*, which was normally assigned to support the fort, was not even present. It was off on a mission in Sag Harbor on Long Island.⁵

3. Selectmen of Saybrook to Governor Jonathan Trumbull, April 26, 1782, Governor Trumbull Papers, 16:103a-b, Connecticut State Library.

4. Louis F. Middlebrook, *History of Maritime Connecticut During the American Revolution* (Salem, Massachusetts: The Essex Institute, 1929), 15. Capt. Adam Shapley to Governor Jonathan Trumbull, July 4, 1781, Governor Trumbull Papers, 14:323b-d, Connecticut State Library. A fort stood on the site since the Pequot War, but has long since vanished. The site of the fort today is not the one that is "recreated." Rather, it was closer to the waterfront, probably on the site of today's Saybrook Point Marina and Resort. Only one company return is known to exist prior to the attack. It was taken upon a review of the company in July 1781. At that time, it mustered one lieutenant, three sergeants, and thirty-seven rank and file. But as it was noted, the "men are but very indifferently provided with Ammunition." The guards were considered "State Troops," members of the militia who agreed to serve for a set amount of time, usually six to eight months, under officers appointed by the General Assembly.

5. Selectmen of Saybrook to Governor Trumbull, April 26, 1782; Middlebrook, *History of Maritime Connecticut*, 230. In August 1781, ten members of the company were detached and sent to New London which was deemed more strategically important. Most became casualties in the subsequent British attack on New London.

Writing to the governor, the three selectmen told Trumbull, "Two [to three] Refugee Boats . . . made an Entrance into Connecticut River in the Night Season" and slipped by the Saybrook fort as well as Kirtland's guards. These two or three boats were likely whaleboats which the Refugees typically utilized. Whaleboats were crewed usually by seven to ten men each, and were open row boats, generally about thirty feet long, equipped with a single mast. The crews were typically armed with swords or firearms, though armament varied from boat to boat. Some were unarmed, relying solely on the weapons carried by the crews, others were equipped with small light cannon and/or swivel guns.[6]

The loyalists were presumably launched from a small British flotilla which had prowled Long Island Sound scouring for vulnerable rebel targets for most of April and May. Two vessels served under the Board of Associated Loyalists; the armed-brig *Sir Henry Clinton*, and the armed sloop *Association*, the third was the British brig *Keppel*, and the final vessel was a galley, whose identify or affiliation is not known.[7]

At most, with two or three boats, the total attacking force of Refugees probably only consisted of twenty to thirty men. This low number assuredly meant that this was not meant to be a large-scale attack. This was typical of all their attacks. They were supposed to get in, acquire all they could, and then make it back to their boats offshore. This was done preferably without alerting the militia. That night, the Refugees, according to the selectman, "Penetrated as far up the River as Eight Miles," placing the point of attack at the village of Pettipaug, which is present-day Essex. This is also supported by the newspaper reports.[8]

Pettipaug was not an entirely random target. Without further information we are left to guess the objective of the raid, but it more than likely had to do with shipping. This is the same reason the British attacked the town three decades later during the War of 1812.[9] With its

6. Selectmen of Saybrook to Governor Trumbull, April 26, 1782; *Connecticut Gazette*, April 5, 1782.
7. *Connecticut Journal* (New Haven), April 4, May 23, 1782; *New-York Gazette, and Weekly Mercury*, May 27, 1782. The vessels involved in the attack up the Connecticut River were the same vessels involved in the attack on East Guilford a month later. The *Sir Henry Clinton* was the second Associated Loyalist vessel by that name; the first sank in 1781. The unnamed galley was either a Refugee vessel or the British galley *Hussar*. The author tends to believe it was the *Hussar*, which operated out of the same base as the *Keppel*, Hart's Island.
8. Selectmen of Saybrook to Governor Trumbull, April 26, 1782; *Connecticut Gazette*, April 5, 1782. While the selectmen placed their farthest penetration point as eight miles upriver, the *Gazette* placed it only at six miles. Even with the discrepancies, both distances place the attack in the vicinity of Pettipaug.
9. For more information related to this attack, see Jerry Roberts, *The British Raid on Essex: The Forgotten Battle of the War of 1812* (Middletown, CT: Wesleyan University Press, 2014). The two raids bear a lot of similarities.

Detail from a 1780 map of Connecticut showing Saybrook (Saijbrook) at the center right along the Connecticut River where it enters the Long Island Sound. Lyme (Lijme) is across the river, while New Haven is to the far left. Pettipaug (Putty Pogue) is north of Saybrook along the river. (*New York Public Library*)

close proximity to the river, the coves around Pettipaug were home to several shipyards that constructed a number of smaller vessels including packets, sloops, schooners, and brigs. Some were privateers, others were merchant ships. The merchant trade was very active up and down the river throughout the war. Connecticut's first warship, the 20-gun brig *Oliver Cromwell*, was built there at Uriah Hayden's shipyard in 1776.[10]

Under the cover of darkness, the British flotilla approached the Connecticut coastline. Anchored a safe distance offshore, the attacking Refugees were carefully loaded into whaleboats. They then quietly rowed towards and then into the mouth of the Connecticut River completely undetected by Kirtland's guards.

As they proceeded upriver, they remained, remarkably, unnoticed. Nearing Pettipaug, they encountered, captured, and then subsequently, according to the selectmen, "Plundered three vessels." These vessels were, apparently, lightly guarded and were easily overwhelmed by the armed Refugees. The attack was done so quietly that it did not even arouse local citizens, nor did it result in calling out the militia.[11]

After capturing the vessels, the Refugees did not land in Pettipaug or even approach the village. According to the selectmen's letter, a detachment may have continued upriver for about another two miles until they reached Brockway Island, a short distance south of the present-

10. The *Oliver Cromwell* was captured by the *Daphne* in June 1779 off Sandy Hook, New Jersey.
11. Selectmen of Saybrook to Governor Jonathan Trumbull, April 26, 1782.

day town of Deep River. But the majority of the attacking force did not venture far from Pettipaug. Sometime between 4:00 A.M. and 5:00 A.M, they turned around and headed back down river towards the flotilla. According to the selectmen, on their return, the Refugees carried with them the three captured vessels along with two other vessels they picked up along the way.[12]

But as morning approached, the situation started to worsen for the Refugees. At around 6:00 A.M., the same time the Refugee boats were passing the ferry crossing site between Saybrook and Lyme, nearly two miles north of Long Island Sound, the sun began to rise. Their cover was gone. The wind, as well as the river tide, were judged to be too low. This was further complicated by river itself. At this point, the river has a deceptively narrow channel, with lots of sand bars and drifts. Under the present conditions, it would be difficult and dangerous to attempt to take off the larger captured vessels. So, it was decided that the larger vessels, along with the prisoners taken aboard them, had to be left behind. Before leaving the vessels, according to the *Gazette*, the Refugees "nail[ed] down the [prisoners] in the cabbin."[13]

It was probably at this time the Refugees took possession of the "Ferry-Boat and one or two other Boats," said the *Gazette*. These would have had an easier time navigating the river than the larger vessels. Determined to gain something by the raid, the ferry boat and other smaller boats were also presumably loaded by the Refugees with the plunder taken from the larger vessels.[14]

Once the prisoners were secured and tradeoff completed, the Refugee boats continued onward down the Connecticut River. Repassing the Saybrook Fort, they avoided any confrontation with either Kirtland's guards or any other militia. From there, they escaped out of the river and into the Sound and safely back to the awaiting British flotilla.[15]

---

12. Selectmen of Saybrook to Governor Jonathan Trumbull, April 26, 1782.

13. Ibid.; *Connecticut Gazette*, April 5, 1782. Special thanks to my friend and naval historian Daniel Walls for helping me better understand these features of the Connecticut River.

14. Ibid. There was really no other reason to take the ferry boat other than to convert it into a supply barge. It would not prove useful or valuable in future coastal attacks.

15. *Connecticut Journal*, May 23, 1782. During such attacks, the Refugees were usually escorted or assisted by larger naval vessels that operated under their control. They probably had at least one awaiting their return to Long Island Sound, but none of the American sources mentioned them. Prior to their attack on nearby East Guilford, present day Madison, the Refugees were seen patrolling Long Island Sound and attacking merchant vessels with two brigs, a sloop and a galley.

The raid on Pettipaug was in all respects a British success, albeit a minor one that had no real effect on the war. Never before during the war had the Refugees been able to penetrate so far into the state. Not only that, but in doing so, they completely evaded the state troops, the militia, and local citizens. Weaknesses in the state's defenses were definitely noted. Casualties were presumably either few or non-existent. While they were not able to take the larger vessels, they took some things with them. The *Gazette* described the captured vessels as a ferry boat and one or two small boats, while the selectman claimed they took two, unidentified, vessels with an untold amount of goods. The two vessels mentioned by the selectmen were probably the smaller boats mentioned by the *Gazette*, implying that the goods taken were loaded on the ferry boat as well as the smaller boats. Had it not been for the wind and tide conditions, at least two more larger vessels, with prisoners, would have assuredly been taken as well.[16]

The success of the raid assuredly embarrassed the militia, the state troops and local government leaders. This was especially true in Saybrook and the reason the letter was sent to the governor. But at least, according to the selectman, it was not the fault of the garrison at the Saybrook Fort. "Our Small Guards," they explained, "in their Situation, were unable to afford any Relief to the Sufferers."[17]

Before drafting the letter to Trumbull, the selectmen had sat down with each other and discussed their best options. At least two of them, William Hart Jr. and Richard Dickinson, were involved in the sea trade and had strong personal interests in protecting the Connecticut River, which they called the "Key to the State." They reminded the governor that if the mouth of the river was not protected, the trade which operated in it "must greatly suffer." At least one, Hart, was a militia officer, and had seen some active service.[18]

In the letter, the three selectmen, first and foremost, asked for additional funding. They complained that due to lack of funding from the state, they were not able to enlist enough troops into Kirtland's company. The town had funded most of the unit themselves and were already stretched financially thin. This was due in part to—and they made specific mention of it—the heavy "Public Tax" the General Assembly had levied on them and the rest of the state. They also begged the governor to order militia from the interior part of the state to Say-

16. *Connecticut Gazette*, April 5, 1782.
17. Selectmen of Saybrook to Governor Jonathan Trumbull, April 26, 1782.
18. Ibid. Hart served as major and commanded the 1st Regiment of Light Horse, a mounted militia unit. The regiment saw action during the Danbury Alarm in the spring of 1777.

brook. Once there, they could better defend the fort as well as allow Kirtland to post more guards along both Long Island Sound and the Connecticut River. The selectmen also recommended they be provided with a six-gun vessel and two additional whaleboats which could support the garrison by patrolling the river and the Sound. They closed the letter by telling the governor that unless supported, if the enemy renewed their attack they could not effectively hold the town and would be forced to evacuate it.[19]

Unfortunately, lacking any further documentation, we do not know how seriously Governor Trumbull, his Council of Safety or the General Assembly took the selectmen's recommendations or if any of them were ever put into action. If they were not, this, sadly, would not have been uncommon. Even other places in the state deemed more strategically important than Saybrook, like New London, which were also constantly asking for more resources and funding, received little or none. To make matters worse, the state, by 1781, was effectively bankrupt and could barely afford to even pay its own soldiers serving in the Continental Army.[20]

The only documented support sent to the garrison at Saybrook was a barrel of gunpowder which was not ordered there until the following June. In all likelihood, the garrison and town of Saybrook received no additional support from the state. They were forced to make do.[21]

Fortunately for them, no further attacks came. Except for a small skirmish at East Guilford, modern-day Madison, about fifteen miles to the west the following month, attacks along the coastline of Connecticut, which had gone on regularly for the better part of six years, ceased. This followed the controversial execution of an American prisoner by members of the Associated Loyalists. As a result, the British commander-in-chief, Sir Guy Carleton, ordered the Associated Loyalists to be disbanded. This alone put an end to the attacks on Connecticut. Despite this, a garrison was kept at the Saybrook Fort for the duration of the war. The fort would not be tested again until the War of 1812 when the British launched their second and most devastating attack on Pettipaug.[22]

---

19. Selectmen of Saybrook to Governor Jonathan Trumbull, April 26, 1782.
20. Richard Buel Jr., *Dear Liberty: Connecticut's Mobilization for the Revolutionary War* (Middletown, CT: Wesleyan University, 1980), 239-281.
21. Leonard Woods Labaree, *The Public Records of the State of Connecticut For the Year 1782 with The Journal of The Council of Safety From January 17, 1782, to December 16, 1782, Inclusive* (New Haven, CT: Quinnipiack Press, Inc., 1942), 4: 254.
22. *Connecticut Journal*, May 30, 1782.

Revolutionary Revenge on Hudson Bay, 1782

⁂ MERV O. AHRENS ⁂

French naval officer Jean Francois de Galaup, Comte de La Pérouse was one of many who actively supported the American Patriots in their war for independence from Britain. La Pérouse's assignments included patrolling the North Atlantic where he directed the capture of numerous British merchant vessels.[1] His early 1781 outbound voyage from France to Boston brought General George Washington a supply of much needed money and official strategic correspondence from the French court.[2] In late summer 1782, La Pérouse commanded an Arctic raid on the commercial interests of Britain. His destruction of the British trading depots on Hudson Bay was very much a part of America's Revolutionary War.

Once large-scale combat with the British erupted in the Boston area in the spring of 1775, Americans were buzzing with ways to weaken and destroy the British presence in North America and abroad. In December of that year, an armed attempt by the recently formed Continental Army under Gen. Richard Montgomery and then-Colonel Benedict Arnold to conquer neighbouring British Canada ended with the failed assault on Quebec. In early spring 1776, a diplomatic approach to win the hearts and support of Canadians and the British colony for the American cause was spearheaded by Benjamin Franklin.

---

1. Dictionary of Canadian Biography (DCB), www.biographi.ca/en/bio/galaup_jean_francois_de_4E.html, accessed April 2, 2020.
2. "Comte de Rochambeau to Gen. Washington, Feb. 11, 1781," National Archives, Founders Online (NAFO), founders.archives.gov/documents/Washington/99-01-02-05033, accessed April 2, 2020.

This attempt also failed. Other leading American minds proposed weakening the British economy by capturing their merchant vessels thereby destroying their trading networks and dramatically increasing their naval insurance rates.[3]

The majority of delegates to the Second Continental Congress in Philadelphia approved the Eastern Navy Board's plan to attack the Hudson's Bay Company's (HBC) ships and trading forts. In April 1779, the Marine Committee of the congress communicated to the navy board, "Your design of sending a force to intercept the Hudson Bay Company Ships and perhaps to surprize and carry their factory meets our approbation - this Committee as well as your Board have had it often in contemplation; we therefore approve of the proposition made by the owner of a Privateer of twenty Guns, and agree that the *Boston*, instead of the *Providence*, shall be join'd with her and sent on the expedition above mentioned."[4] The approval granted by the congress was not acted upon.

Both John Adams and Benjamin Franklin were aware of Britain's lucrative fishing, whaling and fur industries in the north Atlantic and Hudson Bay.[5] Franklin, after assuming his diplomatic role in Paris, prodded American privateer John Paul Jones to be on the lookout for HBC supply and trading vessels with their rich cargoes.[6] In this regard, it is also highly likely Franklin, who worked closely with French Foreign Minister Charles Gravier, Count of Vergennes, sought the assistance of the King of France and his naval ministers. The HBC, anticipating hostilities on the high seas, requested British Admiralty convoy protection. A variety of British warships guarded the company's merchant vessels that crossed forth and back through privateer-infested waters starting in 1778 through 1782.[7]

3. "Samuel Chase to George Washington, Jan. 12, 1776," NAFO, founders.archives.gov/documents/Adams/06-03-02-0203, accessed April 2, 2020. Chase was a close friend of Washington's who later became a Supreme Court justice.

4. "Marine Committee to Eastern Navy Board, April 19, 1777," Committee of the Second Continental Congress; Letters of Delegates to Congress, 1778-1789, 12: 356.

5. "State of Trade with the Northern Colonies, 1-3 November 1768," NAFO, founders. archives.gov/documents/Franklin/01-15-02-014, accessed April 2, 2020. On June 1, 1780, Adams sent a notice to the President of Congress about the expected outbound sailing date for the HBC ships. He learned this information from a May issue of a British newspaper.

6. "Benjamin Franklin to John Paul Jones, July 8, 1779," NAFO, founders.archives.gov/documents/Franklin/01-30-02-0044, accessed April 2, 2020.

7. Norma J. Hall, *Northern Arc: The Significance of the Shipping and Seafarers of Hudson Bay, 1508-1920*, Doctoral Thesis, Memorial University of Newfoundland, February 2009, 416-418.

La Pérouse's interest in Britain's trading activities on Hudson Bay went back at least two years before he conducted his successful raid. In 1780, he proposed to a high-ranking naval compeer that the British on the Bay should be vanquished. His replacement plan called for French forts to be staffed by hardy Frenchmen from St. Pierre and Micquelon, the fishing islands just off the south coast of Newfoundland.[8] This plan, however, did not receive any immediate royal support.

Paradoxically, La Pérouse's chance to earn future royal accolades would come after a major French naval defeat in the Caribbean in April 1782. Although he had earlier shared in several naval victories, it was British Admiral George Rodney's victory in the Battle of the Saintes that put fresh wind in La Pérouse's sails. He joined the battered French squadron as it regrouped at Cap-Francois (Cap-Haitien, in Haiti). During refitting and command restructuring efforts, Louis-Philippe de Rigaud, Marquis de Vaudreuil took command of the battered French Atlantic fleet. Together Vaudreuil and La Pérouse enacted a highly secretive retaliatory strike against the British establishments on Hudson Bay.[9] In late May 1782, La Pérouse set out with three warships, *Sceptre*, *Astree*, and *Engageante*, all under his command. His sailing orders directed him five thousand miles northward to Hudson Bay in an attempt to capture British trading vessels and destroy their bayside depots.

By early August 1782, La Pérouse's warships were anchored very close to British-owned Churchill Fort (Fort Prince of Wales). His ship of the line, *Sceptre*, carried seventy-four cannon and several hundred troops and crew. The two companion French frigates carried additional troops, cannons, attack guns, mortars and bombshells.[10]

Churchill Fort was built at the mouth of Churchill River located about midway along the Arctic western coastline of Hudson Bay. It was

8. A copy of La Pérouse's 1780 plan is in the Archives Nationales, Marine, in Paris. See an English translation at http://www.mhs.mb.ca/docs/mb_history/52/laperousemanu script.shtml, accessed April 2, 2020.

9. Vaudreuil, before leaving France, was probably briefed by the French Ministry of Ports and Arsenals regarding La Pérouse's interest in eliminating the British presence on Hudson Bay. Vaudreuil assumed command of the French fleet after Commodore Comte de Grasse and his flagship, *Ville de Paris*, were captured by the British in the Battle of the Saintes. La Pérouse and Vaudreuil probably harboured revengeful feelings over their recent defeat in the Caribbean, their country's earlier loss of French Canada to the British in 1763 and their forefathers' exclusion from trading on the Bay as dictated by the 1713 Treaty of Utrecht.

10. Captain Christopher recorded in his ship's journal that one of the enemy vessels appeared to be missing its foremast. This damage was likely inflicted earlier by the British in the Battle of the Saintes. See Hudson's Bay Company Archives, Winnipeg, Manitoba (HBCA), C.1/904, August 11, 1782, 31.

operated as a military and trading complex by the HBC headquartered in London, England. The largest structure was a fifty-year-old star-shaped, massive fortress enclosed by a fifteen-foot thick parapet sheathed in cut limestone blocks. Its surrounding rampart was pierced with embrasures for forty cannon of various calibre.[11] By its outward appearance, the fort could easily withstand a sizable attack, but the thirty or so manual labourers within its walls lacked military experience, artillery training and courage.

On August 9, 1782, a small French naval force disembarked into longboats and rowed towards the fort. In the absence of any visible defensive activity, some officers along with marines boldly landed, marched forward and demanded entry. The gates were opened and its governor, Samuel Hearne, after a short parley, surrendered the fortress without a shot being fired.[12] The British commander and most of the workers were immediately taken as prisoners and herded onboard the anchored warships. The French flag was hoisted over the depot and most of its valuables had been stripped by August 11. Larders were emptied and victuals, including the fort's horses, were shuttled back to the ships to replenish their dwindling food supplies. The French loaded onboard many valuable prizes including large quantities of luxurious peltries. Before the attackers departed, the cannons had been destroyed, huge gaps were blown in the stone walls and finally all the wooden structures and the powder magazine had been torched.

La Pérouse's fleet then sailed southeastward about one hundred fifty miles to the company's principal post, York Fort (later called York Factory). This larger, but less substantial armed depot was located very near the mouth of the Hayes River. The shallow, shoal-filled bay downstream from the fort necessitated a water and ground assault from a landing several miles distant. The enemy's threatening appearance was first reported by the crew on August 20 to Capt. Jonathan Fowler, Jr., master of the anchored HBC's supply vessel *Prince George III*. On the evening of August 20 several hundred French troops, their officers and some artillery were loaded into longboats. To reach York Fort the attack flotilla rowed, just beyond the range of Fowler's nine pounder's cannon balls, into the nearby mouth of the Nelson River.[13] After finding a suitable landing site, the advancing troops made a long, difficult overland march through extensive drowned marshlands and small woods. Upon

11. David Grebstad, "The Guns of Manitoba: How Cannons Shaped the Keystone Province, 1670-1887," *Manitoba History* No. 72 (Spring-Summer 2013), 3.
12. There are multiple accounts of Hearne's bloodless surrender of Churchill Fort. See DCB, http://www.biographi.ca/en/bio/hearne_samuel_4E.html, accessed April 2, 2020.
13. See Jonathan Fowler, Jr.'s ship journal, HBCA, C.1/386, 26, August 22,1782.

reaching the fort the following morning with an attack force of several hundred, a leading French officer demanded entry to the fort. Its infirm chief, Humphrey Marten, later recorded, "Before this I had hailed them and told them to halt. At first they took no notice but on my acquainting them that if they did not halt I should be obliged to fire at them they halted. I demanded a parley which was granted. They deliver'd a letter sign'd La Pérouse & [Major] Rostaing offering us our lives & private property but, threatening the utmost fury should we resist. On which I delivered terms of Capitulation which being in the main [were] agreed to; upon Honor I delivered up the Fort. They informed me Churchill was taken [earlier] and blown up."[14]

A second eye witness within York Fort later reported in a letter published in a 1783 London newspaper:

> About 10 o'clock this morning [August 22, 1782] the enemy appeared before our gates; during their approach a most inviting opportunity offered itself to be revenged on our invaders by discharging the guns on the ramparts, which must have done great execution; but a kind of tepid stupefaction seemed to take possession of the Governor [Humphrey Marten] at the time of the trial and he peremptorily declared that he would shoot the first [company] man to fire a gun. Accordingly, as the place was not to be defended he, resolving to be beforehand with the French, held out a white flag with his own hand, which was answered by the French officer's showing his pocket-handkerchief.[15]

The majority of York Fort's sixty or so workers were added to the HBC prisoners already on board the French vessels. Those remaining were ordered onto the *Severn*, one of the company's single-mast sloops commandeered earlier. The seized trading complex was torched, but not before an officer ordered a tent-like shelter to be constructed nearby. His troops then stocked it with large quantities of trade guns, powder, shot, blankets, clothing, food, etc. This humanitarian act by the French provided a small supply of survival goods for the benefit of the surrounding Indigenous families who were being decimated by an outbreak of smallpox.[16]

14. See 1782 York Factory Post Journal, HBCA, B.239/2/81, 3.
15. Edward Umfreville, *The Present State of Hudson's Bay: Containing a Full Description of that Settlement*, Printed for Charles Staker, 1790, 126-27.
16. Matthew Cocking's 1781-82 York Fort journal contains multiple references to the smallpox epidemic that had reached Hudson Bay by summer 1782. Cocking's journal, HBCA, B.239/a/80, can be viewed online by conducting a Keystone Archives - Advanced Search of the Archives of Manitoba at http://pam.minisisinc.com/pam/index.html, accessed April 2, 2020.

The remaining company posts further southeast (Severn, Albany, Moose, etc.) were not destroyed because they were smaller and mostly dependent on York Fort. La Pérouse had concluded that because his ships had lost their anchors in a recent storm, and more than three hundred of his crew were ill, he would not execute any further strikes.

Following the destruction of the two largest bayside HBC trading facilities, the three French warships sailed out of Hudson Bay and through the ice-clogged Hudson Strait. During their outward voyage one of the warships towed the *Severn*, which was crammed with prisoners. While enroute, on board the *Sceptre*, prisoner Hearne's polite mannerisms, intelligence and accomplishments greatly impressed La Pérouse as they dined together at the officers' table. Subsequently, Hearne was granted his freedom and was ordered onto the *Severn*. His release was conditional on his pledge that once in London he would publish his manuscript travel journal that detailed his year-and-a half-long overland trek in 1770-1772 to the Arctic Ocean via the Coppermine River.[17]

The *Severn* was subsequently untethered near Resolution Island just off the southeastern tip of Baffin Island. About thirty HBC prisoners, including Hearne, Humphrey Marten, and the boat crew, began their unplanned, risky voyage of just over four thousand miles across the cold North Atlantic to London via the Scottish Hebrides Islands and North Sea. The remainder of the British prisoners onboard the two French frigates were transported to Brest, France and held as prisoners of war.[18]

Once the *Severn* anchored on October 18, 1782 in Stromness harbour, in the Orkney Islands off Scotland's northern mainland, Hearne sent off his first correspondence to the HBC headquarters. Foremost in his letter would have been his eye-witness account of the devastation executed on the Bay's two largest depots by the French naval force.[19]

However, two very valuable British prizes escaped capture. La Pérouse's forces failed to outsmart two highly skilled and experienced HBC captains whose vessels were very close by during the pillaging and destruction of the trading posts. Capt. William Christopher was in charge of the inbound, cargo-laden *Prince Rupert III*, a 200-ton

17. In 1787 the HBC allowed Hearne the opportunity to ready his travel journal for printing. An edited version, *A Journey from Prince of Wales' Fort in Hudson's Bay to the Northern Ocean*, was published posthumously in 1795.
18. DCB, http://www.biographi.ca/en/bio/marten_humphrey_4E.html, accessed April 2, 2020.
19. Hearne's letter, written at Stromness dated October 18, 1782, was read at HBC headquarters on Nov. 13, 1782. See *Foul Copies of Governor and Committee minutes*, HBCA, A.1/141, 54.

frigate. He first spotted the enemy's fleet as he neared Churchill Fort.[20] About the same time, the French spotted Christopher's approaching vessel and a frigate was dispatched to chase and capture the *Prince Rupert*. The HBC captain was very familiar with the reefs and shallows along the bay's western shore. He used his experience in these dangerous waters to outdistance his pursuer's cannon shots and with the coming of nightfall he escaped. After the chase, Christopher continued northward about one hundred miles and hid out in Knapp's Bay until August 27. Presuming the enemy vessels were long gone, he then sailed back to Churchill Fort and sounded his customary approach signal. When it went unanswered, Christopher immediately left the fort's charred remains behind, turned his cargo-rich ship about and headed back to his company's London headquarters.[21]

Jonathan Fowler, Jr., the senior captain of the second larger vessel, *King George III*, faced a similar threat. On August 25, his crew was just finishing unloading cargo from the ship's hold when the enemy squadron was spotted steering towards York Fort.[22] There was an immediate rush to get all of the inbound supplies off-loaded and transferred to the fort. Simultaneously, boat crews from the fort quickly transferred to Fowler's care the season's huge collection of valuable fur bales, fresh water, and food supplies. Using the cover of darkness to help elude the French threat, Fowler skillfully guided his loaded outbound vessel unscathed through numerous rocky shoals and shallows and started his homeward voyage to London.[23]

A third HBC captain, George Holt, was not as lucky escaping the French. Holt and his crew of twelve men had been busy working their old, seventy-ton sloop, *Charlotte*, on a remote bayside northern trading assignment while La Pérouse's forces were busy destroying the company's forts in the south.[24] Holt, on his return voyage to Churchill Fort, was totally unaware that Captain Christopher had hid from the French in Knapp's Bay and headed south only days earlier. Total shock would have gripped Holt when the blackened ruins of his home base, Churchill Fort, came into view. Faced with life and death survival con-

---

20. Captain Christopher, after he observed the three large ships ahead of him in the distance, made the following note in his ship's log: "made the Ship [*Prince Rupert III*] Clear for Engaging [in battle] & Supposing them (as we very well might) to be Enemies one of them seem'd to have lost her foretop mast." HBCA, C1/901, 31.
21. Captain Christopher's *Prince Rupert III* ship's log, HBCA, C.1/904, 38.
22. Captain Jonathan Fowler, Jr.'s *King George III*'s ship's log, HBCA, C.l/386, 26.
23. Ibid., 28.
24. HBC *London Correspondence Book Outwards*,1767-1795, Microfilm Series I, Reel #38– F.77, A6/11, page 102.

cerns, including shelter, food, clothing and the coming winter, Holt with his crew determined at once to set sail in their aged sloop for company headquarters in London. The desperate crew must have braved many life-threatening challenges as they made their long, perilous voyage across the cold, stormy bay and north Atlantic. Luckily they overcame most of the dangers and on October 18 they successfully anchored their tiny vessel in England's southwestern port of Plymouth.[25]

Holt had defied the odds of reaching his homeland and surely thanked the Almighty for his safe arrival. Immediately he sent off a dispatch to company headquarters in London. His account would have been the first it received that described the burned-out ruins of Churchill Fort. He surely also included in his missive the horrors of their daring voyage and the dreadful condition of his emaciated, scurvy-ridden crew.

Holt anticipated the presence of enemy privateers on the final leg of his voyage from Plymouth to London and therefore requested his company arrange a British Admiralty escort. On November 15, Holt and his crew were part of a London-bound convoy under the protection of His Majesty's twenty-eight gun warship *Nemesis*.[26] As the ships passed the Isle of Wight with the *Charlotte* slightly ahead of the naval escort, two four-pound cannon shots were fired across Holt's bow by French privateer Capt. James Roveau's twelve-gun brig, and ended Holt's freedom. He and his crew were soon prisoners of war and the *Charlotte* was claimed as a prize of war after it anchored at Le Harve, France.[27]

Holt, from his detention quarters in Bolbec, France, requested his employer to pursue a release of himself and his crew. By December 1, still a prisoner, Holt penned an apologetic plea to his captor's friendly American diplomat in Paris, Benjamin Franklin. "The Libty. I take in writing is, to solicit your Friendship; to gain me a pass or a exchange for me to go to England."[28] Holt hoped by mentioning his earlier friendship with some of Franklin's lady friends in London he might

25. Ibid., reverse of page 2. The HBC's reply letter to Holt dated October 22, 1782, acknowledges Holt's arrival on October 18 at Plymouth, England.
26. Ibid., 83. A letter dated December 6, 1782, to Philip Stephens, Esq. (Secretary of the British Admiralty) from Samuel Wegg (HBC Governor & CEO) summarizes Holt's voyage and mentions the HMS *Nemesis*'s beginning escort of the *Charlotte* from Plymouth to London.
27. Ibid., 83, 103.
28. NAFO, founders.archives.gov/documents/Franklin/01-38-02-0298, accessed April 2, 2020.

leverage some assistance. He desperately wanted to get safely back home to his wife and family in London whom he hadn't seen for four years. Because a preliminary peace between the United States and Britain had recently been concluded, it is unknown if Franklin was of any help. Later HBC correspondence with Holt indicated his company would cover the costs of getting everyone back to Britain on the condition the captives honoured their existing contracts and returned to Hudson Bay as soon as possible.[29]

In summary, Vaudreuil's and La Pérouse's planned raid on the largest British-owned facilities dotted along the icy coastline of Hudson Bay fulfilled the aspirations of two countries. The French officers received their accolades from their king and America. News of their success was welcomed in Boston and Philadelphia in early December 1782.[30]

After La Pérouse anchored his ice-battered warship, *Septre*, in the Spanish port of Cadiz on October 13 he reported to King Louis XVI and his ministers. He stated he had inflicted damages on the British estimated to be ten to eleven million livres.[31] His successful siege and humanitarian acts earned him much royal praise, an increase in pay and pension and an illustrious promotion. These rewards came, however, with a huge debt borne mainly by his crew. They had suffered from hunger, scurvy, multiple illnesses, and over one hundred deaths, some caused by the drowning of fifteen men when their longboat overturned in stormy waters in front of York Fort. La Pérouse was reprimanded, however, for his kindness and release of some of the British prisoners. He was praised for his thoughtful generosity shown to the Indigenous families who were reliant on the supplies of the British bayside forts.

Upon receiving news of the loss of Churchill and York Fort, rebuilding plans were immediately formulated by the HBC's Governor and Committee. The damages did not bankrupt the company but yearly

---

29. *Foul copies of Governor and Committee minutes*, HBCA, A.1/141, Wednesday, November 6, 1782, 52, records: "the committee will apply for their protection [from impressment and return to London] on their assurance of continuing in the Company's [contracted] Service [at their posts on Hudson Bay]."

30. "James Madison to Edmund Randolph, December 10, 1782," NAFO, founders. archives.gov/documents/Madison/01-05-02-0166, accessed April 2, 2020. "George Washington to Bartholomew Dandridge, December 18, 1782," NAFO, founders.archives. gov/documents/Washington/99-01-02-10234, accessed April 2, 2020. News of La Perouse's august success in Hudson Bay was received and quickly shared in America.

31. NAFO, founders.archives.gov/documents/Madison/01-05-02-0166, footnote 13; accessed April 2, 2020. The note reads, "La Pérouse estimated that he had destroyed or captured property worth between ten and eleven million livres. The company acknowledged a loss of from seven to eight million livres . . . or half a million sterling."

dividends were not paid to their stockholders for several years. There is no agreement in the historiography of the raid regarding the company being compensated for its wartime losses. Indirectly, it was the Indigenous population that experienced the greatest loss. There was already widespread suffering and fatalities among the Cree peoples surrounding the Bay. Their hardships were further exacerbated by the reprisal on the Bay that was contemplated and planned by the Americans and executed by the French.

The Framers Debate Impeachment

❀ RAY RAPHAEL ❀

July 20, 1787, a clear and pleasant Friday afternoon. Delegates to the Federal Convention, known now as the Constitutional Convention, are addressing a clause in the working draft of what will become the Constitution of the United States. The National Executive, the draft says, will be "*removeable on impeachment and conviction of malpractices or neglect of duty.*" Gouverneur Morris and Charles Pinckney move to strike down the provision. Debate is vigorous, and the consequences enormous. At stake is the critical balance of powers amongst three branches of a new governmental edifice, which could potentially tumble down if that balance is irrevocably disrupted.[1]

The story evolves, as all history does, from backstory. Some seven weeks earlier, during the fifth day of their deliberations, delegates had addressed a resolution in the Virginia Plan, the convention's opening foray:

> *Resd. [resolved] that a National Executive be instituted; to be chosen by the National Legislature for a term of ___ years, . . . and to be ineligible a second time; and besides a general authority to execute the National laws, it ought to enjoy the Executive rights vested in Congress by the Confederation.*[2]

A "National Executive"—this was a dramatic departure from the Articles of Confederation, which had vested all executive authority with Congress. When the first speaker, James Wilson, moved that this new executive office should "consist of a single person," absolute silence descended on the body. For the first and only time during that long sum-

Note: Selections from all resolutions and working drafts are italicized.

1. Madison, *Notes of Debates*, July 20.
2. Ibid., May 29 and June 1.

mer, not one eminent statesman ventured even a passing comment, much less a reasoned position. From James Madison's *Notes of Debates in the Federal Convention of 1787*:

> A considerable pause ensuing and the Chairman asking if he should put the question, Doctor FRANKLIN observed that it was a point of great importance and wished that the gentlemen would deliver their sentiments on it before the question was put.[3]

"A point of great importance"—that was precisely the problem. The new nation had buttressed its very existence upon the cardinal principle that people can and must rule themselves, free and clear of any king or queen. How could it now place one man above all the rest and charge him with executing the myriad affairs of government?

Finally, a few delegates weighed in. John Rutledge "was for vesting the Executive power in a single person, tho' he was not for giving him the power of war and peace." Elbridge Gerry "favored the policy of annexing a Council to the Executive." Wilson explained that he "preferred a single magistrate, as giving most energy, dispatch and responsibility to the office." But Edmund Randolph "could not see why the great requisites for the Executive department, vigor, dispatch, & responsibility, could not be found in three men as well as in one man." A single executive, he warned, was "the fetus of monarchy." Seeking to assuage Randolph and others who took offense at any hint of monarchy, James Madison suggested: "To prevent a Man from holding an Office longer than he ought, he may for malpractice be impeached and removed." This intriguing idea elicited no response, although it would be taken up later. Faced with staunch opposition from Randolph, governor of the nation's largest state, those favoring a single executive decided not to press the issue just yet.[4]

Delegates moved on. How long would the executive(s) serve? Three years and seven years were the only contenders, with seven prevailing. Wilson then proposed that special electors, chosen by the people, would select the executive(s). This was roundly rejected. So, as of June 2, the executive(s) would be chosen by Congress and serve for seven years.

The lengthy term raised red flags. Delegates quickly resolved that the executive(s) could serve only a single term, but this alone did not suffice. "Some mode of displacing an unfit magistrate is rendered indispensable by the fallibility of those who choose, as well as the corruptibility of the man chosen," George Mason proclaimed. (This would hold whether the executive was singular or plural.) Madison added, "It

---

3. Madison, *Notes of Debates*, June 1.
4. Ibid., and William Pierce's notes in Farrand, *Records*, June 1.

was far from being his wish that every executive Officer should remain in Office without being amenable to some Body for his conduct." Others agreed. A motion that the executive(s) would be *"removable on impeachment & conviction of mal-practice or neglect of duty"* passed with no dissent.[5]

That was a game changer. Now that a single executive could be removed, fears of abuse subsided. South Carolina's John Rutledge and Charles Pinckney immediately moved that the executive be *"one person."* This motion passed, seven states to three.[6] The record suggests that we owe the office of the president to the safeguard known as impeachment. Without a path for removal, the framers might never have vested all executive power in a single person.

But on July 20, when removal of the executive came up for review, Gouverneur Morris and Charles Pinckney challenged it. From the outset, Morris, Pinckney, and Wilson had pushed for a truly independent executive, one not beholden to the legislature.[7] They had objected all along to Congress choosing the executive, and Morris now argued that Congress should not be empowered to remove him either. Impeachment, he said, would "render the Executive dependent on those who are to impeach." But what if the chief executive does wrong? Morris's response was slim: "He can do no criminal act without Coadjutors who may be punished."[8]

George Mason's counter argument was more forceful:

> No point is of more importance than that the right of impeachment should be continued. Shall any man be above Justice? Above all, shall that man be above it who can commit the most extensive injustice? When great crimes are committed, he was for punishing the principal as well as the Coadjutors.... Shall the man who has practiced corruption & by that means procured his appointment in the first instance, be suffered to escape punishment?

Benjamin Franklin, ever creative, turned the issue on its head. Impeachment was actually "favorable to the Executive," he determined:

> What was the practice before this, in cases where the chief Magistrate rendered himself obnoxious? Why recourse was had to assassination in which he was not only deprived of his life but of the opportunity of vindicating his character. It would be the best way therefore to pro-

---

5. Madison, *Notes of Debates*, and Pierce's notes in Farrand, *Records*, June 2.
6. Madison, *Notes of Debates*, June 2.
7. For the efforts of Wilson, Pinckney, and Morris to liberate the executive from the legislature, see Ray Raphael, *Mr. President: How and Why the Founders Created a Chief Executive* (New York: Alfred A. Knopf, 2012), 55-62.
8. All quotations for July 20 come from Madison, *Notes of Debates*.

vide in the Constitution for the regular punishment of the Executive where his misconduct should deserve it, and for his honorable acquittal when he should be unjustly accused.

Morris began to bend. He now admitted that "corruption & some few other offenses" should be impeachable, although "the cases ought to be enumerated & defined."

Support for removal powers kept coming. James Madison spoke up:

[It is] indispensable that some provision should be made for defending the Community against the incapacity, negligence, or perfidy of the Chief Magistrate. The limitation of his service was not a sufficient security. He might pervert his administration into a scheme of peculation or oppression. He might betray his trust to foreign powers. The case of the Executive Magistracy was very distinguishable from that of the Legislature or any other public body. . . . In the case of the Executive Magistracy which was to be administered by a single man, loss of capacity or corruption was more within the compass of probable events, and either of them might be fatal to the republic.

As did Elbridge Gerry:

A good magistrate will not fear them [impeachments]. A bad one ought to be kept in fear of them. He hoped the maxim would never be adopted here that the chief magistrate could do no wrong.

And Edmund Randolph piled on:

Guilt wherever found ought to be punished. The Executive will have great opportunitys of abusing his power, particularly in time of war when military force, and in some respects the public money will be in his hands. Should no regular punishment be provided, it will be irregularly inflicted with tumults & insurrections.

Even Morris's cohort, James Wilson, "concurred in the necessity of making the Executive impeachable while in office." But Charles Pinckney, who had had joined Morris in the challenge to impeachment, held firm:

Some gentlemen reasoned on a supposition that the Executive was to have powers which would not be committed to him. He presumed that the powers would be so circumscribed as to render impeachments unnecessary.

While Pinckney's prediction about "circumscribed" executive powers appears naive, Rufus King offered a stronger argument against impeachment:

He wished the House to recur to the primitive axiom that the three great departments of Government should be separate & independent: that the Executive & Judiciary should be so as well as the Legislative: that the Executive should be so equally with the Judiciary. Would this be the case, if the Executive should be impeachable?

And a more nuanced one:

The Judiciary hold their places not for a limited time, but during good behavior. It is necessary therefore that a forum should be established for trying misbehavior. . . . The Executive was to hold his place for a limited term like members of the Legislature. Like them . . . he would periodically be tried for his behavior by his electors. . . . Like them therefore, he ought to be subject to no intermediate trial.

King's argument might have carried more weight if the tenure of the Executive was short, as Morris preferred, but delegates were not inclined to wait six years—the operative term at that moment of the convention—to hold him accountable.

Benjamin Franklin, the venerable sage, closed by referencing civil strife that engulfed the Dutch Republic in the 1780s and was just then reaching its climax. All this might have been eliminated, he argued, had Dutch law provided for an orderly process of impeachment. From Madison's Notes:

Doctor Franklin mentioned the case of the Duke of Orange during the late war. [The American Revolution, which had spread through Europe by 1780.] An agreement was made between France and Holland [Britain's adversaries] by which their fleets were to unite at a certain time & place. The Dutch fleet did not appear. Everybody began to wonder about it. At length it was suspected that the Statholder [chief magistrate, the Duke of Orange] was at the bottom of the matter. This suspicion prevailed more & more. Yet as he could not be impeached and no regular examination took place, he remained in office, and strengthening his own party, as the party opposed to him [the so-called Patriot Movement] became formidable, he gave birth to the most violent animosities & contentions. Had he been impeachable, a regular & peaceable enquiry would have taken place and he would if guilty have been duly punished, if innocent restored to the confidence of the public.

Gouverneur Morris heard it all and came around. Again, from Madison's Notes:

Mr. Govr Morris's opinion had been changed by the arguments used in the discussion. He was now sensible of the necessity of impeachments, if the Executive was to continue for any time in office. . . . No one would say that we ought to expose ourselves to the danger of seeing the first Magistrate in foreign pay, without being able to guard against it by replacing him. One would think the King of England well secured against bribery. He has as it were a fee simple in the whole Kingdom. Yet Charles II was bribed by Louis XIV. The Executive ought therefore to be impeachable for treachery; corrupting his electors, and incapacity were other causes of impeachment. For the latter he should be punished not as a man, but as an officer, and punished only by degradation from his office. This Magistrate is not the King but the prime-minister. The people are the King.

Rarely did a delegate to the Federal Convention, with such candor, admit to changing his mind—and Gouverneur Morris, generally, was as fixed on proving himself right as any of his peers. His change of heart pays tribute to the power of the arguments presented on behalf of impeachment.

The necessity of impeachment would never again be challenged, but it still needed to be fleshed out: Who should impeach, and who should try an impeachment? What should constitute an impeachable offense? What would be the consequences upon conviction?

Six days after the impeachment debate, on July 26, the convention recessed. It appointed a five-member Committee of Detail to transform the various resolutions into a comprehensive document. Reporting back on August 6, this committee gave the single executive a name: "*President of the United States of America.*" It also clarified the process of removal: "*He [the President] shall be removed from office on impeachment by the House of Representatives, and conviction in the Supreme Court, of treason, bribery, or corruption.*"[9] That clause did not come up for discussion until August 27, and then but briefly. Only one speaker weighed in: Gouverneur Morris, who believed that the Supreme Court would be an improper "Tribunal" to try an impeachment. Without waiting for a response, he moved to postpone the matter.[10] This maneuver meant that the venue for an impeachment trial would come before the Committee on Remaining Matters, composed of one delegate from each state. Four days later, Morris was appointed to serve on that committee.[11]

---

9. The final draft of the Committee of Detail is in Madison, *Notes of Debates*, August 6. Working papers of the Committee are in Farrand, *Records*, v. 2, following the July 26 entries.
10. Madison, *Notes of Debates*, and the Convention's Journal, in Farrand, *Records*, August 27.
11. For Morris's maneuvering to get several important matters relating to the executive referred to the committee, see Raphael, *Mr. President*, 100-106.

This committee, reporting back on September 4, dramatically restructured the Executive Branch. Special electors, not Congress, would choose a President, who would serve for four years and be eligible for reelection. The president, not the Senate, would appoint ambassadors and members of the Supreme Court, although the Senate would have to approve them. Morris had long been pushing for such measures, which made the presidency more robust and independent. Further, the committee changed the venue for an impeachment trial from the Supreme Court to the Senate, with a two-thirds supermajority required for conviction—much as Morris had proposed and managed to get tabled a week earlier.[12]

On September 8, the convention considered the change of venue for impeachments. James Madison and Charles Pinckney argued against trial by the Senate; that would make the President totally dependent on Congress, which Morris himself had been complaining about all along. But Morris had changed his mind: "The supreme Court were too few in number and might be warped or corrupted," he argued, while "there is no danger that the Senate would say untruly on their oaths that the President was guilty of crimes of facts." Again, Morris had his way; by a vote of nine states to two, the Senate prevailed. To guard against partisanship, Morris then moved that *"no person shall be convicted without the concurrence of two thirds of the members present; and every member shall be under oath."* This too passed, by the same margin.[13]

On that same day, George Mason questioned what could be considered impeachable in the existing draft: "Why is the provision restrained to Treason and bribery only?" There were doubtless "many great and dangerous offences" and other "attempts to subvert the Constitution" that should qualify. But when he moved to add "maladministration" to the list, Madison immediately objected: "So vague a term will be equivalent to a tenure during pleasure of the Senate."[14]

Mason accepted the critique. In place of "maladministration," he proposed *"other high crimes & misdemeanors against the State"*—more expansive than the short list of treason or bribery, but not totally open-ended. This phrase comes from English common law. A "high" offense did not have to be a heinous one, like a murder, but one that violated

12. For the committee's report, see Madison, *Notes of Debates*, and the Convention's Journal, in Farrand, *Records*, September 4.
13. Madison, *Notes of Debates*, September 8.
14. Ibid.

the trust people had bestowed on an individual in "high" office. It was not a "crime" in the ordinary sense, because common citizens would not be in a position to commit one; it was an offense that stemmed directly from the power of the office. But a "high" crime or misdemeanor did have to be a serious and conscious abuse of that power, not simply a mistake. The word "other" is key: the offense must be on the scale of the specific ones mentioned, treason and bribery. Madison had warned that a president "might pervert his administration into a scheme of peculation or oppression" or "betray his trust to foreign powers." Morris worried about "seeing the first Magistrate in foreign pay." These sorts of abuses could be covered under the general heading "high crimes & misdemeanors." Mason's amendment passed, eight states to three. Unanimously, the convention then agreed to substitute "United States" for "State"—"to remove ambiguity," Madison noted. Impeachment was to be a national affair.[15]

The convention then resolved without debate: *"The Vice President and other civil Officers of the United States shall be removed from Office on impeachment and conviction as aforesaid."* That would include federal judges, who served "during good behaviour." The framers granted judges unlimited tenure to insulate them from the political process, but even delegates who had opposed impeachment of the president favored a constitutionally guaranteed method for removal of judges, if necessary.[16]

Also on September 8, the convention appointed a five-member Committee on Style— James Madison, Alexander Hamilton, Rufus King, William Samuel Johnson, and Gouverneur Morris—to combine everything that had been decided into an almost-final draft. On that committee, Morris served as the penman, and he is generally credited with writing the celebrated preamble to the Constitution: *"We, the People."* Apparently, he also took the opportunity to make an alteration relevant to impeachment: following *"Treason, Bribery, or other high Crimes and Misdemeanors,"* he dropped *"against the United States."*[17] Legal scholars have argued and still argue over this:

• Some say the phrase was redundant. In historical context, the term "high" implied the offense was against the nation, so we should read the final text as if "against the United States" were still there.

---

15. Ibid., and the Convention's Journal, in Farrand, *Records*, September 8.
16. Madison, *Notes of Debates*, and the Convention's Journal, in Farrand, *Records*, September 8.
17. Madison, *Notes of Debates*, and the Convention's Journal, in Farrand, *Records*, September 12.

• Others contend that by deleting the qualifying phrase, Morris was expanding the boundaries for what qualifies as an impeachable offense. On July 20, after he transitioned from an opponent to a proponent of impeachment, he had suggested that "corruption & some other offences . . . ought to be impeachable." Morris fretted over corruption, and he might have envisioned egregious offenses that were not demonstrably "against the United States."

• Still others argue that Morris was a great fan of a strong executive, and he would not have wanted to facilitate a president's removal in any way. In this reading, deleting "against the United States" was purely stylistic.[18]

All this is speculative. The text is what it is, make of it what we will: *"Treason, Bribery, or other high Crimes and Misdemeanors."*

The framers' discussions on impeachment reflect a deliberative process; nobody at the outset envisioned the end result. Gouverneur Morris, in particular, evolved from a leading opponent of impeachment to its chief architect. The process bore fruit. On July 20, as he was changing his mind, Morris wisely suggested that the chief executive "should be punished not as a man, but as an officer, and punished only by degradation from his office."[19] No delegate disagreed, and this limitation on impeachments found its way into the Committee of Detail draft and eventually the Constitution. It was a critical measure. Impeachments would focus on violations of the public trust, with removal from office the sole punishment; by contrast, punishment "as a man" would remain the job of the judicial branch—this might or might not come up later, and it would be handled by the courts. Imagine the turmoil if Congress alone, an avowedly political body, could throw a president in jail. That could undermine people's faith in Constitutional processes and trigger a cycle of retribution. But impeachment, in its final formulation, was intended to avoid horrific alternatives—tumults, insurrections, or assassinations, as Randolph and Franklin feared. It was to be an orderly, albeit unpleasant, business—that was the hope and expectation, at any rate.

The Committee of Style had the last word on impeachment. Here are the relevant sections of its draft, which are included in the United States Constitution:

18. William A. Treanor, "Framer's Intent: Gouverneur Morris, the Committee of Style, and the Creation of the Federalist Constitution," Presentation to San Diego Originalism Conference, February 2019, 111-112, papers.ssrn.com/sol3/papers.cfm?abstract_id=3383183.
19. Madison, *Notes of Debates*, July 20.

ARTICLE II, SECTION 4: *The President, Vice President and all civil Officers of the United States, shall be removed from Office on Impeachment for, and Conviction of, Treason, Bribery, or other high Crimes and Misdemeanors.*

FROM ARTICLE I, SECTION 3: *The Senate shall have the sole Power to try all Impeachments. When sitting for that Purpose, they shall be on Oath or Affirmation. When the President of the United States is tried, the Chief Justice shall preside: And no Person shall be convicted without the Concurrence of two thirds of the Members present.*

Judgment in Cases of Impeachment shall not extend further than to removal from Office, and disqualification to hold and enjoy any Office of honor, Trust or Profit under the United States: but the Party convicted shall nevertheless be liable and subject to Indictment, Trial, Judgment and Punishment, according to Law.

CITATIONS

Most of what we know about the framers' discussions comes from James Madison's *Notes of Debates in the Federal Convention of 1787.* The best print source, annotated by Adrienne Koch and thoroughly indexed, is W. W. Norton's 1987 edition. Several Internet sites, including *ConSource* and *Avalon*, are easily referenced by date. Max Farrand's *Records of the Federal Convention of 1787* includes Madison's meticulous notes, spotty notes by several other framers, and the official *Journal.* Organized by date, Farrand's *Records* can be found at the *Online Library of Liberty.*

The Constitutional Convention Debates the Electoral College

JASON YONCE

In the first two decade of the twenty-first century, the Electoral College has come under harsh, though derivative, criticism as a result of the presidential elections in 2000 and 2016. Comparing the Electoral College at its inception to the Electoral College of 2020 is a distortion. For one, the twelfth amendment ended the practice of affording the presidency and vice-presidency to the first and second place finishers in the electoral vote. Secondly, by 1830, all but South Carolina had adopted the "winner take all" distribution of the electoral vote which, aside from the contentious 1800 election, has been the primary cause of strife than the Electoral College itself.

On the surface, the Electoral College is no more than a double majority check; one of many that are present in the Constitution. The reason for double majorities is simple: changes to government or to laws should require very strong support. This is true not only in federalist systems but in unitary governments as well. In the United States, the first and most easily identifiable majority required is the quorum.[1] Prior to the ratification of the 1787 constitution, the American government's relationship with quorums was problematic at best. The Confederation Congress struggled to produce a quorum even to ratify the Treaty of Paris in 1783. Yet, the Annapolis Convention convened, drafted its recommendations, and adjourned without a quorum in 1786.[2] Other examples of these double—and multiple—majorities in the Constitution

---

1. United States Constitution, Article I, Section 5, Clause 1. The Constitution is notoriously fickle about what a quorum is.
2. Jason Yonce, "The Annapolis Convention Of 1786: A Call For A Stronger National Government," *Journal of the American Revolution*, May 27, 2019, allthingsliberty.com/2019/05/the-annapolis-convention-of-1786-a-call-for-a-stronger-national-government/.

include the passage of bills in two houses and the multilayered process to amend the Constitution.

Even eminent historians have fallen prey to notions that the Electoral College is a uniquely American institution. These historians, along with critics of the institution, place the formation of the Electoral College in a historical vacuum. Systems of using electors were well-known before the Constitutional Convention. Even among the states, indirect suffrage systems—to include the use of electors—were already established.

At the Constitutional Convention of 1787, the debates over the best method of electing the executive branch were subordinate to other discussions about executive power. In fact, as contentious as the Electoral College is today, the actual issue of electing the president was mostly considered a settled matter during the first month of the convention. Both the Virginia and New Jersey Plans, which differed so greatly on the legislative branch, were in unison over the election of the executive. Specifically, the executive—whatever that would be—would be chosen by the legislature. Had it not been for the insistence of three men in particular—Elbridge Gerry, James Wilson, and Alexander Hamilton— it is questionable whether we would even be having a discussion of the Electoral College today. Other framers would grow more prominent in this debate as it ensued.

During the first month of the convention, the committee of the whole pored over the broad strokes of the new government. Questions about the executive were less contentious than those about the legislative but discussions did center around a few primary concerns: how many executives, how long would they serve, could they serve again, who should they be, and can they be removed? The question of "who chooses them" did not take precedence but that is not to say that it avoided discussion altogether.

By May 29, the discussion in the committee of the whole had finally reached the questions concerning the executive and the judiciary branches. Even if the executive branch had not roused quite the same furor that the legislative had, it was the question that spoke to the nature of the new terms of confederation that the convention had hoped to achieve. Perhaps it would have been less prickly to have had an executive council drawn from the states, but the bulk of the opinion leaned toward a unified executive. For states that had maintained a large degree of independence under the confederation government, a unified executive vested in a single person represented a massive shift in the nature of the government. The frequently-underestimated Charles Pinckney of South Carolina and Delaware's George Reed were the expositors of this supreme executive.

On the question of how this executive was to be chosen, the answer seemed obvious to the committee: the congress would select them for a term of seven years. William Paterson's notes are the only set attesting to this selection process, other framers who bothered taking notes for posterity seemed entirely unconcerned with the matter by May 29 and 30. The diversity of opinions on how elections should take place reflected the immense diversity of thought among the states. Each state delegate carried to the convention its preference. Caleb Strong of Massachusetts, as well as other New England Federalists, brought a preference for annual elections and a greater degree of democracy. Other states, like South Carolina, did not popularly elect the governor. James Wilson of Pennsylvania was the most disposed toward popular elections for every branch and house to include the senate.

Elbridge Gerry's opinions were difficult to predict, a common complaint among his contemporaries. Gerry later favored a slightly more democratic approach to electing the executive in contrast to his earlier criticism that "excess democracy" was a scourge to resist. To re-emphasize Gerry's fickle nature, he would change his mind again by the close of the committee's deliberations on June 19. In the interim, Gerry and Wilson drew towards the center of a compromise to allow for electors to choose the executive on behalf of the states' residents.

This idea was not a new one to the framers. Maryland's 1776 constitution created an electoral college to elect its state senate. Maryland was not unique in its undemocratic property requirements for suffrage or to run for office, but their initial constitution, post-independence, left little reason to question aristocratic control. A slate of twenty-four electors—two from each county plus one each from Annapolis and Baltimore—were elected by county freeholders to convene and choose the fifteen members of the senate for five-year terms. They were at liberty to choose the senators from their own ranks as well. If the question of senatorial election roused much debate in the 1776-7 convention, it was not recorded. The first President of the Senate in Maryland was high federalist tobacco planter Daniel of St. Thomas Jenifer. Ten years later, Jenifer attended the Constitutional Convention as a delegate from Maryland.[3]

James Madison and Rufus King objected to this framework initially. Selection by Congress, or through electors, would reduce confidence in the new government. King's notes from the convention calculated how far removed certain positions were away from the people's votes.

---

3. *The Decisive Blow is Struck: A Facsimile Edition of the Proceedings of the Constitutional Convention of 1776 and the First Maryland Constitution* (Annapolis: Hall of Records Commission of the State of Maryland, 1977).

This speaks to the notion that King figured state governors or legislatures would choose the electors, a notion that would later be the case in some states. A president chosen by way of electors, chosen by state legislators, then certified by a national congress hardly seemed pragmatic let alone a system that would instill much confidence that the government truly represented the will of the people. In Maryland there would be yet another layer of electors as well!

Gerry and Wilson's efforts notwithstanding, the matter was settled in committee. The overwhelming number of state delegations rejected popular election of the executive and the use of electors. On June 7, Gerry—perhaps changing his mind or attempting to reinvigorate the discussion via a new proposal—proposed that state governors select the president. The discussion was brief and the committee did not divert from course. The New Jersey Plan came to the floor on June 15 and, despite its many objections to the Virginia Plan, was basically in agreement that the congress should choose the executive.

Outside of the example of Maryland, several European nations had used indirect electors since the middle ages. The best-known example was the Holy Roman Emperor who, since the Golden Bull of 1356, was chosen via powerful electors scattered throughout the continent. While hardly a democratic election of a monarch, the recognition of electors was also, in some manner, the recognition of states and territories within the Holy Roman empire that was later realized in 1648 in the Treaty of Westphalia.

If this seems like a distant and overreaching example of electors to support the idea of an electoral college, it was not so for the constitutional framers. In particular, a young Alexander Hamilton invoked the examples of European electors in his first major speech to the convention on June 19. Hamilton, for all his later esteem, had not spoken much during the first month of the convention, which Madison attributed to his age and political differences from the other New York delegates. Age was inhibiting for some—Jonathan Dayton of New Jersey barely spoke at the convention. For others, like Charles Pinckney, it made little difference. However, Madison was understating the differences between Hamilton and his fellow New York delegates, John Lansing and Robert Yates. Both were unwavering anti-Federalists who later left the convention in protest and rallied a great deal of support against ratification in what would be the closest ratification vote of any state until Rhode Island's in 1790.

Hamilton described "elective monarchies" but carefully avoided the unease associated with the idea of monarchy by stating that these elective monarchies were often in tumultuous governments. Hamilton, more than any other to this point, made the case for what would become the Electoral College. Drawing from Maryland's example, Hamilton also endorsed a similar indirect suffrage scheme for the senate. Once the full convention met in July, however, the Electoral College was again rejected and congressional appointment again moved forward.

Despite these votes, the question of executive elections arose numerous times between July and September. A play-by-play of each instance would be rather redundant. There were patterns within the individual debates that are worth treating generally rather than specifically, but the changes in the state voting blocs prove interesting. By September, only South Carolina and North Carolina continued to oppose any direct or indirect scheme of electing the executive. Even as this majority formed, one debate became intractable: how would states choose the electors? At this point Hamilton had left the convention and would not return again until September. After July 10 none of the New York delegation remained; as noted, John Lansing and Robert Yates had exited the convention in protest. New Hampshire's pair of delegates would not arrive until July 21. Of those that remained, the most vocal members of this debate were James Wilson, Elbridge Gerry, Gouverneur Morris, James Madison, and George Mason. It would be up to Connecticut, in the persons of Roger Sherman and Oliver Ellsworth, to rescue the convention from utter fracture as they did with the warring between the Virginia and New Jersey Plans.

Debate on the executive question quieted for some time while the convention moved on to the judiciary. It would be a recurring, and tiring, theme all the way until September, such that delegates grew restless about presidential selection. Connecticut maneuvered to offer a compromise. While Sherman had not necessarily been opposed to legislative appointment, it was clear by July that the idea was going nowhere even though it has previously garnered support. Connecticut delegates refined the Electoral College idea and proposed the now-familiar formula of apportioning the electors by state. In this first model, states could have one to three electors. Though this motion passed with only a divided Massachusetts and the Carolinas opposed to it, the debate would re-emerge and continue. The Connecticut plan nonetheless became the foundational compromise that united a majority of the state delegations.

To get a sense of what problems the Electoral College solved, one has to shake off any contemporary notions—which goes without saying in historical analyses - but it requires stepping away from the convention itself. The confederation government lacked an executive. Despite

many extraordinary claims to the contrary, the president of the confederation congress was not an executive figure.

If the problem of legislative elections nearly drove the convention
into chaos, the question of electing an executive that had hitherto not
existed would prove even more difficult. This is especially true given
the fears many of the framers harbored of having an executive figure at
all. This probably spurred much of the early support for congressional
appointment of the president. The British had an evolving "head of
government" but what those in the present would think of as a Prime
Minister was foreign to many at the time and repugnant to men who
were even given the title.

There was very little consistency among the states for guidance.
Many states lacked direct election of their governors. South Carolina
did not popularly elect a governor—or presidential electors - until after
the Civil War. Pennsylvania existed under a directorial system with an
executive council like contemporary Switzerland. Outside of James
Wilson, and the example of some New England delegates, the thought
of direct elections was simply unpalatable.

George Mason considered it a paradox that so many of the framers
were agitating for a stronger, more energetic legislature but thought it
would be too corrupt to choose an executive. Yet, the fears of cabal and
legislative intrigue with selecting the executive were likely realistic. It
would hardly be fair to call the executive branch a distinct branch at all
if that were the case. Gerry pitched gubernatorial or state legislative
election as an alternative but this received even less consideration than
direct elections. The fears of leaving the executive too beholden to the
state governments was palpable. That would come near to defeating the
designs of many who had called the convention which had even considered, abortively, to give national veto power over state legislatures.

· While much of the preceding focuses on the internal debate, a look
at state delegation votes is instructive as well. Though the topic of electing the executive ebbed and flowed, a few dates are important for consideration in 1787: June 2, July 17, July 19, July 24, August 24, and
September 5.[4]

Maryland, already comfortable with using electors, and Pennsylvania, whose club of exclusively Philadelphia delegates were friendly to
the idea of popular elections, were reliably on the side of using electors
while the other states were not. With little variation those two states
were always predictable. Equally predicable were the southern states of

4. Information on votes are drawn from Max Farrand, *The Records of the Federal Convention
of 1787* (New Haven: Yale University Press, 1937), 1: 77-31, 149-181 and 2: 29-120, 397-
406.

North Carolina, South Carolina, and Georgia for opposing anything except for congressional appointment. Georgia would prove interesting later.

The other states dithered on the subject. New York was rarely even featured in these votes, and when they were the deep ideological divide between John Lansing and Robert Yates versus Alexander Hamilton kept the delegation divided. As noted earlier, eventually none of them would be present for the convention.

On on July 17 the same basic voting pattern held as it did on June 2. On a third vote, congressional appointment was unanimous. Two days later almost every small state, barring Georgia, had flipped sides. It was around this same time that questions about representation, via the Connecticut Compromise, were finally getting ironed out and probably alleviating much of the anxiety among small states. Jacob Broom of Delaware seconded the motion to vote on the Electoral College both times and Connecticut itself would switch sides to employing electors to vote on the president. Oliver Ellsworth of Connecticut actually initiated the motion on July 19. Questions about the Senate lingered for a few days.[5]

A week later, on July 24, William Houstoun and James Dobbs Spaight, of Georgia and North Carolina respectively, attempted another change to carve out a provision for national appointment of the electors. This succeeded briefly and every small state except for Connecticut voted in favor of the idea. New Hampshire's late arrival complicated matters again because they did not support the use of electors and formed a bloc with the southern states during the August vote. With New York missing, and Massachusetts strangely absent, the even split led to a rejected motion.

Finally, on September 5, the small states except for New Hampshire fell in line and Georgia defected to the Electoral College bloc leaving only the Carolinas. John Langdon and Nicholas Gilman were from two separate factions in New Hampshire politics. Langdon's faction was his own and not particularly inclined toward nationalization; Gilman was more independent friendly to a faction of nationalists.[6] South Carolina's

5. Broom's appearances in the record are infrequent as were his personal documents left to posterity. This and his fight against premature adjournment without a drafted constitution are the only notable mentions, although Broom was fairly successful in both business and politics. See M.E. Bradford, *Founding Fathers* (Lawrence: University Press of Kansas, 1994), 108-109. Bradford lists Broom as an attendee of the Annapolis Convention but this is not borne out in the records of that meeting.

6. Forrest McDonald, *The Economic Origins of the Constitution* (Chicago: University of Chicago Press, 1958), 21-38.

delegation was largely dominated by John Rutledge who opposed the Electoral College, although Charles Pinckney also held great sway with matters and, at least in 1800, appeared to have been friendly to the Electoral College.[7]

Georgia had proven pivotal before on the question of representation. Abraham Baldwin cast the deciding vote on the Connecticut Compromise after befriending the delegation in other votes. Georgia, like New York, had an interesting delegation. William Few was serving concurrently in the Confederation Congress and absent for much of the deliberations until the final signature in September. William Pierce left to engage in a duel after a falling out with a business partner.[8] William Houstoun had been the nay vote to Baldwin's yea on the representation question but was also absent by the end of July.

This was the quandary. Bruce Ackerman noted that popularity played little to no role in the framers' calculus for choosing an executive. He argues that this became a feature of elections after the Adams-Jefferson battle in 1800. Electors seemed like a good middle ground but not if they were simply going to vote for the most popular man in their state. Therefore, it was settled that each elector would cast two ballots and one could not be from his state. This seems to have been an innovation of North Carolina's Hugh Williamson. If this system failed then it became a matter of concern for the House but, in this sole instance, the House would vote in state blocs rather than as individuals. It is worth noting here that the Constitution forbade members of congress from also acting as electors. Even setting aside the problems that have arisen in the ensuing 233 years with the Electoral College, this system was far from ideal. One only has to envision a fifth-place finisher currying enough favor in the new House to suddenly become the president.

While imagining other systems of executive selection in 1787 could be useful as a counterfactual exercise, very few alternatives could be serious. Even analyzing the possibility of direct election would be fruitless given the still-limited suffrage in the period. Congressional appointment is the lone alternative that seemed to have been taken seriously

7. Farrand, III:382-390.

8. Gerald J. Smith, "Abraham Baldwin," *New Georgia Encyclopedia*, University of Georgia Press, November 11, 2005, www.georgiaencyclopedia.org/articles/history-archaeology/abraham-baldwin-1754-1807. Sam Fore, "William Pierce," *New Georgia Encyclopedia*, University of Georgia Press, November 14, 2008, www.georgiaencyclopedia.org/articles/history-archaeology/william-pierce-1753-1789. Also, Lee Ann Caldwell, "Georgia and the U.S. Constitution," Augusta University, accessed May 31, 2020, www.augusta.edu/library/resources/constitution_day/ga.php.

at the convention. This arrangement would still have been a republican method. Roger Sherman pointed out in early July that the Congress were to be the representatives of the people. Gouverneur Morris, who stood flatly opposed to both term limits and congressional appointment, tethered the question to another: impeachment. If there was to be the threat of impeachment then it followed that a powerful enough cabal could simply appoint the president at will and could dangle the threat of impeachment over his head to induce him to do their bidding.

Legislative selection of some sort did have a pragmatic appeal to many of the delegates: it was cheap. Charles Pinckney of South Carolina spoke of "designing men" gaining the presidency in a popular election scheme, but the large geographic expanse of the original colonies made the idea of convening a one-time body to elect the president unattractive given the large distances. Madison was also aware of what a popular election scheme would entail for the south in an election where the three-fifths compromise would hold no leverage. Any election that required forming a majority would benefit the north; the number of southern freemen would be far too few to have any equal footing.[9]

The final report from September 4 combined all of the elements that permitted compromise on the matter of executive elections. As Jack Rakove observed, "the political logic of the electoral college almost exactly replicated the debate over representation." This observation holds true in the latter half of the convention, although by appearances the more pragmatic concerns held more weight in the first.

There were too many questions of intrigue in congressional appointment. Popular election would be a wonderful boon to large states or would benefit a popular tyrant. Even electors, if they were apportioned, could simply be a way for the largest states to wrest all the power. But if the electors were chosen at the state level, they would have to at least consider a single candidate outside of their state and, failing that, the House could vote on the president but not as individuals. For all of the contemporary criticism of the United States' complex electoral mechanism, other countries can pose equally, and arguably more, complicated structures. One need only take a cursory glance at Belgium, The Netherlands, Bosnia-Herzegovina, Lebanon, or Myanmar to feel even more overwhelmed. Laws to get on the ballot in France are equally perplexing. A popular election scheme may be far simpler to grasp, and seem fairer and more democratic overall, but the basic problems of each

9. Jack Rakove, *Original Meanings: Politics and Ideas in the Making of the Constitution* (New York: Vintage Books, 1996), 89-93, 259-75.

system have not changed in 233 years. As one of many mechanisms of consent in the Constitution, it permits some parity among the various states when it comes to electing the President that helps to avoid delegitimizing the election by placing its outcome solely in the urban centers of the country. However, even a cursory glance of the historical record shows that the idea was not exactly sacrosanct in the minds of the Framers and that the Electoral College's creation was borne of political expediency rather than a generally accepted idea of its usefulness. Nevertheless, casting it aside should require dialogue about the possible consequences at least on par with the dialogue that surrounded its creation.

The Yellow Fever Outbreak of 1793: Ten Observations and Lessons

⁂ BRIAN PATRICK O'MALLEY ⁂

"I often thought that the situation of a people in a bombarded city, was not much worse, and on some accounts not so bad; we had no respite night nor day." Writing to a friend Massachusetts, newspaper publisher John Fenno was trying to convey the effect of the 1793 yellow fever outbreak on Philadelphia. "Such a scene was never before realized in this country; and may GOD of his infinite mercy, preserve us from experiencing any thing similar."[1]

Several prominent Philadelphia residents left moving accounts of the yellow fever outbreak, including two publishers. John Fenno was founded the Federalist newspaper *Gazette of the United States* in New York City in 1789. When the federal government moved to Philadelphia in 1790, Fenno relocated with the newspaper. In letters to a friend in his native Massachusetts, Fenno offered a compelling description of life in Philadelphia. Born in Dublin, Ireland, publisher and author Mathew Carey wrote a book detailing the yellow fever epidemic.[2]

---

1. "Yellow Fever: Philadelphia November 14," *Hartford Courant* (Hartford, CT), December 9, 1793; published anonymously, it is the letter of John Fenno to Joseph Ward dated the same day. John Fenno to Joseph Ward, November 14, 1793, in "Letters of John Fenno and John Ward Fenno, 1779-1800, Part 2: 1792-1800," ed. John B. Hench, *Proceedings of the American Antiquarian Society* 90 (1980): 185, www.americanantiquarian.org/proceedings/44517641.pdf (Hench,"Letters, Part 2").

2. Fenno to Ward, November 14, 1793, 182-188, John Fenno to Joseph Ward, September 9, 1793, in Hench, "Letters, Part 2," 173-175; John Fenno to Joseph Ward, October 8, 1793, in ibid., 176-178; for background on Fenno and Ward, consult "Letters of John Fenno and John Ward Fenno, 1779-1800, Part 1: 1779-1790," ed. John B. Hench, *Proceedings of the American Antiquarian Society* 89 (1980): 299, 301, 303-304, www.americanantiquarian.org/proceedings/44539324.pdf; Mathew Carey, *A Short Account of the Malignant*

In response to Carey's claim that black nurses charged exorbitant rates, African American clergymen Rev. Richard Allen and Rev. Absalom Jones cowrote a pamphlet on Philadelphia's African Americans during the epidemic. Allen was later founder (1816) of the African Methodist Episcopal (A.M.E.) Church, and Jones later the first black priest (1802) in the Episcopal Church. In response to the city's desperate need for help, Jones and Allen accepted the work of burial detail and hired five men to assist the effort.[3]

Two rival physicians offered different treatments for yellow fever, but comparably gripping accounts of the ordeal. Benjamin Rush was a champion of bleeding and mercurial purges. Jean Devèze, a French-born refugee from the slave revolt in Santo Domingo (now Haiti) arrived in Philadelphia August 7, 1793. Devèze advocated milder treatments than Rush and his disciples. Despite their different approaches to medicine, the two doctors left similar accounts of a distressed city.[4]

Despite Fenno's hopes that God would spare Americans anything like Philadelphia's yellow fever outbreak, particular incidents might remind Americans of the initial public reaction to the 1980s AIDS crisis or the 2020 Coronavirus outbreak. Here are ten important observations on the 1793 outbreak, some of which may ring familiar today.

I. LIKE EBOLA, YELLOW FEVER IS A HEMORRHAGIC DISEASE

Yellow fever had two phases, separate by one day of remission. The first phase, of three to four days, involved fever, nausea, backache, vomiting and loss of appetite. Jones and Allen recalled that sufferers "were taken with a chill, a head-ache, a sick stomach, with pains in their limbs and back. This was the way the sickness in general began." For many lucky patients, the remission was genuine. For others, the worst of the fever

Fever, Lately Prevalent in Philadelphia... (Philadelphia: Printed by the Author, November 14, 1793), National Institutes of Health, U.S. National Library of Medicine, Digital Collections, https://collections.nlm.nih.gov/catalog/nlm:nlmuid-8710344-bk (Carey, *Short Account*).
3. Absalom Jones and Richard Allen, *A Narrative of the Proceedings of the Colored People During the Awful Calamity in Philadelphia, in the Year 1793...* (1794), in Richard Allen, *The Life, Experience, and Gospel Labors of the Rt. Rev. Richard Allen...* (Philadelphia: F. Ford and M. A. Ripley, 1880), 33-51 (Jones and Allen, *Narrative*).
4. Benjamin Rush, *An Account of the Bilious Remitting Yellow Fever, as it Appeared in the City of Philadelphia in the Year 1793* (Philadelphia: Thomas Dobson, 1794); Jean Devèze, *An Enquiry into, and Observations upon the Causes and Effects of the Epidemic Disease, which Raged in Philadelphia...* (Philadelphia: Parent, 1794), Countway Library of Medicine, Harvard University, Harvard Library Viewer, iiif.lib.harvard.edu/manifests/view/drs:737 4528$1i.

was ahead. Rush warned, "The remission on the third day, was frequently such as to beget a belief that the disease had run its course, and that all danger was over. A violent attack of the fever on the 4th day removed this deception." The second phase of yellow fever, lasting about seven to ten days, can inflict a mortality rate as high as fifty percent. In the second phase, the returning fever is accompanied by damage to the liver and kidneys. The fever can cause delirium; the liver damage often leads to yellowing of the eyes and skin, a discoloration for which yellow fever is named. In the second phase, a sufferer might bleed from the nose, mouth, eyes or urinary tract.[5]

The yellow fever outbreak lasted from August into November of 1793. Benjamin Rush believed that by the second week of September, Philadelphia had "not less than 6,000 persons ill with the fever." Mathew Carey estimated that from August 1 through November 9, Philadelphia suffered 4,031 deaths. In the fourth edition of his narrative, Carey adjusted the total to 4,041; Carey reiterated a caveat from his first edition, that the count from burial registers was not the complete number of deaths. Also consulting burial registries, Rush put the death toll at 4,044.[6]

2. PEOPLE STOPPED SHAKING HANDS

Unaware that mosquitoes spread yellow fever, Americans feared contact with the sick or unwitting carriers. In their fear of contagion, Americans abandoned the custom of shaking hands. Jones and Allen remarked that "friends, when they met in the streets, were afraid of each other." Fenno mentioned "no shaking of hands," "every one stood aloof." Carey wrote, "The old custom of shaking hands fell into such general disuse, that many were affronted at even the offer of the hand." Instead, acquaintances and friends "only signified their regard by a cold nod."[7]

3. FEAR OF CONTAGION MADE THE CITY A GHOST TOWN

Fenno wrote, "The City is now in a manner depopulated—almost every person who can quit it, is gone. I should judge by appearances that full one half of the People are gone—business is in a great degree stagnant." About 20,000 people left the city, Fenno explained, so "business of every kind became suspended, and universal stillness prevailed night & day."[8]

5. Jones and Allen, *Narrative*, 44; Rush, *Account*, 80; "Yellow Fever," May 7, 2019, World Health Organization, www.who.int/news-room/fact-sheets/detail/yellow-fever.

6. Carey, *Short Account*, 107 [not numbered], 108 [not numbered]; Rush, *Account*, 123, 128; 58-59.

7. Fenno to Ward, November 14, 1793, 184; Carey, *Short Account*, 29.

8. Fenno to Ward, September 9, 1793, 174; Fenno to Ward, November 14, 1793, 184.

"The streets every where discovered marks of the distress that pervaded the city," Rush reported. "More than one half the houses were shut up, although not more than one third of the inhabitants had fled into the country. In walking for many hundred yards, few persons were met, except such as were in quest of a physician, a nurse, a bleeder, or the men who buried the dead. The hearse alone kept up the remembrance of the noise of carriages or carts in the streets."[9]

Philadelphia residents made social isolation the norm. Carey wrote, "Of those who remained, many shut themselves up in their houses, and were afraid to walk the streets." When people summoned the courage to take a walk, "the sick cart conveying patients to the hospital, or the hearse carrying the dead to the grave," "soon damped their spirits, and plunged them again into despondency."[10]

4. MANY POPULAR REMEDIES FAILED

Many Americans subscribed to the belief that foul smells communicated disease. Some Philadelphia residents believed the stench of rotten coffee on a wharf started the outbreak. Fenno was sure Thomas O'Hara, a clerk, contracted yellow fever when he passed an open coffin, "took the scent & died the Wednesday following." Even Devèze, who knew the disease was not contagious, believed that its "first cause" was "alterations of the atmospheric air," air that was "more or less adulterated or modified."[11]

Americans resorted to preventives that combatted stench. John Fenno recalled that "every person was seen with a spunge or a bottle at their Nose." Carey reported, "Those who ventured abroad, had handkerchiefs or sponges impregnated with vinegar or camphor, at their noses, or else smelling bottles with the thieves' vinegar. Others carried pieces of tar in their hands, or pockets, or camphor bags tied round their necks." Four thieves vinegar, or "thieves' oil," is vinegar spiked with herbs or spices.

Alas, these precautions were ineffective. Rush noted, "There did not appear to be any advantage from smelling vinegar, tar, camphor, or volatile salts, in preventing the disorder."[12]

5. NEGATIVITY WAS FATAL

Although he knew of exceptions, Carey wrote, "The effect of fear in predisposing the body for this and other disorders, and increasing their

9. Rush, *Account*, 124-125.
10. Carey, *Short Account*, 28, 30.
11. Carey, *Short Account*, 16-17; Fenno to Ward, November 14, 1793, 185; Devèze, *Enquiry*, 12, 16, 20.
12. Fenno to Ward, November 14, 1793, 184; Carey, *Short Account*, 29; Rush, *Account*, 99.

malignance, when taken, is well known." In many cases of yellow fever, Rush was certain that depression was a contributing cause of death. "The deaths which occurred on the 3d, 5th, and 7th days, appeared frequently to be the effects of the commotions or depression, produced in the system on the 2d, 4th, and 6th days." Rush also attributed high mortality among servant girls not only to the rigors of their work, but also "To their being left more alone in confined or distant rooms, thereby suffering from depression of spirits."[13]

Likewise, the reverends Absalom Jones and Richard Allen were shocked by the morbid pessimism that "took hold on the minds of thousands." Jones and Allen believed "dejection and despondence" "aggravated the case of many; while others who bore up cheerfully got up again, that probably would otherwise have died."[14]

Mathew Carey also suspected psychological factors increased mortality. On a recommendation from the College of Physicians, churches no longer rang bells to mark each death. The constant knell, Carey believed, worked only "to terrify those in health, and drive the sick, as far as the influence of imagination could produce that effect, to their graves."[15]

John Fenno opted to stay indoors to shield himself from the demoralizing effect of a desolate city. Fenno explained, "In addition to the numerous carriages employed to carry the dead, there were 8 or 9 Carts constantly employed in carrying out the sick." At one stage of the outbreak, "it was not possible . . . to go the distance of a square without meeting a Corpse, & often 3 or 4." Fenno wrote, "During this sad state of affairs—I was obliged to go into the center of the Town to market, & to the post-office every day—but such was the dismal scene, & so shocking the details from every quarter . . . I therefore left off going into town."[16]

6. MANY PEOPLE WERE HEROIC

The epidemic also exposed both the widespread good citizenship of Americans, and their low expectations of each other. Rush marveled, "It was remarked during this time, by many people that the name of the Supreme Being was seldom profaned . . . Two robberies only, and those of a trifling nature, occurred in nearly two months, although many hundred houses were exposed to plunder, every hour of the day and night." Jones and Allen also remarked that "it is rather to be ad-

---

13. Rush, *Account*, 80, 98.
14. Jones and Allen, *A Narrative*, 45.
15. Fenno to Ward, 184; Carey, *Short Account*, 29, 31.
16. Fenno to Ward, November 14, 1793, 185.

mired that so few instances of pilfering and robbery happened, considering the great opportunities there were for such things."[17]

Beyond the minimal expectation of restraint from lawlessness, many people showed genuine heroism during the epidemic. Fenno wrote, "During our afflictions there were not wanting those heroic, humane & pious minds who think it their duty to brave every danger in the discharge of the offices of Humanity." Likewise, Carey remarked that many men and women, "some in the middle, others in the lower spheres of life," "exposed themselves to dangers, which terrified men, who have hundreds of times faced death without fear, in the field of battle." Carey mentioned the mayor, committee members, doctors and clergy. Carey remarked of the clergy, "Exposed, in the exercise of the last duties to the dying, to equal danger with the physicians, it is not surprising that so many have fallen."[18]

In a proclamation dated September 10, 1793, Mayor Matthew Clarkson called upon "benevolent citizens" to "offer themselves as volunteers" to help the city's Overseers of the Poor, many of whom were sick with fever. On September 14, in a triumph of self-government, a group of residents formed themselves into a committee, with the mayor serving as president. The committee took charge of Bush Hill Hospital, established an orphanage, and regulated matters like burials and poor relief. Carey remarked, "It is worthy of remark, and may encourage others in times of public calamity, that this committee consisted originally of only twenty-six persons, men taken from the middle walks of life, and of the moderate pitch of abilities." Carey noted the committee members "lived together in more harmony than is generally to be met with in public bodies of equal number."[19]

In August, the Overseers of the Poor appropriated a building at Bush Hill, the country estate of William Hamilton. Out of the country, Hamilton left no local agent to challenge such a move. As patients expired, caked in their own waste, attendants lived riotously on the food and comfort items intended for the sick. Carey described Bush Hill as "a great human slaughter house, where numerous victims were immolated at the altar of riot and intemperance."[20]

---

17. Rush, *Account*, 127; Jones and Allen, *Narrative*, 42.
18. Fenno to Ward, November 14, 1793, 185, 186; Carey, *Short Account*, 89-91; 73.
19. *Minutes of the Proceedings of the Committee, Appointed on the 14th September, 1793, by the Citizens of Philadelphia* . . . (Philadelphia: R. Atken & Son, 1794), 1-4, 7 (*Minutes*); J. H. Powell, *Bring Out Your Dead: The Great Plague of Yellow Rever in Philadelphia in 1793* (Philadelphia: University of Pennsylvania Press, 1993 [1949]), 144; Carey, *Short Account*, 57, 58.
20. Carey, *Short Account*, 27, 61.

On September 15, two committee members volunteered to reorganize and superintend the hospital at Bush Hill: Stephen Girard, a French immigrant and wealthy merchant, and Peter Helm, a manufacturer of hoops for barrels. Within a few days, doctors Devèze and Benjamin Duffield offered their services and made daily visits to the sick, assisted by apothecaries who administered medicine according to the doctors' orders. John Fenno extolled Girard and Helm, noting that the two "immediately entered on this service—and a very great alteration for the better took place directly." Of Devèze and Duffield, Fenno wrote, "A French Physician & another a native of this City attended—from this time, nearly one half of the Patients were saved."[21]

J. H. Powell, a twentieth-century historian of the epidemic, depicted the operation of Bush Hill as the triumph of Frenchmen Girard and Devèze over the disciples of Benjamin Rush, of French medicine over Anglo-Scottish practice. Volunteering to help at Bush Hill September 22, Dr. Benjamin Duffield reported to the committee on September 24 that he "finds every thing there in proper order" and "is satisfied with the mode of practice of Doctor Deveze, and the treatment of the sick, and recommends the continuance of the French Apothecaries."[22]

Devèze marveled that Stephen Girard not only inspected the supplies but visited the sick. "He approached them with that philanthropy that proceeds from the heart alone, and which must give the greater lustre to his generous conduct: he encouraged, took them by the hand, and himself administered the medicine I prescribed." Devèze credited Helm with overcoming fear of contagion. "Towards the end of the epidemic, he also visited the apartments and took care of the sick." Devèze also praised the matron of Bush-Hill Hospital, Mary Saville, "principal nurse of the hospital," "a valuable woman," who "deserves the gratitude of the public for the manner in which she acquitted herself in the charge assigned her." Saville volunteered her services on September 17, 1793.[23]

7. MANY PEOPLE WERE DISAPPOINTING

The reverends Absalom Jones and Richard Allen reflected, "Many of the white people, who ought to be patterns for us to follow after, have acted in a manner that would make humanity shudder." Accepting the burden of burial detail, Jones and Allen recalled, "We have picked up little children that were wandering they knew not where (whose parents had been cut off), and taken them to the orphan house; for at this time

21. *Minutes*, 13, 15, 30; Fenno to Ward, November 14, 1793, 184.
22. September 24, 1793, *Minutes*, 30, 32.
23. Devèze, *Enquiry*, 26, 28, 30; Powell, *Bring Out Your Dead*, 165.

the dread that prevailed over people's minds was so general, that it was a rare instance to see one neighbor visit another . . . much less would they admit into their houses the distressed orphan that had been where the sickness was. This extreme seemed, in some instances, to have the appearance of barbarity."[24]

In the initial panic at the contagion, terror prompted friends and relations to desert their loved ones. Carey described servants abandoning humane masters, and masters rushing faithful servants to Bush Hill Hospital on a mere suspicion of the fever. Carey wrote, "Who, without horror, can reflect on a husband deserting his wife . . . in the last agony—a wife unfeelingly abandoning her husband on his death bed," and "parents forsaking their only children—children ungratefully flying from their parents . . . without an enquiry after their health or safety."[25]

Devèze wrote, "In short, the public papers inspired you with terror by pretending to declare the disease contagious." This terror justified, even required, "abandoning the unfortunate victims of this fatal malady, neglected and left alone to expire in all the horror of despair." Devèze pleaded, "Children! mothers! husbands! think of the duty which God has prescribed to you." The doctor warned that if "those for whom alone you ought to live are deprived of the cares they expect from you—think what will be your remorse when they are no more."[26]

John Fenno wrote of "stress and apprehensions" that were "so powerful, that Husbands deserted their Wives; Wives their husbands; children their parents, & *vice versa*." Fenno claimed "this unnatural conduct," in violation of "affection, principle & duty," was "awfully sanctioned" by the "fatal consequences" of loyalty: "Husbands & wives who mutually nursed each other both died in numerous Instances."

Humans were not the only victims of abandonment. Rush observed, "Here and there a dead cat added to the impurity of the air of the streets; for many of those animals perished with hunger in the city, in consequence of so many houses being deserted by the inhabitants who had fled into the country."[27]

The abandonment of loved ones was confined to the initial phase of panic. Of the cases of relations and neighbors abandoning others, Carey wrote, "But I must observe, that most of them happened in the first stage of the public panic. Afterwards, when the citizens recovered a little from their fright, they became rare."[28]

24. Jones and Allen, *Narrative*, 47-48.
25. Carey, *Short Account*, 30-31.
26. Devèze, *Enquiry*, 8, 10, 12, 16.
27. Rush, *Account*, 109.
28. Carey, *Short Account*, 34.

8. PEOPLE FEARED THE SICK

As a Philadelphia resident observed in 1793, an orphanage was necessary because the extended family of bereft children, and the neighbors who knew them, were "shy of them." Fear of the disease meant, in many cases, the children were rejected by surviving relations. Fear of the sick during the yellow fever outbreak was comparable to people's initial response to HIV/AIDS in the 1980s. In 1985, American television evangelist Tammy Faye Bakker (later Messner) spoke approvingly of hugging a person with HIV/AIDS. In 1987, Britain's Princess Diana shook hands with an AIDS patient, without gloves. In the 1980s, simply touching a person with AIDS challenged public sentiment on the disease.[29]

Girard and Devèze rightly believed yellow fever was not contagious. Most Americans, however, dreaded a sick person and feared that a healthy person was an asymptomatic carrier. Even the symptoms of a common cold could provoke public backlash. Carey knew of people showing signs only of "common colds, and common fall fevers," people "only slightly ill" who were forcibly "sent to Bushhill, by their panic-stricken neighbours." An anonymous Philadelphia resident wrote that "each person became afraid of his neighbors, insomuch that if any became sick they were avoided, and many fled from the sick, leaving them in a destitute situation, perhaps shut up in a house, and the neighbors alarmed."[30]

Some acts of rejection exceeded self-preserving avoidance and reached the level of violent hatred. Jones and Allen recalled "an instance of cruelty, which, we trust, no colored man would be guilty of." As Jones and Allen understood the incident, "Two sisters, orderly, decent, white women, were sick with the fever." One sister recovered. "A neighboring white man saw her, and in an angry tone asked her if her sister was dead or not? She answered, 'No,' upon which he replied, 'Damn her, if she don't die before morning, I will make her die!'" The stunned woman managed only a "modest reply," prompting the man to grab a container heavy with water. The unkind neighbor meant to dash her over the head, but an African American intervened on the woman's behalf. (Jones and Allen do not mention the gender of the Good Samaritan.)

---

29. "New-York, September 28: Extract of a Letter from Philadelphia to a Gentleman in Baltimore, dated the 20th Instant," *Hartford Courant*, October 7, 1793, www.newspapers.com/clip/47299036/letter-from-philadelphia-dated-sept/ (Philadelphia to Baltimore, September 20, 1793); John H. Wigger, *PTL: The Rise and Fall of Jim and Tammy Faye Bakker's Evangelical Empire* (New York: Oxford University Press, 2017), 204-205; "How Princess Diana Changed Attitudes to AIDS," BBC News, April 5, 2017, www.bbc.com/news/av/magazine-39490507/how-princess-diana-changed-attitudes-to-aids.
30. Carey, *Short Account*, 62; Philadelphia to Baltimore, September 20, 1793.

9. WHITES OVERLOOKED THE CONTRIBUTIONS, AND THE SUFFERING, OF AFRICAN AMERICANS.

Benjamin Rush, Matthew Clarkson and Mathew Carey acknowledged what the African Americans did for the public good. Sadly, the work of black caregivers was largely invisible to whites. Reverends Jones and Allen labored on burial detail and visited the sick. Black nurses, new to the vocation but eager to help, struggled to care for patients who were delirious with fever. Jones and Allen remarked, "We have suffered equally with whites; our distress hath been very great, but much unknown to the white people. Few have been the whites that paid attention to us, while the colored persons were engaged in others' service."[31]

African Americans were constantly working in the background of the stories whites remembered. John Fenno wrote, "I have repeatedly been in the Street when scarcely an individual was to be seen as far as the eye could extend, except a Negro leading a Herse, or a Chair Carriage, or a Horse Cart with a Corpse—sometimes two in a Cart." Carey remarked that men of fortune, who had given work to hundreds, "have been abandoned to the care of a negro, after their wives, children, friends, clerks, and servants had fled away, and left them to their fate." Likewise, "corpses of the most respectable citizens" went to the grave, "unattended by a friend or relation," "the horse driven by a negro."[32]

Rush recalled, "Funeral processions were laid aside. A black man, leading, or driving a horse ... with now and then half a dozen relations or friends following at a distance from it, met the eye in most of the streets of the city at every hour of the day, while the noise of the same wheels passing slowly over the pavements, kept alive anguish and fear in the sick and well, every hour of the night."[33]

Benjamin Rush's account of yellow fever suggests the gruesomeness and heartbreak of Jones and Allen's work on burial detail. Rush relied on Allen and Jones for details about postmortem effects of yellow fever. The discharge of blood from the nose, mouth and bowels of several corpses necessitated sealing the joints of coffins, to prevent leakage of draining fluids. Allen and Jones witnessed the posthumous tears shed by the corpse of a young woman. Rush gave these descriptions in clinical detail, but they were images of anguish etched in the memories of Jones and Allen.[34]

The reverends described occasions they were summoned to inter a corpse and "found a parent dead, and none but little innocent babes to

31. Jones and Allen, *Narrative*, 43.
32. Fenno to Ward, November 14, 1793, 184; Carey, *Short Account*, 29, 31.
33. Rush, *Account*, 125.
34. Ibid., 113-114.

be seen, whose ignorance led them to think their parent was asleep." The plight of the children and their innocent prattle left the reverends "so wounded and our feelings so hurt, that we almost concluded to withdraw from our undertaking; but, seeing others so backward [in their duty], we still went on."[35]

Jones and Allen mentioned a little girl who chided them, "Mamma is asleep—don't wake her!" The child's reaction to the coffin "almost overcame us." The reverends recalled, "When she demanded why we put her mamma in the box, we did not know how to answer her, but committed her to the care of a neighbor, and left . . . with heavy hearts."

As for allegations that black nurses were neglectful, Jones and Allen implored their readers to consider the difference between "nursing in common cases" and nursing during an epidemic. Many nurses were "up night and day," "worn down with fatigue and want of sleep," "without any one to relieve them." Some patients were delirious, "raging and frightful to behold;" other patients "lay vomiting blood and screaming enough to chill them with horror."[36]

Benjamin Rush encouraged African Americans to offer their help on the mistaken but widespread belief that blacks were immune to yellow fever. Observing a yellow fever outbreak in Charles Town (Charleston), South Carolina in 1748, Dr. John Lining wrote, "There is something very singular in the constitution of the Negroes, which renders them not liable to this fever." In a Philadelphia paper, Rush published an excerpt of Lining's remarks with a declaration of Rush's intent "to hint to the black people" that they had "a noble opportunity" of showing their gratitude to a city that was a center of anti-slavery sentiment, where whites placed blacks "upon a footing with themselves."[37]

Lining, however, did not witness immunity among American-born blacks. In the 1740s, South Carolina's enslaved population was overwhelmingly African-born. South Carolina's enslaved population did not experience natural increase until the 1750s, or perhaps even the 1760s. The people Lining listed as susceptible to yellow fever—whites, mulattoes, Native Americans and people of mixed European and Native American heritage—were born in America or recently arrived from Europe. Lining witnessed blacks who probably survived yellow fever as children in Africa, where the disease was endemic. Yellow fever was

---

35. Jones and Allen, *Narrative*, 46.

36. Ibid., 43.

37. Rush, *Account*, 322-323; John Lining, *A Description of the American Yellow Fever, which Prevailed at Charleston, in South Carolina, in the Year 1748* (Philadelphia: Thomas Dobson, 1799 [1753]), 7.

devastating among adults. Where the disease was endemic, however, yellow fever was a relatively mild childhood illness that provided life-long immunity.[38]

Philadelphia's Free Africa Society offered their services to the city. While Allen and Jones agreed to arrange burials, William Gray organized efforts to recruit black nurses. Carey admitted, "The services of Jones, Allen, and Gray, and others of their colour, have been very great, and demand public gratitude." Benjamin Rush marveled, "Absalom Jones, and Richard Allen, two black men, spent all the intervals of time, in which they were not employed in burying the dead, in visiting the poor who were sick, and in bleeding them and purging them, agreeably to the directions which had been printed in all the news papers. Their success was unparalleled by what is called regular practice."[39]

Despite assurances of their immunity, African Americans suffered from the disease. Rush lamented, "It was not long after these worthy Africans undertook the execution of their humane offer of services to the sick, before I was convinced I had been mistaken. They took the disease, in common with the white people, and many of them died with it."[40]

Despite deaths from the disease, white observers believed yellow fever was more survivable for African Americans than for whites. Rush noted, "The disease was lighter in them, than in white people. I met with no case of hemorrhage in a black patient." Likewise, Carey wrote, "They did not escape the disorder; however, the number of them that were seized with it, was not great; and, as I am informed by an eminent doctor, 'it yielded to the power of medicine in them more easily than in the whites.'"[41]

Jones and Allen took issue with the claim that yellow fever was gentler on African Americans than on Philadelphia's whites. The reverends

---

38. Rush, *Account*, 322-323; Philip D. Morgan, *Slave Counterpoint: Black Culture in the Eighteenth-Century Chesapeake and Lowcountry* (Chapel Hill: The University of North Carolina Press, 1998), 83; Peter H. Wood, *Black Majority: Negroes in Colonial South Carolina From 1670 through the Stono Rebellion* (New York: W. W. Norton & Company, 1996 [1974]), 150-153; Mariola Espinosa, "The Question of Racial Immunity to Yellow Fever in History and Historiography," *Social Science History* 38, no. 3-4 (2014): 445, www.jstor.org/stable/90017043 (Espinosa, "Question of Racial Immunity"); Tim Lockley, "Militarized Slavery: The Creation of the West India Regiments," in *The Many Faces of Slavery: New Perspectives on Slave Ownership and Experiences in the Americas*, ed. Lawrence Aje and Catherine Armstrong (New York: Bloomsbury Academic, 2020), 105.
39. Rush, *Account*, 322-323; Carey, *Short Account*, 77.
40. Rush, *Account*, 97.
41. Ibid.; Carey, *Short Account*, 78.

noted, "In 1792 there were 67 of our color buried, and in 1793 it amounted to 305; thus the burials among us have increased more than fourfold." Jones and Allen asked, "Was not this in a great degree the effects of the services of the unjustly vilified colored people?"[42]

10. NO GOOD DEED GOES UNPUNISHED

In his account of the fever outbreak, Carey alleged "some of the vilest blacks" extorted high wages for their attendance as nurses. Carey wrote, "They extorted two, three, four, and even five dollars a night for attendance, which would have been well paid by a single dollar." A few, Carey noted, had been "detected in plundering" the goods of the ill. Carey strained to control the racist implications of his charges, praising Jones, Allen, Gray, "and others of their colour."[43]

Jones and Allen responded that far more blacks than whites served as nurses, but an equal number of whites were guilty of pilfering. Theft by nurses in general was rare, the reverends noted, but in proportion to their numbers, white nurses were more likely to steal than black nurses. Furthermore, high prices did not result from African Americans charging unreasonable fees. Instead, families outbid each other for the available caregivers.[44]

For Jones and Allen, the image of extortionist nurses hardly represented the black response to the crisis. Jones and Allen described several instances of African Americans who helped the sick without compensation. For instance, "A poor colored man, named Sampson, went constantly from house to house where distress was . . . without fee or reward. He was smitten with the disorder, and died. After his death, his family were neglected by those he had served." Jones and Allen wrote, "We do not recollect such acts of humanity from the poor, white people, in all the round we have been engaged in . . . It is unpleasant for us to make these remarks, but justice to our color demands it."[45]

As for the charges of economic opportunism, Jones and Allen offered a glimpse at their own account of expenses. "The whole amount of cash received for burying the dead, and for burying beds," was £233 10s. 6d. The reverends paid £33 for coffins and £378 total to the five men hired to help with burials. The reverends calculated themselves "out of pocket" £177 9s 8d. This did not include their incidental gifts

42. Jones and Allen, *Narrative*, 44; for a modern historian's rejection of inherited immunity to yellow fever, consult Espinosa, "Question of Racial Immunity," 441-449.
43. Carey, *Short Account*, 77.
44. Jones and Allen, *Narrative*, 36-40, 42.
45. Ibid., 41, 42.

to poor families or the "several hundred of poor persons and strangers" the ministers buried, "for which service we have never received nor never asked any compensation."[46]

In exchange for their efforts, African Americans faced rumors and false accusations from the white community. Whites accused black nurses of opportunism. Jones and Allen faced rumors that they stole beds from the houses of the dead. Even Mathew Carey was disturbed by the many whites who maligned Philadelphia's African American community. Although he raised the allegation of extortion wages, Carey insisted "it is wrong to cast censure on the whole for this sort of conduct, as many people have done."[47]

Perhaps the lessons of the yellow fever epidemic apply in other crises. Social distancing, in times of contagion, should not entail callousness toward the ill. The public can give a thought not only to those tending the sick, but also remember the people society trusts to tend to the dead.

46. Ibid., 35-36.
47. Ibid., 48; Carey, *Short Account*, 77.

Thomas Jefferson and the Public Benefit of Epidemics

GEOFF SMOCK

An epidemic that violently attacks public health—that sickens and takes lives; that cripples our economy; that forces us into our homes; that turns cities into ghost towns—may be unprecedented to the present generation of Americans, but was as commonplace to the Revolutionary generation as was revolution itself. The War of Independence, Shays' Rebellion, the French Revolution, the "revolution of 1800," Yellow Fever outbreaks—be it socio-political or pathogenic disruption, that cohort had seen it all.[1]

To Thomas Jefferson, it was all much of the same. Both classes of phenomena—epidemic and revolution—fell within the same paradigm: they sprung up suddenly, spread rapidly, sowed mass disruption, and look lives.

They also served a larger, noble purpose.

"When great evils happen, I am in the habit of looking out for what good may arise from them as consolations to us, and Providence has in fact so established the order of things, as that most evils are the means of producing some good."[2] With such a mindset—a sort of calloused optimism—he was able to look at the mass carnage of the epidemiological and political upheavals of his time philosophically.

---

1. In Jefferson's view, his election as president in 1800 was "as real a revolution in the principles of our government as that of 1776 was in its form." "To Judge Spencer Roane; Sept. 6, 1819," in Jean M. Yarbrough, ed., *The Essential Jefferson* (Indianapolis: Hackett Publishing, 2006), 250.
2. "To Dr. Benjamin Rush; Monticello, Sep. 23, 1800," in Merrill D. Peterson, ed., *Jefferson: Writings* (New York: Library of America, 1984), 1080.

When many of the elites in his Revolutionary milieu saw their experiment in liberty drowning in the bloodshed of Shays' Rebellion, Jefferson saw the opposite.[3] Washington was "mortified beyond expression"
by the insurrection, the actions of a few malefactors acting as "a scurge
on the major part of our fellow citizens."[4]

To Jefferson, Daniel Shays' rebels weren't villains threatening to
undo the Revolution of '76, but heroes securing it. No country, he declared, "can preserve it's liberties if their rulers are not warned from
time to time that their people preserve the spirit of resistance" when
those liberties are threatened. "What signify a few lives lost in a century
or two? The tree of liberty must be refreshed from time to time with
the blood of patriots & tyrants. It is it's natural manure."[5]

The Sage of Monticello maintained his equanimity in the face of
exponentially greater bloodshed during the French Revolution. Guilty
and innocent alike had met their end underneath the blade of the guillotine, and he deplored their deaths "as much as anybody." The immense loss of life was for a greater good though, it being "necessary to
use the arm of the people, a machine not quite so blind as balls and
bombs, but blind to a certain degree" to achieve the larger endgame of
French liberty. He and everyone else horrified at the bloodletting could
console themselves that the future would "rescue and embalm" the
dead's "memories, while their posterity will be enjoying that very liberty
for which they would never have hesitated to offer up their lives."[6]

Yellow Fever outbreaks, both in Philadelphia in 1793 and then in
other American cities in 1800, were no different.[7] The pestilence was
indeed a "scourge," but would ultimately prove a great benefit by discouraging "the growth of great cities in our nation, & I view great cities
as pestilential to the morals, the health and the liberties of man."[8]

3. For a succinct account of Shays' Rebellion and its effect on American political elites, see
Joseph J. Ellis, *The Quartet: Orchestrating the Second American Revolution, 1783-1789* (New
York: Vintage Books, 2015), 100-104.
4. "To Henry Lee; Mount Vernon 31st October 1786," in John Rhodehamel, ed., *Washington: Writings* (New York: Library of America, 1997), 608.
5. "To William Smith: Paris, Nov. 13, 1787," Peterson, ed., *Writings*, 911.
6. "To William Short; Philadelphia, Jan. 3, 1793," ibid., 1004.
7. For an exemplary summation of the Yellow Fever outbreak of 1793, see Brian Patrick
O'Malley, "The Yellow Fever Outbreak of 1793: Nine Observations and Lessons." *Journal
of the American Revolution*, March 26, 2020, allthingsliberty.com/2020/03/the-yellow-fever-
outbreak-of-1793-nine-observations-and-lessons/. For a larger historical timeline of Yellow
Fever occurrences in the United States, see Susan Brink, "Yellow Fever Timeline: The History of a Long Misunderstood Disease." NPR, August 28, 2016, www.npr.org/sections/
goatsandsoda/2016/08/28/491471697/yellow-fever-timeline-the-history-of-a-long-mis-
understood-disease.
8. "To Dr. Benjamin Rush; Monticello, Sep. 23, 1800," Peterson, ed., *Writings*, 1081.

Not only did population density enable the transmission of biological pathogens, but worse, cultural and political ones. Urban centers were the domiciles of stockjobbers, usurers, dependent mobs, and corruption. This was antithetical to the agrarian republic of free, independent yeomen farmers Jefferson envisioned, making it impossible for Americans to preserve the fruits of their Revolution were they "to get piled upon one another in large cities."[9] A Europe full of over-populated urban centers was proof of this.

As with Shays' Rebellion and the Reign of Terror in France, the lives lost at the malignant hand of the Yellow Fever were sacrifices, albeit involuntary ones, in the cause of deurbanization and, in turn, human freedom. Political revolution "now and then" preserved a "precious degree of liberty" by serving as a caution to would-be despots.[10] By discouraging the growth of cities, viral epidemics advanced the cause of liberty in like manner.[11] The indiscriminate death of thousands was simply a harrowing but ultimately worthwhile price to pay.

At least it was in the mind of Thomas Jefferson.

9. "From Thomas Jefferson to James Madison, 20 December 1787," *Founders Online*, National Archives, founders.archives.gov/documents/Jefferson/01-12-02-0454.

10. "To James Madison; Paris, Jan. 30, 1787," Peterson, ed., *Writings*, 882.

11. Obviously Yellow Fever outbreaks did not stop the process of urbanization in America, but Jefferson wasn't necessarily wrong that epidemics encouraged many to leave cities temporarily and some permanently—whether it be because of Yellow Fever in the late-eighteenth century or Covid-19 in the early-twenty first. See Anne Kadet, "Escape from New York City," *The Wall Street Journal*, April 21, 2020, www.wsj.com/articles/escape-from-new-york-city-11587477601.

Did Yellow Fever Save the United States?

GEOFF SMOCK

To Thomas Jefferson, great plagues were within the genus of republican antibodies. Like the occasional popular insurrection that warned rulers "the spirit of resistance" still existed, a few hundred deaths or so before the pathogenic scythe of a virus discouraged "the growth of great cities in our nation, & I view great cities as pestilential to the morals, the health and the liberties of man."[1]

In the course of their late-life rapprochement, John Adams would gently chide Jefferson for his blasé outlook towards death and disruption. To him, only those who had read of these types of events from afar could serenely accept, let alone praise them. Jefferson, he admonished, had "never felt the Terrorism" of Shays' Rebellion, or the Whiskey Rebellion, or, more importantly, the furor stirred up by French Ambassador "Citizen Genet" in 1793, "when ten thousand People in the Streets of Philadelphia, day after day, threatened to drag Washington out of his House, and effect a Revolution in favor of the French Revolution, and against England."[2]

Barely into Washington's second term, Edmond-Charles Genet's brief foray as French ambassador would rock the United States to its

---

1. "To William Smith: Paris, Nov. 13, 1787," in Merrill D. Peterson, ed., *Jefferson: Writings* (New York: Library of America 1984), 911; "To Dr. Benjamin Rush: Monticello, Sept. 23, 1800," Ibid., 1081. For a broader discussion of Jefferson's views on epidemics, see Geoff Smock, "Thomas Jefferson and the Public Benefits of Epidemics," *Journal of the American Revolution*, May 11, 2020, allthingsliberty.com/2020/05/thomas-jefferson-and-the-public-benefits-of-epidemics/.
2. "To Thomas Jefferson: Quincy June 30th, 1813," in Gordon S. Wood, ed., *John Adams: Writings from the New Nation: 1784-1826* (New York: Library of America, 2016), 557.

political core; leaving one faction convinced that "the flowers of Jacobinical Rhetorick" were leading to blood and anarchy; the other that incipient "Anglomany" was taking America around a cul-de-sac back to British subservience.[3]

The French diplomat had arrived in Charleston in April of '93, just after news that the National Convention had executed King Louis XVI and declared war on Great Britain. Reflecting American enthusiasm for France's struggle, Genet was met with fanfare at every stop along his route to Philadelphia. "It is impossible for anything to be more affectionate, more magnanimous than the purport of his mission," Jefferson gushed. "In short he offers everything & asks nothing."[4]

Suspecting that Genet was, in fact, asking for quite a bit, Jefferson's enthusiasm eluded Washington. He had just issued a declaration of neutrality enjoining all Americans to "adopt and pursue a conduct friendly and impartial towards the belligerent powers."[5] Having only just gained its independence, Washington knew that a country that couldn't even subdue tribes on its frontier faced complete oblivion if pitted against the armed forces across the Atlantic. Neutrality equaled survival, and Genet's conduct was an existential threat to the United States.

Undeterred by Washington's declaration, the impetuous Frenchman violated diplomatic protocol and American sovereignty by issuing direct appeals to the people (with Jefferson's encouragement). Letters of marque bearing his signature were issued to American ships crewed by American sailors to make war against British shipping. Conspiracies were hatched with American civil and military officials in the west to attack Spanish Louisiana and establish an independent republic. Democratic societies were established—first in Philadelphia, then in other cities—to foment popular pressure that would strong-arm Washington into changing course.[6]

By the early summer of '93 Genet was a fire causing the American pot to boil over. Larger and louder crowds—the very same ones Adams reminded Jefferson of in their retirement—were assembling outside

3. "John Adams to Charles Adams: Philadelphia Dec 23. 1793," Ibid., 298; "To James Madison from Thomas Jefferson, 5 May 1793," *Founders Online*, National Archives, founders.archives.gov/documents/Madison/01-15-02-0015.
4. "To James Madison: Phila, May 19, 1793," Peterson, ed., *Writings*, 1008-1009.
5. "Proclamation of Neutrality," in John Rhodehamel, ed., *Washington: Writings* (New York: Library of America, 1997), 840.
6. For a more detailed account of Genet's exploits in America, see Thomas Fleming, *The Great Divide: The Conflict Between Washington And Jefferson that Defined America, Then And Now* (Boston: De Capo Press, 2015), 153-177.

Washington's residence, raucously demanding that America take up France's struggle as France had done for America.

Washington, Federalists, and increasing numbers of Republicans feared that events were escaping their control. "That these societies were instituted by the *artful* and *designing* members . . . primarily to sow the seeds of jealousy and distrust among the people" was beyond dispute for Washington. The "father" of it all was Genet, who "under a display of popular and fascinating guises" had instigated "the most diabolical attempts to destroy the best fabric of human government and happiness . . . that has ever been presented for the acceptance of mankind."[7] Americans' fondness for France was being manipulated, Alexander Hamilton added, "by every art of misrepresentation and deception to be made the instrument first of controuling[,] finally of overturning the Government of the Union."[8]

Vice President Adams, who had borrowed muskets from the War Department to defend his home amidst the turmoil, shared these fears: "I am really apprehensive that if our People cannot be persuaded to be more decent, they will draw down Calamities upon our Country, that will weaken Us to such a degree that We Shall not recover our Prosperity for half a Century."[9]

Yet just when it seemed like it was to fall over the precipice, America was ultimately saved, according to the retired Adams, by an outbreak of Yellow Fever in the capital city. "The coolest and the firmest Minds," he told Jefferson, "have given their Opinions to me, that nothing but the Yellow Fever . . . could have saved the United States from a total Revolution of Government."[10]

Exploding late in the summer, the epidemic sent those who could afford to fleeing from the city and those who couldn't locked inside their homes.[11] By the time it had abated, the Jacobins had taken control of the National Convention back in France and recalled Genet.[12] The imminent threat of insurrection had passed and, according to Adams, it had been Yellow Fever that saved the day.

7. "To Henry Lee: German Town, August 26, 1794," Ibid., 876.
8. "Defense of the President's Neutrality Proclamation, [May 1793]," *Founders Online*, founders.archives.gov/documents/Hamilton/01-14-02-0340.
9. "To Charles Adams," Wood, ed., *Adams: Writings from the New Nation*, 299.
10. "To Jefferson," Ibid., 557.
11. See Brian Patrick O'Malley, "The Yellow Fever Outbreak of 1793: Nine Observations and Lessons," *Journal of the American Revolution*, March 26, 2020, allthingsliberty.com/2020/03/the-yellow-fever-outbreak-of-1793-nine-observations-and-lessons/.
12. The recall came with the near-certainty that Genet would be executed upon his return. He, somewhat ironically, would avoid that fate by living in America as a refugee for the remainder of his life. Fleming, *The Great Divide*, 182-183.

Edmond-Charles Genet in a 1793 portrait.

Was he correct? Did the Yellow Fever epidemic of 1793 save America and its newly-installed constitutional order?

The answer: probably not.

By the time Yellow Fever had exploded in Philadelphia, Genet's own feverish machinations in America had recoiled upon him. Intoxicated by the "perpetual fetes" held in his honor, and convinced that he had become the supreme influencer in American affairs as a result, he had written to Jefferson asserting that Washington was acting beyond his powers as president in malice towards France and, more specifically, that he had no authority to prevent French consuls from commissioning privateers in American ports—or to prevent said ministers from condemning British merchant ships brought back to them.[13] That power belonged to the true representative voice of the people alone: congress. He then compounded his discourtesy by refusing Jefferson's request to prevent a French privateer from sailing from the port of Philadelphia that July.[14]

---

13. As quoted in Stanley Elkins and Eric McKitrick, *The Age of Federalism: The Early American Republic, 1788-1800* (New York: Oxford University Press, 1993), 343; "To Thomas Jefferson from Edmond Charles Genet, 22 June 1793," *Founders Online,* founders.archives.gov/documents/Jefferson/01-26-02-0312.

14. "To Thomas Jefferson from Edmond Charles Genet, 9 July 1793," *Founders Online,* founders.archives.gov/documents/Jefferson/01-26-02-0402.

Desperate to quell the Francophile uproar (and to embarrass Genet's Republican admirers), Hamilton, writing under the pseudonym of "No Jacobin," revealed that it was "publicly rumored in this City that the Minister of the French Republic *has threatened to appeal from The President of The United States to the People.*"[15] Genet had crossed a line, and Hamilton wanted the country to know about it. Many Americans might have felt a fraternity with Revolutionary France, but a great deal more reserved an absolute filial devotion to Washington. For Genet to circumvent him was touch the third rail of the early republic.

Seeing the writing on the wall, Jefferson moved to prevent Genet's impertinence from exploding into a scandal that would humiliate him and the Republican Party. In exchange for not making Genet's threats public, the secretary of state agreed to quietly request his recall. "I adhered to him as long as I could have a hope of getting him right," Jefferson lamented. "Finding at length that the man was absolutely incorrigible, I saw the necessity of quitting a wreck which could not but sink all who should cling to it."[16]

In the span of four months, "Citizen Genet" had gone from being the toast of every town and city on the American seaboard to a wannabe Brutus without friends. The Genet fever running through the streets of Philadelphia had broken, shortly but well-before Yellow Fever filled the void. What had saved the republic—if indeed it had truly needed saving—had not been an epidemic, but the anonymous work of Hamilton, the moderating work of Jefferson, and the reputation of Washington.

American liberty, as it turned out, had abler guardians than a virus.

---

15. "No Jacobin No. I, [31 July 1793]," Ibid., founders.archives.gov/documents/Hamilton/01-15-02-0120.

16. "To James Madison from Thomas Jefferson, 11 August 1793," Ibid., founders.archives.gov/documents/Madison/01-15-02-0049. For Jefferson's role in having Genet quietly removed, see Elkins & McKitrick, *Age of Federalism*, 362-365.

Presidential Power: Thomas Paine, Thomas Jefferson, and the Louisiana Purchase

JETT B. CONNER

In 1813, Thomas Jefferson received a letter from Marguerite Brazier Bonneville, a French emigre and Thomas Paine's former caretaker. Bonneville asked the former president if she could publish Paine and Jefferson's correspondence. Paine had left most of his estate including all of his personal papers to her in his will when he died in 1809. Jefferson declined. "While he lived," he replied, "I thought it a duty, as well as a test of my own political principles to support him against the persecutions of an unprincipled faction [the Federalist Party]." Jefferson indicated that he did not wish to disturb his "tranquility." And he continued: "It is my wish that they should not be published during my life, as they might draw on me renewed molestations from the irreconcilable enemies of republican government. I would rather enjoy the remainder of life without disturbance from their buzzing."[1]

Jefferson's words to Madame Bonneville probably would not have surprised Paine. Still, they surely would have stung. In 1792 Jefferson had written to Paine after receiving copies of his second volume of *Rights of Man*, sent to Jefferson by way of President George Washington while Paine was in Paris. "Our people, my good friend, are firm and unanimous in their principles of republicanism & there is no better proof of it than that they love what you write and read it with delight.

1. Thomas Jefferson to Margaret B. Bonneville, April 3, 1813, *Founders Online*, National Archives, founders.archives.gov/documents/Jefferson/03-06-02-0044; original source: *The Papers of Thomas Jefferson*, Retirement Series, vol. 6, *11 March to 27 November 1813*, ed. J. Jefferson Looney (Princeton: Princeton University Press, 2009), 47.

The printers season every newspaper with extracts from your last, as they did before from your first part of the *Rights of Man* . . . Go on then in doing with your pen what in other times was done with the sword: show that reformation is more practicable by operating on the mind than on the body of man, and be assured that it has not a more sincere votary nor you a more ardent well-wisher than Yrs, &c."[2]

What happened to some of the correspondence between the two men will never be known, because Paine's papers were lost forever. The papers were left upon her death to her son, and Paine's godson, West Point graduate, soldier and explorer Benjamin Lewis Eulalie de Bonneville. His adventures in the American west were made famous by the writings of Washington Irving in the 1830s. Unfortunately, Captain Bonneville's attempt to store Paine's papers in a safe place failed when the barn in Missouri where he left them burned down while he was away. At least, that is the story as told by his surviving widow many years after her husband's death.

Fortunately, much of Paine and Jefferson's correspondence survives, at the Library of Congress in its collection of Jefferson's Papers, and at Monticello. And among those materials are letters between Jefferson and Paine that reveal a mutual interest in expanding the American frontier. The letters, several written by Paine to Jefferson, support the president's decision to acquire the Louisiana Territory.

Interestingly, Paine never ventured further west than Valley Forge and the Schuylkill River. As for Jefferson, though he traveled up the eastern seaboard and, like Paine, spent time in Europe during the formative years of America's constitution-building after the Revolution, he never went further west than his native Virginia. But all one has to do today to learn of Jefferson's fascination with the American frontier is to visit Monticello and walk through the front door to discover the western artifacts and décor in the Entrance Hall.

Jefferson's interest in all things American West—its geography, flora, fauna, fossils, and people, especially native Americans—was unmatched by early American presidents. He was, as Joseph Ellis stated, "in spirit, if not in fact . . . a westerner."[3] And although Paine may not have possessed the same fascination, he too was keenly aware of the potential the largely unexplored western portions of the continent offered for building a strong, independent nation.

2. Jefferson to Thomas Paine, June 19, 1792," *Founders Online*, National Archives, founders.archives.gov/documents/Jefferson/01-20-02-0076-0014; original source: *The Papers of Thomas Jefferson*, vol. 20, *1 April–4 August 1791*, ed. Julian P. Boyd (Princeton: Princeton University Press, 1982), 312–313.

3. Joseph P. Ellis, *American Sphinx: The Character of Thomas Jefferson* (New York: Vintage, 1998), 253.

Both men have been identified with the nascent idea of American exceptionalism, the idea that the American character, and the nation's immense territory, were unique, and gave Americans a rare opportunity unavailable to the territorially and culturally bound nations of old Europe.

After a hiatus in Europe of fifteen years, Paine, the famous author of *Common Sense*, the *American Crisis* and the *Rights of Man*, returned in 1802 to America with the help of Jefferson's encouragement. Jefferson even offered Paine the opportunity to return on a national ship, much to the consternation of the Federalist Party that had come to detest Paine.

Paine had become persona non grata in America for several reasons. In the 1790s he wrote his famous (or infamous to many Americans) theistic work *The Age of Reason* while in France during the Reign of Terror. In two volumes he attacked all organized and revealed religion, including Christianity. The work caused a sensation in America, a very negative one, and caused Paine much grief for the rest of his life.

Adding insult to his own injury, Paine publicly attacked George Washington in a bitter letter he published in the American press, blaming the president for his seeming indifference to his old Revolutionary friend's pleas to help get him out of prison in France during the Reign of Terror. Paine had been caught up in the French Revolution and elected to the French National Assembly. But as a moderate who publicly decried the decision to behead Louis XVI, he was imprisoned by Robespierre during the revolution's most bloody period and awaited what he assumed would be a similar fate. He got lucky when a night jailor failed to properly mark his door while selecting those to be sent to trial and the guillotine the next day.

James Monroe, another Revolutionary friend and at the time an envoy to Paris, succeeded in getting Paine out of the Luxembourg prison after the fall of Robespierre. But Paine never forgave Washington. Washington ignored Paine's letter, and the two men never corresponded again.

For a decade after Paine's attack on Washington, Jefferson did not reply to Paine's letters either. But upon his return to America, Jefferson maintained a cordial relationship with his old Revolutionary friend, at least for a while.

After landing in Baltimore, Paine went directly to Federal City. He had declined an offer from Jefferson to return on a government frigate Jefferson had suggested, because the Federalist press charged that Jefferson was sending the ship, the *Maryland*, just to pick Paine up and bring him back. Rather than give the critics more fuel for their fiery attacks on the president, and him, Paine returned instead on a private vessel. Soon, the two wined and dined while the Federalists fumed.

On December 25, Paine sent Jefferson a Christmas card. "I congratulate you on *the birthday of the New Sun*, now called christmas day; and I make you a present of a thought on Louisiana." Paine suggested that the United States should purchase Louisiana from Napoleon. He was surprised (and disappointed, thinking his idea was original) to learn by Jefferson's reply the next day that "measures were already taken in that business."[4] The quick reply and message were not lost on Paine. It meant that he was, as we would now say, out of the loop.

Spain had ceded Louisiana to France, having taken control of it decades before following negotiations ending the French and Indian War. Recently, the Spanish had closed the port at New Orleans to American traffic, and Jefferson feared the French would soon regain control of New Orleans and continue cutting off American trade on the Mississippi. In that case, in a letter Jefferson sent to Kentucky senator John C. Breckinridge (the senator who introduced the Kentucky Resolutions in Congress, secretly written by Jefferson), Jefferson wrote that the United States would be forced once again to "marry ourselves to the British fleet and nation."[5] So, the president sent envoys to Paris to try to purchase New Orleans and parts of west Florida (the Gulf Coast) from Napoleon.

The story of what happened next is well known. Envoy Robert R. Livingston was surprised by Napoleon's response: He offered to sell the entire Louisiana territory to the United States. Napoleon badly needed the money to fund his pending war plans for England. After Napoleon's failed attempt to put down a slave rebellion in Santo Domingo that cost many French lives, he abandoned his hope of expanding French colonialism in North America and turned his focus once again to Europe. Livingston, and James Monroe who had joined him in Paris, jumped at the deal, exceeding, of course, their authority, not to mention committing U.S. funds vastly exceeding the $2 million that Congress had authorized. The price tag ballooned to $15 million. But that was a bargain the envoys could not refuse. Soon, Jefferson received the wonderful "present" of Louisiana that Paine had mentioned, and the pres-

4. Paine to Jefferson, December 25, 1802, *Founders Online*, National Archives, founders. archives.gov/documents/Jefferson/01-39-02-0197-0001; original source: *The Papers of Thomas Jefferson*, vol. 39, *13 November 1802–3 March 1803*, ed. Barbara B. Oberg (Princeton: Princeton University Press, 2012), 217; Thomas Paine, *The Complete Writings of Thomas Paine*, 2 vols., ed. Philip S. Foner (New York: Citadel Press, 1969), 2: 1431n.

5. Jefferson to Robert R. Livingston, April 18, 1802," *Founders Online*, National Archives, founders.archives.gov/documents/Jefferson/01-37-02-0220; original source: *The Papers of Thomas Jefferson*, vol. 37, *4 March–30 June 1802*, ed. Barbara B. Oberg (Princeton: Princeton University Press, 2010), 263–267.

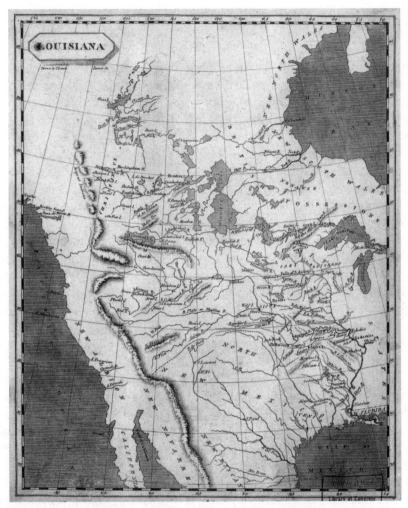

The Louisiana Territory from Arrowsmith & Lewis, *New and Elegant General Atlas*, 1804.

ident now had a huge problem: how to get Congress to ratify the agreement and to pay for it.

But Livingston had told Jefferson he had to act with dispatch, lest Napoleon change his mind. Jefferson did, and the Louisiana Territory was purchased. What is less known is Paine's interest in the business and the efforts he made to support Jefferson's actions. And from his exchanges with Jefferson, it's clear Paine put aside his long-held distaste for unbridled executive power and found a constitutional argument to support his old friend's unprecedented actions.

It was not the first time that Jefferson aggressively exercised executive powers. In the spring of 1801, he sent naval warships without Congressional authorization to the Mediterranean as a show of force to try to stop pirate raids on American merchant shipping by the Barbary states. (Little did he know that Tripoli had already declared war against the United States). American sailors were being captured and held for ransom in an effort to force the United States to pay tribute to the North African leaders in order to ensure safe passage for their ships in the Mediterranean. Although Congress was not in session at the moment, it subsequently approved of Jefferson's action, but without a declaration of war. His action set a precedent for future presidents.

Interestingly, Paine weighed in on that matter, too, in the spring of 1802 before returning to America. He wrote Jefferson from Paris recommending that an American minister be sent to Constantinople, and if the minister was well received "it would be of considerable advantage towards the security of our commerce . . . and [the Barbary states] would, I think, be much checked in their avidity and insolence for war with us if we were on a good standing at Constantinople."[6] A valuable suggestion for a diplomatic approach. But by then, Jefferson's military action against the Barbary leaders had already escalated, with secret plots and a larger group of warships.

Back in America, Paine went to work writing letters to encourage Jefferson's Louisiana Purchase. One of the nagging issues for the president was the question of whether he had exceeded constitutional authority to purchase Louisiana. Though he moved forward with the deal anyway, it bothered him, and he expressed that reservation in a letter to Senator Breckinridge. In the letter, Jefferson admitted his action to purchase Louisiana was unconstitutional without Congressional approval, but then he sought to justify it by claiming that it was similar to a guardian protecting his ward for his good, in this case, for the good of the nation.[7]

Paine offered a constitutional argument of a different kind to justify Jefferson's actions. It was not the first time Paine and Jefferson discussed constitutional issues. As the Marquis de Lafayette reported, "Mr. Jefferson, Common Sense, and myself are debating in a convention of

6. Paine to Jefferson, March 17, 1802," *Founders Online*, National Archives, founders. archives.gov/documents/Jefferson/01-37-02-0062; original source: *The Papers of Thomas Jefferson*, 37: 82–84.

7. Jefferson to John Breckinridge, August 12, 1803," *Founders Online*, National Archives, founders.archives.gov/documents/Jefferson/01-41-02-0139; original source: *The Papers of Thomas Jefferson*, vol. 41, *11 July–15 November 1803*, ed. Barbara B. Oberg (Princeton: Princeton University Press, 2014), 184–186.

our own as earnestly as if we were to decide upon it."[8] The three were in Paris at the time and were discussing newly arrived transcripts of the debates over ratifying the Constitution of 1787 in Pennsylvania.

On August 2, 1803, Paine wrote two letters regarding Louisiana, one to Jefferson and the other to Breckinridge, which he sent to Jefferson to pass along to the senator. In both letters he argued that "the instrument of cession is not of the nature of a Treaty." Paine was reacting to the "federal papers" that were trying to "throw some stumbling block in the way,"[9] and Paine countered their objections to Jefferson's Louisiana Purchase because it necessitated a treaty, by arguing that no treaty applied in this case. In his letter to Senator Breckinridge, Paine had this to say: "Treaties . . . are to have future consequences and whilst they remain, remain always in execution externally as well as internally." But since the United States would be "the sole power concerned after the cession is accepted and the money paid . . . the cession is not a Treaty in the constitutional meaning of the word."[10]

It's doubtful Paine's clever argument held any weight with either the president or the senator. But he had found a way, in this instance, to craft a constitutional interpretation in support of Jefferson's unprecedented action, ever mindful that genuine constitutional limitations generally constrained presidential authority.

There is no question that presidential powers have expanded exponentially in the centuries since Jefferson's presidency. To their credit, founders like Jefferson and Paine cared about the Constitution. And while both struggled to discover arguments to justify the expansion of executive authority in special circumstances, both understood the limitations the Constitution places on the potential abuse of presidential powers.

And that's the way it's got to be.

8. Quoted in David Freeman Hawke, *Paine* (New York: Harper Colophon, 1974), 185.
9. Paine to Jefferson from Thomas Paine, August 2, 1803, *Founders Online*, National Archives, founders.archives.gov/documents/Jefferson/01-41-02-0102; original source: *The Papers of Thomas Jefferson*, 41: 138–140.
10. Paine, *The Complete Writings of Thomas Paine*, 2: 1444.

AUTHOR BIOGRAPHIES

MERV O. AHRENS

Merv O. Ahrens is an independent researcher from Canada who lives immediately adjacent to the Minnesota–Ontario boundary. Following his retirement as an educator he has focused on the early history of his region, including the development of the local fur trade and the geopolitics surrounding the establishment of international boundary in the Lake of the Woods. He has presented his findings at a number of conferences and has authored several journal articles on these topics.

MARK R. ANDERSON

Mark R. Anderson is an independent historian and retired US Air Force officer. He earned his BA in history from Purdue University and an MA in military studies from American Military University. He is the author of *The Battle for the Fourteenth Colony: America's War of Liberation in Canada, 1774-1776*, *The Invasion of Canada by the Americans, 1775-1776: As Told through Jean-Baptiste Badeaux's Three Rivers Journal and New York Captain William Goforth's Letters*, *Down the Warpath to the Cedars: Indians' First Battles in the Revolution*, and contributed to *The 10 Key Campaigns of the American Revolution*.

J. L. BELL

J. L. Bell is an associate editor of the *Journal of the American Revolution*. He is the author of *The Road to Concord: How Four Stolen Cannon Ignited the Revolutionary War* and *Gen. George Washington's Home and Headquarters—Cambridge, Massachusetts*, a comprehensive study for the National Park Service. He maintains the Boston1775.net website, dedicated to history, analysis, and unabashed gossip about the start of the American Revolution in New England. He has been elected a Fellow of the Massachusetts Historical Society, a member of the American Antiquarian Society, and a member of the Colonial Society of Massachusetts.

MICHAEL CECERE

Michael Cecere lives in Williamsburg, Virginia, and is a volunteer interpreter with Colonial Williamsburg and Jamestown Settlement. A retired teacher, he is the author of many books and articles on the American Revolution, primarily focusing on the role that Virginians played in the American Revolution, including *General Peter Muhlenberg: A Virginia Officer in the Continental Line* and *The Invasion of Virginia, 1781.*

Kevin Conn

Kevin Conn teaches advanced placement US history, world history, and German at Delbarton School in Morristown, New Jersey. A graduate of Williams College, he is currently enrolled in the Gilder Lehrman Institute of American History's MA program at Pace University. An avid participant in living history events, he often portrays a soldier in the New Jersey Provincial Frontier Guard, and participates in the annual reenactment of Washington's Crossing.

Jane Hampton Cook

Jane Hampton Cook is a national news commentator on the Fox News Channel, CSPAN, BBC, SKY News and other media outlets. The first female White House webmaster, she is the author of ten books, including *Stories of Faith and Courage from the Revolutionary War* and *Resilience on Parade: Short Stories of Suffragists and Women's Battle for the Vote.*

Jett Conner

Jett Conner is a retired political science professor, college administrator, and academic policy officer for the Colorado Department of Higher Education. He studied the political thought of the American founding period during a National Endowment for the Humanities summer fellowship at Princeton University, and is author of *Thomas Paine* in *John Adams vs Thomas Paine: Rival Plans for the Early Republic.*

Brady J. Crytzer

Brady J. Crytzer teaches history at Robert Morris University. He is the recipient of the Donald S. Kelly and Donna J. McKee Awards for outstanding scholarship in the discipline of history. A specialist in imperialism in North America, he is the author of a number of books, including *War in the Peaceable Kingdom: The Kittanning Raid of 1756, Guyasuta and the Fall of Indian America,* and *Hessians: Rebels, Mercenaries, and the War for British North America.* He is also the host of *Dispatches: The Podcast of the Journal of the American Revolution.*

Douglas J. Dorney, Jr.

Douglas J. Dorney, Jr. is an independent researcher with an interest in the skirmishes and battles among the American militia and British army in the Carolinas. He is currently completing essays on the first British invasion of North Carolina in 1780 and a demographic analysis of the North Carolina Continental Line. He is a licensed architect specializing in higher education, science, and technology projects.

Katie Turner Getty

Katie Turner Getty, an associate editor of the *Journal of the American Revolution,* is a Boston-based lawyer, writer, and independent researcher. She earned her JD from New England Law Boston, cum laude, a BA from Wellesley College with a focus on revolutionary America, and is a graduate of Bunker Hill Community College. For more information, visit her website, www.katieturnergetty.com

Don N. Hagist

Don N. Hagist, managing editor of *Journal of the American Revolution*, is an independent researcher specializing in the demographics and material culture of the British army in the American Revolution. He maintains a blog about British common soldiers (redcoat76.blogspot.com) and has published a number of articles in academic journals. His books include *Noble Volunteers: The British Soldiers Who Fought the American Revolution*, *The Revolution's Last Men: the Soldiers Behind the Photographs*, *British Soldiers, American War*, and *Wives, Slaves, and Servant Girls*. A Rhode Island native and resident, Don works as an engineer for a major medical device manufacturer and also writes for several well-known syndicated and freelance cartoonists.

Alexandre Hinton

Alexandre Hinton is an archaeologist who recieved her BA in anthropology from Stony Brook University. She has periodically worked in the Caribbean, specifically on St. Eustatius, where her research there has focused primarily on maritime archaeological projects in collaboration with The Shipwreck Survey. When she is not in the Caribbean, she spends time in Arizona working for a cultural resource management firm.

Stephen J. Katzberg

Stephen J. Katzberg earned a BA in electrical engineering from MIT and a PhD in electrical engineering from the University of Virginia. A seventh generation South Carolinian through his mother, his interest in the Revolution stems from his ancestor who fought at the Battle of Cowpens.

George Kotlik

George Kotlik studied British Colonial North American History at Oxford University. His interests include Loyalists, the eighteenth-century North American frontier, the Great War for Empire, the Imperial Crisis, and the American Revolutionary War.

Christian M. McBurney

Christian M. McBurney resides in the Washington, D.C. area and is an independent historian. He is the author of *George Washington's Nemesis: The Outrageous Treason and Unfair Court Martial of General Charles Lee during the Revolutionary War*, *The Rhode Island Campaign: The First French and American Operation of the Revolutionary War*, *Kidnapping the Enemy: The Special Operations to Capture Generals Charles Lee & Richard Prescott*, and *Abductions in the American Revolution: Attempts to Kidnap George Washington, Benedict Arnold, and Other Military and Civilian Leaders*. He is also the founder, publisher, and editor of the *Review of Rhode Island History*, at www.smallstatebighistory.com. For more information on his books, see www.christianmcburney.com.

Louis Arthur Norton

Louis Arthur Norton, professor emeritus at the University of Connecticut, has published extensively on maritime history topics, including *Joshua Barney: Hero of the Revolutionary War* and *Captains Contentious: The Dysfunctional Sons of the Brine*. Two of his articles were awarded the 2002 and 2006 Gerald E. Morris Prize for maritime historiography in the Mystic Seaport Museum's LOG. He received the Connecticut Authors and Publishers Association's 2009–2010 and 2010–2011 awards for fiction and essay writing respectively.

Brian Patrick O'Malley

Brian P. O'Malley is a writer and real estate agent in Atlantic Beach, Florida. He earned an MA in history from the University of North Florida, Jacksonville. His writings include editorials in *Folio Weekly* (Jacksonville) and an Op-Ed piece in *The Washington Post*, "Lessons on Iraq From a Founding Father." He writes on historical subjects at http://brianomalley1776.blogspot.com.

Gene Procknow

Gene Procknow is the author of the *Mad River Gazetteer*, which traces the naming of prominent Vermont place names to Revolutionary War patriots. His research concentrations include interpreting the politics of command among the Continental Army major generals; better understanding the Revolution's global aspects; and Ethan Allen and the creation of Vermont. He also maintains a multidisciplinary writer's blog on leadership development and a website to help scholars and students in researching the American Revolution.

Ray Raphael

Ray Raphael is the author of many books, including *The Spirit of '74: How the American Revolution Began*, coauthored with Marie Raphael, *Founding Myths: Stories that Hide Our Patriotic Past*, *Constitutional Myths: What We Get Wrong and What We Get Right*, *Mr. President: How and Why the Founders Created a Chief Executive*, *Founders: The People Who Brought You a Nation*, and *A People's History of the American Revolution*. He is also an associate editor of the *Journal of the American Revolution*. A complete list of his books and articles can be found at rayraphael.com.

Matthew Reardon

Matthew Reardon earned a BA in history and an MA in education from Sacred Heart University. His research interests mainly focus on Connecticut during the American Revolution and the Civil War. He currently serves as the executive director of the New England Civil War Museum and is a middle school teacher in Vernon, Connecticut.

Dayne Rugh

Dayne Rugh is director of education for the Slater Memorial Museum and president of the Society of the Founders of Norwich, in Norwich, Connecticut. He earned a BA in American studies from the University of Connecticut and an MA in museum studies from Johns Hopkins University. His writing has appeared in the *Connecticut History Review*, *Norwich Magazine*, and *Mystic Seaport Museum Bulletin*.

Bob Ruppert

Bob Ruppert is a retired high school administrator from the greater Chicagoland area. He received his undergraduate degree from Loyola University and his graduate degree from the University of Illinois. He has been researching the American Revolution, the War for Independence, and the Federal Period for more than two decades.

Tom Shachtman

Tom Shachtman is the author of more than a dozen non-fiction books, including *Gentlemen Scientists and Revolutionaries*, *Rumspringa: To Be Or Not To Be Amish*, *The Phony War, 1939-1940*, and *Absolute Zero and the Conquest of Cold*. He has lectured at Harvard University, New York University, Stanford University, Georgia Tech, the New York Public Library, the Library of Congress, the Huntington Library, and the Smithsonian Institution.

Michael J. F. Sheehan

Michael J. F. Sheehan earned a BA in history from Ramapo College of New Jersey. He is the senior historian at the Stony Point Battlefield State Historic Site where he has worked since 2008. He is currently writing a book about the history of King's Ferry during the American Revolution. Deeply involved in the Brigade of the American Revolution, he has reenacted and spoken at many historic sites and societies in New York and New Jersey, and is currently serving as a board member for Lamb's Artillery Company.

Jeffrey D. Simon

Jeffrey D. Simon is an internationally recognized author, lecturer, and consultant on terrorism and political violence, and a visiting lecturer in the Department of Political Science at UCLA. He is the author of *The Alphabet Bomber: A Lone Wolf Terrorist Ahead of His Time*, *Lone Wolf Terrorism: Understanding the Growing Threat*, and *The Terrorist Trap: America's Experience with Terrorism*. He earned a BA in history from the University of California at Berkeley, an MA in political science from Indiana University, and a PhD in political science from the University of Southern California. For more information, visit his website, www.futureterrorism.com.

Geoff Smock

Geoff Smock is a native of western Washington. He earned a BA in history from Pacific Lutheran University and a MEd from the University of Washington. He currently teaches middle school social studies and literacy near Seattle.

Ruud Stelten

Ruud Stelten is an archaeologist with a special interest in the colonial period. Born in the Netherlands, Ruud earned a PhD in archaeology from Leiden

University, focusing on maritime archaeology in the Dutch Caribbean. He has lived and worked in the Caribbean since 2011, where he has conducted numerous archaeological research projects, taught hundreds of students, and set up his own museum. He is currently the director of The Shipwreck Survey, an organization he founded to conduct maritime archaeological research.

ANDREW WATERS

Andrew Waters is a writer, editor, and land conservationist residing in Spartanburg, South Carolina. He is the author of *To the End of the World: Nathanael Greene, Charles Cornwallis, and the Race to the Dan* and *The Quaker and the Gamecock: Nathanael Greene, Thomas Sumter, and the Revolutionary War for the Soul of the South.*

RICHARD J. WERTHER

Richard J. Werther is a retired CPA and history enthusiast living in Novi, Michigan. He studied business management at Bucknell University in Lewisburg, Pennsylvania.

ERIC WISER

Eric Wiser earned a BA in history from Loyola University-Chicago where he was a member of the Phi Alpha Theta National Honor Society in History. He taught at the secondary-education level and is a certified public accountant in the state of Illinois having also studied accountancy at DePaul University.

JASON YONCE

Jason Yonce is a graduate from Pittsburg State University where he completed his thesis work under the direction of Dr. Chris Childers. His interests include the later careers of the constitutional framers, constitutional history, and post-Reconstruction Southern politicians. He lives in Alexandria, Virginia.

INDEX